Sayings of the

Christian Prophecy in the Syn

M. EUGENE BORING

Professor of New Testament
The Graduate Seminary
Phillips University

CAMBRIDGE UNIVERSITY PRESS

CAMBRIDGE

LONDON   NEW YORK   NEW ROCHELLE   MELBOURNE   SIDNEY

Published by the Press Syndicate of the University of Cambridge
The Pitt Building, Trumpington Street, Cambridge CB2 1RP
32 East 57th Street, New York, NY 10022, USA
296 Beaconsfield Parade, Middle Park, Melbourne 3206, Australia

First published 1982

Printed in Great Britain by
Redwood Burn Ltd, Trowbridge

Library of Congress catalogue card number: 81-18022

ISBN 0 521 24117 0

TO KAREN

CONTENTS

PREFACE

Several years ago Dr Leander Keck, now Dean of Yale Divinity School, led a series of stimulating seminars at Vanderbilt University on various aspects of the study of the historical Jesus. One such seminar nourished my interest in the effort to account for the expansions made to the sayings of Jesus by the early church, especially by Christian prophets. I pursued one aspect of this topic in a doctoral dissertation under Professor Keck's supervision. I continue to be grateful for his help, not only as an erstwhile dissertation advisor but as friend and encourager through the years, long after the obligations of *Doktorvaterschaft* have passed away.

The following monograph is a new work, in continuity with my dissertation but not simply a revision of it. The scope has been expanded to include the trajectory of Christian prophecy from the earliest post-Easter days through the completion of the synoptic gospels. The method has been refined, especially in dialogue with members of the Society of Biblical Literature's Seminar on Early Christian Prophecy, which met annually from 1972 through 1977. Professors David Aune, Ramsey Michaels, Gerald Hawthorne and Lloyd Gaston were especially helpful conversation partners during this time. Professor Fred Craddock, now of Emory University but my colleague at Phillips University during the writing of this work, found time in his full schedule to read the first part of this manuscript. I am grateful for what I have learned from all of them.

Two periods of study in Göttingen, 1972–3 and the winter semester of 1979, provided library resources, time for reflection and writing, and an engaging atmosphere in which to work. I am grateful for the hospitality of Professors Hans Conzelmann, Georg Strecker and Ulrich Luz, and for the helpfulness of *Wissenschaftliche Assistenten* Bernhard Gelderblom (1973) and Udo Schnelle (1979). I also remember with gratitude the friendly interest in my project of Professor Joachim Jeremias, who read part of my manuscript in 1973. Both research leaves in Göttingen were provided by Phillips University. I hereby express my thanks to the University, and especially to President Joe R. Jones and to Dr James F. Caton, Dean of the

Graduate Seminary, for their encouragement, in word and deed, of our faculty's research and writing.

Professor Robert McL. Wilson has also been a friend since student days. To him and to Dr M. E. Thrall I express my gratitude for their careful and considerate editing and for accepting this study into the SNTS Monograph Series.

In recent years the synoptic problem has again become the focus of lively interest, so that no study dealing with synoptic gospel materials may simply ignore the question of the literary relationship of the gospels. I consider the synoptic problem to be still something of a problem, an open question within which dogmatism and absolutism are not appropriate. I also consider the general outline of the two-source theory to be our best working hypothesis at the present, and the following work has been conceived and executed within that framework. While this study does not attempt an argument for the two-source theory, the manner in which the materials with which I have worked seem to me to cohere best within the framework of this hypothesis has strengthened my own opinion that some variation of the two-source hypothesis is correct, one which makes more room for the continuing influence of oral tradition and for more than one edition of various documents.

Unfortunately, I have not been able to utilize Dr David Hill's helpful book, *New Testament Prophecy* (Atlanta: John Knox Press, 1979), which did not appear until this manuscript was complete. I likewise regret that I have not been able to see Professor David Aune's forthcoming book on Christian prophecy, though he has graciously shared portions of his manuscript with me.

The Graduate Seminary
Phillips University
May 15, 1980

ABBREVIATIONS

AB	Anchor Bible
AGSU	Arbeiten zur Geschichte des Spätjudentums und Urchristentums
ATANT	Abhandlungen zur Theologie des Alten und Neuen Testaments
ATR	*Anglican Theological Review*
BBB	Bonner Biblische Beiträge
BEvTh	Beiträge zur Evangelischen Théologie
BTh	Bibliothèque de Theologie
BU	Biblische Untersuchungen
BWANT	Beiträge zur Wissenschaft vom Alten und Neuen Testament
BZ	*Biblische Zeitschrift*
BZNW	Beihefte zur Zeitschrift für die neutestamentliche Wissenschaft
CF	Cultures et Foi
CGNTC	Cambridge Greek New Testament Commentary
CH	*Church History*
DBS	*Supplément au Dictionnaire de la Bible*
ET	*Expository Times*
EvTh	*Evangelische Theologie*
FRLANT	Forschungen zur Religion und Literatur des Alten und Neuen Testaments
GB	Gospel of Bartholomew
GT	Gospel of Thomas
HC	Hand-Commentar zum Neuen Testament
HNTC	Harper's New Testament Commentaries
HTKNT	Herders Theologischer Kommentar zum Neuen Testament
HTR	*Harvard Theological Review*
HUCA	*Hebrew Union College Annual*
HzNT	Handbuch zum Neuen Testament

IB	*The Interpreter's Bible*
ICC	International Critical Commentary
IDB	*Interpreter's Dictionary of the Bible*
Int	*Interpretation*
JBL	*Journal of Biblical Literature*
JBLMS	Journal of Biblical Literature Monograph Series
JJS	*Journal of Jewish Studies*
JR	*Journal of Religion*
JThCh	*Journal for Theology and Church*
JTS	*Journal of Theological Studies*
KBANT	Kommentare und Beiträge zum Alten und Neuen Testament
KEK	Meyer, Kritisch-exegetischer Kommentar über das Neue Testament
LCC	Library of Christian Classics
LCL	Loeb Classical Library
MNTC	Moffatt New Testament Commentary
NCB	New Century Bible
NIC	New International Commentary
NIGNT	New International Greek New Testament Commentary
NovT	*Novum Testamentum*
NovTSupp	Supplements to *Novum Testamentum*
NTD	Das Neue Testament Deutsch
NTS	*New Testament Studies*
OTL	Old Testament Library
PGC	Pelican Gospel Commentaries
RGG	*Die Religion in Geschichte und Gegenwart*
SBL	Society of Biblical Literature
SBLDS	Society of Biblical Literature Dissertation Series
SBS	Stuttgarter Bibel-Studien
SBT	Studies in Biblical Theology
SNTS	Society for New Testament Studies *Monograph Series*
SPB	Studia Post-Biblica
SUNT	Studien zur Umwelt des Neuen Testament
TBl	*Theologische Blätter*
TDNT	*Theological Dictionary of the New Testament*
THNT	Theologischer Handkommentar zum Neuen Testament
TLZ	*Theologische Literaturzeitung*
TR	*Theologische Rundschau*
TZ	*Theologische Zeitschrift*
UNT	Untersuchungen zum Neuen Testament
WC	Westminster Commentaries

WDF	Wege der Forschung
WUNT	Wissenschaftliche Untersuchungen zum Neuen Testament
WMANT	Wissenschaftliche Monographien zum Alten und Neuen Testament
ZNW	*Zeitschrift für die neutestamentliche Wissenschaft und die Kunde der älteren Kirche*
ZThK	*Zeitschrift für Theologie und Kirche*

PART ONE
The rediscovery of Christian prophecy

1 INTRODUCTION

The problem

The early church used the name 'Jesus' and such christological titles as 'Christ' and 'Lord' to refer both to the historical figure Jesus of Nazareth and to the risen Lord of the church's faith. The historical person remembered and attested-to in the tradition was thought of as the same person experienced as present in the church's life and worship. Accordingly, such phrases as 'word(s) of Jesus' and 'saying(s) of the Lord' had a potential ambiguity from the very beginning. On the one hand, 'word(s) of the Lord' could refer primarily to a 'historical' saying, as for example in Luke 22: 61; Acts 20: 35 or I Cor. 11: 23—5. Such sayings are here called 'historical' not because they necessarily represent a verbatim report of what Jesus of Nazareth once actually said but because they are represented as the words of a past historical figure. They may have been subject to additions or modifications in the course of the traditioning process or conceivably may have been created from whole cloth. But the saying is transmitted in the community and reported in the New Testament as something that the pre-Easter Jesus once said, and it is by virtue of this purported *Sitz im Leben Jesu* that the saying is here called 'historical'.

On the other hand, such a phrase as 'word(s) of the Lord' may refer to the post-Easter address of the exalted Lord to his community, spoken, for example, through a Christian prophet, as in the Apocalypse. Such sayings not only may comprise new, post-Easter revelations; they may also take up and re-present words from the tradition, including words of Jesus of Nazareth. They are here called 'prophetic' because they are presented in the community not as what Jesus of Nazareth once *said* but as what the post-Easter exalted Lord now *says*.

How did the earliest church deal with this ambiguity of the tradition of Jesus' sayings? Generally speaking, did they in fact make the distinction between 'historical' and 'prophetic' sayings, hearing them as different kinds of sayings of Jesus and keeping them in separate categories? Or was the distinction blurred, intentionally or unintentionally, with the result

1

that there was a fluid interchange between 'historical' and 'prophetic' sayings? Is this distinction partly or entirely a modern one? Or can this issue be dealt with *in general* at all?

This problem, and alternative answers to it, first clearly emerged in New Testament studies with the advent of form criticism. Rudolf Bultmann and Martin Dibelius gave opposite answers to the question of whether the early church distinguished between 'historical' and 'prophetic' sayings of Jesus. Bultmann saw a fluid interchange between these two types of tradition. In this discussion I will call this the 'fluid-tradition' view. Dibelius saw a firm distinction made by the earliest church between 'historical' and 'prophetic' sayings of Jesus. I will call this the 'controlled-tradition' view. Before beginning my own study, I will note the sharpening of the contours of the debate, which has continued to the present along the lines first marked out by Bultmann and Dibelius. Each position will be considered in turn.

Rudolf Bultmann and the fluid-tradition perspective

Rudolf Bultmann was convinced that form criticism must go beyond observations on form and lead to historical judgments regarding the authenticity of the material being examined. His approach was to assume that the synoptic tradition of Jesus' words was church material and to place the burden of proof on those who argued for its authenticity. Only material that is distinctively non-Jewish and non-Christian can safely be attributed to Jesus.[1] Only a few sayings survived Bultmann's examination,[2] so that he was left with a large amount of *Gemeindebildung* on his hands that called for explanation.

Christian prophets were brought into the discussion by Bultmann to help explain how it could be that so many sayings of Jesus were created by the church.[3] Bultmann did not begin with a study of the phenomenon of Christian prophecy as such and thereby become convinced that Christian prophets contributed sayings to the synoptic tradition, but seems to have hit upon Christian prophecy as he sought an explanation for the creativity of the church. Whether this was serendipity or rationalization is still debated.

Although Bultmann was not the first to suggest that part of the synoptic-sayings tradition originated as the sayings of Christian prophets,[4] he was certainly the first to bring the phenomenon of Christian prophecy into conjunction with that of the growth of the synoptic tradition in any comprehensive way. Bultmann tended to make generalizations about the 'utterances of the Spirit' and 'sayings of the risen Lord', in order to account for the wholesale expansion of the tradition that he believed he saw, and only rarely to identify particular sayings as oracles of Christian prophets.[5] He never gave supporting evidence as to why a particular saying should be considered the product of Christian prophecy rather than some other kind of secondary expansion: scribal, midrashic, didactic, redactional etc. This is due in part to the fact that Bultmann's hypothesis regarding Christian prophets did not grow out of his study of the texts but was brought in to help justify his negative conclusions regarding the historicity of the bulk of the sayings-tradition. But there was another factor in the development of his view that may be evaluated more positively, namely, his view of the tradition.

Bultmann believed that the early church generally regarded the tradition of the words of Jesus as the vehicle of the voice of the *risen* Lord. Not only were Jewish and Hellenistic materials that originally had nothing to do with Jesus commandeered and edited into the tradition to serve as the rule of the exalted Christ, even historically-authentic dominical sayings were not heard as the recorded teaching of a past historical figure but as the voice of the exalted Lord.[6] The common denominator for authentic pre-Easter sayings and various types of post-Easter material, including oracles of Christian prophets, is word of the risen Lord, not word of (the historical) Jesus. Thus Bultmann believed that the church, 'indeed with full awareness of the fact',[7] incorporated into its tradition of dominical sayings elements that had their origin elsewhere than the pre-Easter Jesus and that it was never concerned to keep these in separate categories. This common basis for the tradition facilitated interchange between its various elements; sayings of the historical Jesus could be heard as sayings of the risen Lord and vice versa. Bultmann contended that whatever vagueness may be contained in this idea was not his but was inherent in the manner in which the early church handed on the tradition of the risen and present Lord.

Since Bultmann saw the tradition itself as a vehicle of the Spirit and oriented toward the risen Lord, this permitted him to operate without a sharply-focused definition of Christian prophetism. He never defined Christian prophecy, nor did he attempt to characterize Christian prophets. It is not clear whether he equated such expressions as 'word of the risen Lord' and 'Christian prophecy', or whether he regarded the latter as a more specific phenomenon than the former. He seemed to draw no clear line between (1) charismatic prophets consciously delivering oracles in the name of the risen Lord, (2) the more 'ordinary' preaching of the gospel and (3) the promulgation of the tradition/word of the risen Lord in the community at large. All came under the one rubric, 'word of the Lord'.

Bultmann's seminal idea has become widely accepted, so that one readily finds synoptic sayings of Jesus attributed to Christian prophets in scholarly literature both from within the Bultmann school and outside it.[8] His students have developed his original insights in two directions.

First, Bultmann's idea that it is the risen Lord who speaks in every level of the tradition has been consciously adopted and reflectively elaborated as a hermeneutical principle by individual scholars such as Julius Schniewind and has become one of the foundational principles of the post-Bultmannian stream known as the New Hermeneutic. The vague line that separated historical and prophetic sayings in Bultmann's understanding of the early Christian tradition has altogether disappeared; the analogous blurred distinction between Christian prophets and other members of the *pneuma*-charged early church has likewise evaporated entirely. The early church's purported lack of interest or capability in distinguishing pre- and post-Easter sayings of Jesus, and Bultmann's perception of it as such, is in neither case considered to be the result of shoddy historical work but an insight into the nature of gospel material itself.

Schniewind acknowledged Bultmann as his exemplar and consciously extended his approach. He argued that, though there are considerable secondary elements in the tradition, it is of little significance to distinguish them from primary elements; for every word of the tradition is both the *kerygma* of the exalted Christ and the result of the historical impact of the man Jesus, whether spoken by him or not — thus making the question of authenticity a 'second-rank question'.[9] The prophetic phenomenon posited by Bultmann has been broadened out by Schniewind to embrace the whole community in its whole history, up to and including the writing of the gospels. The idea of prophetic *additions* to a *tradition*, already vague in Bultmann, has become so diffuse in Schniewind as to become almost meaningless. While this way of looking at the gospels may have theological value, it has become useless as a means of understanding the history of the growth of the tradition. This is clear from the facts that, while Schniewind acknowledged considerable secondary elements in the tradition, he was rarely concerned to identify or account for them, and that, though he believed the tradition was handed on by *Wortcharismatiker*, he never directly attributed a specific *logion* to a Christian prophet.

Another of Bultmann's pupils, Ernst Fuchs, likewise accepted the idea that the risen Jesus spoke by Christian prophets whose words were sometimes added to the tradition.[10] But this is almost incidental to his basic viewpoint, which is that the virile word of Jesus entered into the language stream and begat language true to itself in the church — language that was properly considered the word of *Jesus* though first spoken by his representatives after Easter. Although Fuchs portrayed the early church as having prophets, it was not just they who spoke the authentic post-Easter word of Jesus. '*Whoever* [emphasis mine] understood himself out of this situation [the situation created by the fact that Jesus brought God into language] would bring Jesus Christ into language.'[11] What was unclear in Bultmann has become explicit in Fuchs: the goodly fellowship of the prophets has become co-extensive with the Christian community, the prophetic phenomenon can simply be identified with 'das Ereignis der Predigt'.[12]

Ernst Käsemann developed Bultmann's insight in another direction and has been his most productive student in giving substance to the suggestion that Christian prophets are responsible for parts of the synoptic sayings tradition. Unlike Schniewind and Fuchs, he did this not by further softening the focus of Bultmann's insight until it diffused into the whole tradition and the whole community, but by attempting to sharpen the focus to reveal the phenomenon of prophecy more clearly, to differentiate it from other elements in the community and to give evidence of the prophetic origin of synoptic sayings in particular cases. Although Käsemann sometimes continued the Bultmannian practice of simply declaring secondary *logia* to be prophetic without more ado, in one important group of sayings — 'sentences of holy law' — he offered a careful rationale for his assertions.[13]

Martin Dibelius and the controlled-tradition perspective

An alternative to Bultmann's way of viewing the development of the sayings tradition was offered at the outset from within the form-critical school by Martin Dibelius and has been continued by his successors. Dibelius believed there were basically two types of sayings-material that circulated in the early church:[14] (1) the tradition of the words of the historical Jesus and (2) 'sayings of Christian exhortation', which were 'regarded as inspired by the Spirit or by the Lord'. He terms the former category 'regulatory' and the latter 'inspirational'. Although the 'regulatory' materials were amplified by homiletical additions and modifications to keep the tradition relevant to changing situations, these additions were minimal and did not change the basically historical character of the tradition.[15] Jesus' words continued to be heard as the authoritative word of the teacher of Nazareth given in the past, a kind of Christian *halacha*. The 'inspirational' materials existed alongside the regulatory sayings but in clear distinction from them.[16] These 'inspirational' sayings would include sayings of Christian prophets but apparently only to a minimal extent. They are mostly Christian parenesis, infused with the 'spirit' of the Lord but not generally thought of as sayings of the risen Jesus in any prophetic way. Only once in all his writings did Dibelius make *Propheten-rede* a constituent part of that *Predigt* which was the 'Anfang aller geistigen Produktion im Urchristentum', and even here the bare mention of Christian prophecy was not developed or followed up.[17]

Although Dibelius saw the early church as attempting to keep the two types of sayings-materials separate, he considered it inevitable that occasionally one would be mistaken for the other, so that there was some interchange between the two traditions, and a post-Easter hortatory saying 'through the Spirit' would be 'mistaken' for an authentic regulatory word of the historical Jesus. Dibelius gave no examples of this principle, labeled it 'error' and said that the number of 'genuine' words of Jesus was increased by only a 'few spurious ones'.[18]

Dibelius assumed this view of the tradition as a working hypothesis and never presented a specific rationale for it. The way he would have supported this view may be deduced from his general observations. Dibelius seems to have been led by the present structure of our New Testament, which contains the sayings-tradition of Jesus in the pre-Easter framework of the gospels and reflects the parenetic materials in the letters, to posit two quite separate channels of transmission for the two types of material. There is a bit of irony in the fact that one of the founders of the discipline that turned our attention to the pre-gospel form of the tradition should still tend to think of the sayings-tradition as enclosed in the 'life of Jesus' framework, when it was precisely the work of men such as Dibelius himself that first let us see how the material might have functioned and been heard as it circulated as individual units and collections before Mark first put them into an explicit pre-Easter framework. The achievement of Mark, in creating the gospel form and thereby binding the word of the Lord to the pre-Easter Jesus, has not been sufficiently appreciated.[19] This apparently unconscious yielding to the momentum of a pre-form-critical perspective has continued to have its effect, despite the studies of Q and the Gospel of Thomas, which show that the sayings of Jesus were not always heard within an assumed pre-Easter frame of reference.

Dibelius' assumption of separate channels of transmission for 'regulatory' and 'inspirational' sayings is still no cause to think of them as isolated from each other, however, for he posited the same *Sitz im Leben*, the teaching ministry of the church, for both kinds of material.[20] The basic reason for Dibelius' arguing that the 'authentic' tradition of Jesus' words was not contaminated to any considerable extent by post-Easter *Gemeindebildungen* seems to be that he imagines the former to be a rather rigidly-formed tradition, fixed quite early and under the control of eyewitnesses. There is a certain tension between Dibelius' view of the manner in which he conceives most of the tradition from and about Jesus to have been handed on, by 'unliterary men awaiting the end of the world,'[21] and the transmission process he envisages for the sayings of Jesus. To support his view Dibelius would have needed to have posited some sort of trained academy of repeaters who kept watch over the purity of the tradition from the beginning.

Some later scholars have sensed this problem and have attempted to correct it by positing just such a *Sitz* for the transmission of the tradition. Harald Riesenfeld and his student Birger Gerhardsson have made the most sustained attempt to argue that the tradition of Jesus' words was handed on in a carefully-guarded rabbinic fashion from the time of Jesus until its incorporation into the gospels. They based their argument almost entirely on rabbinic material, rather than on the materials in the gospels themselves. Their occasional attempts to support their case from the New Testament were sometimes painful, e.g. when they argued that ἱστορῆσαι Κηφᾶν in Gal. 1: 18 means Paul submitted to an 'ordination examination' at the hands of Peter, who tested whether Paul had unlearned his rabbinic Torah and replaced it with the memorized tradition from Jesus, during what Gerhardsson considers to have been Paul's three-year period of preparation in Arabia.[22] An openness to the general view proposed by Riesenfeld and Gerhardsson has been expressed by some, who see the phenomena of the synoptic gospels accounted-for better by what the evangelists did to a stable tradition, as illuminated by redaction criticism, than by what happened to the pre-gospel tradition, as pictured by the earlier form critics.[23] Others have welcomed this view of the tradition as an answer to the 'excesses' of form criticism and as an affirmation of the trustworthiness of the gospel materials.[24] But for the most part, the attempt to fill in the gap between Jesus and the gospels with a Christian rabbinic academy that transmitted a carefully-guarded tradition has met with severe criticism.[25]

Even if the view of a Christian rabbinic academy extending from Jesus to the synoptics could be made tenable, there is still room within such a theory to allow for prophetic expansion of the tradition. Gerhardsson states:

'We must take into account that at least some teachers — and haggadists in particular — placed special emphasis on certain of their sayings, delivering them with particular care just because they considered them to be particularly "wise" words which they had "received" in moments of inspiration. The critical attitude of the Tannaitic and Amoraic rabbis to new prophetic revelation and the like ought not to be allowed to obscure this phenomenon.'[26]

Early Christianity was not nearly so suspicious of prophetic phenomena as the rabbinism posited by Gerhardsson, so the tradition of Jesus' words could have been augmented by prophetic sayings even if transmitted in a Christian rabbinic structure. There is thus no basis for an *a priori* denial of the prophetic expansion of the synoptic sayings tradition on the basis of the tradition process itself, however it is conceived.

A further reason for Dibelius' affirming a strict separation between 'historical' and 'prophetic' sayings is that he limited the latter to those that by virtue of their content seemed to be spoken by an exalted heavenly figure and not by the earthly Jesus. He gives only three examples: Matt. 11: 25–30; 18: 20; 28: 18–20; the latter, of course, not purporting to be a saying of the pre-Easter Jesus.[27] Although Dibelius regarded the speeches in the Fourth Gospel as mainly prophetic material,[28] he apparently believed only a modicum of such material could have penetrated the synoptic tradition. Seeing the tradition from this point of view simply begs the question, for the issue is precisely whether the 'historical' sayings of Jesus were *also* heard as the word of the exalted Jesus who spoke in and through the traditional sayings, so that a sharp distinction between pre- and post-Easter sayings of Jesus was not made, which in turn would have left the tradition more open to expansion by the inclusion of prophetic sayings. This assumption leads him to posit the combination of 'historical' and 'mythological' (his term for 'prophetic') sayings as having taken place only late in the tradition process, in the time of the Fourth Evangelist.[29]

Dibelius had originally worked out his analysis of the synoptic tradition prior to, and independent of, Bultmann, and though subsequent editions of *Die Formgeschichte des Evangeliums* did engage in dialogue with Bultmann's work, Dibelius neither made any substantial modifications to his own view nor attempted to disprove Bultmann's. Later scholars who saw the development of the tradition in a manner similar to Dibelius were unable to ignore the growing acceptance of the Bultmannian view and attempted both to undergird the controlled-tradition view and to point out what seemed to them to be the errors of the fluid-tradition view. The additional issues that have emerged in the debate may be summarized as follows.

The issues in the present debate

(1) The Bultmann school has been accused of assuming what is to be proved and seeking to establish the case by assertion and repetition. David Hill charges that the hypothesis of the prophetic expansion of the traditional sayings 'is at best only a hypothesis, but one which has been elevated to the level of assumed fact by reason of its frequent reiteration'.[30]

Bultmann's evidence for his position was in fact startlingly skimpy, and Hill effectively dismantles it, showing, for example, that Odes Sol. 42.6 ('For I have risen and stand by them, and speak through their mouth.') cannot without further ado be assumed to illustrate the experience of first-century Palestinian Christian prophets.[31] Likewise Fritz Neugebauer urges that it is incumbent upon any theory that the sayings-tradition accepted post-Easter additions to present a credible description of the historical events that occasioned this expansion.[32] This the Bultmannians have not done. Christian prophets cannot be called in as a solution to the problem posed by the apparent prolific productivity of the community as long as their role is simply assumed. Neugebauer shows the fallacy of the formula 'not from the historical Jesus, therefore from a Christian prophet', which is often implicit — and sometimes even explicit — in such discussions.

In the entire history of the issue, whenever the discussion has centered on whether or not a particular saying was from a Christian prophet, the categories 'to make plausible' and 'to make probable' have often been mistaken for each other. These are different not just in degree but in kind. The former is a matter of logic and internal consistency; the latter deals with a concrete phenomenon for which historical evidence is necessary. A great gulf is fixed between 'could have' (even 'could well have') and 'probably did'. But establishing that something logically *could have* been the case still leaves open the question of whether it probably *was*, and this question must be dealt with in terms of historical evidence. The critics of the Bultmannian view have rightly charged it with substituting logical assumption, not to say presumption, for evidence.

Any new attempt to deal with the problem of Christian prophecy and the synoptic tradition should realize that it will be expected to provide evidence for its assertions, from case to case. 'Repetition alone cannot persuade.'[33]

(2) A second issue that has emerged concerns the nature of the pre-gospel traditioning process. Again David Hill succinctly states a reservation held by many: 'In putting forward their view of the creative role of prophets in respect of *logia Iesou*, Bultmann and those who follow him have not taken with sufficient seriousness the part played by tradition in the early Christian community, and the importance of the Twelve as witnesses of the tradition of Jesus' words.'[34] It had already become apparent in the earliest form-critical studies of Dibelius and Bultmann that the view one has of the tradition and the traditioning process between Jesus and Mark is a significant factor in whether or not one sees Christian prophets as having added to the sayings-tradition. Thus É. Cothonet, for example, in one of the most complete discussions of Christian prophecy available, treats the question of the role of prophets in the formation of

the gospel tradition very briefly and dismisses it somewhat peremptorily because of the role he believes the apostles and tradition to have played in early Christianity.[35] Other scholars also express objections, not on the basis of a study of the alleged prophetic *logia* themselves but on the view of the tradition process implied by the theory. While E. F. Scott's romanticist picture of omnipresent eyewitnesses keeping watch over the purity of the tradition is palpably incredible,[36] and Vincent Taylor's retort that 'If the [Bultmannian] Form-Critics are right, the disciples must have been translated to heaven immediately after the resurrection'[37] is more rhetoric than reason, the advocates of this point of view from Dibelius to the present have made it clear that any theory of prophetic expansion of the tradition implies a theory not only about Christian prophecy but about the nature of the tradition process itself. Some scholars, for example, are quite comfortable with the view that Christian prophets drew sayings of Jesus *from* the tradition, which they re-presented as sayings of the risen Lord, adding to them and modifying them to make them more relevant to changing situations, but reject the idea that entirely new sayings were created which were then added *to* the tradition.[38] These scholars fail to make clear whether the tradition process is supposed to have had some means of accepting altered and expanded (peshered) sayings *back* into the tradition and distinguishing these from sayings created *de novo*, which it refused to accept, or whether Christian prophets themselves are supposed to have expressed their oracles only in the form of modified traditional sayings. This only illustrates that, for the most part, generalizations have been made on all sides of the discussion without the issues having been focused sharply enough to facilitate clear debate. While there is presently no consensus about the nature of the traditioning process and the relation of Christian prophets to it, if any, some things relevant to our present study may be confidently stated:

(i) While the spectrum of opinion on the issue is wide, even the view that sees the tradition as most rigidly controlled still allows for the possibility of prophetic expansion, as indicated in the discussion of Riesenfeld and Gerhardsson above.

(ii) Even those students of the prophetic-creativity issue who lean toward the controlled-tradition view tend to draw back from the extreme form expressed by Riesenfeld and Gerhardsson. Each step away from that position makes prophetic expansion even more likely.

(iii) All parties in the debate still tend to see the material too much through post-Markan eyes. It was Mark who first put the units of sayings-material into a firm pre-Easter framework as an element in his creation of the gospel form. Thus Neugebauer's protest that words of the risen Jesus would not have been confused with words of the historical Jesus, because the *Gattungen* gospel and apocalypse are essentially different, is well taken but anachronistic.[39] Of our New Testament documents, only the letters of Paul let us see directly how the tradition of Jesus' words was handled in (at least one stream of) pre-Markan Christianity. *Nothing is settled by appealing to I Cor. 7: 10ff.*[40] A more illuminating example is I Thess. 4: 15—17. Although what we have here is most likely an oracle of a Christian prophet, some would see it as — in Paul's view, and/or in actuality — a pre-Easter saying of Jesus.[41] But that the matter is even debated should indicate the ambiguity of whether any given isolated dominical saying is even purportedly pre- or post-Easter. On the other hand, that it can even be argued that some or all of the traditional sayings usually assumed to have been understood by Paul as from the pre-Easter Jesus (I Cor. 7: 10; 9: 14; 11: 24—5), all of which I would regard as 'historical' sayings, were in fact understood by him as revelations of the exalted Lord[42] illustrates the same point: in the early decades of the church isolated sayings of the Lord were not always clearly identified as to their alleged point of origin. It may be that Mark, for his own good reasons, first forced this issue upon us. But if we would see the matter as it was in the period with which we are concerned and hear the sayings of Jesus as they were heard in the first four decades of the church's life, we must learn to bracket out the necessity of immediately trying to hear a saying in *either* a pre-Easter *or* a post-Easter frame of reference, for this imposes an alien categorization on the materials. If it should be objected that in such pre-Markan units as apothegms, words of Jesus are already placed in a life-of-Jesus frame, we need to acknowledge that the pre-Markan tradition did have some tendencies in this direction. But the Markan view was only embryonically and unreflectively present. In such units, it was the saying of Jesus that was primary[43] and sometimes tended to create a past-historical frame for itself. That no genuine historicizing of the sayings occurred in this anecdotal process may be seen from the fact that past and present flow together in the scenes portrayed in the apothegms: those who engage Jesus and are addressed by his sayings are the contemporaries at once of the Jesus portrayed in the apothegm and of the tellers and hearers of the story in their post-Easter situation.[44]

(iv) The question of the nature of the pre-gospel tradition and of the traditioning process is presently an open question. But no one may insist that studies of the nature of Christian prophecy and the role and function of Christian prophets should be brought to a halt until the tradition question is solved. Independent studies investigating evidence that may link individual synoptic sayings to Christian prophets can and should proceed apace. Studies of individual sayings with the issues of Christian prophecy in mind become evidence in a fresh appraisal of the tradition process. Meanwhile, no one may postulate a view of the tradition process that makes it *a priori* impossible for prophetic material to have been included in the tradition. *Any new attempt to deal with the problem of Christian prophecy and the synoptic tradition must study the relation of prophets to the tradition process.*

(3) A third issue that has emerged from the debate of the last generation concerns the relation of the specific phenomenon of Christian prophecy to the general presence of the Spirit in earliest Christianity. The Bultmann school is charged with a vagueness in its view of what prophecy was and how it functioned, analogous to the charge made regarding its view of the tradition process. David Hill objects that all 'inspired' people are not prophets and quarrels with Bultmann's tendency to regard all varieties of charismatic speech (except *glossolalia*) as instances of one phenomenon, any of the products of which might be confused with traditional words of Jesus. Hill argues that not even all prophets may be lumped together and questions whether the prophet *per se* was one who promulgated the kind of declarations that might be taken as sayings of the historical Jesus.[45] Likewise Gerhard Delling insists that we should distinguish carefully between prophetic revelations through the Spirit, which he finds in, e.g., I Cor. 15: 51 and Rom. 11: 25, and words of the risen *Jesus*, which purportedly could blend in with the synoptic tradition.[46] Both Delling and Hill claim that research should attend to such distinctions as are made in Acts, which distinguishes the Spirit's addressing someone and utterances of the glorified Lord.[47] The issue may be illustrated by one final point: Neugebauer argues that in the first-century Palestinian situation prophetic material was never anonymous but was always handed on under the name of its author, so that the nature of prophetic speech precludes its being confused with the traditional words of the historical Jesus.[48] Whether the assertion is true or not is here beside the point. (In my opinion it is not; see below, pp. 128—30.) Neugebauer is correct in charging Bultmann with asserting considerable prophetic expansion of the tradition of Jesus' words without making any careful study of what prophetic utterance itself was like in the first century. This was a defect of Bultmann's approach, for he backed into a consideration of Christian prophets without making a study of them *from* which his hypothesis might more legitimately have proceeded. *Any new attempt to deal with the problem of Christian prophecy and the synoptic tradition should define its terms and*

characterize the prophetic phenomenon as exactly as possible, making
historical distinctions.

(4) Finally, the debate has brought to light the issue of which sources
may be appealed to, and how they may be used, in speaking of early
Christian prophets. Bultmann and his followers have rightly been charged
with being too lax, even casual, on both points. Bultmann's own rather
easy assumptions concerning the nature and character of early Christian
prophetism allowed him to combine a few references from the Apocalypse
and the Odes of Solomon as illustrations of a point he did not consider to
be in need of proof. Not only has David Hill made a devastating critique of
the shaky foundations of the Bultmannian form of the argument[49] but his
own studies of our primary New Testament example of Christian prophecy
have also shown that one may not simply assume that the Apocalypse
portrays a type of Christian prophets who would have coined new
synoptic-like sayings of Jesus.[50] Delling made the same point about Paul
and Acts.[51] Since the theory of prophetic expansion of the synoptic
tradition arose out of form-critical work on the materials of the synoptic
tradition itself, little need has been felt by the Bultmann school to use
other sources as a control of, support for, or even critique of, the theory
itself. Even those followers of Bultmann who have attempted to provide
evidence for the prophetic origin of individual sayings, such as Käsemann,
have done so almost entirely in terms of form criticism. This is not to be
disparaged; form criticism first suggested the theory and can continue to
provide evidence for it in individual cases. But due to the circularity
inherent in the method when it is used to make historical judgments, form
criticism alone can neither prove the theory of prophetic expansion of the
synoptic tradition in general nor prove any particular saying to be of
prophetic origin. The critics of the Bultmannian program have raised a
justified objection.[52] *Any new attempt to deal with the problem of*
Christian prophecy and the synoptic tradition must use sources beyond
the synoptic material itself, and other methods in addition to form
criticism, and must offer a rationale for both its sources and its method.

We are now in need of a fresh study of the material of the New
Testament itself, seeking what data there are to support the following
hypotheses:

(1) Christian prophets were present in the early church prior to the
writing of the gospels.

(2) They delivered utterances that were heard and transmitted as
sayings of the risen Jesus.

(3) Such sayings were mixed with sayings of the historical Jesus and
with other sayings purporting to be from the pre-Easter Jesus.

(4) Some of these sayings of the risen Jesus that found their way into the synoptic tradition may be identified with a fair degree of probability.

(5) A history of the interplay between sayings of the risen Jesus and the tradition of Jesus' words can be discerned. Such a history, noting the major moments in the interaction between the traditions of the exalted and the historical Jesus, is important for understanding not only the sayings themselves but also the gospel forms in which they are now contained.

Such a study must begin with a clear definition of terms, a delineation of the sources to be utilized and a discussion of the method to be pursued. This is attempted in the next three chapters.

2 DEFINITIONS

Research on early Christian prophecy has proceeded thus far without any generally accepted definition of terms. This corresponds to the usage of the Hellenistic world, where the προφητ- word-group was applied to a wide variety of figures, functions and products.[1] This is also true of the New Testament itself, where προφήτης, προφῆτις, προφητεία, προφητεύω and προφητικός are not used univocally, although the range of meanings is not so wide as in the Hellenistic world generally.

This situation makes it imperative that any discussion of early Christian prophecy should be prefaced by a definition of terms. This is, of course, not a claim to settle in advance what Christian prophecy 'really' is, but a step in the facilitation of communication. In the present instance we are concerned to study the phenomenon represented by those Christians in the early church who spoke in the name of the risen Lord. The definition needed here, then, should seek to define, in functional terms, this phenomenon with which we are concerned, rather than to analyze the usage of a word-group in a body of literature. Some studies of early Christian prophecy have been too dominated by the occurrence or non-occurrence of the word προφήτης. It has been assumed that the most viable procedure is to accumulate all the instances of the occurrence of the προφητ- word-group, reduce their usages to a least-common denominator and use the result as the definition of 'prophet'. This procedure is something of a guard against arbitrary definitions but is more appropriate to the making of a dictionary than to the study of a phenomenon. But unless it is assumed in advance that the phenomenon we wish to study is always bound to a particular terminology, and vice versa, we must not limit our study to the texts that use the προφητ- vocabulary. Not should the definition attempt to be a full characterization of the phenomenon. We shall later find it useful to draw up a profile attempting to delineate the characteristics typical of early Christian prophets. But this characterization can come only after the group one wishes to characterize has been defined; the characterization should not be confused with the definition itself.

Especially to be avoided is the procedure of gathering up all the instances of the προφητ- word-group, listing the characteristics of the persons thereby indicated and using the resulting composite as definitive for the meaning of 'prophet'.

A functional, phenomenological definition, as proposed here, also excludes the procedure of choosing one source that portrays προφῆται in a certain manner and using this portrayal as the definitive picture of Christian prophecy.[2] David Hill, for instance, lets I Cor. 14 be definitive for what Christian prophecy 'really' was, then on this basis raises the question as to whether the Apocalypse should in fact be called Christian prophecy. This would be analogous to using II Samuel and I Kings as the normative sources from which to derive a definition of נָבִיא , then questioning whether Jeremiah should in fact be called a prophet. Like-wise, a definition in terms of the content of the prophetic utterance itself is to be avoided. It may be that there are characteristic items of content that the oracles of early Christian prophets have in common, but this is a judgment that should be withheld prior to resolving the issue of who belongs to the category 'prophet'.

Similarly, if we wish to examine prophetism as a function and phenomenon in early Christianity, we should not define 'prophet' initially in terms of an 'office'. The relation of the prophetic phenomenon to a prophetic office, if any, and the relation of prophets to apostles, teachers and other ministers of the word, is a matter that must be discussed as the phenomenon is brought to sharper focus, but can remain an open question in preliminary definitions. Our initial working definition should therefore be brief, simply stating the *sine qua non* function of the prophet. The following is my initial working definition: *The early Christian prophet was an immediately-inspired spokesman for the risen Jesus who received intelligible oracles that he felt impelled to deliver to the Christian community.*[3]

It was these figures in the early church who might have promulgated oracles that came into the synoptic tradition as sayings of Jesus. These are the persons I have in mind in using the word 'prophet', whether or not the προφητ- terminology was used of them or by them. In order to be as clear as possible, some terms in the definition need to be elaborated.

By 'immediately inspired' I intend not only to affirm the common view that the claim to inspiration is the *sine qua non* of prophecy, but, since 'inspiration' is used in a variety of senses, to indicate that the prophet claims that what he is saying or writing represents the present, immediate voice of the deity. No statement about the state of consciousness in which the prophet receives the oracles is intended. Nor is the definition intended to exclude the prophet's utilization of sources, traditional materials or the reflections of the prophet himself, all of which may be involved in the delivery to the community of what he perceives to be directly revealed from the risen Lord.

By using the term 'risen Jesus' in the definition, I do not intend to draw any sharp distinctions among Christian prophets who portray themselves, or are portrayed, as speaking for God, the risen Jesus or the Holy Spirit. In early Christianity in general, and particularly in the prophetic experience, these were not always distinguished (Rom. 8: 8–10; Rev. 1: 1–2; 2: 1, 7). If there were prophets in the early church who understood themselves as speaking the word of *God* in some way that distinguished this from the word of the risen Christ, it is likely that their oracles would not have been regarded as sayings of *Jesus* and would not have been combined with traditional sayings of Jesus. If there were such prophets, they are not included in the above definition and are not dealt with in this study; for the distinctive element of Christian prophets was precisely that they spoke to their present in the name of the risen Lord, who was a recent historical figure. So far as I am aware, the history of religions offers no parallels to this phenomenon.

The uniqueness and importance of the phrase 'spokesman for the risen Jesus' in our definition will be clarified by the examination of alleged parallels. Plutarch, for example, refers to Ἐπικούρου προφῆται.[4] Fascher indicates that not only Epicurus but Plato and other philosophers had groups of προφῆται who carried on their teaching after their death, and suggests: 'Da der tote Philosoph dabei als Gottwesen gedacht werden kann ... so ist in unserem Ausdruck ein kultisches Moment enthalten.'[5] Similarly, in discu ' 'on the discourses of the Fourth Gospel, B. H. Streeter toys with the idea that Plato's promulgation of discourses, which he places in the mouth of his deceased teacher Socrates, is something of a parallel to the prophetic phenomenon in the New Testament.[6] But no one, Fascher and Streeter included, would suggest that Plato intended to claim that the recently martyred Socrates was now exalted and speaking to his disciples in the *Dialogues*. Plato's writing of discourses for Socrates is rather to be seen as his attempt to delineate what Socrates would have said, a development of his teaching on the horizontal level, going back to the inspiration of the historical Socrates and thus properly attributed to him in some sense. The relation of the Pastorals to Paul is thus a better analogy to this than is that of the Fourth Gospel to Jesus. It was an elaboration of the dead teacher's doctrine, not 'the word of the exalted Socrates', that was proclaimed by his 'prophets'.

Sigmund Mowinckel has argued that a phenomenon similar to Christian prophetism was present in the transmission and expansion of the sayings of the Old Testament prophets.[7] He argues that this is seen especially in the Servant Songs of II Isaiah; for here, he maintains, is to be found a cultic circle of disciples who met after the sacrificial death of their teacher,

> '... in which the life, death, and saving significance of the Servant would be preached ... with his resurrection. Here it would be natural to put into the mouth of the Servant words about the promises associated with his call ... and, as it were, to allow him to appear himself in the prophetic circle and proclaim the conviction which God had given him and was now giving them, that his cause would triumph, and would lead to Israel's conversion, ingathering, and restoration, and to the spread of true religion among all the people. This cultic interpretation enables us to understand the use of the first person in the Second and Third Songs.'

Mowinckel contends that 'there are other examples in the history of religion of a central figure of this type being introduced as speaking in the first person in a cultic circle', but the examples he gives are all Christian.

In response to this, it must first be said that Mowinckel's view as a whole suggests that the relationship of Jesus and the early church has been read back into the Old Testament materials. But even if he is correct in his understanding of the relationship of the disciples of II Isaiah to their dead teacher, we still do not have a real parallel to early Christian prophetism; for it is inconceivable that the disciples of II Isaiah would put their dead master – even if 'resurrected' – in the place of the deity in the prophetic experience, though this is exactly what happened in the case of Jesus and the early church. To the disciples of II Isaiah, אמר יהוה (e.g. 49: 5) could never mean 'our dead and exalted teacher says', but only 'Yahweh says', as in the Old Testament prophetic idiom universally. The tradition of II Isaiah is rather a matter of an imaginative prophetic continuation of the earthly teacher's message, in which Yahweh alone is regarded as the agent who inspires the prophets to speak. There is thus no parallel here to the distinctive element in early Christian prophetism.

The same may be said of the speeches placed in Moses' mouth in Deuteronomy. H. J. Kraus may be quite correct in his argument for a continuing 'Mosaic prophetic office' in the cult, so that 'in particular the speeches of Moses in Deuteronomy would be seen to be not fiction or a surreptitious authorization, as has often been stated, but the proclamation of the Mosaic prophetic office which is based on the decree in Deut. 18: 15–18, and which took the place of Moses himself'.[8] But again, it is a matter of a cult prophet playing the role of Moses, through whom the word of *Yahweh* comes, not a word of the 'exalted Moses', nor 'Moses speaking in me' on the analogy of II Cor. 13: 3, and thus no parallel to Christian prophecy. All of which is to say: Christian prophetism presupposes a christology that is not found elsewhere.

Integral to the definition of Christian prophecy is the phrase 'the Christian community'. This phrase is intended to distinguish the prophet from the mystic, on the one hand, and the magicians and fortune tellers of whatever sort (even if these were also sometimes called προφῆται!) who claim to dispense supernatural information to individuals, on the other. Prophecy as here defined is a church phenomenon. This does not mean that it is necessarily a congregational, cultic phenomenon – this question is to be left open. But it does indicate that the figures who claim our interest in this study have their setting in the life of the Christian community (and that their oracles are related to the life and affairs of that community) rather than being freelancers who speak to individuals on personal matters.

Christian prophecy as defined above is also specifically intended to be distinguished from three related phenomena in early Christianity, although each of these three is sometimes included in discussions of Christian prophecy:

(1) The specific phenomenon of early Christian prophecy is to be distinguished from the general 'prophetic' character that the early πνεῦμα-filled Christian community possessed. The matter cannot be settled by appealing to Acts 2: 4, 16ff and claiming that 'it is a specific mark of the age of fulfillment that the Spirit does not only lay hold of individuals but that all members of the eschatological community without distinction are called to prophesy'.[9] To be sure, it was universally assumed in early Christianity that all Christians possessed the Spirit. There were, in fact, many circles in which the late-Jewish equation πνεῦμα = πνεῦμα τῆς προφητείας had an enduring influence. The prophet in the strict sense is not as sharply marked-off from the rest of the community as in the Old Testament and Judaism. The emergence of such a community, in which every member did have a kind of prophetic potential, does make the identification of prophetic figures in the strict sense more difficult. But there is ample evidence that even those early Christians, such as Paul and Luke, who affirmed that every member of the community was empowered by the Spirit (Acts 2: 38; 19: 1–7; I Cor. 12: 3, 13) still did not regard every Christian as a prophet but rather distinguished the general gift of the Spirit from the specific manifestation of prophecy (Acts 13: 1; 11: 27–8; 15: 32; 21: 9–11; I Cor. 12: 29; 14: 29), even though both associate the Spirit with prophecy (Acts 2: 17–18; 13: 1–2; 19: 6; 21: 10–11; I Thess. 5: 19–20; Rom. 12: 6; I Cor. 14 throughout, especially verse 37).

An example of the blurring of this important distinction may be seen in Eduard Schweizer's discussion of the church in the background of the Gospel of Matthew. After arguing, correctly I believe, that Matthew and his church were not hostile to charismatic phenomena *per se*, Schweizer comments that: 'In its preaching the church is a church of prophets.'[10] Surely he intends to assert that prophets in the strict sense were active in Matthew's church and that in general the preaching of such a church would be characterized by a kind of authority associated with the community's belief in its possession of the Spirit, but not that every sermon preached in the community was immediately-inspired in the sense of our definition, or that every person in the community made such a prophetic claim for himself. In this essay I have attempted to avoid using 'prophetic' for this broader understanding of a 'prophetic community'.

(2) Similarly, the specific phenomenon of early Christian prophecy is to be distinguished from the general phenomenon of the risen Lord's speaking through the Jesus-sayings handed on in the tradition of the church. Since the earliest days of form criticism, it has been rightly urged that the tradition of Jesus' sayings, containing both authentic sayings from the historical Jesus and the *Gemeindebildung* assumed to be from the historical Jesus, was often heard in the early church not as the remembered words of a great figure of the past but as the present word of the exalted Lord.[11] This would have been true regardless of whether the tradition was repeated by a genuinely prophetic figure or not – it was something inherent in the nature of the tradition, when combined with the community's faith in Jesus as the risen Lord. But this general contemporizing mode in which the tradition was generally heard in the early church must not be equated with, or confused with, the phenomenon of Christian prophecy as defined above.

(3) And, finally, the specific phenomenon of early Christian prophecy is to be distinguished from the general phenomenon of the living Christ who speaks through Christian preaching and testimony, as this is understood in several streams of Christian theology.[12] This popular theological conception of Christian preaching is expressed, for example, in Karl Adam's dictum that 'Christ speaks in the sermon of every country priest.'[13] But this is an understanding of the nature of the preaching event and of the text that is heard in the sermon, and moves on another plane than our discussion here, involving other categories than those we are using in dealing with a particular *religionsgeschichtlich* phenomenon in the first few Christian generations. The exponents of this understanding of the nature of the preaching event would affirm that it may happen irrespective of whether the preacher understands himself in prophetic terms as we have

defined them above. Indeed, this 'prophetic' understanding of the preaching event usually assumes that the preacher does not understand himself as such a prophet and that nothing like 'immediate inspiration' is involved. It is a matter of the sovereignty of the Word itself, or of the exalted Christ himself, having nothing to do with prophecy as a specific phenomenon in early Christianity.

Yet this understanding of the general phenomenon of Christian preaching has caused some blurring of the lines that separate it from prophecy *per se*. In addition to such comments as Schweizer's discussed above, one finds, for example, C. K. Barrett interpreting John 16: 8 as referring to 'the spirit-inspired utterances of Christian preachers'.[14] Should one conclude that Barrett understands this text as referring to Christian prophets as we have defined them or only that the Spirit, in the view of the Fourth Gospel, is active in the 'normal' preaching activity of the church? This latter view has been advocated especially by Bultmann and others in his wake[15] and may be partially responsible for the failure of the majority of Johannine scholars even to consider the possibility that John intends to picture the ministry of Christian prophets (in the strict sense) in his own community. Thus the question of definition leads to the question of which sources may be used for reconstructing the lineaments of early Christian prophecy, and to that question we now turn.

3   SOURCES

The method proposed for this study calls for the construction of a characterization of early Christian prophecy as defined above that can then be used as a heuristic tool for locating the possible influences of oracles of Christian prophets on the developing synoptic tradition. The issue of which sources may be used in such a reconstruction is a basic methodological point, which requires a full discussion before proceeding. We have no direct sources for those prophets who purportedly contributed to the gospel tradition except as their oracles may now be contained in the gospels as sayings of Jesus. Our reconstruction must therefore be based on indirect sources, which reflect and refract the phenomenon in various ways. This makes it important that a rationale should be given for each indirect source that is used, since the inclusion or exclusion of any given document may alter the completed profile of early Christian prophecy.

We may legitimately seek illumination on the figure of the early Christian prophet from any material in the Hellenistic world that has significant points of contact with any of the features of prophecy as defined above. Apart from Christian documents, these would comprise three categories of materials: the Hebrew Scriptures and the prophetic materials of both Judaism and paganism of the Hellenistic period. While nothing approaching a complete discussion of prophecy as expressed in these three bodies of material should be attempted here, a few brief comments about the relation of these materials to our study may be appropriate.

Old Testament prophecy and Christian prophecy

The working definition above obviously portrays Christian prophecy as similar to classical Old Testament prophecy, the primary difference being that the risen Jesus plays the role of Yahweh in the prophetic configuration. It is also clear that the Old Testament as used in early Christianity would often have had an influence on how prophecy was thought of, especially in those circles that understood the gift of prophecy present in the church as the eschatological outpouring of that same prophetic spirit which had inspired the Old Testament prophets. As will be apparent below, there are many points of contact between prophecy as it is understood in the Old Testament and as it is expressed in early Christianity. Thus several scholars consider 'Israelite' rather than 'Greek' prophecy to be foundational for their portrayal of early Christian prophecy.[1] While this may be a valid conclusion to stand at the end of an argument supported on other grounds, it cannot be a presupposition for reconstructing early Christian prophecy; nor can the Old Testament be used as a source for such reconstruction, without further warrant from within the Christian writings themselves.

Contemporary Judaism and Christian prophecy

The prophetic spirit was alive in the Judaism from which Christianity was born. To be sure, the dogma that prophecy had ended in the time of Ezra or Alexander was dominant in some circles.[2] This dogma has been accepted at face value and generalized to include all first-century Judaism by some Christian scholars.[3] How early, and how widely, this theory was accepted in first-century Judaism, and to what extent it affected religious experience, continue to be disputed points. Some would see the dogma as held during the early Christian decades by only a minority, the Pharisaic religious elite of Jerusalem, while folk religion continued to enjoy prophetic experiences.[4] Others would see the dogma as having had only a theoretical and terminological character, so that even those who held it might nonetheless experience prophetic phenomena, although they were not labeled as such.[5] In any case, first-century Judaism knew no dearth of prophetic figures, in the sense of persons who claimed to speak the word of God by inspiration. The *Bath Qol* was heard even by those rabbis who believed it could not take precedence over traditional *halacha*.[6] Gamaliel is reported to have received revelations from the Holy Spirit (= the Spirit of Prophecy), Johanan b. Zakkai prophesied to Vespasian that he would one day become emperor, and other rabbis gave inspired predictions of the future.[7] Though by no means a major element in rabbinic religious experience, a significant number of prophetic phenomena may be documented even in those circles where the dogma of the end of prophecy might be expected to have been most influential. We should not, therefore, be surprised to find an abundance of evidence for prophets and prophecy in those circles where the rabbinic dogma was less influential, namely among the Zealots, Essenes and other apocalyptically-oriented groups, as well as in first-century Jewish folk religion in general (though conspicuously absent among the Sadducees). Ulrich Müller has shown that it was the prophetic circles behind the production of some Jewish apocalypses that kept alive Old Testament prophetic forms, which were then taken over by early Christian prophets.[8] The variety and pervasiveness of prophetic phenomena in first-century Judaism have been documented by others and will not be repeated here.[9]

Qumran illustrates the presence of prophecy in one Jewish fringe group. The Teacher of Righteousness functioned as a prophet. The presence of prophecy at Qumran has been denied because the word נָבִיא was never applied to the Teacher or anyone else in the sect, or because the community was so oriented to rigid structure, study of Scripture and keeping of the Law that the prophetic spirit could find no place.[10] Each of these objections is wide of the mark. The former objection simply illustrates the fallacy of binding the phenomenon of prophecy to a particular vocabulary. The absence of the word נָבִיא is due not to the absence of prophecy, but to the theology of the sect that reserved the term exclusively for the prophets of Scripture and for the eschatological prophet still to come. The latter objection presupposes that prophecy can only exist in the absence of structured authority, an assumption not borne out by our sources. The Qumran community manifests a combination of the charismatic and organizational, of ardor and order, not unlike some early Christian communities. The Teacher of Righteousness is a Jewish prophet analogous to an early Christian prophet in our definition. The Habakkuk Commentary portrays him as one who speaks from the mouth of God (2.2–3), who is taught by God himself, who has poured out his Spirit upon him (7.4–7). In the *Hodayoth* 'the most distinctive individual element is the conscious-ness of having received a divine revelation',[11] even according to Burrows, who regards prophecy as absent from Qumran. The Teacher's charismatic enlightenment obviously results in a message that must be shared with the community. This line of argument has been developed by a number of scholars,[12] so that we may use the Qumran materials as having originated within, and been preserved by, a prophetic community in the same locale as, and partially contemporary with, early Christianity, and in particular we may regard the writings of the Teacher of Righteousness as those of a prophet.

Jewish prophecy in the first century was not of course limited to Palestine and Hebrew- or Aramaic-speaking Jews. Hellenistic Judaism too had prophets in its ranks. Within the extant materials deriving from the Hellenistic synagogue, Philo offers the most information concerning the prophetic phenomenon. Philo's extraordinarily frequent discussions of the nature of prophecy should be taken as a sign that he considered himself occasionally to experience prophetic inspiration. How representative Philo is of Hellenistic Judaism generally, and how his discussions of prophecy in particular are to be interpreted, are both disputed points.[13] From the Palestinian Jewish sources we learn that Christianity was born in a context where prophecy was alive; from Philo and other Hellenistic Jewish sources, such as elements of the Sibylline Oracles,[14] we learn that Christianity spread into a Hellenistic world where prophecy existed to some extent before and alongside it in the Hellenistic synagogue.

Pagan—Hellenistic prophecy and early Christian prophecy

Neither synagogue nor church introduced prophets to the Hellenistic world. The inspired spokesman for the gods, the oracle-giver, the ecstatic mouthpiece for the deity, frequently called προφήτης, was a familiar figure to the Graeco-Roman populace. This has often been described and documented by others and need not be repeated here.[15] Although a few members of the early *religionsgeschichtliche Schule* attempted to prove that early Christian prophecy was derived from this pre-Christian Hellenistic prophecy, that argument has been effectively refuted and will not concern us here.[16] The same may be said for the claim of Walter Schmithals' 'brilliantly one-sided pan-Gnosticism' that early Christian prophecy originated from the borrowing of a congregational office (*Gemeindeamt*) from Gnosticism.[17]

The three categories of materials discussed above have been introduced not in order to argue that they may be used as sources in the reconstruction of a profile of early Christian prophecy but for precisely the opposite reason. Christian prophecy must be portrayed from Christian sources. This is not to dismiss *Religionsgeschichte* out of hand but to insist that we should not first form our ideas of prophecy and prophets from non-New Testament or non-Christian sources, then impose these ideas on Christian materials. Christian prophecy as defined above is sufficiently different from anything outside the church as to exclude our trying to understand it as *simply* a subheading under prophecy in the Hellenistic world in general. In formulating our characterization, we need to be aware of materials from and about prophets in the Old Testament, Judaism and Hellenism. Christian prophecy is not utterly discontinuous from non-Christian prophecy. Non-Christian materials should be used in a secondary, analogical way for illustration and illumination of a picture, the main contours of which have already been firmly drawn on the basis of the New Testament sources themselves.[18]

One further disclaimer needs to be made before discussing the sources to be used. John the Baptist and, especially, Jesus were prophetic figures who obviously had some impact on the emerging Christian prophetism. Detailed studies describing the prophetic traits of each have been produced.[19] But since the pictures of John and Jesus as prophets come to us only in the forms that have been supplied by the community, and since these forms are themselves shaped not only by the impact of the figures of Jesus and John but also by the community's experience of prophecy, there is no way to use the portrayals of the prophets John and Jesus independently as sources for our reconstruction. So materials from and about John and Jesus can only be discussed as the documents in which they are now contained are discussed. This is an implication of the principle that Christian prophecy is to be reconstructed from Christian sources.

We need to consider only those sources that might in some way illuminate Christian prophecy as it appeared in the period prior to the destruction of Jerusalem in 70 C.E. Working with the hypotheses that the Q-material began to congeal in written form by 50 C.E. and was virtually complete before 70, that Mark was written within a very few years either side of 70, and that many of the materials in the 'M' and 'L' strata of the tradition antedate 70, one concludes that the only materials in the synoptic gospels that are post-70 are the later elements of the 'M' and 'L' strata and the redactional contributions of the evangelists themselves. Thus practically all the synoptic materials that could have originated from, or been significantly shaped by, Christian prophets must be earlier than 70 C.E. Further, the destruction of the holy city tended to precipitate a fixation of the traditions, which was in fact the beginning of the canon process.

This means that after 70 it would have been more difficult for prophetic oracles to be accepted into the tradition of Jesus' words than before. Without drawing rigid chronological distinctions, we may delimit our search to pre-70 Christian prophets. This cannot mean, however, that we are interested only in sources written before 70 but rather that we are only interested in sources that can throw some light on Christian prophecy in the pre-70 period.

In the case of each document discussed below, I intend in this chapter only to investigate whether each may legitimately be used as a source for our reconstruction of pre-70 Christian prophetism. No attempt will be made here to glean from these sources the information that will be used in the reconstruction itself, which is the task of Part Two of this study.

Revelation

The Apocalypse is our most obvious, and most extensive, example of Christian prophecy among the sources relevant to our task. It is clear that the author claims to write προφητεία (1: 3; 19: 20; 22: 7, 10, 18–19), the repeated τῆς προφητείας τοῦ βίβλου τούτου being epexegetical genitives, 'the prophecy that this book is'. It is also clear in 22: 9 that the author designates himself as a prophet. The equation in 22: 9 and 11: 18 of δοῦλος and προφήτης would then make the most probable interpretation of the ambiguous τοὺς ἑαυτοῦ δούλους τοὺς προφήτας in 10: 7 a reference that includes Christian prophets. This further means that δοῦλος in 1: 1 was probably understood by John to be the same as προφήτης, so that the revelation was given τῷ δούλῳ αὐτοῦ Ἰωάννῃ, precisely 'to John his prophet'. Thus although it is correct that John never uses the word προφήτης explicitly of himself, this is incidental, for his claim to be a prophet is clear.

But even if the terminology were not present, Revelation would still be prophecy in terms of our functional definition. This book is throughout the address of the risen Lord to his church, delivered through his immediately-inspired spokesman. John's use of traditional imagery and materials is no cause to deny that he is himself a visionary whose revelations are the direct result of his encounter with the risen Christ, an encounter that he places in the same series as the Old Testament prophets' revelatory experiences from Yahweh. Nor is it the case that genuine Christian prophecy in which *Jesus* speaks is found only in chapters 2–3, the rest being the typical Jewish apocalyptic revelation from God by an angel.[20] Rather, the book as a whole is ἀποκάλυψις Ἰησοῦ Χριστοῦ, as the subjective genitive of 1: 1 indicates. The revelatory chain θεός – Χριστός – ἄγγελος – δοῦλος (προφήτης) of 1: 1 also indicates that God, the exalted Christ and the revelatory angel are neither to be isolated from one another nor to be contrasted with each other, but are elements of the same revelatory experience. This is seen, for example, in the series of quotations in 21: 9, 15; 22: 1, 6, 8, 9, 10, 12, which, if the strict logic of the series is followed, has the *angel* saying 'Behold, I am coming soon', which is obviously to be taken as a word of the exalted Jesus. This is also seen in the structure of the book itself. From 6: 1 on, the book unfolds as the seals of the sealed scroll are broken one by one. But this sealed book, which originates from the hand of God, is now in the hand of the exalted Jesus and is opened only by him. In this way, though the apocalyptic form of sealed scroll and interpreting angel is retained, it is subordinated to the understanding of revelation in Christian prophecy, in which the risen Lord himself speaks through his prophet.

It is to be remembered that our definition of prophecy is formal and functional, not material. This means that the categories 'apocalyptic' and 'prophecy' are not necessarily to be opposed to each other and particularly that the question of whether Revelation is 'apocalyptic' or 'prophecy' is misdirected. That apocalyptic materials can be incorporated in a Christian prophetic framework is clear from the above. That John specifically intends to break with apocalyptic, formally defined, and replace it with the direct address of the Lord who speaks in the present, is clear from 22: 10, where John's own προφητεία τοῦ βίβλου τούτου is marked off from all pseudonymous apocalyptic purportedly revealed to some ancient worthy. Revelation is thus a valuable example of one kind of early Christian prophecy.

The value of Revelation as a source for reconstructing early Christian prophecy is not exhausted by the fact that it is itself our most lengthy example of one kind of prophecy. Revelation also reflects the ideas and practice of John's church with regard to prophecy. For example, 10: 8 – 11: 13 pictures the eschatological prophet as he was understood in John's church, using traditional images that let us see their understanding of the essential features of the prophetic figure and ministry, and Rev. 2–3 lets us see not only John's oracles but something of the way the prophetic ministry was practiced and the response to it in the churches of Asia Minor.

Revelation was written to seven churches in Asia from the nearby island of Patmos, by one who had ministered in the area long enough to become a revered leader in this group of churches. Yet there are clear indications that many of the prophetic materials and ideas contained in the book originated earlier, in a Palestinian setting. That the author is a Jewish Christian is apparent from the Old Testament and apocalyptic materials that form the substance of his writing, and from his antipathy to those who claim to be Jews but are not (2: 9; 3: 9). Beyond this, that the author was originally a Palestinian-Jewish Christian has been often and persuasively argued from the linguistic peculiarities of the book, which indicate that the author's native language was not Greek but a Semitic language. R. H. Charles thought it possible to demonstrate that 'he wrote in Greek and thought in Hebrew, and frequently translated Hebrew idioms literally into Greek', and identified the Seer as 'a Jewish Christian who had in all probability spent the greater part of his life in Galilee before he emigrated to Asia Minor'.[21] A recent study has confirmed Charles' linguistic argument and even those, such as Heinrich Kraft, who reject the particulars of the argument, acknowledge that the author of the Apocalypse had Hebrew or Aramaic as his native tongue.[22] Akira Satake has presented a detailed argument that not only John himself but the churches of Asia Minor in which the Seer was at home represent a transplanted Palestinian Christianity forced from Palestine at the time of the war of 66–70 C.E. I find his argument basically convincing.[23]

If Revelation had been written prior to 70, it would be a sterling witness to pre-70 Palestinian Christian prophetism. J. A. T. Robinson is among those who have attempted to revive the nineteenth-century case for dating the Apocalypse this early.[24] Although he has pointed out the assumptions of many recent scholars who may suppose too easily that the commonly-accepted dating in Domitian's reign no longer needs defending, Robinson's own attempt to overthrow the dominant view can hardly be said to have succeeded. His argument relies too much on legendary external testimony and on his confidence in his ability to extract reliable information regarding dates from it; he doesn't allow enough weight to the influence of the Nero *redivivus* myth in the 90s.

If renewed examination of the issue should ultimately vindicate the date proposed by Robinson, the value of Revelation as a source for the project undertaken in this essay would be enhanced. I am presently convinced, however, that the final form of Revelation was written *c.* 95 C.E., with perhaps a re-editing of sections of chapters 13 and 17 slightly later in the reigns of Nerva and Trajan.[25]

The value of Robinson's discussion for the issue pursued here is that it reveals how much material in Revelation is oriented to pre-70 Palestine. Dating Revelation in 95 does not mean that it was created *ex nihilo* at that time. Numerous authors, including Robinson, have pointed out the substantial traditional elements in Revelation, so that the conclusion is justified that John stands in a tradition of Christian prophecy, a tradition originating in the life of the church in pre-70 Palestine.[26] This means that in the Apocalypse we have not only an example of one kind of Christian prophetism in Asia Minor near the end of the century, but also a source that can be judiciously used as in some sense a witness to pre-70 Palestinian Christian prophecy. This does not mean, however, that we may simply assume that John is in all respects typical of other prophets and generalize from features of Christian prophecy found in Revelation. Some of the differences pointed to by David Hill may be accounted for by the fact that John is necessarily absent from the churches he is addressing and therefore composes his prophecy in written form.[27] The key passage to which Hill points as evidence that John delivers his message to the community 'prophets', who then mediate it to the church (22: 16), is difficult to interpret — Charles and Kraft both understand it otherwise. And such passages as 22: 9 indicate that John sees himself as a member of a brotherhood of prophets instead of a unique figure different in kind from them. While it is true that we cannot simply read our description of early Christian prophecy off the surface of Revelation, we may use Revelation critically, in conjunction with other sources, as one source in our delineation of pre-70 Christian prophetism.[28]

Paul

Paul's letters are valuable sources for the reconstruction of early Christian prophecy because they contain our only canonical *discussion* of prophecy, because they portray Paul's own prophetic self-understanding and because they contain prophetic formulae and oracles from Paul himself and other early Christian prophets. Each of these aspects will be discussed in turn.

Our earliest New Testament document concludes with a Pauline exhortation not to despise prophesying, I Thess. 5: 19—21. Paul appears as the advocate of the prophetic gift. Brief as it is, this instruction of Paul is important in that it shows that prophecy is already present at the earliest point at which we can observe the Hellenistic church, indeed, that it has already undergone a certain development, the stages of which can be charted: initial appearance of prophecy at Thessalonica, some sort of excesses, which caused at least some of the Thessalonians to reject or disdain it, and Paul's promotion of their re-evaluation and critical acceptance of it. The grounds of their suspicion of prophecy are not clear but may be related to the eschatological agitation that troubled the church at Thessalonica. Especially if II Thessalonians is from Paul, but even if not, it may be that Christian prophets had prematurely predicted the coming of the Lord and had been discredited by the resultant confusion. But, here as elsewhere, we learn nothing concrete about the content of the preaching of prophets in Paul's churches from what his letters have to say regarding prophecy in a particular church.

Our most extensive discussion of Christian prophecy is found in I Cor. 12—14. As in I Thessalonians, the discussion has a polemical tone, again revealing Paul as the advocate of prophecy, this time over against an inappropriately high valuation of *glossolalia*. There is little indication of the content of the Corinthian prophets' oracles to be gleaned from this passage. Its value for our reconstruction is rather that it permits us to examine Paul's own extended discussion of the nature of Christian prophecy, portraying how *he* understood it.

The brief reference to prophecy in Rom. 12: 3—8 is valuable in that it is not addressed to a situation where prophecy is, in Paul's estimation, misunderstood or devalued. Rather than polemics, a fundamental assumption of Paul's comes to expression here, namely that wherever there is a church the Holy Spirit is at work, and wherever the Spirit is, there is to be found a (the?) principal manifestation of the Spirit, the gift of prophecy. Indeed, prophecy is the only constant in Paul's 'lists' of $\chi\alpha\rho\acute{\iota}\sigma\mu\alpha\tau\alpha$ (I Cor. 12: 8—11, 28—30; 13: 1—2; Rom. 12: 6—8) and, when the gifts are 'ranked', appears second only to apostleship or, from another point of

view, love. These texts from three different letters, taken together, show
that Paul is not forced into discussing prophecy by its occurrence in his
churches, and that for him it is not a 'problem' to be dealt with but a
constituent part of the church itself. We will see below that this makes
Paul's discussions of the nature of the prophetic gift the more valuable for
our delineation of early Christian prophecy.

Is Paul himself to be numbered among the early Christian prophets?
The importance of definition becomes apparent once more in determining
how this question is to be answered. If prophecy is defined in advance in
religionsgeschichtlich terms, which make ecstatic speaking a prerequisite
of prophecy, then Paul must be excluded. Thus Lindblom, who operates
with *religionsgeschichtlich* methods, classifies Paul as a teacher, not a
prophet.[29] If a particular form of address, such as addressing his readers or
hearers using the name of Christ in the first person, is made the *sine qua
non* of Christian prophecy, then Paul must be excluded, for he does not
use that form.[30] But if prophecy is defined functionally as above, then
Paul is a prophet, for he is an immediately-inspired spokesman for the
risen Lord, who receives revelations that he is impelled to deliver to the
Christian community (cf., e.g., I Cor. 2: 13; 5: 3–4; 7: 40 (and, in the
light of this 'postscript', cf. the preceding verses); 14: 6, 37; II Cor. 2: 17;
12: 1–9, 19; 13: 3; Gal. 1: 12; 2: 2; I Thess. 2: 13; 4: 1–2, 15–17.)
Samuel Sandmel's statement, that 'In my judgment, no term better serves
initially to classify the convert Paul than the word "prophet" ', would be
widely accepted from a variety of points of view.[31]

To be sure, Paul never calls himself προφήτης, nor is he called such by
others. In this he is no different from the author of Revelation, who functions
as a prophet without applying the title to himself. In both cases, it is function,
not label, that is important. The absence of the title in Paul's case is
accounted for by his insistence that he is ἀπόστολος. But ἀπόστολος in the
early church, and especially in Paul, is modeled largely on the role of the
prophet in Israel as God's representative and spokesman, who has been
called and commissioned by God himself. Paul's account of his call in Gal.
1: 15–16 is replete with prophetic allusions and shows that he understands
himself in the succession of prophets. Ἀπόστολος is frequently paralleled
by δοῦλος, the meaning of which, when Paul uses it of himself, extends
beyond its general meaning in reference to all Christians and expresses his
claim to the same office as that held by those Old Testament δοῦλοι θεοῦ,
the prophets. Further, Paul does not use ἀπόστολος in the sense of one
χάρισμα among many – not even the chief one – but as an office that
comprehends the other χαρίσματα, including prophecy, in itself. As an
apostle he speaks in tongues (I Cor. 14: 6, 18) and works miracles (II Cor.

12: 12; Gal. 3: 5); as an apostle he can and does prophesy (I Cor. 14: 6;
I Thess. 4: 15–17).

The fact that Paul was a prophet does not mean that Paul's letters are
to be seen *en bloc* as Christian prophecy. It is true that a general prophetic
standpoint characterizes all of Paul's preaching and writing. It is the word
of the crucified and risen Jesus that comes to speech in Paul's writings.[32]
But this hardly means that material from Paul's letters may be quoted
indiscriminately as examples of early Christian prophecy! Rather, we must
sort out the variety of ways in which the prophetic nature of Paul's
ministry has impressed itself upon his letters. There are principally four of
these.

(1) Paul's prophetic self-understanding is occasionally reflected in his
letters only incidentally, by his vocabulary, manner of expression and
choice of materials. Just as a scribe or priest will incidentally adopt a
scribal or priestly style and use scribal or priestly materials, even when not
dealing with scribal or priestly lore, so Paul the prophet may reflect his
prophetic viewpoint in those passages where he is neither discussing
prophecy, nor quoting prophetic revelations *per se*. For example, I Thess.
4: 7–9, a passage of general parenesis, has a number of words and concepts
particularly appropriate to prophetic ministry: the note of 'solemn fore-
warning' (προείπαμεν ὑμῖν καὶ διεμαρτυράμεθα, cf. RSV), the idea of
divine calling (ἐκάλεσεν ἡμᾶς ὁ θεός), the idea that to reject the warning is
not simply to reject the human messenger but to reject the God who sent
him, the reference to the Holy (= prophetic) Spirit, the idea that the
hearers 'have no need to be instructed' because they are all 'taught by
God' (θεοδίδακτοι).[33] In I Cor. 4: 1, in describing himself as among the
ὑπηρέτας Χριστοῦ καὶ οἰκονόμους μυστηρίων θεοῦ, Paul incidentally gives
a description of Christian prophets. The unusual use of ἀκοή (in Gal. 3:
2, 5 and Rom. 10: 17–18) for the prophetic message, meaning the same as
κήρυγμα, is best understood as a technical term of prophetic origin.[34] The
Romans passage has additional prophetic overtones: 'the message that is
preached comes from the word of Christ' (JB), reading Χριστοῦ with the
best MSS and taking it as at least a semi-subjective genitive, the prophetic
connotation of φθόγγος (cf. φθέγγομαι in Acts 4: 18, ἀποφθέγγομαι in
Acts 2: 14; 26: 25), and the general thrust of the passage to the effect that
people do not take the preaching task on themselves but are *sent*, are all
expressions of the prophetic point of view. The capital illustration of this
kind of material in Paul is I Cor. 2: 6–16. A number of scholars argue that
this passage is an expression of the prophetic consciousness.[35] Although
these verses are not a prophetic oracle *per se*, their subject and background
is the prophetic revelation that lives in Paul's mission, and they may be

used with critical caution in describing prophecy as it appeared in Pauline Christianity.[36]

(2) A second, concrete way in which Paul's prophetic self-understanding has impressed itself on his letters is found in the number of prophetic forms and formulae that Paul uses even when he is not quoting a prophetic oracle. Extensive sections of his writings sometimes seem to be shaped, consciously or unconsciously, by forms that have their home in prophetic speech. Particular forms such as 'the prophetic judgment form' and 'sentences of holy law' have been discussed in isolated articles; recently a comprehensive and detailed study of this aspect of Paul's writing style has appeared in a monograph by Ulrich Müller.[37] Müller's argument is as follows: Paul was a prophet. He did not write his letters but spoke them orally, bringing his congregation before his mind's eye as he spoke. One would therefore expect Paul's oral style of prophetic address to influence the form and style of his letters. This is confirmed when we find prophetic formulae in his letters, formulae that are recognized as prophetic because of their occurrence in the Old Testament, Jewish prophecy and Christian prophecy as we otherwise know it. A weakness of Müller's book is that this last point is undeveloped, for he relies almost entirely on Revelation and I Cor. 14 to provide him with his picture of Christian prophecy. Still, Müller's work is a step forward from the arbitrariness that has prevailed in this regard. He is careful to delineate the criteria by which he picks out prophetic elements in Paul's letters,[38] a kind of methodological care almost unknown in discussions of Christian prophecy. These criteria are: (i) introductory and authorization formulae, (ii) function and content, i.e. material that represents a divine decision to be delivered to the community, (iii) traditional speech-forms of prophets (Old Testament, Jewish, Christian), (iv) the congruency of the text in question with our picture of early Christian prophecy as we otherwise know it, (v) the congruency of the text with oral prophetic speech-patterns, (vi) a sudden departure from the literary style of the context. Müller uses these criteria to identify prophetic speech in Paul's letters, including both the incidental fragments of prophetic forms that are not a part of a prophetic oracle *per se* and the oracles themselves. The particular prophetic formal elements in Paul's letters will be discussed at the relevant points in our reconstruction in the following chapter; here we are only concerned to point out in advance that such elements exist and ought not to be overlooked in such a reconstruction.

(3) Paul's use of traditional sayings of Jesus also illustrates his prophetic self-consciousness. This too is discussed in the relevant section of the next chapter and is mentioned here only to point out its usefulness as a source of insight into the functioning of early Christian prophecy.

(4) Most valuable of all the types of prophetic material that may be isolated in Paul's letters are those passages where we probably have the inspired revelations of Paul himself or of some other early Christian prophet. The list of such purported oracles that can be gleaned from the literature on Paul is rather extensive: Rom. 8: 19–22; 11: 25–6, 31–2; 13: 11–14; 16: 17–20; I Cor. 3: 17; 7: 10, 29–31; 11: 23–5; 13: 13; 14: 38; 15: 20–9, 51–2; 16: 22; II Cor. 5: 20–1; 11: 13–15; Gal. 1: 9–10; 5: 21*b*; Phil. 2: 6–11; 3: 17 – 4: 1; I Thess. 2: 15–16; 4: 15–17; 5: 1–11 (II Thess. 2: 3–12). Although many of these verses do bear certain marks of Christian prophecy as we will characterize it below and express something of Paul's prophetic self-consciousness, in most instances a convincing case has not been made for the verses concerned being in fact the oracle of some Christian prophet – indeed most such statements are rather casually made with little or no supporting evidence. Thus most of these passages would seem rather to belong to our categories (i) and (ii) above. The major portion of such material, if used at all, will be regarded as illustrating the general prophetic nature of Paul's ministry rather than as examples of prophetic revelations. There are three passages, however, that have repeatedly been acknowledged as prophetic oracles on the basis of form, style and content: Rom. 11: 25–6,[39] I Cor. 15: 51–2[40] and I Thess. 4: 15–17.[41] Of course, all such identifications of prophetic material in Paul's letters will in the nature of the case remain short of certainty, since Paul never explicitly identifies any text as a revelation from the risen Lord to him or as a quotation from another Christian prophet. Even in I Thess. 4: 15–17, where this is most nearly the case, the nature of the quotation is not absolutely clear. In all work of historical reconstruction such as is being attempted here, subjectivity cannot be entirely eliminated, and conclusions will remain in the realm of probability. However, in view of the arguments presented by those scholars referred to in the notes, Rom. 11: 25–6; I Cor. 15: 51–2 and I Thess. 4: 15–17 can be reasonably considered as having originated as revelations of the risen Lord and will be used in our reconstruction as examples of pre-70 Christian prophetic material.

Paul's prophetism was once widely regarded as being of a piece with Hellenistic prophecy generally.[42] Although the Hellenistic factor in Paul's doctrine of the Spirit is not to be absolutely denied, more recent study has correctly observed that Paul's understanding of prophecy is not simply a reflection of prophetic phenomena as experienced in his churches but stands in tension with it. Already in I Thess. 5: 19–20, but especially in the running debate of I Cor. 12–14, Paul is exalting a kind of prophecy that he advocates over against an understanding of prophecy in his churches. The criticism of Paul by his opponents in II Cor. 10: 10; 11: 6 probably represents their charge that he lacked facility in extempore speaking, which facility was the mark of the true pneumatic. For the Corinthian prophets, the Spirit was irresistible, but for Paul the spirits of the prophets were under the control of the prophets themselves (I Cor. 14: 32). For the Corinthians, the prophet was autonomous, but for Paul others must weigh and 'confirm' what is said (I Cor. 14: 29). The Corinthians espoused a super-realized eschatology, against which Paul advocated the old Jewish-Christian apocalyptic understanding kept alive by Christian prophets (I Cor. 15). The Corinthians had rejected the category 'new people of God' and had substituted an individualistic anthropology, but Paul's understanding of spiritual gifts is corporate, so that their only purpose is edification of the body (I Cor. 12: 7, 27–8; 14: 4, 12).

How is this tension between Paul's understanding of prophecy and that of his churches to be explained? At first, an explanation from within Hellenism itself was sought. Hans Leisegang attempted to see Paul as opposing the extremes of Hellenistic enthusiasm in his churches on the basis of a higher Greek understanding, which opposed νοῦς to πνεῦμα. But Leisegang's forced exegesis of I Cor. 14, in which he attempts to separate νοῦς and πνεῦμα, assigning the former to Paul and the latter to the Corinthians alone, only illustrates the untenability of this position.[43] Rather, Paul is to be seen as standing in a prophetic tradition. This tradition has its roots in the Old Testament-Jewish understanding of prophecy and represents the understanding of prophecy and prophets as they were manifest in some streams of the early Palestinian church. Paul has been influenced by this tradition, which was a major factor in molding his own concept of prophecy. Paul is pictured in Acts as having been in close association with prophetic figures of the early Palestinian church: Barnabas (Acts 4: 36; 13: 1 – 15: 40, esp. 13: 1–2; Gal. 2: 1, 9, 13; I Cor. 9: 6), Silas/Silvanus (Acts 15: 22, 32; 15: 40 – 18: 17; II Cor. 1: 19; I Thess. 1: 1 (II Thess. 1: 1)), Agabus, the daughters of Philip, and other anonymous prophets (Acts 11: 27–30; 21: 9–14; cf. 16: 6; 20: 23; 21: 4). Although some details of the Acts representation may have been colored by legend or Lukan *Tendenz*, there is no reason to deny this picture as a whole. Further, Paul's obvious preference for prophecy among the gifts of the Spirit in the discussion in I Cor. 14 expresses the point of view dominant in Palestinian-Jewish Christianity, in which the Spirit is pre-eminently the spirit of prophecy. The particular contrasts between Paul's understanding of the prophetic gift and that of the Corinthians must have made him appear as something of a traditionalist to them. Paul's connection with this prophetic tradition probably extends even to the occasional preservation and transmission of an oracle that originated in early Palestinian prophecy.[44] It is now widely accepted, on the basis of evidence thoroughly argued, that when Paul confronts and responds to an understanding of Christian prophecy different from his own, he is not simply responding *ad hoc*, but that the tradition within which he stands comes to expression in his response.[45]

This does not mean that one can simply generalize from Paul to 'early Christian prophecy', still less that Paul can be used as a normative picture of Christian prophecy by which others are measured. But it does mean that material from Paul's letters can be used, in critical comparison with other sources, as one source from which information may be gleaned about those prophets who may have influenced the synoptic tradition of Jesus' words.

The Deutero-Pauline letters

If Ephesians and/or the Pastorals are by Paul himself, then obviously they are to be used as sources for early Christian prophecy in the same ways as the other Pauline letters. If they are not from Paul, as is here judged to be the case, these letters may be expected to portray prophecy as it was understood in the Pauline churches of the second and third generation, but to yield at most a minimum of new information about those early Christian prophets whom we are seeking to characterize. Since it is possible, however, that even these late products of developing Pauline Christianity may contain some memories and impressions of the ministry of Christian prophets in earlier times, they should not be dismissed *a priori* as sources for our reconstruction.

The three explicit references to προφῆται in Ephesians are all to Christian prophets rather than to Old Testament figures. This is clearly the case in 3: 5 and 4: 11, where a church context is specified, but is hardly less obvious in 2: 20, where word order and the fact that both ἀπόστολοι and προφῆται are embraced under one article argues for church prophets. It is just as clear, however, that these are not prophets in the time contemporary with the author but belong to a period already past. In 3: 5, the revelation given to the prophets calling for a startling new departure is now something presupposed and celebrated but no longer debated. In 2: 20 prophets are regarded, along with the apostles, as forming an essential part of the founding generation of the church but not necessarily a part of its present ministry. The reference to prophets in 4: 11 should be seen within the temporal framework assumed by the author, representing 'Paul's' time, but not the author's, who no longer knows either apostles or prophets personally. The manifold charismatic gifts of Paul's own time are here reduced to apostles, prophets, evangelists and pastor-teachers as representative of the whole group enumerated in I Cor. 12—14 and Rom. 12. Since apostles and prophets belong to the 'founding' period, the ministry in the author's own church seems to be composed of εὐαγγελίσται and ποιμένες καὶ διδάσκαλοι, the latter probably thought of as one office. The earlier charismatic ministry is remembered with gratitude, but it is only a memory and has given way to a more structured, ordered ministry in the later Pauline churches. No materials are preserved in Ephesians that originated as the oracles of the earlier charismatics. There is no awareness that the existence of prophets in the earlier church was a problem as well as a blessing. The author is simply grateful that in the early days of the church the exalted Christ bestowed this gift upon the young church, for the memory persists even in the author's time that a theological decision of momentous import, the decision to include the Gentiles within the church, was a matter of post-resurrection revelation ἐν πνεύματι to apostles and prophets. This fading-away of the prophetic gift, strictly defined, seems to have happened without a crisis, without any suspicion or denigration of the prophetic phenomena. This is seen not only in the reverence in which he holds the earlier prophets but in the fact that the author's vocabulary concerning revelation and the spirit is related to the earlier prophetic vocabulary, though no longer limited to the prophetic phenomenon *per se* (e.g. 1: 9, 17). Expressions originally at home in the circles of Christian prophets have been broadened to describe the Christian life generally. This means that the author stands in a tradition in which Christian prophecy was once active, the effects of which can still be perceived to some minimal extent in this later deposit.

Likewise in the Pastorals, prophecy is primarily a remembered phenomenon from the Pauline past, rather than a vital part of the Pastor's own church. There may still be some stirrings of the prophetic spirit manifest in the references in I Tim. 1: 18; 4: 14 and II Tim. 1: 14, but if these refer to the time of the author, and are not simply embellishments portraying Timothy's ministry in accord with its assumed time-frame, then the gift of prophecy is regarded with more than a bit of suspicion. The point seems to be that the prophetic charisma should lead to regular ordination and, in fact, operates properly only within the legitimately ordained channels and in connection with the deposit of tradition (ἡ παραθήκη). The dearth of reference to the Spirit, so frequent in Paul, has significance not only for the question of authorship but in illustrating the non-pneumatic nature of the Pastor's *Sitz im Leben*. The chief function of the ministry is the teaching of orthodox doctrine, handing on the tradition of the past, not the reception of new 'words of the Lord'.

Claims that prophetic oracles are found in the Pastorals are uniformly unsupported by evidence. The prophetic spirit is considered incompatible with the emphasis on 'divine order'. The 'prophecy' of I Tim. 4: 1–3 is not a real word of the Lord that comes into being in the author's own time but only a literary device to indicate that heresy did not come upon the church by surprise but was foreseen and 'prophesied' by the earlier apostle. Just as the Pastor's ideas of the relation of Christian prophecy and ordination seem to have been shaped by his reading of Acts 13: 1–3, so his view that earliest, heresy-free Christianity already prophesied the apostasy of succeeding generations seems to have been influenced by Acts 20: 29–30. We may therefore expect the Pastorals to be even less valuable than Ephesians as sources for the reconstruction of early Christian prophecy.

Acts and the Gospel of Luke

Acts is our only New Testament document that purports to describe prophets in the pre-70 Palestinian church. Agabus stands out most clearly (11: 27–30; 21: 1–14) as one who is not only called προφήτης by Luke but fits my functional definition of prophecy as well. Judas and Silas are prophets (15: 32). Philip has four daughters who prophesy (21: 9). Anonymous prophets proclaim their message by the Spirit, a term used interchangeably in such contexts with 'Holy Spirit', 'Spirit of the Lord' and 'Spirit of Jesus', showing that it is the exalted Christ who is thought of as active in the prophetic event (16: 6–7; 20: 23; 21: 4).[46] A group of prophets and teachers at Antioch includes Barnabas and Paul (13: 1–2). That Luke intends to include Barnabas among the prophets seems to be clear both from the grammar of this text and from 4: 36; whether or not Paul is called a prophet in 13: 1–2 is not absolutely clear.[47] At the least, Paul is associated very closely with church prophets and is described by Luke as functioning as a prophet (9: 3–6; 13: 9–12; 16: 6–9; 18: 9–10; 22: 6–21; 26: 9–20; 27: 23–4).

   In addition to this portrayal of particular individuals who manifest the prophetic gift, Luke understands that the Spirit has been poured out on the whole church, and this Spirit is pre-eminently the Spirit of Prophecy (2: 17–18, 38; 4: 31; 6: 10; 16: 6–7). This means that, though Luke does recognize certain persons in the church who function consistently as prophets (whom he so designates), he does not draw a sharp line between prophets and non-prophets. Whoever in the church acts in the power of the Spirit is something of a prophet. This in turn means that even in those scenes where prophets are not specifically mentioned, but where the Spirit is active in some extraordinary way, the figures may be portrayed prophetically. Key examples would be 5: 1–11 and 10: 1–47, where Peter is portrayed as directed by the Spirit, for whom he serves as spokesman. This does not mean, however, that generalizations may be made from such passages in regard to early Christian prophecy or even in regard to Luke's understanding of it. Those passages in which Luke clearly intends to portray prophets should serve as guides. But since Luke does not draw firm lines between these and his secondary descriptions of the prophetic Spirit at work, these latter may also be used in a supplementary way.

Luke uses traditions that portray prophets in early Palestinian Christianity and portray the earliest church as a whole as charged with the prophetic Spirit.[48] But this does not mean that a description of pre-70 Palestinian prophets can be read off the surface of the text of Acts. Luke does not create his statements about Christian prophets *ex nihilo*; he does adapt his tradition to his own *Tendenzen*. For Acts to be of optimum usefulness to us in our reconstruction, we must be aware of these.

The Lukan theological perspectives that might from case to case have influenced his portrayal of Christian prophecy are principally four.

(1) Luke is interested in portraying the church as the continuation of the Old Testament people of God, which leads him to portray Christian prophets (and Jesus) as standing in the succession of Old Testament prophets, whom they resemble. Agabus' binding himself with Paul's belt, for instance, is reminiscent of the symbolic acts performed by Isaiah, Ezekiel and Jeremiah (Acts 21: 10–14; cf. Is. 20: 2–6; Ezek. 4–5; Jer. 13: 1–11). John the Baptist is introduced in Luke 3: 1–3 in the same way that Old Testament prophetic books are introduced (Is. 1: 1; Jer. 1: 1–2; Ezek. 1: 1–3; Hos. 1: 1; Amos 1: 1; Micah 1: 1; Zeph. 1: 1; Hag. 1: 1; Zech. 1: 1). In the speculations about Jesus' identity reported in Luke 9: 8, 19, Luke each time adds ἀρχαῖος to the term προφήτης contained in his source. All this indicates a conscious intent on Luke's part to stylize his descriptions of prophets to conform to those of his Bible. Of course, it may well be that early Christian prophets did in fact resemble their Old Testament counterparts on several points. But since Luke seems to frame his language deliberately on Old Testament models, such elements in Luke's descriptions may sometimes be redactional rather than traditional. Decisions will have to be made from case to case.

(2) Luke's portrayal of the prophets in Acts, including Paul, is uniformly non-eschatological. Agabus' prediction of a famine that would cover the whole οἰκουμένην was probably originally *the* famine that is often a part of the eschatological drama, but Luke has historicized it and reduced it to Judea. Similarly, Paul's oracles, which in his epistles are always eschatological, are in Acts this-worldly predictions of the historical

future (20: 22–3, 29–30; 27: 22–3). Luke has a demonstrable tendency to historicize the eschatology of his sources,[49] and this tendency should be kept in mind when evaluating his portrayal of Christian prophets.

(3) Luke chiefly values the prophetic phenomenon manifest in the early church for its evidential value rather than for the content of Christian prophetic oracles themselves. *That* persons in the early church prophesy is a proof that the eschatological gift of the Spirit is present in the church and that the church therefore is to be understood in continuity with the Old Testament people of God (2: 14–18; 19: 1–7). *What* the content of these 'prophecies' is matters little to Luke. It may not be mentioned at all, as in 19: 7, or need not be obeyed, as in 21: 4. Luke's interest in prophecy does not extend to the careful preservation and handing on of prophetic oracles themselves. To the extent that this is present in Luke, it is incidental to Luke's purpose or represents an interest of the pre-Lukan tradition.

(4) Although prophetic phenomena are frequent in Acts, Luke allows the prophets only a fringe role in the leadership of the church. So far as church structure and order are concerned, Luke has an early catholic *Tendenz*. He celebrates the presence of prophecy in the church as a supernatural validation of the church's claim to be the people of God but is hesitant to portray charismatics as playing too great a role in the actual policy-making decisions of the church. This role is filled primarily by 'apostles and elders'. In 13: 1–3 prophets are explicitly involved in a major new departure in the history of the church, though no new policy is set there. Luke's own perspective is seen more typically in Acts 10, where the new policy *vis-à-vis* the Gentile mission comes by a revelation to Peter, in a scene filled with prophetic nuances. However, Peter is not called a prophet but an apostle, and his action is officially ratified by the other apostles and the Jerusalem church in chapter 11.

Acts 15: 1–35 portrays a similar circumstance, in which prophets in the pre-Lukan tradition seem to have played a greater role in the decision-making process than is now apparent in the Lukan edition of the event. First, the problem is posed for which the will of God is sought. But instead of 'inquiring by a prophet', the disputants go to Jerusalem to the 'apostles and elders', a couplet used by Luke five times in this context to emphasize the role of the 'official' leaders in the decision-making process (15: 2, 4, 6, 22, 23). Judas and Silas, whom Luke designates as prophets (15: 32), are 'leading men among the brethren' (15: 22), though they are portrayed by Luke as playing no role in the decision. They are entrusted with delivering the letter, which is called παράκλησις, a word with prophetic overtones. The letter contains the phrase 'it seemed good to the Holy Spirit and to us', which corresponds to the typical process by which oracles were received by prophets and the διάκρισις function of the whole community by which they were validated. The decision itself was arrived at on the basis of speeches by Peter, Paul and Barnabas, all of whom are prophetic figures; but it is James, a non-prophet, to whom Luke assigns the role of declaring the verdict. The interpretation of the Old Testament to apply to the present, another prophetic characteristic,[50] also plays a role. Thus we have a scene permeated by prophetic phenomena, which is described by Luke in such a way as to give the prophets only a subsidiary role.

Luke has an obvious disdain for the Hellenistic type of pagan prophet, whom he refuses to dignify with the revered Old Testament term προφήτης.[51] He does not wish to portray the life of the church as penetrated by ecstatic types resembling pagan 'prophets'. Although he has a somewhat romantic appreciation of the prophetic ecstasy of the earliest church, seen for example in his adding καὶ προφητεύσουσιν to the Joel quotation in Acts 2: 18, he no more wishes to promote it in the life of the church of his own generation than he wishes to perpetuate the earliest church's 'communism' of 4: 32–6. Luke is by no means anti-prophetic. But he describes the role of prophets as operating within a firm structure controlled by apostles and elders. This *Tendenz*, like the others, must be kept in mind when using Acts to describe early Christian prophecy.

Not only Acts but also the Gospel of Luke manifests Luke's cautious appropriation of prophetic imagery. As in the other synoptic gospels, the Lukan Jesus predicts the emergence of prophets in the church – though in the Lukan form prophets are complemented by apostles (11: 49–51). Little help is to be gained, however, for the project of reconstructing the characteristics of early Palestinian Christian prophets from such incidental remarks about Christian prophets in Luke. A more fertile field for our project may be found in the Lukan portrayal of Jesus, whom Luke intentionally pictures as a prophet. The image of the prophet had already been impressed on the traditional materials about Jesus prior to Luke. Indeed, it is very probable that the historical Jesus himself manifested prophetic characteristics. But Luke, and/or the peculiarly Lukan tradition ('L'), emphasizes the prophetic nature of Jesus' ministry. Jesus is made to represent himself self-consciously as a prophet, who compares himself with prophets of the Old Testament (13: 33; 4: 25–7). 'Prophet' is a valid christological category for Luke, which is seen in the fact that Jesus is pictured in 'L' materials as a prophet, with no suggestion that this is an inadequate description or misunderstanding (7: 16, 39; 24: 19; cf. Acts 3: 22–3). The description of the ministry of the risen Christ in 24: 13–49 is especially relevant for our purpose, in that not only is the resurrected

Lord called a prophet but the post-Easter speaking of the risen Lord is
graphically portrayed. Although the older form of the story has been
altered to express Lukan theology (e.g. the flesh-and-bone nature of the
resurrection body, verse 40; the pre-*ascension* setting), the older form,
told in prophetic categories, still shines through.

Whence comes this predilection for portraying Jesus in prophetic garb?
Some of it, at least, must be attributed to the influence of the Old
Testament on Lukan theology. To the extent that this is the explanation,
there would be little in the Lukan portrait of Jesus of value for reconstructing the image of Christian prophets in earliest Christianity. But it is
likely that Luke's image of prophecy was shaped not only by his reading
of the LXX but also by the impression made on him or his tradition by
prophets in the church. Jesus in Luke resembles not only his predecessors
in the Old Testament but also his successors in the church.[52] It seems
likely that there is some material of value for our project contained in the
Lukan description of the prophet Jesus, but it is difficult to sort out which
elements of this description may be attributed to the remembered
prophetic ministry of Jesus, which to the church's casting of Jesus in the
role of a prophet and which to the Lukan view of prophecy, which has
itself been influenced both by the Old Testament and by the phenomenon
of prophecy in the church. In the nature of the case, this source must be
used with extreme care, and no conclusions may be based on it alone.

There is, however, another source in the Gospel of Luke that might be
of great value for our reconstruction. The outburst of oracular hymnody
that surrounds the birth of Jesus in the Lukan narrative is replete with
prophetic materials. Elizabeth is filled with the Holy Spirit, which is
identified as the Spirit that inspires prophecy, and with a loud cry –
another mark of prophecy – she pronounces a prophetic utterance (1: 41,
42–5). The Magnificat is spoken by one on whom the Holy Spirit has
come (1: 35) and who speaks as a Christian prophetess. The Benedictus is
called a prophecy, by one filled with the Holy Spirit (1: 67–79). Simeon is
one filled with the Spirit who receives divine revelations (2: 25–6), so that
2: 29–32, 34–5 should be regarded as prophetic utterance. No direct
words of the prophetess Anna are preserved, though her general
characteristics as a prophetess are clear. The words of the angel in 1: 14–
17 and 32–3 also have oracular–hymnic qualities, and, as we shall see in
chapter 8, angels are a vehicle of Christian prophecy.

The complicated question of the sources and history of the tradition of
the materials in Luke 1–2 may be left aside for our purposes. However the
critical issues presented by these chapters may be resolved, it seems clear
that (1) Luke is not here composing *ab ovo* but is rewriting a source or

sources, (2) which come from pre-70 Jewish Christianity in at least one stage of their development; (3) these materials represent Elizabeth, Zechariah, Mary, Simeon and Anna to be functioning as prophets; (4) the content of these oracles and conduct of the personages may be taken as representative of what some pre-70 Jewish Christian communities considered to be appropriate for prophets, the oracles perhaps being the very oracles of Christian prophets preserved and used in worship. The prophetic connections of these materials have been noticed before but they have never been consistently used in a reconstruction of early Christian prophetism. A valuable source has been overlooked.

The hypothesis of this study is that oracles of Christian prophets are found among the sayings of Jesus preserved by Luke and the other evangelists. But it would be a defect of method to attempt to include such purported sayings of Christian prophets among the sources to be used in our reconstruction, since a main purpose of this reconstruction is to provide a means of identifying such oracles in the synoptic tradition of Jesus' words. To avoid such circularity, synoptic sayings of Jesus purported to originate from, or be shaped by, early Christian prophets must be excluded from the sources used in reconstructing pre-70 Christian prophecy. But even without the use of purported sayings of Christian prophets contained in Luke, both Luke and Acts offer a variety of materials and insights that may be used in our reconstruction.

The Gospel of Matthew

If it remains unclear whether or not Luke is personally engaged with Christian prophets, there can hardly be any doubt in the case of Matthew. In several instances, Matthew (or peculiarly Matthean tradition, the traditions most characteristic of the Matthean church) has altered the tradition that came to him to make it apply more directly to the phenomenon of Christian prophecy. When Matt. 5: 12 is compared to Luke 6: 23, it is apparent that a general statement about ancient prophets has now, in Matthew's church, come to address Matthew's hearers as themselves standing in the prophetic succession. In 7: 15—23, general exhortations to the Christian community, in which neither the word nor the idea of prophecy appears, have been altered to deal specifically with the problem of (false) prophecy in the Matthean church by including the insertion of specifically prophetic terminology in verses 15 and 22. In 10: 41, a *logion* peculiar to Matthew, dealing specifically with the reception of Christian prophets, concludes the missionary discourse. The Q-*logion* in Matt. 23: 34—6, paralleled in Luke 11: 49—51, is in its Matthean form more clearly a reference to Christian prophets.[53] Matthew has a large number of sayings in the form 'sentences of holy law', which, as will be argued later, is characteristic of Christian prophets.

Ernst Käsemann has argued, in two influential essays, that Matthew and his church are not themselves proponents of Christian prophecy.[54] Käsemann regards the kind of prophetic leadership of congregations that he discerns in Matthean materials as possible only very early, in the period immediately after Easter, in the rural churches of Judea. Matthew himself is regarded as a rabbinic type who opposes the claim of charismatic enthusiasts to announce the word of the risen Lord. In Käsemann's view, it is only Matthew's interest in law that causes him to preserve so many of the prophetic 'sentences of holy law'. Käsemann concedes that 10: 41 does reflect something of a church order, but it is a primitive one, no longer representative of Matthew's own church, which is developing a Christian rabbinate.

Eduard Schweizer has roundly criticized Käsemann's view in a number of different essays, arguing that, far from being skeptical about charismatic phenomena in the church, Matthew's understanding of discipleship is modeled on that of the prophet, so that the Matthean church is a 'church of prophets'.[55] Matthew's objection to 'false prophets' is not to their prophetic claims *per se* but to their ἀνομία. The value of Schweizer's work is that he has shown convincingly that Christian prophecy is at home in the Matthean church. A problem here is that Schweizer never defines what he means by 'prophet', except by the equally vague term 'charismatic'. His implied definition is broad enough to include all the members of Matthew's church, so that even the difference between 'scribe' and 'prophet' disappears.[56]

Numerous other students of Matthew, however, have come to regard the Matthean church as including Christian prophets as a definite group within its leadership.[57] Efforts to extract a precise description of Matthew's church order and the nomenclature used for it from his gospel have thus far remained unconvincing, but it seems clear that prophets did play a distinct role in the leadership of Matthew's church, however this leadership was structured and named. Matthew was apparently able to embrace his whole community in the thrice-repeated προφῆται καὶ δίκαιοι (10: 41; 13: 17; 23: 29). His interest in this phrase is apparent in that the latter two instances are the result of Matthean modifications of his source in order to obtain this couplet, and in his alteration of one of the occurrences of προφήτης in 23: 35 to δίκαιος in order to complement the occurrence of προφήτης in 23: 34 and thus obtain another προφήτης/δίκαιος pair. If δίκαιος is indeed a 'quasi-technical term' for 'teacher' in the Matthean church, as argued by David Hill, then we have here the Matthean church order, a ministry composed of prophets and teachers, with the lay people being represented by 'little ones' throughout.[58] Hill's argument that righteous = martyrs = witnesses = teachers is too tenuous, however. The fact that in 13: 17 and 23: 29 the phrase refers to Old Testament worthies is probably the clue to its meaning in Matthew. As the Old Testament congregation was composed of prophets (leaders) and righteous (pious people, lay people), so Matthew sees his own church. This does not, of course, mean that teachers played no role in Matthew's church. The contrary would be indicated by Matthew's σοφοὶ καὶ γραμματεῖς in 23: 34 and by the little self-portrait in 13: 52 — Matthew himself is such a teacher. The relations of such prophets and teachers in Matthew's church remain unclear but they do not seem to have been in opposition. Teachers functioned in a church, the recognized leadership of which was characterized by the term προφῆται.

While the exact nature of the church order of Matthew's community must remain an open question, the role of Christian prophets within this structure has been portrayed by the work of Alexander Sand in a manner that does most justice to the data.[59] Like Schweizer, Sand sees prophecy as *the* category in which Matthew interpreted discipleship to Jesus as such. But the Matthean community also knows a relatively small number of 'wandering' prophets, prophets who were not independent freelancers but delegated missioners of the Matthean church. In addition, there was a larger group of congregational leaders in the church, who were not 'wandering' but resident in the congregation, who recognized that discipleship to Jesus was to be practiced in prophetic terms. They performed prophetic functions in the community, including speaking in the name of the risen Lord. These are not sharply distinguished from the disciples in general but they did form a recognizably distinct group. This is the picture of prophecy in the Matthean church that I accept. It would seem, therefore, that peculiarly Matthean statements about Christian prophets, and traditions representing the Matthean church, might be used in characterizing prophecy in Palestine—Syria in the last third of the first century.

To a lesser degree, and with less precision, Matthew's description of the disciples may be used to delineate the contours of Christian prophecy in his church, for Matthew emphasizes expressly that the disciples are prophets. It is clear that Matthew has no interest in developing a picture of the Twelve as 'apostles'. He only uses the term once, in a tradition taken over from Mark 10: 2. The verb ἀποστέλλω is no technical term in Matthew. Rather, the Twelve are pictured as prophets (5: 10–12; 10: 41; 13: 17), the model of discipleship for those prophet-disciples whom the risen Jesus will send into his church (23: 34). In four of the five major discourses, Matthew has described the disciples as prophets or compared them to the Old Testament prophets. This obviously does not mean that all that is said about the disciples in Matthew may be transposed uncritically into a description of Christian prophets. But it does mean that when Matthew is thinking particularly of the prophetic ministry of the disciples, the redactional emphases of his description may be examined for their prophetic aspects. A particularly helpful instance is the discourse instructing the disciples concerning their mission in 10: 1–42. Frank Beare and others have shown that Matthew conceives this scene in terms of the risen Lord sending forth his prophetic messengers.[60] Most commentators have contented themselves with referring to the Jewish juridical principle, 'a man's representative is as himself'. But, as argued by Birger Gerhardsson and É. Cothonet, the background of this discourse is not juridical but prophetic.[61] The tasks with which the missioners are charged in 10: 1 are the same as those that Matthew has already related to Christian prophets in 7: 22. The discourse ends with a specific reference to Christian prophets, 10: 41–2. The missioners are portrayed as preachers (verse 7) who on occasion are inspired by the Holy Spirit (verses 19–20), who are charged with saying what the Lord reveals to them that they should proclaim (verses 26–7). These prophetic references at the beginning and end of the discourse, as well as the indications of prophetic speech within the discourse itself, indicate that Matthew here gathers up material that has had its *Sitz im Leben* in prophetic circles within the community and sets it forth as a manual of conduct for those Christian prophets and teachers on their missionary journeys in behalf of the church. In a later chapter, we will examine this speech-complex to see whether it contains material that originated as Christian prophecy. For the present, I am only calling attention to the fact that the discourse should be considered as a viable source for composing a description of Christian prophecy as Matthew understands it.

On the other hand, one should be hesitant to use the elements peculiar to Matthew's description of Jesus as material for depicting early Christian prophets. Unlike Luke, Matthew seems to have no particular interest in portraying Jesus as a prophet. Διδάσκαλος is the title that others use for a church office, but Matthew reserves it exclusively for Jesus. Jesus calls himself προφήτης only once (13: 57), in a traditional saying taken over from Mark, and is called prophet by others only in 16: 14; 21: 11, 46, all clearly misunderstandings of Jesus' true identity. There are no indications that Matthew was guided by the role Christian prophets played in his community as he shaped his own presentation of Jesus as the one διδάσκαλος and καθήγητης for the community (23: 8–10). There is only one exception to this. As in the case of the post-Easter speaking of Jesus in Luke, the final scene of the gospel in which the disciples are commissioned is obviously a scene in which the risen and exalted Lord is portrayed as speaking. It is important to recognize that it is the exalted Lord who addresses his church here, not simply the resurrected Jesus who converses with his disciples shortly after the resurrection, as in 28: 9—10. This is apparent both from the stance from which the address is given — 'all authority in heaven and earth has been given unto me' — and from the fact that there is not, and cannot be, any later 'ascension' of the Jesus who here speaks — 'I am with you always, to the close of the age.' Whether the words of Jesus here given originated as the oracle of a Christian prophet is a question that will be explored later. The words of commissioning bear many marks of Matthean editing, so the final form of the saying must be attributed to Matthew himself.[62] This means that, whatever the origin of the original saying, its present setting and reworking by Matthew lets us see at least how Matthew thought of the risen Christ as speaking, and these words may therefore be added to the other elements in Matthew that may be used as sources for describing Christian prophecy in the Matthean church.

The Didache

It is probable that the Didache, or one of its major sources, originated in the same general area as the Gospel of Matthew and is thus an independent witness to the prophetism of the church in the region of Syria. The latest full-scale commentary on the Didache, that of Jean-Paul Audet, argues this case thoroughly.[63] Audet also argues that the bulk of the Didache was composed prior to 70. If this dating could be accepted, the Didache would be a more direct reflection of the prophets we will attempt to describe than any of our other documents and would be our best source for reconstructing pre-70 Palestinian Christian prophets. Audet's particular theory has not won widespread acceptance, however, so that the date, integrity and provenance of the Didache all continue to be disputed. Although no consensus seems to be emerging, there is extensive agreement on the following position, which is adopted in this study.[64] (1) The Didache is principally composed of two sources: the Two Ways in chapters 1—5 and the Manual of Church Order in chapters 6—15. (2) Each of these is itself composed of traditional material older than the source itself. (3) The Manual of Church Order (which contains all the explicit references to Christian prophecy) was originally of Syrian provenance. (4) The Manual is to be dated in the last third of the first century, perhaps in the earlier part of this period. This means that the majority of those who disagree with Audet's dating of the Didache as a whole still date the section that is relevant for our purpose at very nearly the same time and place as does Audet.

The Manual of Church Order comes from a Christian community that both honors prophecy and has come to experience it as a problem. This is the reason for the intense interest of the author(s) in prophecy, an interest that causes the instructions on prophets to be elaborated far beyond what is said about ἀπόστολοι and διδάσκαλοι. These instructions do not seem to be all of a piece, indicating that they came into being from different hands over an extended period. For example, the prophet is considered to be above question when he speaks ἐν πνεύματι, so that to challenge him is the unforgivable sin (11: 7), and yet some things that he says are not to be tolerated, even if said ἐν πνεύματι (11: 12). The criterion of true prophecy is whether he teaches according to the truth (11: 1); but even that prophet who teaches according to the truth is a false prophet εἰ ἃ διδάσκει οὐ ποιεῖ (11: 10). Such inconsistencies denote a developing tradition rather than composition by a single author. Some of the instructions regarding Christian prophets probably come from the editor of the Manual in the last decades of the first century. Others indicate earlier efforts of the same community to deal with the problem of true and false prophecy. We are justified, then, in taking Didache 10–15 as a source for Syrian-Christian prophets of the late first century, which may even contain pre-70 material.

The Gospel and Letters of John

'It is not at all sufficiently emphasized that John must be seen in the historical and theological context of Christian prophecy.' 'To ignore the phenomenon of prophecy is to study the Fourth Gospel apart from its environment.' These declarations from Käsemann and Streeter respectively[65] are now rather widely shared by a number of students of the Johannine literature, who believe that the Johannine community contained a significant group of Christian prophets among its leaders. This hypothesis appears to be solidly based on good evidence. Without becoming embroiled in the complicated question of how many authors are responsible for the Gospel and Letters of John, we may confidently regard them as emerging at different points from the same 'circle' or 'school'. In addition, at least the minimal statement of Charles should be accepted, that 'the Apocalypse and the Fourth Gospel were in some way related to each other'.[66] Whether or not the author of Revelation is regarded as a member of the Johannine 'School', the numerous points of contact between the gospel and the Apocalypse, pointed out by Charles and others, indicate interaction between the evangelist and Christian prophecy, since the Apocalypse

obviously was written by a prophet. The letters too come from a circle
that was familiar with the prophetic phenomenon and was beginning to
experience some manifestations of it as problematic, without denying its
validity *per se* (I John 2: 20, 27; 4: 1–3). And since the 'we' of I John
cannot be separated from the 'we' of the Fourth Gospel, we would expect
a priori that the gospel would also originate from a circle in which the
prophetic ministry was very much alive. The internal evidence of the
gospel bears out this expectation. The Johannine portrayal of both the
Paraclete and Jesus seems to be influenced by the author's perception of
the ministry of Christian prophets in the Johannine church. I have elsewhere given a detailed argument for this.[67] Thus both Jesus and the
Paraclete, as John portrays them, can be used as sources for the reconstruction of early Christian prophecy.

The idea that John himself is something of a Christian prophet, himself
an embodiment of the Paraclete, has not become widely accepted, though
argued rather frequently.[68] Streeter went beyond the general affirmations
of Sasse, Weinel and Windisch and attempted to picture the prophet-
author as having 'heard' what the risen Jesus was saying in the discourses
with his 'prophetic ear', somewhat romantically describing the aged
prophet–elder 'slipping into a mystic trance', in which the meaning of the
delay of the *parousia* was revealed to him by the reinterpretation of earlier,
traditional, words of Jesus, and attempting to support such imaginative
projections by, for example, the fact that more Aramaisms occur in the
discourses than in the narrative parts of the gospel.[69] More recently, David
Aune has argued on other grounds, and without romanticism, that actual
auditions of Christian prophets are contained in the Johannine discourses.[70]
While questioning whether the exact manner of revelation can be described
as clearly as Streeter and Aune think, I would include myself in that
growing number of students of the Fourth Gospel who believe that the
Johannine discourses are to be explained not as the result of John's having
christianized and historicized a pre-existing source, but as the result of a
long process of development in the preaching of the Johannine community,
a process in which Christian prophets were active.[71] During this process of
development, no sharp line was drawn between sayings of the historical
Jesus and post-Easter revelations, which is what one would expect from
the description of the ministry of the Paraclete (John 14: 25–6; 16: 12–
13). The author of the Fourth Gospel was himself such a Christian prophet,
but one who was concerned, as were other members of his school, that the
message of the risen Jesus should remain bound to the event of the fleshly,
historical Jesus. It is precisely for this reason that the evangelist does not
set forth his message in letter form, as did Paul, nor in a collection of

sayings of Jesus, as did the Q-community, and especially not in the form of revelation-discourses of the exalted Lord, as did the gnostics, but in the *gospel* form. Even though the exalted Christ and the historical Jesus blend into each other in John's portrayal, the earthly Jesus and his word are never simply replaced by the word of the exalted Christ, so that John does not sacrifice history to mythology. John is thus properly to be seen as a Christian prophet, but of a peculiar type, who already sees the problem involved in the typical prophetic form and presents an alternative based on extensive theological reflection. Partly for this reason, and partly because at this stage in the discussion to regard John as a prophet and elements of the Johannine discourses as of prophetic origin represents a question-begging violation of method, this point will not be pursued here, nor will the discourses of the Fourth Gospel be used as examples of Christian prophecy in our reconstruction. Even without my doing this, the Johannine materials offer us a wealth of insight concerning the nature of Christian prophecy.

To know the date and provenance of the Johannine writings would be helpful for our purpose but these are not crucial issues. What is crucial is to see that John stands in a tradition, a tradition that is ultimately of Palestinian origin.[72] The day when John could be characterized as a lone creative genius is now long past. John works creatively within a tradition that places him in direct lineal descent from early Palestinian Christian prophets. The Gospel and Letters of John may be used not only to describe the Christian prophetism of the time and place of the Fourth Evangelist himself, whenever and wherever that may have been; they may also be used, when critically balanced with other sources, to help reconstruct the contours of that Christian prophetism that was active nearer the source of the tradition which finds its deposit in the Johannine writings and other early Christian literature.

Hermas

In the *Shepherd of Hermas* we have a Christian document, emanating from the Roman church in the first half of the second century, that both characterized the ministry of Christian prophets within the church (Mand. XI) and repeatedly represented itself as being the revelation of the Holy Spirit or Son of God to his church in the latter days (e.g. Vis. IV. 1.3; Sim. IX. 1.1). The author never refers to himself as a prophet, but this is incidental for our purposes, for if the self-description of the document is taken at face value, the author precisely conforms to the functions of Christian prophecy in our definition. If the 'prophecy' of the author is regarded as only a literary device, we would have in the author's self-description an imaginative portrayal of the way the prophetic phenomenon was conceived to be by one not existentially involved in it. In view of the fact that prophecy is still a live phenomenon in the author's church, which he at least observes (Mand. XI), this would still be of some value. There are some marks of genuine prophetic self-consciousness, e.g. the revelation of a second chance of repentance in view of an impending persecution and the imminent return of the Lord (Vis. III. 1.9). But even if the author does have some personal prophetic experiences, for the most part his writing is a tedious, labored, uninspired and uninspiring work, formally in the prophetic category but written by one for whom prophecy is already a traditional phenomenon that may be stereotyped.

The threads that connect Hermas with those early Christian prophets who are the subjects of this reconstruction are long and thin, if present at all. These connections are enhanced by the favored view today that Hermas belongs to Jewish Christianity. J.-P. Audet has even won some supporters for his view that Hermas was born of Jewish parents who had grown up in the Qumran community, then had fled to Italy during the war of 66–70.[73] On the other hand, the most recent study of Hermas argues that he is of Hellenistic origin and is at home with Hellenistic concepts of prophecy, which he both accepts and struggles against.[74] In Reiling's view, the Jewish-Christian elements in his writing are only a result of the Jewish-Christian tradition into which Hermas came at his conversion. In any case, Hermas' writings have enough traditional Jewish-Christian content to be possibly of value for our reconstruction. They should not be excluded as a source in advance, since it could be that the image of prophecy and prophets of earlier Jewish Christianity had impressed itself onto the tradition that came to Hermas and formed part of that understanding of prophecy which shaped both his own ministry and his response to other prophets of his time.[75] At the most, however, we may expect to glean only a minimum of material for our purposes from Hermas. In him, we hear the last faint echoes of the 'old' prophecy. After him, references to prophecy in the church are oriented to the New Prophecy of Montanism, either in affirmation or in repudiation — and in either case are too far removed from those early Christian prophets who might have augmented the synoptic tradition of Jesus' words to offer us anything for our reconstruction.

Summary

Only the eight sources discussed above are to be used in reconstructing that early Christian prophecy which might have contributed to the expansion of the tradition of the sayings of Jesus.[76] These may be summarized as follows:

(1) Revelation: an example of early Christian prophecy.

(2) Paul's letters

(i) Paul's discussion of prophecy in his churches, particularly at Corinth.

(ii) Paul's own prophetic self-consciousness.

(iii) Oracles from Paul himself and other early Christian prophets contained in his letters.

(3) The Deutero-Pauline letters

(i) Description of prophecy contemporary with the writing (minimal).

(ii) Memory of prophecy of earlier generations.

(4) Luke—Acts

(i) The Gospel's and Acts' descriptions of Christian prophets.

(ii) Luke's portrayal of Jesus.

(iii) The descriptions of prophetic phenomena in the birth story.

(5) The Gospel of Matthew

(i) Descriptions of Christian prophets.

(ii) Descriptions of the disciples, especially in 10: 1—41.

(iii) The commissioning by the risen Lord, 28: 18—20.

(6) The Didache's description of Christian prophets.

(7) The Gospel and Letters of John

(i) John's portrayal of the Paraclete, influenced by Christian prophets.

(ii) John's portrayal of Jesus, influenced by Christian prophets.

(iii) The Letters' description of Christian prophets.

(iv) The author himself as a Christian prophet.

(8) Hermas

(i) Hermas himself as a prophet.

(ii) Hermas' description of prophecy.

All the above sources can be used for depicting early Palestinian Christian prophets, without assuming in advance that any of the sayings of Jesus now contained in the synoptic gospels are from Christian prophets. A broad base of sources is at our disposal.

4 METHOD

The contours of our understanding of Christian prophecy must be shaped
by what we learn from the eight sources discussed in the preceding chapter.
We should not evaluate the data concerning Christian prophecy in these
sources by some presupposed ideal of what Christian prophets were or
should have been. This picture should only emerge at the end of the
reconstruction, not dominate the formation of it. Nor should we permit,
at this stage of the investigation, our understanding of early Christian
prophecy to be influenced by synoptic sayings of Jesus supposed to have
originated from Christian prophets.

All the above sources, in varying ways and to various degrees, reflect
and refract the phenomena of early Christian prophecy. But no one of
them contains, in such a way that it can be read off the surface, a portrayal
of those early Christian prophets who were active in the early days of the
formation of the synoptic tradition and whose oracles may be preserved
within it. A workable method must make use of all the relevant information
contained within these sources to reconstruct the features of a type or
types of Christian prophecy that none of them directly attest. Although
our sources are, relatively speaking, widely scattered in both time and
place, the expectation that they might still yield a coherent picture of the
prophetism of an earlier time and different place is not unrealistic because,
as the above discussion indicates, several of these sources stand in that
stream of tradition which emanated from Palestine and flowed into the rest
of the Hellenistic world, and reflect this tradition in their representation of
Christian prophecy. In this regard some words of Hans von Campenhausen,
written of the apostles and early Jerusalem Christianity, are equally
relevant to early Christian prophecy:

'We possess hardly one word which can, in its present form, be ascribed
with certainty to their circle ... First and foremost, however, one thing
is quite incontestable, namely that the primitive community was the
point from which the whole succeeding development began ... Those

who came after interpreted the tradition they received, and in so doing they naturally from the very first also transformed it, and in numerous ways placed it in a different light; but they did not invent it, and therefore their evidence concerning it can still be of use to us ... If we wish to recover the true circumstances in all their living, complex reality, we must set aside the rigid formulas and concepts of a later age, and start by breaking down or at least teasing out the community into the individuals and groups which the records show to have been the leading elements within it.'[1]

The method proposed in this study calls for the construction of a characterization of early Christian prophecy that may be used as a means of identifying those synoptic sayings of Jesus that may have been created or shaped by early Christian prophets. The characterization will be constructed as follows: the data regarding Christian prophecy contained in each of our sources will be projected carefully backward and Palestineward, to the extent that this is possible. That is, the attempt will be made to determine the traditional picture of prophecy that has left its impression on each source, by allowing for the *Tendenzen* and situation of each author. The second step will be to base our characterization on those features of Christian prophecy that are common to, or typical of, several of our sources. The list of characteristics so obtained may be considered as traditional and/or general features of Christian prophets, providing us with a characterization logically, and frequently chronologically, prior to all our sources. In addition, some features that do not have multiple attestation, but nevertheless seem to present some early or typical trait of Christian prophecy, should be included. This characterization should be as complete as possible, regardless of whether or not the various items in it seem to have any point of contact with synoptic *logia* suspected of being of prophetic origin. This characterization should not attempt to be an objective profile of the Christian prophet as an individual but should include his social and ecclesiastical context, since by definition the prophet is not an isolated figure but operates within a community.

The features characteristic of Christian prophecy may not be unique to prophets. To restrict the characterization to such features produces a minimal and distorted picture. The prophet may share some features with the apostle and the teacher, for example. It may sometimes be the case that the clustering of a number of features, none of which is of itself particularly prophetic in nature, is the characteristic prophetic feature. Also, a function shared by prophets and others may be performed by prophets in a characteristic manner, so that it is not the function itself but the way it is done that is prophetic. We shall see below that this is the case in the interpretation of Scripture, for example.

The characterization that results from this approach will of necessity be something of a composite, since a combination of indirect sources is used, but it must be a critically-constructed composite. The danger of drawing data from a variety of times and places to produce a conglomerate figure who in fact existed in none is recognized, and such a flat-surface, timeless, composite portrait resulting from a non-historical phenomenological approach is explicitly rejected. David Tiede's discussion of θεῖος ἀνήρ research implies an analogous danger in the investigation of Christian prophecy:

'Bieler aggregated so many features into his composite portrait of the typical "divine man" that it would be difficult to find any hero in antiquity to whom at least several of these qualities were not attributed, and it is perhaps as difficult to find a pre-third century A.D. portrayal of any figure which supplies its hero with Bieler's complete catalogue of the characteristics of the "divine man".'[2]

Christian prophecy research can learn from θεῖος ἀνήρ research to avoid indiscriminately using materials from the whole Hellenistic world to construct a prophetism-in-general. This would be like drawing materials from various locations throughout the Old Testament and ancient Near East to reconstruct an Old Testament cultus-in-general, a procedure rightly rejected by Hans-Joachim Kraus, who argues for a history of the cult rather than a phenomenology of it. Some words he has written regarding the study of the Old Testament cultus are also appropriate to our enterprise:

'We need to look carefully at the blocking of the stream of tradition brought about by the sources at certain times. In the literary reservoir of the "sources" the traditions as they flow together are given a definite form corresponding to the institutions of worship contemporary with the source. On the other hand, however, we have to give close attention to the elements in the tradition as such, for they often maintain — even in the more recent forms of the sources — their own life and point back to older, even to the oldest origins.'[3]

The study of apocalyptic, of the 'Johannine School', and especially of Old Testament prophecy, has also provided similar methodological problems, to which helpful solutions have emerged analogous to that proposed here.[4] A composite figure may legitimately be constructed, but historical distinctions must be maintained. This means that we may anticipate finding some variety in the kinds of prophetic figures that functioned within pre-70 Christianity. Prophecy was no more a monolith in the church than it was in Israel. But just as Amos, Hosea, Isaiah and Micah, though quite different from each other, still form a recognizable entity, 'the eighth-century prophets', which as a group is distinct both from Israelite prophecy of preceding and following centuries and from extra-Israelite prophecy, so it was with early Christian prophecy: although it embraces some variety, we may legitimately speak of a general category, 'early (pre-70) Christian prophets', who are distinct both from non-Christian Hellenistic and Jewish prophets and from later Christian prophets, if the evidence seems to support such a reconstruction. It is this general *typus* that will be characterized in Part Two of this study.

It should be acknowledged in advance that there is no proof that the *typus* described corresponds point by point to pre-70 Christian prophets as they actually existed. To ask for that is to ask for what in the nature of the case is impossible. But the description here offered is still a more satisfactory basis for discussing the characteristics of early Christian prophets than generalizations from one source, or radically hypothetical reconstructions extrapolated from *logia* supposed to come from Christian prophets, or despair about our ability to say anything at all about pre-70 non-Pauline Christianity. While not demonstrable, the reconstruction offered in the following chapters is less arbitrary than alternative approaches and is correctible in that it provides an itemized basis for continuing discussion of the phenomenon of early Christian prophecy.

Since the Book of Revelation is our only unambiguous primary source for first-century Christian prophecy, we will usually begin the discussion of each feature of our reconstruction with data from it. The Book of Revelation is used simply to get the topic for discussion before us, not as a norm. But neither is any other one source to be used as a 'norm'. The reconstruction is intended to be based on the common features of a number of independent sources. This means that sometimes the point will be made in contrast to Revelation, on the basis of other sources, if these are judged to be more typical. As each point is introduced in relation to Revelation, it will be supplemented and/or altered by information from the other sources, the goal of each section being to determine what early Christian prophets were like on that particular point.

To the extent that this reconstruction is successful, it will have provided a valuable contribution to our understanding of early Christianity in and of itself, independent of its value (or lack of it) as a means of locating sayings of Christian prophets in the synoptic tradition. But in the comprehensive perspective of this study, the reconstruction is not an end in itself but the means of firming up our statements about the contribution of Christian prophets to the synoptic tradition.

After the characterization is completed, the next step will be to compare it carefully with each of those synoptic sayings of Jesus that meet two criteria. First, they must be able to be seen as having existed independently of a narrative context, even if they are now contained in narratives. This includes even apophthegmata, which are now integrated into narrative units but may have been inserted into them or even have generated them.[5] Secondly, they must be considered to be secondary, i.e. church products (at least in their present form), rather than words of the historical Jesus, on other grounds than their similarity to Christian prophecy. It should be explicitly noted that there were other means of expansion of the tradition besides the prophetic, e.g. scribal, and that the formula 'not from Jesus, *therefore* from a Christian prophet' is to be rejected. Since Jesus was himself something of a charismatic figure, who is frequently portrayed in the gospels as a prophet, sayings cannot be declared secondary only on the basis that they bear certain marks of prophecy. Authentic sayings are also likely to manifest prophetic traits. The questions of authenticity and of prophetic origin should be kept separate and the latter introduced only after a judgment has been given on the former. In questionable cases, of course, it may happen that a number of characteristics of Christian prophecy in a saying the authenticity of which is difficult to decide may help to resolve the issue by tipping the scales in favor of *Gemeindebildung*. Secondary sayings that have points of contact with the characteristics of early Christian prophecy may be considered to be of prophetic origin with some degree of probability.

In the course of Part Three of this study it will become apparent that the typical way of posing the question: 'Is this saying from the historical Jesus or from an early Christian prophet?' is too simple an approach, and that the question needs to be refined, since Christian prophets may have influenced the developing synoptic tradition at more than one point, in more than one way, including reshaping sayings that originated from the historical Jesus. These nuances of the issue may be left aside for the present, however, since before further discussion of the relation of Christian prophets to the synoptic tradition will be fruitful, the delineation of pre-70 Christian prophecy needs to be presented, and to that task we now turn.

PART TWO

A characterization of early Christian prophecy

5 THE PROPHET AS A CHURCH FIGURE

The extent of prophecy in early Christianity

Prophets were widespread in the early church, not being limited to any one geographical area, sociological grouping or stream of theological tradition. This is already apparent from the variety of settings of the eight sources that provide the evidence for our reconstruction. In addition, several of these explicitly indicate that prophecy was not an isolated phenomenon peculiar to only a few congregations. The Seer of Revelation speaks generally of prophets as constituting an integral part of the world-wide church (11: 18; 16: 6; 18: 24; 22: 9). Paul supposes that there are prophets in the Roman church, though he has never been there (Rom. 12: 6). Acts locates prophets in Jerusalem, Antioch, Caesarea, Tyre and, with excusable exaggeration, 'every city' in Greece, Macedonia and Asia (13: 1; 15: 32; 20: 23; 21: 4, 10). Ephesians looks back upon a first-generation church that was generally characterized by the presence of prophets (3: 5). While in some cases the writer's perception of the whole church may be colored by his own church setting, the evidence is sufficient to indicate that in the early church prophets were neither rare nor parochial.

The prophet within the church

Modern historical study of early Christian prophetism was given fresh impetus by the writings of Adolf Harnack, who wrote under the spell of the then recently-discovered Didache. Harnack understood the Didache to portray a 'Two-fold Ministry', in which apostles, prophets and teachers (all charismatics) were a universal, itinerant ministry, and bishops and deacons were a settled, congregational ministry.[1] Harnack's enthusiasm for the new discovery permitted him, not without violence, to read this schematization into the New Testament and all his sources. Quite apart from the method-ological error of generalizing from one source, it is not at all as clear as Harnack supposed that the prophets represented by the Didache are of an exclusively wandering type. The first mention of prophets (10.7) occurs in the context of prescribed prayers for the cup, the loaf and the meal, and simply says τοῖς δὲ προφήταις ἐπιτρέπετε εὐχαριστεῖν ὅσα θέλουσιν, with no suggestion that such prophets are anything but local figures. The extended discussion of ἀπόστολοι καὶ προφῆται in Did. 11 may be understood in terms of traveling prophets but need not be so, and certainly may not be the basis for interpreting ambiguous references in other sources as describing an itinerant prophetic ministry. Only ἀπόστολοι are clearly spoken of as coming to the congregation from without; ψευδοπροφῆται is used of those ἀπόστολοι who are judged to be frauds, but this seems to be because ψευδοπροφήτης is a general pejorative term that may be applied to a variety of types of fraudulent church leaders,[2] not because the author of the Didache is making the equation ἀπόστολος = προφήτης. Nothing in this chapter explicitly refers to peripatetic prophets; everything said of apostles refers to their coming and going. Only at Did. 13.1 do we have a reference to a prophet coming into the community from outside, but here it is a matter of his taking up residence among the congregation as a part of it, receiving his living from it, without any indication even here that he had previously had an itinerant ministry. He could just as well have been a prophet resident in another congregation who had relocated. That there probably were wandering prophets is not excluded. But the evidence in these texts for making itinerancy of the essence of early Christian prophetism seems slender indeed.

As we shall see, this picture of the 'wandering' prophet of the Syrian churches, based primarily on Harnack's interpretation of the Didache and reinforced by questionable analogies to the wandering Cynic preachers and θεῖος ἀνήρ types, has had a continuing influence on the interpretation of Christian prophecy. But when our sources are approached without the pre-judgment that prophets were primarily 'wandering charismatics', another picture emerges. The prophet-author of Revelation writes to seven churches (1: 4), which may well mean that he did not reside at one place but traveled from church to church. But he writes as a known insider who introduces himself simply as 'John' and expects a hearing, not as a 'wandering' stranger who does not belong within the churches he addresses. To be sure, he takes his stand with the exalted Lord over against the congregation he addresses, but this is because he is a *prophet*, not because he is an outsider to the local churches. On the contrary, the rich use of tradition and liturgical materials from the congregational worship presents John as one very much at home within the settled, ordered life of the Christian community, rather than as a traveling prophet who intrudes his oracles into a community to which he does not essentially belong.

Paul, like John, is an example of a prophetic figure who, though he travels from place to place, is still to be seen as a constituent member within the church where he is located. Paul identifies with the congregations to which he ministers, takes his stance within them, is by no means a 'wandering' itinerant who troubles the life of the 'settled' churches. And Paul's understanding of the prophetic ministry is that it is a ministry of, and within, the church. God places προφήτας ἐν τῇ ἐκκλησίᾳ (I Cor. 12: 28). Prophecy is repeatedly mentioned in the midst of a discussion of the corporate life of the church (Rom. 12: 6; I Cor. 11: 4–5; 12: 10; 14: 1–39; I Thess. 5: 20). Everything in the extended discussion in I Cor. 14 indicates that the prophets in Corinth are resident members of the community, not wandering bearers of an individualistic charisma. Even so, there is a tension between Paul's understanding of prophecy and the understanding of πνεῦμα held by the Corinthians, in that theirs tends toward individualism, while Paul rejects an individualistic anthropology in favor of the community, the new eschatological people of God, as the bearer of the Spirit. Here, Paul reflects the earlier Palestinian church, which grew out of a Judaism that, nurtured on the Old Testament promises, looked forward to a community of the Spirit. Paul is here a witness to the idea of prophecy held by early Palestinian Christianity.

The evidence of Acts is more ambiguous. The fact that prophets are pictured as moving from place to place (11: 27–8; 15: 32; 21: 10) has led some scholars to speak of prophets in Acts as 'wandering' rather than 'settled'.[3] Whether this idea would even have arisen if the picture of 'wandering prophets' had not been injected into the discussion by Harnack's interpretation of the Didache is a moot point. In any case, it should be observed that Acts also represents the prophets as 'settled' (13: 1–2; 19: 6; 21: 4, 9). In 20: 23, Paul and his company are pictured as traveling and receiving prophetic testimony from the – presumably 'settled' – prophets 'in every city'. In Acts the only figures specifically called prophets who are also represented as traveling are Judas, Silas and Agabus (15: 32; 11: 27–8; 21: 10). Judas and Silas are not 'wandering' prophets but are sent as delegates from one congregation to another and on missionary trips (15: 32, 40). And even Agabus is not depicted as an extra-church individual prophet but as one who is at home within the churches he visits, perhaps calling one of them, the Jerusalem congregation, his 'home church'. If the precision of our definition of prophet be relaxed somewhat, to include all those who speak the word of the Lord by virtue of a special inspiration of the Holy Spirit, the case for 'wandering' charismatics who intrude into 'resident' non-charismatic local churches becomes even more difficult to support from Acts. Those represented in Acts as functioning as prophets, though not specifically called such, do incidentally travel, as one might expect of early missionary-ministers; but rather than having itinerancy as an essential aspect of their ministry, they are pictured as residing with a local church for extended periods of time, though they also change locations and make missionary trips (Barnabas, 4: 36; 11: 22–6, 30; 13: 1 – 15: 39; Stephen, 6: 8 – 7: 60; Philip, 8: 4–40; 21: 8; Paul, 9: 1–22; 13: 1 – 28: 31, esp. 13: 1; 16: 6–9; 18: 9–11; 22: 6–11, 17–21; 23: 11; 27: 23–34; the apostles generally, chapters 2–5; and even Christians generally (cf. Luke's addition of καὶ προφητεύσουσιν to the Joel quotation), 2: 17–18). The fluidity of these categories in Luke's thought makes it quite clear that he cannot be used as evidence for an itinerant prophetic ministry that 'wanders' about encountering non-prophetic churches. The prophetic phenomenon, in general and in particular, is located by Luke firmly within the Christian community.

Matthew also portrays Christian prophecy as an inner-church phenomenon. As in Acts, prophets indeed travel (10: 1–42), but are not to be characterized as itinerant, because they are sent out by the church in response to the prayers of the congregation (9: 38). They are sent out not to intrude on 'settled', non-charismatic congregations but to heal and preach to the unconverted. Thus Matt. 9: 37 – 10: 42 is a Matthean version of a scene like Acts 13: 1–2. That there were prophets who came to the Matthean congregations from outside (7: 15–23) is, of course, not disputed. But it is not clear that these were wandering, individualistic prophets; they could just as well be seen as the representatives of some other branch of Christianity. In any case, Matthew regards them as ψευδοπροφῆται, and they should not be regarded as characteristic of the Matthean community.

The authors of the Gospel and Letters of John belong to a close-knit community within which the πνεῦμα/παράκλητος comes to expression as Christian prophecy. The false prophets who are opposed are not free-lancers but erstwhile members of John's own community and members of some opposing confessional community, as is indicated by I John 2: 29; 4: 1.[4] If II and III John come from the same community as the Gospel of John and I John, the traveling preachers to be rejected are not charismatic individualists but representatives of another confessional community; just as, conversely, the representatives of the Elder's own community are rejected by the opposing communities (II John 9–11; III John 7–10).

Our other sources confirm this view unanimously: Ephesians regards prophets as one of the ministries *within* the body or the very foundation of the structure of the church (4: 11–12; 2: 20–2). The author of the Pastorals is doubly-anxious to incorporate προφητεία within the regular church life, for it is either identified with that which is received at ordination (I Tim. 4: 14), or seen as fulfilled in the ministry of one who is regularly ordained (I Tim. 1: 18). Hermas stigmatizes as ψευδοπροφῆται those who give private revelations to individuals in response to questions, i.e. who attempt to operate as prophets outside the congregation, while προφῆται speak *in the congregation* in response to prayers addressed to God. Christian prophets cannot manipulate their gift; it is not at their disposal but functions within the community as a part of its worship (Mand. XI.1–21). All the above should indicate that the 'wandering' aspect of early Christian prophecy has been greatly exaggerated in the secondary literature on Christian prophecy and, while not absent, is by no means typical. Unlike the θεῖος ἀνήρ and wandering Cynic preacher, the *typus* of Christian prophet who might have influenced the synoptic tradition of Jesus' words was not an extra-church transient loner on the fringes of stable congregational life but was typically interior to, and participant in, that life.[5]

In our working definition of Christian prophecy, we have emphasized that prophecy functions within the church. This does not mean that Christian prophecy had no message for, or influence upon, those outside the congregations. There is some evidence that outsiders are also addressed by the prophets' message, but there is no evidence that would modify either our working definition or our description above of prophets as essentially inner-church figures. Paul can picture a scene in which outsiders are addressed by prophetic preaching (I Cor. 14: 24–5) but this is because they are visiting within a Christian congregation. The Apocalypse pronounces judgment on the unbelieving outside world (e.g. the oracle against 'Babylon' in 18: 1–24), but this is only 'overheard' by the world, in a prophetic message prepared to be delivered in the congregation (1: 3–4). Or, on the other hand, when 'the world' seems to be addressed by the Seer, as in 8: 13, this is primarily an indirect message to the church, to the extent that it has become like the unbelieving 'world'. Similarly with the Paraclete, which is an inner-church ministry sent *not* to the world but to the believers but which functions in such a way that it brings judgment on the unbelieving world (John 16: 7–11). The prophetic ministers in Acts (Paul, Barnabas and Silas, but not Agabus) do address 'the world' directly, as do the prophets among the missionaries in Matthew (10: 40–1). In such cases, the prophet is directly engaged with the world, but this is because the prophet belongs to the church, and the church is engaged with the world. I am not contending that the prophet was any more isolated from the world than other Christians were, only that prophecy is basically an inner-church phenomenon, that when the prophet addresses the world he does this not independently but as a member of the church from within which he makes his address. The prophet has no independent message directly to the world but stands with the church over against the world.

Prophets as a distinct group within the congregation

In the Jewish community from which early Christianity sprang, the Holy Spirit was considered pre-eminently the Spirit of Prophecy. The conviction of the early church, like that of Qumran, was that it was the eschatological community upon whom the eschatological gift of the Spirit had been poured out. The community as a whole, not just the select few, were the bearers of the Spirit. It is thus readily understandable that the idea could become diffused in the early church that all Christians were prophets, at least ideally or potentially. John the Seer is a prophet; yet, as Eduard Schweizer points out, 'precisely in his capacity of bearer of the Spirit he is only a brother and comrade of all the other church members (1: 9)', and the μαρτυρία in which the whole church is engaged is the πνεῦμα τῆς προφητείας (19: 10).[6] This leads Schweizer to conclude that 'the whole Church is understood in principle at least as a church of prophets', a conclusion that has been shared by several others.[7] However, the phrase 'in principle at least' and similar qualifiers are to be noted and under-scored. John is obviously a prophet in a way that distinguishes him from most others in his church, a point made also by Schweizer.[8] And this appears to be typical of our sources. Paul expects that anyone in the Corinthian church can prophesy, by virtue of having been baptized into the body of Christ where the Spirit is common to all (I Cor. 12: 13; 14: 1, 39); but he does not expect an affirmative answer to his question 'are all prophets?' (12: 29), as even the grammar attests (μή instead of οὐ). Luke begins his story of the church by affirming programatically that, unlike the experience in Israel, now the Spirit of Prophecy has been poured out ἐπὶ πᾶσαν σάρκα, adding an emphatic καὶ προφητεύσουσιν to the citation from Joel (Acts 2: 17—18). Yet as the story continues, it is apparent that only some are designated as prophets (11: 27—8; 13: 1—2; 15: 32; 21: 9—11); though, as we have seen, the line between particular prophets and other members of the Spirit-filled community, who also may speak by inspi-ration, is not drawn *too* sharply. The situation in the Matthean community is best summarized by Alexander Sand, who regards prophecy as *the* category that Matthew uses to present discipleship as such, but in terms of three concentric circles: (1) a small number of missionary prophets, who were the central core of (2) a larger number of resident prophets, who are not *sharply* distinguished, i.e. not in any 'clergy/laity' sense, from (3) disciples in general in Matthew's church.[9] Although it seems to me that the thrice repeated προφῆται/δίκαιοι pair (10: 41; 13: 17; 23: 29) does suggest more distinction between prophets as such and other disciples than Sand's presentation indicates, I would agree that prophecy is not discontinuous with Christian life generally in the Matthean church. So also in the Johannine church: the παράκλητος/προφήτης is a manifestation of that Spirit in which all believers participate, yet not all members of the community perform the particular prophetic functions represented by the παράκλητος.[10] Hermas (Mand. XI) also seems to provide evidence for both a designated group of prophets within the congregation and the potential for any member of the congregation to be filled with the Spirit and begin to speak by inspiration. All our other sources evince a clear distinction between the prophets and the body of believers as a whole (Eph. 2: 20; 3: 5; 4: 11–12; I Tim. 1: 18; 4: 14; Did. 11–13).

This dual perspective, in which the community as a whole has a prophetic self-understanding, although within the community only relatively few actually emerge as prophets, is also found at Qumran.[11] The existence of such an understanding of prophecy in the environs within which early Christianity originated, and the same understanding documented at several widely-separated points in later first-century Christianity, would indicate that this was also the understanding of prophecy in that early Christianity which we are attempting to reconstruct. This early Christianity was a prophetic community in which the line between prophets and non-prophets was not firmly drawn. Yet, when we speak of early Christian prophets, we are not talking about some amorphous entity vaguely diffused throughout the church. Although, as we have seen, early Christian prophets were not solitary individuals outside the churches, neither are they simply to be identified with the community as such. Without being an official 'order', they are a recognizably distinct group within the early church, who may be identified by characteristic features.

Prophetic utterance as tested by the community of faith

That early Christian prophets were not independent figures over against the community is seen in the fact that their revelations were tested by the community, which also possessed the Spirit. A preliminary reading of our primary instance of Christian prophecy, the Apocalypse, seems to indicate that the prophets of John's church may have stood over against the community at large as the sole possessors of the Spirit. 'Spirit' and 'church' are repeatedly contrasted with each other (2: 7, 11, 17 etc.) and the whole community seems to be divided into 'Spirit' (prophets) and 'Bride' (church) in 22: 17. Further, the Revelation seems to be launched into the churches as a projectile to be obeyed, without any indication that it is to be criticized and evaluated by the community. No doubt something of the authentic prophetic consciousness comes to expression here. The prophets did not pose issues for discussion by the community but delivered the unqualified word of the Lord. This is the prophetic mode. We should not expect the prophetic address itself to present us with a discussion of how the prophetic phenomenon was dealt with by the community. And yet even in Revelation there are some important clues in this regard. In addition to the common ground the Seer shares with the church, which we have discussed above,[12] it is to be noted that John begins and ends with an appeal to the hearer really to hear (1: 3; 22: 17). 'He asserted that the truth of his message had been fully endorsed by the angel, the Spirit, and the Messiah. He appealed to every reader and every congregation to join in the circle of endorsement. Presumably this appeal succeeded; otherwise this book would doubtless have joined many other early Christian documents in oblivion.'[13] This argument by Paul Minear is to be taken seriously: the book itself indicates that the author understood the churches he addressed to be fully capable of evaluating claims to Christian truth, including specifically the evaluation of prophetic claims, and that he expected them to do so (2: 2, 6, 14, 15, 20).

Of all our sources, Paul is the most theologically reflective on this problem. He never introduces the subject of prophecy without including affirmations of the community's capability of, and responsibility for, the evaluation of claims to revelation. It is instructive to examine these in their chronological order.

I Thess. 5: 19–22

The proverb-like statements of verses 21–2 are joined to the exhortations concerning the Spirit in verses 19–20 to form one unit. The earliest mention of prophecy in the New Testament is an apostolic admonition that it should not be despised. Whether the Thessalonians were tempted to disdain prophecy in favor of the more spectacular gifts of ecstatic speech, as was later the case in Corinth, or to belittle inspired speech because it threatened to become irrational ecstasy or apocalyptic enthusiasm, can no longer be determined. The parallel exhortation against quenching the Spirit probably indicates the latter. Paul finds himself in the situation of commending prophetic speech to those who are suspicious of it. But while prophetic claims are not to be dismissed, neither are they to be uncritically accepted. The congregation is not at the mercy of pneumatic claims, for it possesses the Spirit not only because it includes pneumatics in its midst but as a total community (4: 8). Paul's original preaching to them in the power of the Spirit was complemented by their reception of the word by the same Spirit (1: 5–6).

I Cor. 2: 6–16

No exegesis of this difficult passage will be attempted here. I would only declare my agreement with that large number of scholars who see the issue of pneumatic speech at Corinth as already being dealt with here.[14] The introductory thanksgiving element in the letter had already hinted that the speech gifts of the Corinthians are a major concern of the letter as a whole, so we should not attempt to confine Paul's reflection on that subject to chapters 12–14. Christian prophecy and its role in the community are already in view here, expressed in the dual concern that the community does in fact receive revelations from beyond itself by the Spirit, and that the community can and should evaluate such revelations by the Spirit resident in the community as a whole. Both these concerns are embodied in the pivotal verse 13, which Robert Funk paraphrases: 'In so doing we are combining or comparing spiritual things with spiritual things, and thus discerning the spirits, i.e. engaging in substantive criticism. For the Spirit not only confers wisdom and spiritual gifts, but stands in critical judgment upon wisdom and spiritual gifts.'[15]

I Cor. 12–14

The issue that has surfaced in the preceding texts becomes the object of a full-blown discussion in this key section of I Corinthians. In 12: 3 the point is not only that an 'objective norm' of sorts is given by which the authenticity of inspired speech can be recognized, but that the whole community that confesses 'Jesus is Lord' is thereby authenticated as a community of the Holy Spirit and is therefore capable of evaluating claims to pneumatic speech. In the light of the preceding, the gift of διάκρισις πνευμάτων in 12: 10, closely associated with the gift of prophecy, should continue to be understood as the Spirit-given gift to the community to evaluate the claims to revelation by the Spirit.[16] This text should be seen in conjunction with 14: 29, where οἱ ἄλλοι are to exercise διακρίνειν on what a prophet has said. Although it is not clear whether 'the others' refers to the community as a whole or to the other prophets, it is clear that a prophetic declaration in the community is not to be simply received uncritically at face value, but that others besides the receiver of the revelation are to exercise discriminating judgment in behalf of the community, and that this discrimination is itself a charisma of the one Spirit. Although Paul values prophecy as the highest charisma excepting only ἀγάπη, he also knows that even inspired speech claiming to be the word of the Lord himself can be inflicted on a hapless community as the product of human arrogance, and thus writes in 13: 9: ἐκ μέρους γὰρ γινώσκομεν καὶ ἐκ μέρους προφητεύομεν. 'Direct revelation' is still historical, relative, to be tested; still does not lift the prophet or apostle above the finite human condition; is still 'a treasure in earthen vessels, to show that the transcendent power belongs to God and not to us' (II Cor. 4: 7).

Rom. 12: 6

In a reflective mood, looking back on the stormy struggle with the Corinthians concerning pneumatic speech, Paul instructs the Romans that prophecy should be κατὰ τὴν ἀναλογίαν τῆς πίστεως. The preceding discussion, and the corporate nature of the Christian life that is implicit throughout the context of this phrase, should confirm the insight of numerous recent interpreters that in this text the norm of prophetic speech is *fides quae creditur*.[17] While this could never mean for Paul that there was an objective rule of faith that could be used to squelch the word of the Spirit – Paul's view of πίστις was too dynamic for that – it does mean that prophecy functions only within the corporate life of the community's faith, which forms the context for evaluating it.

Prophetic revelation functioned this way in Paul's own ministry. As a prophet, he was absolutely convinced that he had had a revelation from the risen Lord (Gal. 1: 11–12), yet if it did not correspond to the gospel that had been preached to the Galatians and received by them, it was to be rejected, even if preached by Paul himself or an angel from heaven (Gal. 1: 8–9). Paul makes a journey to the Jerusalem church leaders, a journey that he believes he has been led by a divine revelation to make, to present the gospel to them, which he also believes is revealed from the risen Lord. He both believes that churchly confirmation of his revelation is necessary (μή πως εἰς κενὸν τρέχω ἢ ἔδραμον; 2: 2) and has the prophet's confidence that his revelation is valid. This is also clearly seen in the closing words of Paul's discussion of Christian prophecy in I Cor. 14: 37, in which he confidently submits his own word to the judgment of the prophets and pneumatic community at Corinth to be acknowledged as a word of the Lord, with the insistence that they had *better* do so (I Cor. 14: 37–8)!

Although only Paul gives a thorough discussion of this issue, our other sources indicate that prophetic revelation was dealt with in a similar or analogous way in the churches they represent. It is remarkable that, though Acts has a high view of prophetic revelation (13: 1–3; 11: 28–30; 16: 6–9; cf. 3: 22–3), revelation that is acknowledged to be from the Spirit seems to be simply ignored; at least it does not alter the decisions of the persons addressed (20: 22–3; 21: 4, 10–14). I am implying not that these scenes are precisely historical but that Luke's understanding of the prophetic phenomenon included both an affirmation of the revelation as having come from the Spirit and a judicious weighing of the message by the recipients; and that it was this combination of revelation-plus-response-by-the-community that was considered the revelatory event, and not the Spirit-inspired oracles alone. This is captured in one Lukan phrase in 15: 28: ἔδοξεν γὰρ τῷ πνεύματι τῷ ἁγίῳ <u>καὶ ἡμῖν</u>.

The issue of testing prophetic revelation is not directly discussed in the Fourth Gospel, but the way that instruction from the Paraclete is described does give criteria that the community may apply to purported revelations, in that he will bring to the church's remembrance the tradition of Jesus' words (14: 26) and will bear witness to Jesus himself (15: 26). The community addressed in I John itself has the Spirit (3: 24; 4: 13) and has no need for anyone (outside the community) to teach it, because it itself has the χρίσμα (2: 27; cf. αὐτοὶ γὰρ ὑμεῖς θεοδίδακτοί ἐστε; I Thess. 4: 9). It is thus capable of discerning the validity of various claims to revelation by the Spirit, in part by means of the creedal confession that 'Jesus Christ has come in the flesh', but also because it knows itself to be a Spirit-endowed community that confesses this faith (4: 1–3; cf. I Cor. 12: 1–3).

The Matthean community also acknowledges the continuing voice of its risen Lord, making himself known through Christian prophets, but knows that it must test such claims. In 7: 15–20, Matthew himself seems to have taken up a traditional *logion*, 'you shall know them by their fruits', and applied it specifically to the problem of prophecy. Similarly in 7: 21–3, ἀνομία is the community's criterion to sort out false claims to revelation. The Didache probably reflects the church in the same geographical area as Matthew as it struggles with the prophetic claims in its midst, and is almost humorous in its effort both to respect the Spirit of Prophecy (11.7: 'Do not test or examine any prophet who is speaking in a spirit, "for every sin shall be forgiven, but this sin shall not be forgiven".'), and to avoid being taken in by illegitimate claims to revelation by the application of rough and ready rules to distinguish true prophets from false (11.8–12). The same verbs are used to describe this testing process as those New Testament writers use: δοκιμάζω (11.11; cf. I Thess. 5: 21; I John 4: 1); κρίνω and διακρίνω (11.7, 11–12; cf. I Cor. 12: 10 and 14: 29); πειράζω (11.7; cf. Rev. 2: 2). Even in the early second-century Roman church, this same traditional manner of responding to inspired speech in the congregation was still practiced, according to Hermas' eleventh Mandate.

Since our sources, mostly literarily independent, all manifest essentially the same relationship between the congregation and its prophets, we may confidently assume that this relationship obtained also in that early stream of Palestinian-oriented Christian prophecy with which we are concerned. The prophetic charisma was widely honored; everywhere it was honored it was also judiciously criticized by a community that did not consider the prophets within it as the sole bearers of the Spirit. This aspect of prophetic ministry is important in considering whether or not Christian prophets might have contributed to the developing tradition of sayings of Jesus. While the process of evaluating the claims to speak the word of the risen Jesus should not be thought of in legal, official, systematic terms (boards did not meet after each 'revelation' to decide on its validity), the evidence suggests that this process should be thought of as neither arbitrary nor haphazard. The Christian prophet had neither the opportunity nor the authority to insert his own post-Easter revelations willy-nilly into the church's collection of sayings of Jesus.[18] The community itself was the arbiter of what was a saying of the Lord and what was not. The common denominator between the traditional sayings of Jesus and new prophetic sayings of the risen Lord was the community itself, the bearer of the tradition. This calls for a study of the relation of Christian prophecy to the tradition and the tradition process. But first we must examine the relation of prophets to worship, to determine if the worship life of the church might be the setting within the community in which prophecy and tradition have their vital interaction.

Christian prophecy and worship

Within the community of faith, prophecy functioned in a 'public', communal setting rather than in a private, individual setting. Prophecy was a function of the community gathered for worship. This is vividly documented by the Apocalypse, which came as a revelation on the day when the congregation assembles for worship (1: 10), indicating that even the enforced separation of the prophet from his church does not negate what must have been the usual circumstance, that the prophet received his revelation in association with the community's worship. The Apocalypse is written to be read in worship to the gathered congregation, in the absence of the prophet himself (1: 4). It begins with a greeting of grace and peace (1: 4), closes with a benediction (22: 20), and is permeated throughout with worship materials, of which 4: 11; 5: 9–13; 11: 17–18; 12: 10–12; 15: 3–4; 19: 1–5, 6–8 are only the more explicit examples, since the whole prophecy is conceived within a cultic framework that unites the heavenly and earthly cultic spheres.[19]

All Paul's specific references to prophecy in I Corinthians are included in the extensive discussion of public worship that stretches from 11: 2 through 14: 39. Paul regards prophecy as occurring in worship, as a ministry performed before the gathered congregation, and only there. Presumably prophets might receive revelations at other times – though there is nothing in Paul that makes even this assumption necessary — but these revelations do not function as *prophecy* unless and until they are delivered to the community, for whose edification they are intended (14: 3). A fundamental difference between tongues and prophecy for Paul is this difference between personal edification and the edification of the whole community (14: 4). A prophecy must become the subject of the διάκρισις of the wider community (12: 10; 14: 29). The close relationship between prayer and prophecy in I Thess. 5: 19—20, and the possibility of the community's disdaining of prophetic utterance, probably also indicates the worship setting of prophecy in Paul's thought. The possibility of prophets giving private revelations to individuals outside the setting of the gathered congregation is utterly alien to Paul. The communal view of prophecy was maintained in the Pauline tradition that related pneumatic speech to the worship setting (Col. 3: 16; Eph. 5: 18—20; I Tim. 1: 18; 4: 14).

Prophets in Acts function in gatherings of the community that are sometimes specifically designated as worship settings (11: 27—9;[20] 13: 1—3; 15: 1—32; 19: 1—7; probably 21: 10—14), though other references are not so clearly so (16: 6—9; 20: 23; 21: 4). The prophetic figures of Luke 1—2 are all associated with a worship context, and their oracles have a liturgical ring. Whether the Fourth Gospel and its understanding of the Spirit's leading of the Christian is related to the worship life of the congregation is a disputed point that cannot be debated here.[21] I am most persuaded by those students of John who argue that the speech material as we have it bears the marks of having been handed on, continually re-formed and used in the liturgy of a worshipping community.[22] John does not pursue 'worship' as a theological theme, but his materials bear the marks of being grounded in worship as their *Sitz im Leben*. I have argued elsewhere that the Paraclete is not the individualistic teacher within the heart of every Christian but a functional ministry within the Johannine community.[23] It is clear that in the Didache the prophets are expected to lead in worship (10: 7) and are seen as filling the role of 'high priests' to the community (13.3), with nothing suggesting that prophets function outside the worship setting. This latter view is explicitly opposed in Hermas, who considers the context of worship by the holy community as the *sine qua non* of all legitimate prophecy (Mand. XI.1—9), while false prophets avoid congregations (Mand. XI.13). When this almost-unanimous evidence of the New Testament and early Christian literature is placed beside the fact that in Israel, Judaism and paganism there was frequently a connection between prophecy and the cult,[24] we may be justified in concluding that this was the case with early Christian prophets as well.

This supposition is strengthened by an examination of the relation of prophecy to tradition.

Christian prophecy and tradition

A widespread stereotype of Christian prophecy pictures it as divorced from tradition. Some representative statements:

'All prophecy rests on revelation, I Cor. 14: 30. The prophet does not declare what he has taken from tradition or what he has thought up himself.'[25]

'This [early Palestinian Christian] prophecy spoke independently of the Scriptures and the developing tradition.'[26]

'Die Verkündigung orientiert sich primär an dem überlieferten Wort Gottes, während die prophetische Rede unmittelbar aus der Dynamik des heiligen Geistes hervorbricht.'[27]

'Weil die Prophetie nicht wie die "Lehre" aus der Tradition schöpft, sondern auf Offenbarung beruht, besass die Feststellung der Echtheit eines Prophet vom Anfang an grösste Bedeutung.'[28]

If this understanding of prophecy were valid, the hypothesis that Christian prophets added to the synoptic tradition would hardly be supportable. Prophecy so conceived is so isolated from tradition, and its products so unlike traditional material, that it would be difficult to imagine significant mixing of the two. This understanding of prophecy is a significant factor in the reluctance of some New Testament scholars to accept the relation of Christian prophets to the synoptic tradition. It is a misunderstanding. The supposed separation of prophecy from tradition is not derived from the sources. Recent studies of Old Testament prophets have revealed how congenial the use of tradition is with the claim to speak directly for the Lord.[29] In Jewish apocalyptic, which forms part of the background of early Christian prophecy, the seer typically understands himself as standing in a long tradition and does in fact use traditional materials, even when communicating genuine visionary experiences.[30] In the Judaism from which early Christianity was born, the prophets were not thought of as inspired innovators, who brought radically new revelation, but as strong links in the chain of tradition, who only presented afresh what was already Israel's traditional lore.[31] It might be expected that prophecy that originates from such a context will make no particular attempt to insulate itself from the church's tradition.

All the evidence that indicates that Christian prophecy typically functioned in the worship setting also serves to bring prophecy into proximity to the tradition, for it was in the setting of worship that the tradition was handed on. This axiom of form criticism of the gospels need not be pressed to mean that the sayings of Jesus were recited exclusively in the liturgy but only that the public gatherings of the community, of which worship was a part, formed the general setting in which the tradition was transmitted. Even the distinction between the worship setting and the school setting should not be firmly drawn; the school community was also a worship community.[32] In general, tradition and Spirit should be seen as belonging together in early Christianity, except in some Hellenistic streams of *Enthusiasmus* that are opposed by Paul.[33] But more than this general conclusion may be drawn: the evidence of our sources indicates that Christian prophets were not only active in the cultic setting in which the tradition of Jesus' words was transmitted, but were sometimes involved in the process of transmission themselves.

It is a commonplace of research on the Apocalypse that the Seer expresses his revelatory experiences using materials that have in great part come to him from the church's tradition.[34] In the first place is to be noted the extensive amount of Old Testament materials of which he makes use, without ever expressly quoting a single passage. John's interpretative technique will be discussed later; here the significant point to be noted is that John's prophecy reveals that his mind is steeped in the traditional materials that were handed on and used in the church's worship, and that there is no tension between the vertical dimension of 'revelation' and the horizontal dimension of 'tradition'. The Old Testament materials are not cited as the historical evidence of a past authority but become the present address of the risen Lord. Every page of Revelation is replete with examples; an especially clear one is 18: 1–8, where words and sayings from several Old Testament books are woven into oracles that are presented as voices from heaven to the Seer. The prophetic charisma expresses itself through the appropriation and re-presentation of traditional materials. These materials also include forms taken over from apostolic letters that have been read in the liturgy of the church (e.g. 1: 4–5; 22: 21), the appropriation, modification and re-presentation of oracles from earlier Christian prophets, which had been preserved and transmitted in the cult; and perhaps material from non-Christian prophets (e.g. 11: 1–13; 17: 1–18).[35]

Of central significance for our purpose, of course, is the fact that among the traditional materials that find expression in the Seer's revelation from the heavenly Lord are reflections of sayings that were handed on in the church as sayings of the historical Jesus. The *extent* to which this was the case is disputed, but there are some clear examples that make it apparent that the Seer does know sayings of Jesus that the synoptic gospels place in the mouth of the pre-Easter Jesus (e.g. 3: 5 = Luke 12: 8 par.; 2: 7 = Mark 4: 9 par.). Especially when seen in the light of other evidence presented here, this phenomenon should prove that the two traditions, the sayings of the 'historical' Jesus and the revelations from the 'exalted' Jesus, were passed along in proximity to each other, the setting for both being the worship life of the congregation. Revelation further documents that sayings associated with the historical Jesus could become sayings of the risen Jesus. It is passing strange that this fact has sometimes been readily acknowledged by students who deny that the flow could go the other way, so that sayings of the exalted Lord were included in some circles with the sayings of the historical Jesus, because the early church purportedly kept these categories 'distinct'.[36] Revelation was written after the gospel form, in which sayings of Jesus were explicitly incorporated into a pre-Easter frame, had become common. As 'gospel' and 'prophecy' became more fixed literary forms, the Christian message began to flow in channels that did tend to identify sayings of Jesus as 'pre-' or 'post-Easter' by virtue of the literary form itself. This was already happening by the end of the first century, with the result that John has fewer sayings attributable to the 'historical' Jesus than one might expect. The small amount of such material in Revelation does establish the point here argued, however, and makes it the more probable that a generation earlier the line between pre- and post-Easter sayings of Jesus was even less distinct, and that Christian prophecy of that era was even more related to the sayings of the pre-Easter Jesus.

Form criticism is making it clearer and clearer that Paul's letters contain an extensive amount of traditional material, including creeds, hymns, parenesis and liturgical material, much of which had its *Sitz im Leben* in the worship life of the church.[37] I will not labor that well-established point here but will discuss the relevant aspects of Paul's use of traditional sayings of the earthly Jesus. As in the case of the Apocalypse, the extent of this is disputed, with some students finding hundreds of allusions to synoptic sayings of Jesus.[38] While allowing that Paul undoubtedly did know more sayings of Jesus than he explicitly quotes, though apparently not a *great* many more, for reasons of methodological clarity we will limit our discussion to those texts where Paul explicitly refers to 'words of the Lord':

I Cor. 7: 10: παραγγέλλω, οὐκ ἐγὼ ἀλλὰ ὁ κύριος
I Cor. 7: 12: λέγω ἐγώ, οὐχ ὁ κύριος
I Cor. 7: 25: ἐπιταγὴν κυρίου οὐκ ἔχω
I Cor. 9: 14: οὕτως καὶ ὁ κύριος διέταξεν

I Cor. 11: 23–6: ἐγὼ γὰρ παρέλαβον ἀπὸ τοῦ κυρίου ὃ καὶ παρέδωκα
ὑμῖν

I Cor. 14: 37: ἃ γράφω ὑμῖν ὅτι κυρίου ἐστὶν ἐντολή

I Thess. 4: 15–17: τοῦτο γὰρ ὑμῖν λέγομεν ἐν λόγῳ κυρίου

It is immediately noticeable that all these references are from I Corinthians, which alone among Paul's letters contains a discussion of Christian prophecy, with the sole exception of I Thess. 4: 15–17, which itself is Christian prophecy. This itself should suggest some relationship between Christian prophecy and the tradition of Jesus' words. There is no indication that the prophets at Corinth drew materials from the sayings-tradition; their revelations seem to be entirely the spontaneous inspirations of the moment, received during worship without previous reflection (14: 26–32). But the Corinthian idea of prophecy is more ecstatic than Paul's. Over against the Corinthian enthusiasm, Paul places an understanding of prophecy that is closely related to the church's tradition. The understanding of prophecy held by Paul, and Paul's own functioning as a Christian prophet, includes not only the reception of words from the risen Lord but the taking up of sayings of Jesus from the tradition and re-presenting them, sometimes in modified and reinterpreted form, as the present address of the risen Lord. This is obvious from the second remarkable aspect of the above list: 'word of the Lord' for Paul includes sayings that could derive either from the historical or from the risen Jesus, with no attempt made to distinguish them. The subject from whom the sayings derive is designated ὁ κύριος throughout, whether this is supposed to be the historical or the exalted Jesus. There is no set introductory formula for a saying from the historical Jesus to distinguish it from sayings of the risen Lord, e.g. nothing remotely resembling the γέγραπται used for Scripture citations. We have already discussed the exaggerated importance sometimes attached to 7: 10–12 in this regard,[39] but it may be further noted that 7: 40*b* and 14: 37 must be considered in any understanding of Paul's disclaimers in 7: 12 and 7: 25 pertaining to his having a command of the Lord. Paul's own apostolic–prophetic γνώμη is a result of the inspiration of the risen Lord who is the Spirit (Rom. 8: 9–10; II Cor. 3: 17); what the apostle–prophet writes is itself ἐντολὴ κυρίου. So Paul does not distinguish traditional sayings of the historical Jesus from the inspired products of church prophets as clearly as is sometimes supposed. Rather, what I Cor. 7: 12 and 25 tell us is that on these subjects Paul has no *traditional* saying of the Lord to appeal to. These texts do not state that the Lord in the traditions here appealed-to is exclusively the historical Jesus, and the way ὁ κύριος is used indiscriminately in the above list to introduce sayings that could originate from either the pre- or the post-Easter Jesus implies the exact opposite: Paul does not distinguish these and makes no effort to distinguish the sayings of the one from the other. Gerald Hawthorne points out in this connection that:

> 'Paul in referring to the Last Supper (I Cor. 11: 24–5) quotes Jesus as saying "This is my body, which is for you; do this as a memorial of me" (verse 24). Later he says that in the same way the *Lord* Jesus took the cup after supper and said "Do this, as often as you drink it, as a memorial of me" (verse 25). Then, without a break or any indication that the Lord had stopped speaking, the text continues (verse 26): "For as often as you eat this bread and drink the cup you proclaim the Lord's death until he comes ..." In fact the conjunction "for" ($\gamma\acute{\alpha}\rho$) ties the two statements so closely together that one has to take special note that verse 26 begins Paul's exposition of the Jesus-words, and is not a continuation of the Jesus-words. Here, then, in the liturgy of the eucharist, commingle traditional words of Jesus with prophetic words of the risen Lord. Little or no concern on Paul's part to distinguish between them is evident.'[40]

This ambiguity is clarified in the *Apostolic Constitutions*, VIII. 12.16, where these words are put into Christ's mouth, with the change '*my* death, till *I* come', thereby making the transition from prophetic church saying to purported saying of the historical Jesus complete.

From all this it is clear that Paul does have a tradition of sayings of the Lord, a tradition that includes both sayings of the historical Jesus in various degrees of reinterpretation and sayings of the risen Lord derived from Christian prophets. Paul's gospel is both tradition-receiving and tradition-creating. The way Paul handles the oracle of the risen Lord in I Thess. 4: 15–17 shows that it was included in the tradition from which he drew; it was not created *ad hoc*. And his instruction that the oracle should be used to comfort the Christians of Thessalonica, as the letter becomes a part of their tradition (4: 18; cf. 5: 27), indicates that he expected the saying to continue to live in the church's tradition. Paul does not understand prophetic speech to be only a momentary inspiration, spoken into the air, to quickly disappear. Paul the prophet passes on a tradition of prophetic speech, which he expects to continue to be passed on. It is no accident that Paul's discussion of charismatic speech in Corinth is prefaced by an appeal to a traditional creedal affirmation of the historical Jesus as decisive (12: 3), and is immediately followed by a declaration of the gospel as expressed in the oldest traditional form (15: 1–3). Prophecy and tradition are not only co-ordinates in Paul's ministry, they are inextricably interwoven with each other.

A different picture is given in Acts, where prophets are portrayed by Luke as having no relation to church tradition. Only Judas and Silas are incidentally engaged in passing along church decisions reached in Jerusalem (15: 32; cf. verse 28). Agabus' revelations are particular disclosures of the future to an individual or congregation and are preserved in Acts in the same way that conversations are preserved, not because prophets are thought of as drawing from or creating church tradition. The prophets of Acts certainly have nothing to do with the transmission of Jesus' words. No doubt there were prophets such as Agabus is represented to be. But the uniform presentation of prophets in Acts as a-traditional is to be attributed primarily to Luke's theology.[41] It is a remarkable fact that no one in Acts, including apostles and teachers, is concerned to pass on the sayings of Jesus. In Luke's understanding, the church is not led by remembering the teaching of Jesus, which belongs to the time prior to Easter, but by the Spirit. The sole reference to a saying of Jesus in all of Acts is 20: 35 – a saying not found in the Gospel. It is important for the reader to have the teachings of Jesus, as they are preserved at the proper *heilsgeschichtlich* point in the πρῶτος λόγος, the Gospel of Luke, but the sayings of Jesus are not a significant feature in the history of the early church as depicted by Luke. It is not unexpected, then, that Luke's prophets in Acts are unrelated to the tradition of Jesus' own words. On the other hand, the prophetic figures in Luke 1–2 do seem to be related to the tradition, in that the oracles they deliver draw from traditional materials and then become church tradition, so that even in Luke–Acts there is still some reflection of the early prophets' relation to the tradition. The tradition underlying Luke's editing indicates that Christian prophets should therefore be seen as having formed a part of that group that Luke labels ὑπηρέται τοῦ λόγου (Luke 1: 1), which formed one of the links in the tradition from Jesus' day to Luke's.

The prophet–Paraclete of the Fourth Gospel is bearer of tradition and medium of new revelation from the risen Lord in one and the same person (14: 26; 16: 12–13). The picture of Christian prophecy offered by the Johannine materials indicates a fusion of tradition and present revelation. The author of the gospel himself functions as such a prophet, uniting the tradition from Jesus with the present address of the risen Jesus in an inseparable bond. Likewise the author of I John is an exponent of both tradition (1: 1–3) and continuing revelation (2: 26–7), so that relation to the tradition can even be used as a criterion of true and false prophecy (2: 24; 4: 1–3). In John the tradition is made present by the charisma; the charisma is made valid by the tradition; a prophet who is not something of a traditionalist is a false prophet.[42]

The connection that we find in our sources between prophets and tradition is supported by recent studies of prophecy from a sociological perspective.[43] Gerd Theissen in particular has argued that the sayings of Jesus were transmitted in part by prophetic bands at the edge of society and church.[44] Theissen's view that traditions were transmitted by charismatics is well-documented and is to be accepted. His view that sayings of Jesus which include a call for radical abandonment of home and family could only have been handed on by a homeless group on the fringe of society and church need not be accepted: Amos's words were preserved even by a community that never did quite succeed in establishing justice in the gate. Thus, though prophets were not as 'wandering' as he is inclined to believe, which I have argued above, this does not invalidate his insight regarding the transmission of tradition by charismatics. In the early church too, the Jewish dictum held true: 'From the day whereon the temple was laid waste, prophecy was taken from the prophets and given to the sages. Not everyone who opens "Thus saith the Lord" is a prophet, just as not everyone lacks prophetic gifts because he opens "It is written" ' (Baba Bathra 12*a*).

The significance of the above investigation for our particular project is threefold: (1) since prophets have a positive relation to the tradition, functioning in the setting of the life of the church in which the sayings of Jesus were transmitted, and drawing materials from the tradition with which to express their revelations, it is not *a priori* unlikely that they also contributed to the tradition. (2) It is likely that the transmission process itself will sometimes bear the characteristic marks of Christian prophecy, so that the cluster of materials within which a saying is handed on, or the particular shape of the context of a saying, may be used as evidence that the saying has been created, or shaped, by Christian prophets. (3) Quite apart from the question of whether individual sayings were coined or re-formed in ways so characteristic of Christian prophecy that they may now be recognized as constituting a prophetic stratum within the tradition — a question that is to be explored in Part Three below — the prophets' relation to the tradition process may have influenced the tradition of Jesus' words taken as a whole. Not only may particular sayings bear the marks of Christian prophecy, the tradition *en bloc* may have become something different from what it would have been without its connection to prophecy, if, for example, it had been handed on by traditioners who were altogether of the rabbinic or scribal type. Günther Bornkamm has made a very important point in this connection: the various renderings of Jesus' words in the tradition point to their prophetic use as the word of the living Lord to various situations.[45] To point to the tendency of popular, oral tradition to alter, adorn and omit is not in itself an adequate explanation for the phenomena, though of course these laws of popular oral tradition also had their effect on the gospel tradition. But the fact that the 'there and then' of Jesus' word is taken up into the 'here and now' of his addressing the church is to be seen as one of the primary means of accounting for the variety of forms in which a saying of Jesus appears in the tradition. If this had regularly happened in the recitation of the sayings of Jesus in worship under the influence of the prophets who were present there, even non-charismatic interpreters of the tradition, such as Matthew and Luke, would have had a model for handling the Jesus-tradition that could not be reduced to deductive logic, the laws of oral tradition or midrashic interpretation, though all of these were factors. Because of the prophets' role in the tradition process, the tradition as a whole bears something of a prophetic character, whether or not we are able to isolate particular sayings that have been influenced by Christian prophets.

Prophets and teachers

The preceding discussion makes prophets appear quite similar to teachers, as teachers in the early church are commonly understood. As we shall see, prophets are to be distinguished from typical teachers on one crucial point, but first the line of evidence that we have uncovered indicating their similarity needs to be pursued. To begin with, the Christian teacher is a rather vague figure in early Christianity, just as is the case with the early Christian prophet. We may not begin by supposing that we have an assured description of the functions, characteristics and status of the early Christian teacher, which may be used as a foil for characterizing early Christian prophecy. Although we no doubt have much material in our New Testament that comes from or through the hands of early Christian teachers, both directly, in the sense that they might have written some of our New Testament books, and indirectly, in that their products (catechesis, parenesis, *testimonia* collections, collections of stories and sayings of Jesus etc.) are utilized by New Testament authors, we have not a single book that explicitly declares itself to be διδαχή or διδασκαλία, or to be written by one exercising the office of a διδάσκαλος. James is the nearest to this (3: 1). Here we are in a situation analogous to that which obtains in the discussion of Christian prophecy. But one unknown cannot be clarified by comparing it to another unknown. Rather, the investigation of each should proceed together. It is, of course, not my purpose to launch a full-scale investigation of the early Christian teacher here — though that task needs to be done by someone — but to note how alike prophets and teachers are in our sources.

Like the prophets, teachers are often regarded as charismatics, who do not simply function on the basis of native gifts or acquired learning but are constituted as teachers by the Holy Spirit. This is certainly the case with Paul (I Cor. 12: 28; Rom. 12: 7), as well as his followers (Eph. 4: 11; cf. II Tim. 1: 11). Teaching is described as a charisma given by the Spirit in I John 2: 26–7. That our sources are far from unanimous in this would suggest that teaching was not regularly seen as a charismatic function, but in some streams of early Christianity this was the case. All prophets were charismatics, but not all teachers. But charisma *per se* did not distinguish prophets from teachers.

Prophets and teachers are often closely associated in our sources. Again, this is the case in Paul (I Cor. 12: 28; Rom. 12: 6–7) and his followers (Eph. 4: 11), who place prophecy and teaching in the same series. Acts (13: 1) and the Didache (13.1–2; 15.1–2) mention them together as forming a unit. Further, prophets are sometimes explicitly described as teaching (Rev. 2: 20; Did. 11.10; John 14: 26) so that the reception of prophecy results in 'learning' or 'instruction' (I Cor. 14: 19, 31). Whether Matthew identifies teachers with prophets or only associates them very closely is debated; in any case, he does not distinguish them sharply. Qumran's Teacher, who functions prophetically, is only one example of the way in which the offices of prophet and teacher had already merged in the thinking and life of first-century Judaism, a fact that probably colored the way in which both prophecy and teaching were conceived in earliest Christianity. Among recent writers there seems to have been a fresh perception of the way the functions of prophecy and teaching shade into each other, with the result that the prophet is now seen as much more a teaching figure than formerly.[46]

All the above discussion indicates that the picture of teachers who hand on the firmly-guarded tradition of the sayings of Jesus in one context, while charismatic prophets deliver their inspired, ephemeral revelations from the risen Jesus in another, is based on fantasy. The horizontal, traditioning function of the church's ministry operated conjointly with the vertical, revelatory aspect. Prophets and tradents were partners engaged in a complementary and mutually-enriching ministry of the word; prophet and tradent were sometimes the same person.

I now come back to the important distinction between prophets and teachers. Prophets and teachers should not be simply identified without qualification. There were non-charismatic teachers as well as charismatic; only the charismatic teachers were similar to Christian prophets. And not all charismatic teachers spoke in the name of the risen Lord; their charismatic ministry of the word most often came in the form of parenesis, inspired interpretation of the Scriptures similar to that of the Teacher of Righteousness at Qumran, the revelation of Spirit-given 'mysteries' that come in some other form than as sayings of the risen Jesus. But when an inspired teacher delivers his teaching by taking up a traditional saying of Jesus and re-presenting it as the present word of the Lord, reinterpreted and modified to speak to the new situation, or when new instruction is given in the form of sayings of Jesus that had not previously been a part of the church's tradition, then the teacher is functioning as a prophet according to our definition and should be considered a prophet whether this term was used of him or not. Thus, for example, when Johnston and Müller prefer not to call the Paraclete a prophet, but an 'inspired teacher', the difference between their view and mine is only terminological, and the Paraclete, even as they describe him, represents the ministry of Christian prophecy.[47]

6 THE PROPHET AS 'HOMO RELIGIOSUS'

The prophet as pneumatic speaker

It is only in view of the ecclesiastical setting of Christian prophecy and the prophet's relation to the church's tradition and teaching ministry that we now turn to a consideration of the prophet as πνευματικός. Certain understandings of terms such as 'inspired', 'enthusiasm' and 'ecstatic', when applied to Christian prophets, make it difficult to conceive of such figures uttering words that could be added by the community to its tradition of sayings of Jesus. Thus both a definition of terms and an investigation of our sources with these definitions in mind are needed before declarations concerning the possible 'ecstatic' nature of early Christian prophecy can be meaningful.

I agree with Johannes Lindblom that all prophets function with the conviction that they receive direct revelations from the deity.[1] Such revelations are received in a psychic state that might, with Lindblom, be called 'der revelatorische Zustand', 'the revelatory state', which embraces the entire spectrum between an ecstatic trance, in which consciousness and volition are lost, and strong intuitive certainty, in which the prophet is in full possession of both his reflective and volitional powers. This corresponds to Reiling's delineation of three types of ecstasy, in the first of which both will and consciousness are lost, in the second of which will is eliminated but consciousness remains, the prophet passively observing that the deity speaks through him. But in the third type 'both will and consciousness remain intact and the prophet speaks what is revealed to him as a divine message', a state that may be experienced as 'little more than an elated feeling'.[2] In view of the discussion to follow, I think it is better to limit the term 'ecstasy' and 'ecstatic' only to Reiling's first two types, i.e. the portion of Lindblom's spectrum in which consciousness and/or volition is lost, and to adopt the careful working definition of James Dunn:

> 'By "ecstasy" I mean here an unusually exalted state of feeling, a condition of such total absorption or concentration that the individual

81

becomes oblivious to all attendant circumstances and other stimuli, an experience of intense rapture or a trance-like state in which normal faculties are suspended for a shorter or longer period and the subject sees visions or experiences "automatic speech", as in some forms of glossolalia.'[3]

So defined, prophecy was generally an ecstatic phenomenon in the Hellenistic world. In classical times there had existed a distinction between μάντεις, who were enthusiastic, ecstatic recipients of revelation from the divine world, and προφῆται, who were basically interpreters and proclaimers of revelation. Μάντις has an ecstatic element in the root idea of the word itself that is completely lacking in προφήτης. But the following complaint from Plato shows that even in classical times this theoretical distinction was not always maintained:

'God gave unto man's foolishness the gift of divination (μαντικήν) ... no man achieves true and inspired (ἐνθέου) divination when in his rational mind (ἐννοῖ), but only when the power of his intelligence is fettered in sleep or when it is distraught by disease or by reason of some divine inspiration (ἐνθυσιασμόν) ... It is not the task of him who has been in a state of frenzy, and still continues therein, to judge the apparitions and voices seen or uttered by himself ... Wherefore also it is customary to set the tribe of prophets (τῶν προφητῶν γένος) to pass judgment upon these inspired divinations; and they, indeed, themselves are named "diviners" (μάντεις) by certain who are wholly ignorant of the truth that they are not diviners but interpreters of the mysterious voice and apparition, for whom the most fitting name would be "prophets of things divined" (προφῆται μαντευομένων).'[4]

In later Hellenistic times this distinction was hardly maintained at all, and as frenzied enthusiasts were often called προφῆται, prophets were described as mantics. Lucan gives a typical description of this widespread understanding of what happened to the seer/prophet in the moment of revelation: the god takes over the body of the seer and drives the human spirit out. The man himself loses consciousness, is ἔκφρων; νοῦς is no longer in him. He is not responsible for what he says, cannot prevent himself from speaking and cannot interpret what he has said.[5] Lucian and Vergil fill in the picture by describing the violent physical phenomena that accompanied the state in which oracles were both received and delivered: rolling eyes, foaming mouth, pounding heart, gasping breath, all of which shows that the term *mania* was meant seriously.[6]

The first writer known to us to develop a comprehensive syncretistic understanding of the prophetic experience is Philo of Alexandria, who explained biblical prophecy in terms of Hellenistic enthusiasm. He was the first to use ἔκστασις in a technical sense, which he understood in its literal etymological sense: ἐκ-στάσις is when the human mind *stands outside* in order that the divine spirit may enter. 'The mind is evicted ... mortal and immortal may not share the same home.'[7] Ἐκ-στάσις is thus the corollary of ἐν-θεός: vacating the premises to make room for the divine speech. 'When the light of God shines, the human light sets.'[8] Thus in describing Moses, he identifies speaking by enthusiasm with prophetic speech: καὶ λέγων ἅμα ἐνθουσίᾳ μεταμορφούμενος εἰς προφήτην.[9] It is noticeable that in Philo's discussion of Old Testament passages dealing with prophecy he shuns the LXX expressions ἅγιον πνεῦμα or πνεῦμα θεοῦ and replaces them with words such as ἐνθουσία, ἔνθους γίνεται, θεσπίζει, θεοφορηθείς, ἐπιθειάσας, κατεχόμενος, with which προφητεύειν is sometimes mingled or interchanged. For example, where the LXX of Num. 24: 2 has καὶ ἐγένετο ἐπ' αὐτῷ πνεῦμα θεοῦ, Philo has ἔνθους γενόμενος ἀναφθέγγεται.[10] Philo considers the authors of all Old Testament books to be prophets, who receive their revelations in Dionysian ecstasy, so that, for example, the prophet of Deut. 18: 15–18 will only say what is given him but will not understand it.[11] Plato, Lucan, Lucian, Vergil and Philo only illustrate a point that could be documented many times over: prophecy was generally an enthusiastic, ecstatic phenomenon in the Hellenistic world.

We are in a different world when we read the documents that represent early Christian prophecy. In regard to ecstatic experience, there is a clear contrast between typical Hellenistic prophets and the type of prophecy manifest in our sources. Our primary example of first-century Christian prophecy, the Apocalypse, offers no descriptions whatsoever of the author's psychic state or extraordinary physiological or psychological phenomena during the reception of the revelations. The revelatory state is not encouraged or manipulated by any external act. The initial entrance into the revelatory state, and subsequent moments within it, are described with the simple ἐν πνεύματι (1: 10; 4: 2; 17: 3; 21: 10). There is a conscious avoidance of the religious vocabulary of ecstasy that profane Greek and syncretists such as Philo customarily use as synonomous expressions for πνεῦμα. In Revelation, the state of being ἐν πνεύματι is an extraordinary state, the state in which things can be seen and heard that are not available to the natural man, but I would hesitate to describe this state as an ecstatic experience, because it is not involuntary but is expressed in terms of the author's own conscious intent, including the reflective use of traditional materials. There is an element of 'ecstasy' in the reception of the revelation, in that the Seer does genuinely see visions and hear voices, but in the delivery of the message the Seer is consciously reflective and intentional, not merely the vehicle for some supernatural power. This corresponds to Reiling's 'third type' of ecstasy, which I would prefer not to call ecstasy at all, since this tends to confuse the experience of early Christian prophets with that of Hellenistic prophets. 'Immediate inspiration' is the term I prefer for the Christian prophet.[12] Since the Seer's writing is consciously intentional and reflective, we may confidently assume that, had he not been separated from the congregation, his oral delivery of his prophecy to the congregation would likewise have been conscious and intentional, though recognizably 'inspired'. In all of this he corresponds to the prophets of the Old Testament, whose heir he is.

Paul is obviously embroiled in a discussion with the Corinthians on the validity of ecstatic speech. The Corinthians prefer the more ecstatic gift of tongues, in which the speaker utters words incomprehensible to men (14: 2), speaking mysteries in the Spirit (14: 2), uttering speech that is not intelligible (14: 9), in which the mind of the speaker is not engaged (14: 14), and are critical of Paul because his speech is not sufficiently 'spiritual', by which they mean ecstatic (II Cor. 10: 10). Paul is tolerant of this manifestation of the Spirit in the congregation (14: 5, 18, 39) but exalts prophecy at the expense of *glossolalia* (14: 1–3, 5, 18–19, 23–5, 39–40). Yet it is clear that by 'prophecy' Paul intends something less ecstatic than the Corinthian view of prophecy. The Corinthians had associated *glossolalia* and prophecy, considering the latter only an inferior version of the former. Paul not only inverts this valuation, he distinguishes them in kind, not simply in degree, and rejects the common Hellenistic view that prophetic speech is *validated* by *glossolalia*.[13] He redefines prophecy in the act of commending it to them. The crisis in the Corinthian understanding of charismatic speech that provoked all of I Cor. 12–14 occurred when an ecstatic prophet, speaking intelligibly but under the compulsion of the supernatural power, proclaimed ἀνάθεμα Ἰησοῦς (12: 3). This expression probably originated from an enthusiastic prophet within the 'Christ party', a sub-group within the Corinthian congregation that claimed immediate revelation from the heavenly Spirit—Christ and disdained the earthly human being Jesus of Nazareth. Though many Corinthians were apparently generally sympathetic to this christology, this radical statement delivered 'in the Spirit' seemed to some to be going too far, and they asked Paul about it.[14] Paul responded to their query by arguing that in their pre-Christian religious life they had also experienced ecstasy (12: 2), so that ecstasy as such is no guarantee that what is said in the ecstatic state is true. Claims to Spirit-inspired speech are to be measured by the confession of faith (12: 3), by the community itself, which contains persons gifted by the Spirit with the ability to discriminate between competing claims to

Spirit-endowed speech (12: 10; 14: 29), and by love (13: 2). Such a stance shows that Paul does not regard prophecy as an ecstatic phenomenon in the Hellenistic sense, and that the Corinthians are inclined so to understand it. This is borne out by Paul's descriptions of prophecy, which is a matter of τῷ νοΐ λαλῆσαι in contrast to εἰς ἀέρα λαλοὖντες (I Cor. 14: 8, 9). For Paul, μαίνεσθαι (14: 23) is a stinging rebuke, not a goal to be sought after, as it was in the Bacchic experience of the Dionysian cult.[15] It can be no accident that neither here nor anywhere else in the literature of the early church is the μάντις – μαίνεσθαι vocabulary used of the prophetic experience. Paul's discussion assumes προφητεία to be a rather sober, understandable, meaningful language that leads to οἰκοδομή. There is no mention of trances, visions or any kind of externally-observable phenomena. The prophet, like the speaker in tongues, is in control of himself and can be silent – though he may have to be reminded that this is the case (14: 27–32).

Paul dissociates ecstatic experience from prophecy, but not because he is unacquainted with the former. When pressed, he can document ecstatic experiences of his own (II Cor. 12: 1–5) but he does not call them prophecy; rather he contrasts such experiences with the kind of prophecy he commends. It was a rare experience, incommunicable, which he is reluctant to talk about and sees no edifying value in sharing with the church: different at every point from Paul's understanding of prophecy.

Paul's understanding of the prophetic experience is to be seen against the Old Testament – Jewish – rabbinic background, rather than as a reflection of the Hellenistic enthusiastic view of prophecy. This means that while prophecy is not ecstatic for Paul, it is more than humanly motivated and empowered preaching; for it is a manifestation of the Spirit (I Cor. 2: 6–13; 12: 7, 10; 14: 1; Rom. 12: 6; I Thess. 5: 19), which means a supernatural manifestation of divine power. The prophet is πνευματικός but not ἐνθυσιασάμενος.

This characterization consistently fits prophecy elsewhere in our sources as well. The Pauline School seems to have preserved Paul's own high estimate of prophecy as a gift of the Spirit, combined with a suspicion of ecstatic phenomena.[16] The author of the Fourth Gospel may have prophetically 'seen' and 'heard' some of the materials in his gospel, or at least included materials that had come into being in such prophetic experiences. He certainly conceives his own gospel to be a product of the revelatory πνεῦμα. But in John there is no thought of the sporadic coming of the Spirit, the extraordinary nature of his manifestations, ecstatic phenomena or miraculous acts. Nothing in the Paraclete sayings suggests that speech given by the Spirit is characterized by enthusiastic frenzy, but rather the opposite. Hermas is careful to distinguish the true Christian prophet from the pagan *mantis*: the prophet is inspired by the Spirit but does not become mantic (Mand. XI.2–9). The Didache reveals a community in which the idea is alive that whatever a prophet does 'in the Spirit' must be accepted, because it is entirely the Spirit with which one is dealing and not the will of the prophet himself. But though this understanding of prophecy is seductively present in the community represented by the Didache, it is altogether clear that the Didache itself rejects this understanding of prophecy. The community is indeed to recognize that it is dealing with more than mere human speech in the oracles of the prophet (10: 7; 11: 7, 11), but the Spirit-inspired prophet is also one who is himself to be held accountable for his speech, since he is not simply the passive vehicle of the Spirit (11: 8–12). In our terms, inspiration is acknowledged, but not ecstasy, as the authentic revelatory mode. Luke–Acts is our most 'Hellenistic' source on this point, in that it reports many dreams and visions as a common *modus operandi* of the Spirit's communication with the church and, alone of our sources, even uses the terminology of ἔκστασις in a positive sense (Acts 10: 10; 11: 5; 22: 17). But even Luke never describes the effects of such 'ecstasy' in the Hellenistic terms of Lucian and Philo and never relates such 'ecstatic' experiences to the prophets he describes.

We conclude that in our sources prophets are uniformly believed to be empowered by the Holy Spirit. Prophecy is never simply identified with the ordinary ministry of preaching, which is carried out in the context of the presence of the Spirit that is common to all Christians, but is always a special manifestation of the Spirit. But our sources never describe prophecy in ecstatic terms. Since this was also generally the case in that Judaism from which early Christianity sprang, it is almost a certainty that those early Christian prophets we are attempting to characterize were spokesmen for the risen Lord who understood themselves to be particularly inspired by the Holy Spirit to deliver their message and were accepted by the church as such. But they were not frenzied enthusiasts, and their charismatic claims complement, rather than contradict, their relation to the teaching ministry and the tradition that we have documented above. The pneumatic aspect of early Christian prophecy thus gives us no reason to be hesitant about the possibility of Christian prophets' influence on the developing synoptic tradition. Rather, it gives us a helpful identifying mark of prophetic material. In the light of the above, we may expect some prophetic material in the synoptic gospels to be concerned with the Spirit, in particular with the idea that the Spirit gives to the church the capacity to speak with boldness.

The prophet and miracles

Πνεῦμα as discussed above is not to be understood in the idealistic sense but as a term denoting the divine power operative in those who possess it. Consequently, those who possess the Spirit not only speak by divine power but often also manifest other supernatural abilities. It is a truism of *Religionsgeschichte* that inspired speech rarely appears alone but is usually accompanied by other extraordinary powers, sometimes in the prophet himself, sometimes in his associates. Prophecy and miracles are correlates, both in the Hellenistic religious world and in Judaism.[17]

Our sources do not manifest a uniform attitude toward the relation of prophecy and other forms of miraculous activity. It is probably the case that the prophets familiar to the Seer of Revelation perform miracles, but the evidence for this is indirect: the prophets portrayed in 11: 3–12 are endowed with miraculous power (11: 5–6, 10), but it is difficult to penetrate the Old Testament imagery and apocalyptic symbolism with which the passage is laden to discern the specific traits of those prophets in John's church who were the occasion of this description. Certainly John knows that *false* prophets work miracles (13: 11–15, with 16: 13; 19: 20; 20: 10), but this does not mean that he rejects the miraculous element in prophetic ministry *per se*. Rather, John probably considered miracles a feature of prophetic ministry but not a proof of the truth of the prophet's message.

In Paul's understanding this dialectic is sharply focused. He too believes that the one Spirit that inspires prophecy also gives the gift of miracles (I Cor. 12: 8–11, 28–30). He thinks of these gifts as ordinarily being distributed among the congregation in such wise that, if one has the gift of prophecy, he may not necessarily have the gift of working miracles, and vice versa. Still, the association between prophecy and miracles is present in Paul's understanding, and not only in that they are mentioned together in lists of charismatic gifts. Such lists are not intended to distinguish discrete gifts sharply from each other, as may be seen from comparing the various lists, but to illustrate the variety of ἐνεργήματα of the one Spirit. Paul is a prophet (I Cor. 14: 6) who works miracles (II Cor. 12: 12). My present purpose is not to develop Paul's theological critique of the claims that were made for the miraculous (I Cor. 13: 2; II Cor. 10–13) but to note that, in spite of this critique, prophecy and miracles are closely related even in Paul. Matthew, too, is unimpressed by miraculous phenomena *per se* and acknowledges that prophets who perform miracles are not thereby validated as true prophets (7: 22–3). His polemic is not against associating miracles with prophecy, however, for the missionaries sent out by Matthew's community include prophets in their number, and such missionaries are commissioned not only to proclaim the word but to work miracles (10: 1, 41). Luke 7: 16 and 24: 19 consider miracles, mighty deeds, even raising the dead, as marks of the true prophet, and not only the words he speaks. The Fourth Gospel also knows a connection between miracles and prophets (6: 14; 9: 17), although the portrayal of the Paraclete—prophet does not include miraculous gifts as part of the picture. John's picture of the prophet Jesus includes miracles as a fundamental element not only because of the sources used by the evangelist but because miracles happen in the prophetic community. In the Didache the tension between working miracles and speaking the word has been relaxed, and prophets appear only as ministers of the word, with miracles being assigned only to the eschatological deceiver (11.3–10; 16.4). But the association of prophecy and miracles occurs often enough in our sources to suggest that early Christian prophets were often thought of as working miracles and functioned in a charismatic setting, where not only Spirit-empowered speech but Spirit-empowered miracles were expected and experienced. An interest in such miraculous phenomena may then be taken, with other evidence, to indicate that a *logion* considered secondary on other grounds may derive from, or have been influenced by, Christian prophets.

The prophet's sense of call, authority and mission

The prophet speaks with a sense of immediate authority resulting from his conviction that he has been personally commissioned by the deity to deliver a message to the people.[18] This sense of mission is one of the primary distinguishing factors between mystics and prophets: the mystic seeks his God, longs for undifferentiated union with him, while the prophet is persuaded that the deity has sought and commissioned him. Unlike the Greek προφῆται, who developed no sense of mission or claim to full personal authority because they tended to surrender their personality and consciousness to the deity, the biblical prophets of both Israel and the church emphasize the authority and purpose of the missioner, not his 'union' with the sender.

This awareness of authority and mission is characteristic of all our sources. The author of the Apocalypse recounts his call and commission (1: 9–19), identifies his word with the word of the Spirit and the risen Christ (2: 7 etc.), places his writing on a par with the Scriptures (1: 3), contrasts his own immediate authority with that of the apocalyptists by writing in his own name (1: 4) a book that is not to be sealed up (22: 10, contrast e.g. Dan. 12: 9) or tampered with under threat of divine retribution (22: 18–19). Throughout his writing he neither pleads nor cajoles, but announces and commands with a sense of unqualified authority. Although Paul usually designates his own authority as that of ἀπόστολος rather than προφήτης, we have seen that there is every reason to consider Paul as a representative of early Christian prophecy. Paul's account of his call is expressed in terms borrowed from the prophets (Gal. 1: 15 = Jer. 1: 5; Is. 49: 1), as is his sense of compulsion in regard to his mission (I Cor. 9: 16 = Jer. 20: 9) and his self-consciousness of mediating the divine authority in his own ministry (II Cor. 10: 8; 13: 10 = Jer. 1: 10). It is thus better to speak of Paul's 'call' than his 'conversion'.[19] The immediate authority with which prophets act in Acts is illustrated by Agabus, especially in the introductory formula τάδε λέγει τὸ πνεῦμα τὸ ἅγιον (21: 11). Prophetic speech is also reflected in the terminology used by Luke to describe those who spoke with the power of the Holy Spirit: ἀποφθέγγομαι (Acts 2: 4, 14; 26: 25) and παρρησία/παρρησιάζομαι (Acts 9: 27, 28; 13: 46; 14: 3; 18: 26; 19: 8; 26: 26). This latter term is a point of contact with the Gospel of John, which uses παρρησία as a characteristic term for Jesus' speech and action, an indication of his immediate authority in which the prophets of the Johannine community also participated (7: 26; 10: 24; 11: 14; 16: 25, 29; 18: 20). The Fourth Gospel lays special emphasis on the 'sending' of Jesus (ὁ πέμψας με or a variation thereof used twenty-seven times), whereby we may not only see the original prophetic authority of Jesus described, but also an indirect reflection of the prophetic ministers of John's community, since the Paraclete is repeatedly described as 'sent' (14: 26; 15: 26; 16: 7), as are the disciples (13: 20; 20: 21). The Johannine community knows a circle of prophets who claim a direct commission and authority from the risen Lord. This is also the case in Matthew. Without pre-judging the question of whether the discourse in Matt. 10 contains materials *from* Christian prophets, it clearly represents the risen Christ as sending forth his missioners, including prophets, with his own authority (10: 1, 40–1). Commentators often content themselves with referring to the Jewish juridical principle concerning the שָׁלִיחַ , 'a man's representative is as himself', and see the chapter in terms of apostolic authority.[20] But Cothonet correctly points out, in agreement with the work of Gerhardsson on this text, that the background is not juridical but prophetic.[21] This corresponds to the picture in 28: 16–18, where the community knows that it is sent forth in mission with all the authority of the risen Christ, who speaks to it and is present within it. Likewise in the Didache, the prophets obviously claimed, and were accorded, great authority (10.7; 11.4–11; 13.3–6; 15.1–2).

Early Christian prophets, then, ought not to be thought of as pneumatic eccentrics, who were regarded as curiosities within the life of the early church, but as ministers of the word who spoke with an unqualified authority on subjects that could only be handled with hesitation by their uninspired brethren. Being subject to the judgment of the community does not relativize the authoritative form of the prophet's speech, which is delivered with a sense of absolute authority. Consequently, the form and tone of such sayings would be very like the sayings of Jesus himself (Matt. 7: 29) and distinguishable from the sayings of ordinary Christian teachers and scribes. This is doubly significant for our project, in that such sayings would the more readily be blended into the tradition of Jesus' sayings, on the one hand, and may the more readily be distinguished from non-prophetic additions to this tradition (scribal, redactional, midrashic etc.) by this authoritative form and tone, on the other.

The symbolic actions of the prophets

The prophets of the Old Testament drew no sharp line between prophetic word and prophetic action, so that their 'symbolic actions' were not merely illustrations or vivid portrayals of their message but were themselves prophetic words that, once enacted, set the process of fulfillment in motion (Jer. 13: 1–11; 19: 1–13; 27: 1 – 28: 14; Is. 20: 2–4; Ezek. 4; 5; 12; Hos. 1; 3).[22] There is some indication of a similar way of embodying their message among Christian prophets, but it is not always clear whether this is because early Christian prophets did in fact use symbolic actions, or whether our sources have described Christian prophets in Old Testament terms. In Revelation, there is the additional complication of attempting to distinguish what is purely visionary apocalyptic imagery and what may have some counterpart in the ministry of the prophet-author himself. Eating the scroll (10: 8–11) and measuring the temple (11: 1–2) probably belong only to the realm of vision, and the angel's throwing of the stone into the sea as a symbol of Babylon's fall (18: 21) is probably a reflection of the prophetic symbol in Jer. 51: 63–4; nevertheless a Christian prophet whose thinking is so thoroughly permeated with such an understanding of the nature of prophecy probably engaged in such symbolic acts himself. Likewise, while there is no explicit evidence that Paul or the prophets in his churches performed acts of prophetic symbolism, still one may ask how Paul 'pronounced judgment in the name of the Lord Jesus' (I Cor. 5: 3–5) and how the Corinthian church, in which prophets were active, 'delivered this man to Satan'. If Acts 21: 10–11 accurately portrays Agabus, and is not simply Luke's casting him into an Old Testament mold, then we have one clear example of such symbolic action by an early Christian prophet. The passage at least reveals that Luke or his tradition understood such prophets to have functioned in this way. The shaking-off of the dust of the feet in Matt. 10: 14, though a fairly common act to express the disavowal of fellowship, in the Matthean context has the connotation of a prophetic threat performed by missioners who include prophets in their number (10: 41) and may indicate that church prophets known to Matthew performed such power-laden rituals. Even the baptism of John was probably more symbolic act in the prophetic sense than sacrament in the church sense. The σημεῖα of Jesus in the Fourth Gospel are part of his revelatory, prophetic ministry: a symbolic presentation of his word, not miraculous proof of its truth. Though John himself strikes a profound theological note here, this understanding may have been partially shaped by the prophets of John's church who performed such symbolic embodiments of their word. The Didache's intriguing reference to a prophet ποιῶν εἰς μυστήριον κοσμικὸν ἐκκλησίας (11.11) who, if he is a 'tried and true' prophet, is to be allowed to do such, but is not to be imitated, probably refers to some bizarre symbolic acts or improprieties of worship.[23] The 'old' prophets, who are appealed to as precedents, could be Christian prophets of a previous generation, but more likely the strange acts of Old Testament prophets are invoked as justification of the behavior of contemporary ones. The evidence is slight and sketchy but may indicate that one characteristic trait of early Christian prophets was that they sometimes performed dramatic acts to communicate their message.

The 'ascetic' life-style of the prophets

As a person determined by the Spirit, the prophet rejects the cultural norms and lives a life in tension with the values and moral life of the culture of which he is a part. Of course, this is true to a greater or lesser extent of all members of the community called by the Spirit. But within the community it is particularly true of those who are self-consciously prophets. They seem to have lived a particularly austere life, rejecting the usual manner of life with its involvement in family, occupation and the accumulation of wealth. This is what I intend by 'ascetic' and not some withdrawal from the world based on philosophical or theological dualism. There is no evidence for a hermit-like withdrawal from the world, and the evidence presented above regarding the involvement of the prophets in the life of the community shows that prophetic 'asceticism' should not be understood in this way. We should rather think of a somewhat 'ascetic' class living within the congregation but distinguished from their fellow Christians by their commitment to poverty and their rejection of family life, somewhat like a parish priest in the Roman Catholic Church, except that their 'orders' are entirely a matter of the Spirit, and their authority is charismatic rather than institutional.

This general picture of the ascetism of early Christian prophets has been affirmed by a number of scholars,[24] but it remains to fill in this picture with details and evidence from our sources. The Seer on Patmos gives us no specific indication of his economic condition, but his appreciation of poverty and condemnation of wealth (2: 9; 3: 17; cf. 18: 1–24) suggest his orientation clearly enough. Paul's view of himself as a prophet on this point is complicated by his self-understanding as an apostle. It is clear that as an apostle he has the right to support from the churches, yet for his own reasons he has renounced this right and sometimes earns his own keep, and sometimes accepts gifts from churches (I Cor. 9: 1–18; II Cor. 11: 7–11; Phil. 4: 10–17). How Paul's prophetic self-consciousness is involved in this is not clear; it is clear that Paul has abandoned the usual course of 'making a living' and is sometimes in poverty as a result of his prophetic calling, and that this is something that distinguishes him from the general body of Christians and even from other 'apostles'. Luke's focus on the poor in his gospel (1–2; 4: 18–19; 6: 20–1; 12: 13–21; 14: 12–14; 16: 19–31; 18: 18–25; 19: 8; 21: 1–4) is somewhat modified in Acts, where with obvious relish he shows the church adding to its membership such persons as a Roman centurion, a business woman from Thyatira, 'not a few of the leading women' of Thessalonica and men and women 'of high standing' in Berea (10: 1–48; 16: 14–15; 17: 4, 12). Luke does not portray the church of Acts as such to be oriented toward the life of poverty. It is somewhat striking, then, to note that the prophet Barnabas is one who has sold (only some of?) his property (4: 36), and that none of the prophets of Acts are described in the bourgeois terms Luke is so pleased to use of the church at large. The commitment to poverty of early Christian prophets may shine through Luke's tradition here, as it does in the gospel. The prophets of the Didache obviously are not engaged in normal occupations but are dependent on the congregations for support, even taking precedence over the poor: they are the poorest of the poor and more deserving of support because their poverty is not simply misfortune but is inherent in their prophetic vocation (11.8; 13.3–4). In Hermas, only the ψευδοπροφῆται receive fees for their oracles; the true prophet ἑαυτὸν ἐνδεέστερον ποιεῖ πάντων τῶν ἀνθρώπων (Mand. XI.8). All of this corresponds to the general sociological description of the prophet as a religious *typus*,[25] and to the general poverty characteristic of early Palestinian Christianity, and makes it quite likely that the typical early Christian prophet was characterized by the renunciation of wealth and worldly goods. The interest in fasting that is sometimes mentioned as a prophetic trait (Luke 2: 36; Acts 13: 1–2; Vis. II.2.1; III.1.2, 10.6, 14.23) is therefore probably not a part of the revelatory technique, since in any case the prophetic capacity was not thought to be subject to manipulation but was a part of their austere life-style.

Sexual abstinence also seems to have frequently been a prophetic commitment. Geze Vermes has assembled some interesting material documenting this view among the rabbis:

> 'According to the Talmud, Moses freely decided to terminate cohabitation with his wife after he received his call from God. He reasoned that if the Israelites, to whom the Lord spoke only once and briefly, were ordered to abstain from women temporarily, he, being in continual dialogue with heaven, should remain chaste permanently.
>
> One of the early rabbinic commentaries on Numbers treats the same theme from the woman's standpoint. Moses' sister, Miriam, noticing her sister-in-law's neglected appearance, asked her why she had ceased to look after herself. Zipporah answered, "Your brother does not care about the thing." (Siphre on Num. 12: 1 [99]) The same passage of the document also notes that when it was announced that the two Israelite elders, Eldad and Medad, had started to prophesy, Miriam overheard Zipporah's muttered remark: woe to the wives of these men.'[26]

Although this tradition comes from the second century C.E., Vermes is assured that it is also representative of rabbinic ideas contemporary with those prophets we are characterizing, from the fact that Philo also makes use of it:

> 'Moses cleansed himself of "all the calls of mortal nature, food and drink and intercourse with women. This last he had disdained for many a day, almost from the time when, possessed by the Spirit, he entered on his work as a prophet, since he held it fitting to hold himself always in readiness to receive the oracular messages"' (*De Vita Moses*, 2.68–9).

It is well known that the Essenes, particularly at Qumran, also understood abstinence from sex to be an ingredient of the holy life belonging to the prophetic vocation. The presence of this understanding in such diverse streams of first-century Judaism makes the celibate life of the prophetic figures John the Baptist and Jesus easily understandable, even in a culture that placed a premium on early marriage, and suggests that Christian prophets emanating from such a context would understand their calling as a life of celibacy. As we shall see later, this life-style was integral to early Christian prophetic eschatology, not to a renunciation of the world as itself inherently evil.

Traces of this presumed trait of early Christian prophets remain in our sources. Rev. 14: 1–5 exalts the celibate life, though John is no thoroughgoing ascetic; the prophetic 'ideal' is reflected here, not a general theme of world renunciation, which is completely foreign to the Apocalypse. Luke associates virginity and the prophetic vocation very closely (Luke 1: 26–55; 2: 36–8; Acts 21: 9). Paul understands that apostles and the brothers of the Lord have the right to marry, and as an apostle he has that right. However, he and the prophet Barnabas are not married (I Cor. 9: 5), which may reflect their prophetic ministry, though Paul himself does not make this connection explicit. The successors of Paul, claiming the authority of prophetic revelation, *opposed* abstinence from marriage (I Tim. 4: 1–5), but this may be because Paul's earlier prophetic–eschatological idealization of the unmarried state (I Cor. 7: 25–40) was no longer understood eschatologically, but as a part of the general gnostic rejection of the world. The Didache makes no reference to wives or families of the prophets, but this does not, of course, prove that they were celibate. There are some ambiguous texts in the Didache that fall into place, however, on the assumption derived from the other sources that prophets were typically unmarried. The criterion for distinguishing true prophets from false in 11.8, that the true prophet ἔχῃ τοὺς τρόπους κυρίου, might well refer to his celibate state. The approved prophet who is to be permitted ποιῶν εἰς μυστήριον κοσμικὸν ἐκκλησίας, so long as he does not instruct others to do the same, may refer to the 'spiritual marriage' of some prophets to their female traveling companions, who may have interpreted the μυστήριον of Eph. 5: 32 in this way, as well as appealing to the prophet Hosea (Hos. 3: 1–3).[27] In the light of the other evidence regarding the celibate expectations of Christian prophets, these two problematic texts seem best explained as dealing with prophets who attempted to avoid living strictly by this norm. Hermas' general aversion to sex and fascination with sexual matters, illustrated for example by his describing the holy spirits, the powers of the Son of God, as virgins (Sim. IX.13), is probably to be attributed not only to his personal psychology but to his understanding of the prophetic vocation. There is some significant evidence, then, that early Christian prophets typically were committed to poverty and sexual abstinence, and we may expect to find that sayings originating from, or shaped by, such prophets may sometimes manifest this commitment.

7 THE PROPHET AS HERMENEUT

The thesis of this chapter is that early Christian prophets functioned as interpreters of Scripture in the light of contemporary events, and as interpreters of events in the light of Scripture. Scripture and event go together. The pairing of revelation-by-word and revelation-by-event is the unmistakable structural analogy that binds together the theology of the old covenant and its documents, on which early Christianity was founded, and the new, eschatological covenant, of which the early Christian prophets understood themselves to be ministers. We separate Scripture and event only for purposes of clarity in discussion, with the understanding that each is interpreted only in the light of the other.

The prophet as interpreter of Scripture

The Judaism with which early Christianity shared a common Bible exhibited two, fundamentally different, hermeneutical stances toward Scripture. While there were graduations and minglings of these two stances, for clarity I will describe them as polarities. The one, which may be designated 'scribal—rabbinic', perceives the Scripture to be an authoritative, objective, external collection of documents that contain deposits of God's eternal truth. These documents can and should be quoted, interpreted and commented-on by proper interpretative methods, a process that allows the word of Scripture to illumine the interpreter's present. Scripture is by no means regarded as a dead letter in this view. It speaks the word of God to the present by being quoted and interpreted. Some New Testament authors, such as Matthew, use the Scriptures within this hermeneutical framework with great effect (1: 23; 2: 6, 15, 18, 23; 4: 15–16; 8: 17; 12: 18–21; 13: 35; 21: 5; 27: 9–10). This approach distinguishes clearly between the word of Scripture and the word of the interpreter, between 'text' and 'sermon', between the 'then' of Scripture and the 'now' of proclamation. The Scripture is an external object that is interpreted by means of an external method, a method that may be articulated and examined by others. One's interpretation may be examined and evaluated as to its methodological correctness.[1]

95

The other hermeneutical stance may be called 'pneumatic—apocalyptic', in which Scripture is taken up into the present word of the interpreter and becomes indistinguishable from it. The text is not quoted but internalized and re-presented as the word of the interpreter himself, that is, of the Spirit whose word he speaks. Text and interpretation are fused; the 'then' of Scripture and its addressees is collapsed into the 'now' of the interpreter and his congregation. There is no objectifiable method that the interpreter may present to his hearers for consideration, to justify the correctness of his interpretation. Rather, the interpreter seems to have meditated on Scripture as illuminated by the history of his own time until the text spoke its own word to him, which he perceived as a word of revelation and delivered with the authority of one who is not a secondary interpreter of a text but an immediately-inspired spokesman through whom the text finds a new voice.

Such pneumatic—intuitive exegesis of texts began in Israel soon after the exile and is exemplified in Joel, who is thoroughly versed in the ancient prophecies but, instead of quoting them, bodies forth his interpretation of their current word as his own inspired word of the Lord.[2] In Daniel, this development is already full blown, so that we see a prophet who self-consciously functions as an inspired interpreter of the old Scriptures for a new day (9: 1—24). This self-understanding is characteristic of all Jewish apocalyptic that regarded itself as prophetic.[3] Jewish prophets who derived their oracles from inspired exegesis of Scripture persisted throughout the first century, as IV Ezra and the Zealot prophecies described by Josephus make clear.[4] Qumran offers the most illuminating example, for there the Teacher is definitely a prophet who speaks 'revelation' (גלה) directly 'from the mouth of God' (מפי אלהים IQpHab 2.2—3) but is just as clearly an exegete whose 'revelation' is 'interpretation' of the prophetic texts (גל.ה is used interchangeably with פשר).[5] Even a rabbi such as Akiba, who normally made no claims to inspiration, could, in the light of the advent of Simeon bar Kosiba, declare that the 'star out of Jacob' of Num. 24: 17 had now arrived. This is analogous to those early Christian prophets who reinterpreted the Scriptures in the light of their faith that the Messiah had come in Jesus of Nazareth. Even the great majority of rabbis whose handling of the Scripture was non-charismatic and who were personally far removed from prophetic experience nonetheless understood the prophets to be interpreters of Scripture: the Old Prophets had been such, and the Eschatological Prophet, when he arrived, would function as an interpreter of Scripture.[6] Not only was the identification of prophecy and inspired exegesis at home in several streams of Palestinian Judaism, but Philo and Josephus show that this view was shared by Hellenistic Jews as well.[7] And Fascher has collected considerable evidence that demonstrates that prophets in the pagan world frequently delivered their oracles by means of the interpretation of written documents. Plutarch, for example, describes an oracle-giver who reads from a manuscript but receives his inspired interpretations of this manuscript directly from the deity, so that he is in this sense a προφήτης, a proclaimer of new revelations.[8]

All of this evidence is introduced not because it proves anything about the character of early Christian prophecy, for it does not; this must be done on the basis of the Christian sources themselves. But since some contemporary readers still tend to think of inspired prophets as speaking on the basis of spontaneous emotional outpourings — a *typus* quite common in the Hellenistic world, as we have seen — it is helpful to know that in the Hellenistic world, and especially in that Judaism from which early Christian prophecy sprang, 'prophet' and 'interpreter of the Scripture' were very congenial concepts.

When we turn to the early Christian sources and inquire concerning the nature of Scripture interpretation present in them, we are touching an area that is of fundamental importance in the development of New Testament theology. C. H. Dodd has shown that, without denying that New Testament theology has a substantial Hellenistic element, its substructure is built upon the Old Testament and the conviction that what is written there is now being fulfilled in the ministry of Jesus and the life of the church.[9] His thesis is that whoever explained the Scriptures to the early church was the real architect of New Testament theology. The church's understanding of itself as the true and ultimate people of God, its christological understanding of the essentially non-messianic life of Jesus (measured by traditional messianic expectations) and its understanding of Jesus' death as a redemptive act that led to his glory and exaltation were all derived from its new understanding of the Scripture — assuming, of course, that something happened to evoke this reinterpretation. The event was interpreted by Scripture, just as the Scripture was interpreted by event. Since the basic creative interpretation had already been done by the time of Paul, who presupposes it as familiar, Dodd correctly argues that we must look in the period prior to Paul. And though Dodd acknowledges that there may have been some anonymous creative thinkers between Jesus and Paul, he prefers to accept the witness of the New Testament itself (Luke 24) that 'it was Jesus Christ Himself who first directed the minds of His followers to certain parts of the Scriptures as those in which they might find illumination upon the meaning of His mission and destiny'.[10]

It may be granted to Dodd that Jesus himself may have given the original impetus toward a fresh understanding of the Old Testament in view of contemporary events. All the evidence that indicates that Jesus saw the End as rapidly approaching would carry with it as its corollary that he saw the promises of the Scriptures as being in the process of fulfillment. Apocalyptic is by nature an interpreter of prophecy. But to whatever extent this interpretative process was begun by Jesus, it was greatly extended and elaborated in the earliest church, as is seen from the fact that most of the *testimonia* reflect a post-Easter perspective. When we ask who in the earliest Christian community might have been responsible for this inspired, authoritative interpretation of the Scriptures as the vehicle for expressing the ultimacy of the events surrounding Jesus (Jesus as the eschatological savior-figure; the church as the eschatological community), one group comes readily to mind, in view of our previous discussions: early Christian prophets. Käsemann and others have declared that church prophets did indeed serve as the inspired–intuitive interpreters of the Scripture for the earliest church, and are thus key figures in the formation of New Testament theology.[11] I shall give evidence for the correctness of this assertion below. If this assertion can be substantiated, we have an important insight into the problem of how the proclaimer became the proclaimed, a bridge from the teaching of Jesus to the theology of the early church; for these Christian prophets would both take up the traditional message of Jesus, re-presenting it as the word of the exalted Lord, and affirm the redemptive eschatological significance of the person of Jesus himself, uniting both in a proclamation given in Jesus' own name. Jesus the self-proclaimed (by post-Easter Christian prophets who interpret the Jesus-event via Scripture) emerges as a middle term between Jesus the proclaimer (of the Kingdom of God during his pre-Easter ministry) and Jesus the proclaimed (in the post-Easter *kerygma* of the church). We have struck on a significant point. We must now inquire what evidence there is in our sources for relating Christian prophets to the interpretation of Scripture.

I turn first to Revelation. The twenty-fifth edition of the Nestle–Aland Greek text prints in bold type every direct quotation and clear allusion to the Old Testament texts. In Revelation, 499 such usages of Old Testament materials are found, an average of 11.3 per page. The Westcott–Hort text, which uses a similar procedure, has approximately the same number of allusions indicated. E. C. Selwyn, who is slightly more generous in listing texts in which the Old Testament allusion is not clear, finds a total of 518 instances![12] By any reckoning, it is clear that the Apocalypse is saturated with words and phrases from the Old Testament. It is not our purpose here to go into the details of how the Seer interprets the Old Testament; the sheer amount of Old Testament material shows that here Christian prophecy functions primarily by interpretation of the Scriptures. Heinrich Kraft hardly overstates the matter when he asserts that for every statement in the Apocalypse the Seer has a Scripture source, which he reinterprets and sets forth afresh in the light of the Christ-event.[13] The manner in which John does this is important and may be illustrated by the way in which Old Testament allusions and quotations are handled in the third edition of *The Greek New Testament* of the United Bible Societies. The editorial policy of this edition is to call to the reader's attention, by printing in bold type, 'only those passages which are clearly quotations from the Old Testament, ... eliminating references to words and phrases which are only allusions or literary echoes'.[14] The result is that in all the twenty-two chapters of Revelation, not a single Old Testament reference is indicated, either by bold type or in the 'Index of Quotations'. This is correct procedure in terms of the edition's editorial policy, however misleading it may be regarding John's use of the Old Testament, for in fact the prophet—interpreter never once formally cites an Old Testament passage. To have done so would have bifurcated the inner unity between his own prophetic word and the prophetic word of his texts. The prophet no longer experienced the inspired texts as a *past* voice of the Lord that was to be 'applied' to the *present* experience of the congregation. The texts became the vehicle for communicating the present word of the risen Lord. They are thus not quoted, but re-presented in new forms and combinations so that neither the past/present distinction nor the subject/object distinction is maintained.

The way the Scriptures are used in Revelation indicates a community intensively occupied with Scripture, which suggests in turn that there were definite persons in the community charged with its interpretation. John was one such person, and apparently in a role of leadership, but the extent to which familiarity with Scripture and the prophetic mode of handling it is presupposed makes it unlikely that he was the only such interpreter in the community. We may postulate a group of prophetic interpreters to whom the community looks for guidance in interpreting the Scripture.[15]

It is not so clear from Paul that the prophets of the Corinthian congregation were involved in interpreting Scripture, since Paul gives us only hints of the *content* of Corinthian prophecy. It has been argued by Cothonet that the παράκλησις of I Cor. 14: 3 indicates charismatic exegesis of Scripture, and by Rousseau that the λόγος σοφίας and λόγος γνώσεως of 12: 8 intend the same,[16] but these arguments generate little credence. Probably prophecy at Corinth was too enthusiastic to be related closely to exegesis of the Scriptures. It is when we turn to Paul himself as a prophet that the connection between prophecy and exegesis is first posed by the Pauline materials. As a prophet, Paul functioned as an interpreter of the Scriptures to the church for the last times. He interprets the Old Testament in the light of the contemporary eschatological events, and these events in the light of the Old Testament, as for example his treatment of Adam in Rom. 5 and I Cor. 15, his treatment of Abraham in Gal. 3–4, his treatment of the exodus events in I Cor. 10, and the plethora of Old Testament interpretation in his *heilsgeschichtlich* exposition of Rom. 9–11 make clear.[17] The Old Testament sayings and narratives were not written for their own sake but for the παράκλησις of Christian believers (Rom. 15: 4), a παράκλησις of which Christian prophets are also the agent (I Cor. 14: 3). He reinterprets the Old Testament as τύποι, not, however, as τύποι of soul-events as does Philo, but as foreshadowing the Last Times, which he believes now to have dawned. The interpretation of Scripture in the eschatological times is not left to human logic and inference but is accomplished by the eschatological gift of the Spirit. There is no doubt that Paul considered his own interpretations to have been given him by the Spirit. It is the Lord who is the Spirit who gives to Paul that freedom to see the Christian events already revealed in the Old Testament, which are veiled to the Jews precisely because they do not have this κύριος/πνεῦμα (I Cor. 2: 6–16; II Cor. 3: 15–17). That Paul's own oracles sometimes came to him, and were formulated in conjunction, with his exegesis of Scripture is to be seen from the quotations related to them in Rom. 11: 25–7 and I Cor. 15: 51–5. Further, the use of ἐρευνάω of the Spirit who gives revelations (I Cor. 2: 10) in this prophetic passage corresponds to the דָּרַשׁ of rabbinic exegesis (cf. John 5: 39) and points to the connection here posited between Christian prophecy and the interpretation of Scripture.

E. Earle Ellis has pointed out an interesting phenomenon that bears positively on this point. Four Old Testament quotations in Paul contain the phrase λέγει κύριος imbedded within the quotation itself; in three of these the quotation has another introductory formula and λέγει κύριος is an addition within the Old Testament text.[18] In every case the citations vary both from the MT and the LXX, and that not only in additions and omissions but in substantive changes to the text as well. Such changes could be accounted for by the use of a text that agrees with neither the MT nor the LXX, but more likely reflect the kind of free peshering of the text done by the pneumatic community at Qumran and by the prophet-author of Revelation. Ellis points out that λέγει κύριος itself is a badge of prophetic pronouncement in the Old Testament, and 'its presence in the New Testament probably has an equivalent significance and may give a clue to understanding the role which the New Testament exegete – or better, the New Testament prophet — considered himself to fill'.[19] The fact that Paul added his own introductory formula to a quotation that already contained a λέγει κύριος formula not a part of the Old Testament text indicates that some of Paul's quotations are used by the apostle in a form already known and used in the early church, i.e. from a collection of *testimonia* bearing the interpretative and formal characteristics of New Testament prophets. In these three quotations we have some of the literary remains of just those early Christian prophets whose profile we are attempting to reconstruct. Each of the passages readily fits into the category of Christian prophecy: Rom. 12: 19 speaks of that eschatological recompense which, as will be argued below, was characteristic of the Christian prophets' message; I Cor. 14: 21 occurs in the midst of a discussion of Christian prophecy and bears the prophetic marks of prediction and lamentation; II Cor. 6: 16—18 is a compilation of texts from the Old Testament that would be very suitable for the proclamation of the way of life in the eschatological community by a Christian prophet.

It would seem, then, that, formally speaking, there were two ways of appropriating the Scriptures as the word of the risen Lord. Revelation exemplifies the first, by which Old Testament material is incorporated in the address of the risen Jesus to the church, without explicit quotation formulae. Paul illustrates the second, in which Old Testament material is taken up, reinterpreted and to some extent re-formed, then re-presented as the word of the Lord (Jesus) by incorporating within the quotation a λέγει κύριος formula. This latter method, as argued by Ellis, would in itself prove little, but it may be taken as a convincing corroboratory bit of evidence for the prophetic aspect of Paul's own ministry, his contact with, and reflection of, Christian prophets who were before and beside him, and the relation of Christian prophecy to interpretation of Scripture here argued on other grounds.

Luke's descriptions of those he specifically designates as prophets give no indications that prophets function as interpreters of Scripture, unless Agabus' prediction of famine may be taken as originally an eschatological oracle derived from a reinterpretation of Old Testament prophecies. The incidental references to inspired speech in the Gospel and Acts paint quite another picture. The prophetic figures of Luke 1—2 deliver oracles that, like the Apocalypse, contain many Old Testament allusions, indicating that they were derived from charismatic interpretation of Scripture, the Magnificat and Benedictus being almost entirely composed of Old Testament phrases. The προφητεία of Acts 2 is replete with Old Testament interpretation of an eschatological perspective, applying the promises of the End of the ages to the events of Jesus' life, death and resurrection.

The issue in Acts 15 is resolved prophetically by an interpretation of the Old Testament that declares its fulfillment in contemporary events. M. Dumais' unpublished two-volume thesis argues that Acts 13: 16–41 has as its basis a Christian prophet's charismatic interpretation of Scripture.[20] Luke 24: 13–32 portrays the whole process by which the risen Lord gave to the church its new understanding of the Scriptures in one scene filled with motifs from Christian prophecy: Jesus is called a prophet (24: 19); the travellers are reproved for not believing the prophets (24: 25), *all* of whom are emphasized (24: 27); the scene is a cultic one in which there is table fellowship, blessing, breaking and distribution of bread (24: 30); the 'burning' of their hearts as he opened to them the Scriptures perhaps reflects the response to fervent charismatic preaching. Luke knew that the church did not receive its new understanding of the Scriptures in one day, just as he knew that the church did not perceive the risen Lord sending it on a mission to all nations on the first Easter Sunday (24: 47; cf. Acts 1–15). Each of these was the result of a gradual process of prophetic insight in the early church, as depicted in Acts. Yet Luke also knew that the church's new insight into the Scriptures did not come about by a deductive process, nor by the application of an objective method to the text, but was the direct gift of the risen Lord. Christian prophets who speak in the name of the risen Jesus as they interpret the Scriptures to the church are portrayed in Luke 24: 13–35.[21]

The Fourth Gospel quotes the Old Testament explicitly relatively few times, but, like the Apocalypse, prefers to weave Old Testament allusions into the structure of its presentation without formal quotation.[22] Interpretation of Scripture is a charismatic function in the community of the Fourth Gospel, for the Paraclete–prophet has the interpretation of Scripture as one of his functions. The post-resurrection gift of the Spirit, the remembrance of Jesus' words and the understanding of Scripture are all related in 2: 22 and 12: 16 (cf. 2: 17; 7: 39; 14: 26; 20: 9). The function of Scripture is to bear witness to Jesus (1: 45; 5: 39), which is identical to the function of the Paraclete (15: 26). The predictive function of the Paraclete is also to be related to Scripture exegesis (16: 13), since prediction among early Christian prophets was generally eschatological, in conjunction with their understanding of Scripture, rather than historical prediction of mundane events, as Revelation and Paul make clear.

In Hermas revelation takes place through a study of the Scriptures: ἀπεκαλύφθη μοι ἡ γνῶσις τῆς γραφῆς (Vis. II.2.1). The matter is less clear in the Didache, but here too the prophet's teaching function probably includes the exposition of Scripture in view of the way the author–editor himself understands διδαχή to combine sayings of Jesus, Old Testament commandments and church teaching. As in I Clem. 22, the Old Testament may be quoted in the Didache as the word of the Lord (Jesus).[23]

The evidence of our sources, seen against the Jewish background from which early Christian prophecy developed, gives us ample reason for believing that the earliest Christian prophets frequently spoke the word of the risen Lord as a result of their inspired interpretation of the Scripture. The eschatological mood of earliest Christianity both required and produced more than a scholastic exposition of the sacred text. The Spirit had been poured out to reveal that the Old Testament promises were now in the process of realization. The Spirit, which was the common possession of all members of the community, made the community open to the new interpretations, and the Spirit's gift of prophetic insight was focused in relatively few inspired spokesmen, i.e. prophets, in whose hands Scripture became a living book, speaking directly of and to the present. The prophets handled the text with a new freedom, even reshaping it to fit more clearly the fulfillment that they saw happening before them, just as did the Qumran interpreters. Speaking from the Old Testament text in a way that was no longer bound to its words means that reflection on the Scriptures may have influenced the formation of New Testament texts in such a way that this influence is no longer to be documented simply by explicit quotation or direct allusion to an Old Testament text.[24] No claim is made that prophetic speech was universally related to Scripture, even in that free sense described here, but the evidence indicates that this was indeed frequently the case, and may be used as one identifying mark in the quest for prophetic oracles now imbedded in the synoptic tradition as sayings of Jesus.

The prophet as interpreter of events

'The Old Testament is a history book.' With this terse manifesto Gerhard von Rad affirms that even the prophets of the Old Testament should not be regarded as purveyors of inspired information from heaven, but inter-preters of the meaning of the historical events in which they and their hearers found themselves.[25] The prophet in Israel did not begin with a personal experience of revelation, as though prophecy were an episode in the life of an individual, but with an event that shaped the life of both prophet and congregation and bound them together. Amos declared Yahweh's judgment on the historical acts of nations, including his own, and this on the basis not of an ahistorical, individualistic, mystical experience but of the claim of divinely-given insight into the meaning of contemporary history: the illusory prosperity occasioned by the advance of Assyria, which would soon bring destruction to Israel. Isaiah has a similar hermeneutical function in relation to the same historical crisis for Judah, Jeremiah to the advance of Nebuchadnezzar, II Isaiah to the rise of Cyrus with its accompanying events, Joel to the locust plague, Haggai to the drought, Daniel to the persecution by Antiochus IV. And Moses is considered the prophet *par excellence* (Deut. 18: 15–18; Hos. 12: 13) not because he goes into trances and delivers revelations from the heavenly world but because he reveals that the event at the Reed Sea was not simply good fortune but the saving act of God. The prophets of the Old Testament are typically interpreters of the historical deeds of Yahweh, who does nothing without revealing his סוֹד to עֲבָדָיו הַנְּבִיאִים (Amos 3: 7). The prophet is that figure in the community who is enabled, by the Spirit, to recognize the otherwise mute, surd-like events of history as acts of God, to interpret their meaning and to proclaim them to the community. He is hermeneut not only of the tradition (and/or Scripture), but of the event, in which God also speaks, but which is mute or un-intelligible until interpreted and given voice by the prophet. The revelatory *Gestalt* typical of the Old Testament consists of three interdependent elements: event, interpretation by a prophetic figure and reception by the community. The revelatory event is not self-contained within the prophet, but he is the essential mediator if the event is to be revelatory to the community. In itself, the event is opaque, or, at the most, ambiguous; the event needs the prophet before God's word is heard in it. But neither is the word of the prophet a purely vertical word from heaven directed at the point of man's life; the prophetic word always operates by engagement with the horizontal line of that history which forms the essential context, and often the content, of the prophet's message.

The prophet's insight into the meaning of events as God's act is not a rationalistic process, but an intuitive, pneumatic, 'ecstatic' one.[26] There is a non-deductive gap between history and *Heilsgeschichte*, between event as such and revelation. Although the revelation is there in the event, it remains hidden until seen and proclaimed by the prophet. This prophetic 'seeing' is not a matter of the prophet being a more astute observer of the historical scene than his contemporaries, but a charismatic illumination of the event as the revelation of God, a revelatory insight quite beyond the power of, and sometimes contrary to the will of, the prophet. The prophet's interpretation of the event becomes revelation when it is heard and acknowledged as such within the community. This can happen only as a confession of faith on the part of the community, which acknowledges both event and interpretation interdependently as the Word of God. Such is the Old Testament understanding of prophecy. Its connection of prophecy to history represents a prophetic type *sui generis* in the ancient world. There were many shamans, prophets, soothsayers and diviners in the ancient Near East, as later in the Hellenistic world, but only in Israel does prophecy represent the claim that the deity has addressed the prophet for the purpose of conveying a message to others, a message that interprets history in its totality as in the control of the deity who speaks, which revelatory word draws history and previous revelatory moments into a unity.[27]

This style of prophecy, which functioned by interpreting current events as part of the eschatological *Heilsplan* of God, extended into first-century Judaism. Not only is this evidenced at Qumran (e.g. the Habbakuk Commentary), but the prophets described by Josephus were also of this sort. Though he attempts to describe the outbreak of prophecy just prior to the outbreak of the war in C.E. 66 as simply the enthusiasm of revolutionary fanatics, his descriptions reveal that such men as Jesus ben Ananias, the Egyptian prophet, and the prophet who gathered 6000 men in the temple court during the last battle for Jerusalem were apocalyptic prophets who saw in the war's events the beginning of the final act of the drama of salvation (*Wars* II.261–2; VI.285–300). If early Christian prophets were also more in the succession of Old Testament prophets than continuous with Hellenistic prophets, then the revelatory *Gestalt* of event/prophet/community would obtain in the early church as in Israel. We have seen that early Christian prophets were not individualists but operated in the context of a community that tested and acknowledged their revelations. We must now examine the evidence that might indicate that their *modus operandi* involved interpretation of events.

The Apocalypse was born of a historical crisis in the life of the church, a threat of imperial persecution that had already claimed one victim, Antipas of Pergamum, a 'test case' who had already been executed (2: 13). In such a situation, the absurd meaninglessness of the events that seemed imminent was more of a threat to the faith than the events themselves. With prophetic insight, John sees that the threatening persecution, the historical reality in which he and his church must live out their lives, is not 'a tale told by an idiot, full of sound and fury, signifying nothing', but the last act in the drama of God's redemptive history. It is to 'his servants the prophets' that the 'divine mystery' ($\mu\nu\sigma\tau\dot{\eta}\rho\iota o\nu$ $\tau o\hat{\nu}$ $\theta\varepsilon o\hat{\nu}$) has been revealed (10: 7), which means that the prophets are those who, by the Spirit, recognize and proclaim the contemporary events to be integral to God's saving act. John is less inclined to cosmological speculation and more closely related to history than the typical Jewish apocalypse, although he expresses his prophetic insight in traditional apocalyptic imagery. John has a prophetic word to say because of his interpretation of the historical event that confronts him, and he is able to do this not only from the resources of Scripture and apocalyptic tradition, in which he is immersed, but fundamentally because of his and his predecessor-prophets' interpretation of *the* historical event of Jesus Christ. The prophet's call for the churches of Asia to 'conquer', i.e. witness faithfully even to the point of martyrdom, but without violent resistance to the imperial power (2: 7, 11 etc.; 2: 10), is based on the christological insight that in the face of the same imperial power Jesus 'conquered', i.e. surrendered his life (1: 17–18; 3: 21; 5: 5–6 etc.). Not only so, the prophet continues to reinterpret the meaning of the event of Jesus of Nazareth to his contemporaries, even in new categories. The book as a whole is a fresh ἀποκάλυψις Ἰησοῦ Χριστοῦ not only in the sense that Jesus is the speaking subject in Revelation, but also in the objective genitive sense. This is particularly so in the christological affirmations that begin each of the seven letters, in which the risen Lord identifies himself by means of christological affirmations that are particularly relevant to the crisis of the Asian churches as they faced impending persecution. For example, Jesus calls himself ὁ μαρτὺς ὁ πιστὸς καὶ ἀληθινός (3: 14), a title that had hitherto never been used of Jesus but was particularly meaningful in the situation of a 'confessing church'. Here is illustrated the creative role of Christian prophets in the formation of christology, a subject amplified in the Appendix, pp. 239–50. This is apparently the significance of the author's own key statement concerning the prophetic role in 19: 10: ἡ μαρτυρία Ἰησοῦ ἐστιν τὸ πνεῦμα τῆς προφητείας. This genitive is properly regarded by Charles and others as an objective genitive,[28] as in the first part of the verse, and would mean that in John's view the very essence of Christian prophecy is testimony to Jesus. But the view that this is a subjective genitive also fits very well both the context and John's other instances of this phrase in 1: 2, 9 and 12: 17, as argued by Caird and others.[29] The genitive construction here seems to have both subjective and objective aspects and may have been chosen to express the unique aspect of Christian prophecy in which the risen Christ is both subject and object, both proclaimer and proclaimed. The event of Jesus of Nazareth thus becomes the touchstone of authentic prophecy, as in I Cor. 12: 3; I John 4: 1–3 and Rom. 12: 6, so that prophecy is not freed by the Spirit to declare just any content but is bound to the event of Jesus of Nazareth, which it *interprets* but does not simply *repeat*. Christian prophets go beyond what the historical Jesus himself actually said and did, but it is testimony to *this* event that makes them Christian prophets. 'Fundamentally the exalted earthly Lord cannot make himself present in the word that denies his history.'[30]

So also in the Fourth Gospel: the risen Christ is himself the interpreter of the event of Jesus' life and death as he speaks through the Paraclete. When the Johannine Jesus promises with reference to the Paraclete: ἐκεῖνος μαρτυρήσει περὶ ἐμοῦ (15: 26), this is analogous to the μαρτυρία Ἰησοῦ affirmed to be the essence of prophecy in Rev. 19: 10: to declare the saving significance of Jesus, to reveal the act of God in him. Despite all the retrojection of the exalted Christ's glory and the church's faith into the pre-resurrection ministry of Jesus in the Johannine account, there are unmistakable signs that the prophet—evangelist knows that during Jesus' lifetime even his close disciples did not recognize the significance of his person and work (1: 10–11; 2: 17, 22; 7: 5, 39; 12: 16; 13: 7; 14: 20, 29; 16: 12, 20–6; and the Paraclete passages 14: 16–17, 26; 15: 26; 16: 7–11, 13–14). In the author's view, it was after the resurrection, in conjunction with a fresh understanding of Scripture given by the Spirit, that Jesus was recognized and declared to be the Christ. It should be noted that the only occurrence of προφητεύω in the Fourth Gospel (11: 51) reveals the form that prophecy takes for John, namely the divinely-given interpretation of the meaning of the life and death of Jesus, and not merely prediction.

When we turn to the data preserved in Paul's letters, we find nothing to indicate that the prophecy of the Corinthian enthusiasts was related to historical events, except as they were influenced by Paul's own views of prophecy. Rather, prophecy at Corinth seems to have been a spontaneous occurrence in worship, not particularly related to events of the past, present or future. But when Paul encounters the charismatic speech of the Corinthians, his efforts to mold it into forms that he considers to be authentic prophecy indicate that Paul stands in that traditional stream of Christian prophecy which related prophecy to the interpretation of events. Beginning with the Corinthians where they were, enthralled with the mysterious goings-on that were occurring in their worship, the thrust of Paul's discussion is that prophecy, as the most valuable χάρισμα, belongs to that person who can translate the numinous events happening in their midst into meaningful, edifying language (I Cor. 14: 1–5, 26–9). The prophet has insight into the meaning of the act as God's act and declares this meaning to the community in intelligible language. For Paul, interpretation is thus seen to be of the essence of Christian prophecy. It has, in fact, not been sufficiently noticed that Paul seems simply to equate the gifts of interpretation and prophecy. Thus 14: 5: μείζων δὲ ὁ προφητεύων ἢ ὁ λαλῶν γλώσσαις, ἐκτὸς εἰ μὴ διερμηνεύῃ, ἵνα ἡ ἐκκλησία οἰκοδομὴν λάβῃ. The RSV translates the underlined phrase 'unless someone interpret'. But there is no τις (not even in the variant readings, all of which indicate that it is the tongue-speaker himself who interprets), and 14: 13 clearly indicates that it is the speaker-in-tongues himself whom Paul desires to be

the interpreter. The KJV, ASV, NEB, Moffatt, Goodspeed, J. B. Phillips
and Jerusalem Bible all translate the Greek better by identifying the
speaker-in-tongues himself as the one who interprets. Verse 5 indicates
that if the one speaking in tongues *interprets* his speech, he is of equal
value to the congregation as the prophet. It should be noted that Paul
designates the content of the tongue-speech as μυστήρια (14: 2). Thus the
διερμηνεύειν of μυστήρια is considered by Paul to be the same as
προφητεία. Although Paul's understanding of the χαρίσματα is not so
mechanical that it can be represented mathematically (the gifts have overlapping functions and are not always to be sharply defined from each
other), something of Paul's thought on this point is captured by the
following equations:

$$\pi\nu\epsilon\hat{\upsilon}\mu\alpha \longrightarrow \gamma\lambda\hat{\omega}\sigma\sigma\alpha = \mu\upsilon\sigma\tau\acute{\eta}\rho\iota\alpha$$
$$\mu\upsilon\sigma\tau\acute{\eta}\rho\iota\alpha + \delta\iota\epsilon\rho\mu\eta\nu\epsilon\acute{\upsilon}\epsilon\iota\nu = o\grave{\iota}\kappa o\delta o\mu\acute{\eta}$$

but:

$$\pi\nu\epsilon\hat{\upsilon}\mu\alpha \longrightarrow \pi\rho o\phi\eta\tau\epsilon\acute{\upsilon}\epsilon\iota\nu = o\grave{\iota}\kappa o\delta o\mu\acute{\eta}$$

therefore:

$$\pi\rho o\phi\eta\tau\epsilon\acute{\upsilon}\epsilon\iota\nu = \mu\upsilon\sigma\tau\acute{\eta}\rho\iota\alpha + \delta\iota\epsilon\rho\mu\eta\nu\epsilon\acute{\upsilon}\epsilon\iota\nu = \gamma\lambda\hat{\omega}\sigma\sigma\alpha + \delta\iota\epsilon\rho\mu\eta\nu\epsilon\acute{\upsilon}\epsilon\iota\nu.$$

Prophecy is a two-stage process, involving the reception of the revelation
(μυστήριον) and the translation of it into edifying speech. Tongues are
inferior to prophecy precisely because the μυστήρια are received and then
expressed without being 'translated' or interpreted. The tongue-speaker
gives vocalization, but not conceptualization, to the μυστήρια he has
received, in which his πνεῦμα, but not his νοῦς, is active (14: 14–19). In
responding to the Corinthians, Paul seems to have been working from a
prior understanding of the nature of prophecy derived from his Jewish
heritage via early Palestinian Christianity.

In the prophetic oracles contained in Paul's letters, some of which may
be revelations to Paul himself, the element of revelatory interpretation of
the μυστήριον is also prominent. This μυστήριον is the eschatological plan
of God, which is already being worked out in contemporary events: an
understanding that is part of the prophetic stream of tradition emanating
from the Old Testament and especially from Daniel, where the prophets
are those who understand the רָז , the μυστήριον, of the saving plan of
God, which is already in operation. Thus the oracle of Rom. 11: 25–7 is
called a μυστήριον, which refers not to an esoteric secret but to the
eschatological significance revealed to the prophet of a historical event in
the redemptive plan of God. Paul here speaks as a pneumatic who has

special prophetic insight into God's historical saving process.[31] The connection with a historical event, the general rejection of the gospel by Israel, is to be noted here. The event does not mean what it seems to mean on the surface; its true eschatological meaning is perceived only by the prophet. Here it is seen that prophecy does not speak from a vacuum but is bound to history; it interprets events, revealing their *heilsgeschichtlich* significance. In I Cor. 15: 51–2, the event that the revealed μυστήριον interprets is the resurrection of Jesus. In I Cor. 2: 6–16, the prophetic Spirit gives the interpretation of the event of Jesus' crucifixion, thus making it a revelation. The bare event is ambiguous; it is the Spirit that reveals that it is from God and that leads to proclamation in words given by the Spirit (2: 12). This is a portrayal of the prophetic function.

Paul's view is continued in Ephesians, where the author regards the inclusion of the Gentiles in the church as the μυστήριον revealed ἐν πνεύματι to apostles and prophets. This event, which was understood to be a part of the eschatological *Heilsplan Gottes* (Is. 2: 2–4; 19: 24–5) is identified with the present event in church history. This identification of contemporary historical events with the eschatological redemptive events is remembered to be the work of the first-generation men of prophetic insight, the apostles and prophets (2: 20; 3: 5). Here, as in Acts 10 and 15, which also have prophetic overtones, an accurate memory of the earlier function of Christian prophets is preserved. So also in Acts 2, the interpretation of Scripture is interwoven with the interpretation of the life, death and resurrection of Jesus as God's decisive saving act, and it is emphasized that this is prophecy (2: 17, with the addition of an extra καί προφητεύσουσιν to the Old Testament text in 2: 18). The prophetic figures of Luke 1–2 recognize and proclaim the salvific character of events that to the natural eye are absolutely ordinary (1: 43, 68–9, 77; 2: 29–32, 38). This does not mean that everyone who writes theologically-understood history, such as Luke himself does in Acts, is thereby a prophet. Luke's is a secondary theological interpretation of a history that early Christian prophets had already taught the church to see as theologically significant. The initial insight must be charismatic, which can then be theologized by others. Luke here stands in the same relation to the events he records as do Ephesians and the Pastorals to Paul.

The prophets of the early church, like their Old Testament counterparts, do not spin their messages out of the air, nor from their 'experiences', but begin with a given: concrete events that have happened and are happening. The content of the prophets' messages was not a *creatio ex nihilo*, but a fusion of interpretation of event and interpretation of Scripture. These characteristics can be used, in conjunction with others, in identifying Christian prophetic speech in the tradition of the sayings of Jesus.

The prophet as interpreter of the sayings of Jesus

We have seen that the prophet stands within the stream of tradition handed on by the church, that this tradition included the sayings of Jesus and that prophets functioned in conjunction with this tradition, both influencing it and being influenced by it. We have seen that our sources contain evidence that words of Jesus were taken up by Christian prophets and re-presented as sayings of the risen Jesus. This would suggest that Christian prophets also functioned as interpreters of the sayings of Jesus within the church, elaborating and modifying traditional sayings to express the word of the risen Lord more clearly to the present situation. A number of students have come to this general conclusion, though it is rarely supported in particular cases with evidence.[32] There were others besides prophets in the community who elaborated the traditional sayings of Jesus. The thirteen types of alterations of the parables during the period of oral transmission that Jeremias had documented,[33] for example, and the redactional activity of the evangelists, show that there was a variety of interpretative ways of making the tradition more relevant to the present, without any claim to be speaking prophetically for the risen Lord. In Part Two of this study we will examine the evidence that indicates that Christian prophets did in fact sometimes take up a traditional saying of Jesus, modify and elaborate it in characteristic ways (prophetic 'peshering') and re-present it as a word of the risen Lord. In such sayings, there will be no sharp line between pre-Easter words of Jesus and words of the risen Lord through the prophet. We must not come to the gospel sayings of Jesus with the *a priori* view that the sayings of Christian prophets therein, if there be such, will be totally new creations; for the prophet may have served as hermeneut not only of the Scriptures and the times, but of the sayings of Jesus as well.

8 MATERIAL CHARACTERISTICS OF EARLY CHRISTIAN PROPHETIC SPEECH

(1) Eschatological parenesis

Eschatological-apocalyptic content

It was widely accepted in first-century Judaism that the Spirit (= the Spirit of Prophecy) was essentially the eschatological gift, so that when prophets reappeared, this itself would be a sign of the dawning End. Any talk of prophecy was by definition eschatological. This view was the common denominator of both those circles that affirmed the presence of the prophetic Spirit (e.g. Qumran) and those that denied it (many streams of rabbinic tradition). Thus Jewish prophecy of this period has a consistently eschatological content. This is seen, for example, in the declarations of the Teacher of Righteousness, who interprets the Scriptures as directly describing the things happening to the (present) last generation, הַבָּאוֹת עַל הַדּוֹר הָאַחֲרוֹן (IQpHab 7.1−2; cf. 2.7). The contemporary understanding of prophecy is also seen in the apocalyptic promises of those prophets, described by Josephus, who proclaimed the deliverance of God in the very days that the Romans were destroying the city and the temple. He considers them 'suborned by the tyrants to delude the people, by bidding them await help from God, in order that desertions might be checked' (*Wars*, VI.285−6). It is far more likely that these were apocalyptic prophets who saw in the Roman devastation the death-throes of the old age and the sure prelude to the new (cf. II.258−9, 261−2; VI.312). The portents he enumerates were taken as signs of *hope* by the populace: a star like a sword stood over the city; a comet appeared for a full year; a cow brought to sacrifice gave birth to a lamb in the temple court (*Wars*, VI.30). Josephus sees these as signs of political, this-worldly doom. But the populace, at the instigation of the prophets, understood these as apocalyptic signs, as the throes of nature immediately preceding the advent of the victorious End Time, as in IV Ez. 5: 4−9.[1]

Within this milieu, where prophecy was by definition eschatological, early Christianity arose. It was in conjunction with the conviction of the early church that the Last Times had dawned that prophets emerged within it. One of the primary presuppositions for the Apocalypse is that the author and his hearer/reader are living in the Last Days of history, that the eschatological events described will take place soon (1: 1, 3; 2: 16, 25; 3: 11, 20; 6: 11; 10: 6–7; 11: 2; 12: 6, 12; 17: 10; 22: 6, 7, 10, 12, 20). This fundamental orientation of the prophet should not be suppressed in the interests of supposedly making the book more relevant for later readers. The guilt of all preceding generations is summed up in the last generation (13: 1–2; 18: 24). Within this *massa perdita*, where even the traditional people of God have deserted him, the church exists as the holy remnant of the End Time which alone can hear the prophetic word, in accordance with traditional prophetic understanding.[2]

The prophetic oracles included in Paul's letters are uniformly of an eschatological nature (I Thess. 4: 15–17; I Cor. 15: 51–2; Rom. 11: 25–7). Käsemann's insight regarding Paul's affirmations in I Corinthians, originally somewhat startling, has become almost commonplace: Paul was an advocate of the old apocalyptic Palestinian tradition, in opposition to the excessive 'realized eschatology' of the Corinthian enthusiasts.[3] In this respect, Paul becomes almost a direct witness to the eschatological nature of early Palestinian Christian prophecy. The eschatological orientation of prophecy is fundamental to Paul, not a quirk of his response to a local situation at Corinth. Also at Thessalonica, exaggerated eschatological enthusiasm, based on Paul's original prophetic preaching, had led to excesses among local prophets, resulting in a disdaining of all prophecy, which Paul found it necessary to correct (I Thess. 4: 15–17; 5: 19–20).[4]

The older eschatology shines through Luke's consistently non-eschatological descriptions of Christian prophets. Agabus was probably more eschatological than Luke's depiction reveals: σημαίνω indicates not that straightforward, unambiguous speech such as Luke represents it to be (by regarding the predicted famine to be a mundane historical disaster), but that mysterious, prophetic speech such as is used by the Pythia at Delphi,[5] and is used specifically in Rev. 1: 1 to refer to eschatological events. Likewise, the words μέλλω, λίμος μεγάλη and ὅλη οἰκουμένη represent traditional apocalyptic expressions and betray the original apocalyptic nature of Agabus' oracle.[6] All the oracles of the prophetic figures of Luke 1–2 strike the eschatological note. In 1: 76–9 particularly, the προφήτης is the forerunner of the eschatological epiphany of God.

With the exception of the Pastorals and the Didache, which give only minimal indications of their understanding of the content of Christian prophecy, all our remaining sources testify to the eschatological nature of Christian prophecy. The παράκλητος of the Fourth Gospel declares eschatological data: κρίσις, δόξα, τὰ ἐρχόμενα. Since the Fourth Evangelist himself has only a modest interest in futuristic eschatology, this characterization of the proclamation of the Paraclete underlines the fact that for the Fourth Evangelist too, prophecy and eschatology were co-ordinates. Ephesians, like Acts, indicates in an indirect and unconscious way that Christian prophets declared the eschatological time to be breaking in, when they point out that it was by prophets that the inclusion of the Gentiles (a part of the eschatological drama) was revealed to be the will of God.[7] Hermas announces the last chance to repent in relation to the impending second coming of the Lord (Vis. II.2.5; III.8.9). On the basis of the above evidence, we may anticipate that oracles of early Christian prophets in the synoptic tradition, if there are such, will manifest an eschatological orientation and frequently contain specific items of eschatological content.

This general eschatological-apocalyptic character of early Christian prophecy is itself characterized by particular features that may help us to identify the sayings of Christian prophets in the synoptic tradition.

'οἰκοδομὴ καὶ παράκλησις καὶ παραμυθία' (I Cor. 14: 3)

The eschatology of the early Christian prophets was not formulated for its own sake but as the foundation for, and in inseparable union with, parenesis. The church was not edified by sharing speculative apocalyptic information about the future but by the call to a certain way of life that was the outcome of the eschatological vision of the prophets. In this, early Christian prophecy was more akin to Old Testament prophecy than to late-Jewish apocalyptic. This contrast should not be drawn too sharply, however, for the Jewish apocalyptic tradition that formed part of the context for the emergence of early Christian prophecy was itself more concerned with ethical exhortation than is sometimes taken to be the case[8] Our sources indicate that the eschatology of the prophets functioned not as curiosity-satisfying speculation but as pastoral edification. The Book of Revelation is, despite its adumbration with apocalyptic imagery, a pastoral letter offering encouragement and instruction to Christians seeking the will of God for their lives during a particular crisis. 'It is clear that the document would never have been written apart from John's desire to produce changes in thought and behavior.' This assertion by Paul Minear is supported by his analysis of eight different literary forms, which appear throughout the book, by which John develops the hortatory aspect of his prophetic book.[9]

When Paul sums up the content of prophecy as οἰκοδομὴ καὶ παράκλησις καὶ παραμυθία, he clearly indicates the hortatory and parenetic goal of prophetic speech (14: 3; cf. 14: 31). It would appear that the word παράκλησις particularly has a prophetic, eschatological overtone in Paul, for he concludes the prophetic saying of I Thess. 4: 15—18 with ὥστε παρακαλεῖτε ἀλλήλους ἐν τοῖς λόγοις τούτοις and encourages the Thessalonians with the exhortation παρακαλεῖτε ἀλλήλοις καὶ οἰκοδομεῖτε (I Thess. 5: 11), in a passage that is replete with prophetic references. Similarly, Paul's own prophetic oracles are for the purpose of building up the Christian life of his churches, as is seen from the parenetic notes that express the implications of the oracles in I Cor. 15: 51—2 (verse 58) and Rom. 11: 25—7 (verse 25).

Luke represents the prophet Simeon as waiting for the παράκλησις of Israel, which he recognizes and proclaims to be present in the advent of Jesus (Luke 2: 25). In this text the prophetic παράκλησις is the encouraging, edifying word of the present fulfillment of the hopes of the community, along with the assurance that the yet-to-be-fulfilled hopes will certainly be fulfilled. Luke understands 'βαρναβᾶς' to be a nickname given to Barnabas because of his facility at prophetic preaching, i.e. υἱὸς παρακλήσεως (Acts 4: 36),[10] which indicates that he understood a close relationship, if not identity, between προφητεία and παράκλησις. We have seen that Luke's description of the Apostolic Council reflects prophetic phenomena,[11] and that the Decree, which is called a παράκλησις, is delivered by prophets who further παρακάλεσαι the people (Acts 15: 31—2). Here, the prophetic παράκλησις functions for the edification of the community because, as in Revelation, it is the concrete word of God addressed to a particular problem for the present moment.

The Fourth Gospel does not use the verb παρακαλέω or the noun παράκλησις, but the prophet-author chooses παράκλητος as the appropriate term to designate the ministry of Christian prophets in his community.[12] The announcement of the fulfillment of the messianic hopes, as in Luke 2: 25 above, which constituted a basic element in Christian prophetic speech, is one of the overtones of the term παράκλητος. The parenetic aspect of Christian prophecy is also seen later in Hermas, who uses apocalyptic form and style but whose purpose is parenetic throughout. It would appear, therefore, that eschatological parenesis in general, with παράκλησις-terminology in particular, is sufficiently evidenced in our sources to indicate that it was a traditional prophetic element and was probably characteristic of earlier Christian prophets.

Persecution and suffering

The motif that the true prophet must suffer, and that he proclaims suffering as the lot of the faithful, is also an aspect of the eschatological message of the prophet. In the Old Testament some prophets suffer as an integral part of their prophet vocation — Ezekiel and Jeremiah come immediately to mind — but suffering is not characteristic of prophetism as such. On the contrary, in some circles the prophet was pictured as quite beyond the realm of ordinary human suffering, by virtue of his divinely-given miracle-working capability, as in the Elijah—Elisha cycle of stories. But with Jeremiah as the beginning-point, there developed in late-Jewish literature the firm idea that the true prophet must suffer as a badge of his authenticity. Isaiah, for example, who strides through the pages of the Old Testament rather triumphalistically, is pictured as the suffering martyr in the literature of the first century C.E.[13] When this tendency combined in Christian prophecy with the apocalyptic view that terrible sufferings must come to the faithful as a prelude to the End, the Christian prophetic tradition became marked with many references to persecution and suffering.

It is understandable that Christian prophets were in fact persecuted. Their claim to have the eschatological Spirit was blasphemous in the ears of those whose theology denied that it was possible for the Spirit to be present; yet the prophets were in possession of, or sometimes appeared to be possessed by, *some* 'spirit'. Thus there inevitably arose the counter-claim among the Jewish opponents of early Christianity that the speaking of those who claimed to possess the eschatological Spirit was in fact the raging of those possessed by demons (cf. I Cor. 14: 23; John 7: 20; 8: 48, 52; 10: 20—1).

In the understanding of the prophet-author of Revelation, the true prophet is the one who in word and deed lets the meaning of Jesus' suffering and death become manifest as the saving act of God in Jesus, which is the point of orientation for the Christian's own manner of life. If the traditional interpretation of 1: 9 is correct, John writes as one who has himself suffered the official rejection and persecution of the state, and his message to the church abounds in references to present and anticipated sufferings (2: 9—10, 13, 22; 3: 10; 6: 9; 7: 14; 12: 11—17; 13: 7; 16: 6; 17: 6; 18: 24; 20: 4). The repeated promise to ὁ νικῶν (2: 7, 11, 17, 26; 3: 5, 12, 21), when seen in the light of 5: 5—6, obviously refers to those believers who have been faithful in the face of persecution even to the point of death (cf. 2: 10; 12: 11). In particular, the prophets are singled out as being the objects of persecution and victims of suffering (10: 8—11; 11: 1—8 (cf. verse 10); 16: 6; 18: 24).

In a manner that is closer to the prophet of Revelation than is usually recognized, Paul also understands his present time as the dawn of the Last Days, which must include persecution and suffering for the saints, so that his prophetic message too is characterized by references to suffering, a motif that is also continued in the Pauline school (I Thess. 3: 3*b*—4; I Cor. 7: 25—31; cf. II Thess. 1: 4—7; II Tim. 3: 12). It may be that in I Thess. 2: 14—15 we have an explicit reference to the Jewish persecution of precisely those early Palestinian Christian prophets whom we are attempting to characterize. This passage is frequently regarded as a post-Pauline interpolation, and, when it is considered Pauline, the prophets referred to are usually considered to be Old Testament prophets.[14] However, in view of the unusual word order (Jesus — prophets — Paul), and the context in which Paul is speaking of recent events in Palestine, and the several allusions to Christian prophets among the Thessalonians (1: 6; 4: 8, 9, 15—18; 5: 11, 19—20), the possibility must be kept open that Paul is here referring to Jewish persecution of those earliest Christian prophets who identified Jesus with the Son of Man, which is also reflected in other New Testament data (Acts 6: 8 — 8: 3; Matt. 23: 34; John 16: 2).[15] The explanation for the several non-Pauline features that do appear in this text may not be that this is a post-Pauline interpolation, but that Paul takes over a pre-formed piece of tradition, which reflects the *Gerichtsrede* characteristic of early Christian prophets, as argued by Ulrich Müller.[16]

When Luke is describing some prophetic figure *qua* prophet, such as Agabus, there is no suggestion that rejection and suffering are inherent in the prophetic vocation. Agabus, in fact, is a rather commanding figure. But this may be due more to the minor role that *theologia crucis* plays in Luke's own theology, particularly his reluctance to portray those endowed in a special measure with the Spirit as *thereby* designated for suffering. However, some of those incidentally identified as prophets (Paul, Barnabas, Silas, 13: 1—2; 15: 32) do suffer repeated rejection and persecution as a characteristic mark of their ministry (Acts 13—14; 16—28). And the ministry of Jesus is portrayed in prophetic terms that make one point clear: *no prophet is acceptable*, period.[17]

The early Christian prophetic conception of God's messengers as persecuted and suffering sheep rests on Jer. 11: 18—19, then on Is. 53. So in Matt. 7: 15, the self-understanding of early Christian prophets is represented: the true prophet is sheep-like rather than wolf-like, oppressed rather than oppressor. This is also the meaning of Matthew's (or his tradition's) allegorizing addition to the Parable of the Great Supper, in which the messengers from the king (= the prophets, including Christian prophets) are abused and killed. The peculiarly Matthean elements in 23: 29—36 also suggest that in the Matthean church the prophet was known to be a rejected, persecuted figure.

The rejection and persecution of the true prophets is only the penultimate reality, however. With prophetic insight, the prophets are such that in the *eschaton* those who are rejected now will be accepted, and those who are considered blessed now will learn that they are rejected. This note of the eschatological reversal of roles is sounded by both the author of Revelation and Paul, who see it as already occurring in the rejection of the Jews and acceptance of the Gentiles (Rev. 2: 9; Rom. 11: 25), and by the oracles in the Lukan birth narratives, which celebrate the rejection of the rich and the acceptance of the poor (Luke 1: 52–3). We might anticipate that this theme too would surface in Christian prophetic sayings in the synoptic tradition.

Rebuke of immorality and announcement of judgment

Reinhold Niebuhr was thinking primarily of the prophets of Israel when he declared that the essence of all prophetism is the note of 'againstness' – the prophet speaks against the people in the name of the people's own God.[18] Yet this description fits the prophets of earliest Christianity as well, for their eschatological orientation came to expression in yet another form: the rebuke of immorality and the pronouncement of judgment on sinners within and without the community. The Apocalypse is throughout a prophetic rebuke of immorality and unfaithfulness and a pronouncement of judgment upon those who do not repent (e.g. 2: 23; 3: 10; 13: 10; 16: 6; 22: 12, 18–19). This is not a moralizing rebuke from a self-righteous stance; the Seer does this as the spokesman for the eschatological judge who is already making himself present in his prophetic word. In this the author of the Fourth Gospel stands close to the Apocalypse, for he emphasizes that a primary function of the $\pi\alpha\rho\acute{\alpha}\kappa\lambda\eta\tau\sigma\varsigma$ is to $\dot{\epsilon}\lambda\acute{\epsilon}\gamma\chi\epsilon\iota\nu$ the unbelievers, and the basis for it is the eschatological judgment pronounced on $\dot{\sigma}$ $\acute{\alpha}\rho\chi\omega\nu$ $\tau\sigma\hat{\upsilon}$ $\kappa\acute{\sigma}\sigma\mu\sigma\upsilon$ $\tau\sigma\acute{\upsilon}\tau\sigma\upsilon$ (16: 8–11). The identical word $\dot{\epsilon}\lambda\acute{\epsilon}\gamma\chi\epsilon\iota\nu$ used of Christian prophets in I Cor. 14: 24 should be noted. The legal connotation of $\pi\alpha\rho\acute{\alpha}\kappa\lambda\eta\tau\sigma\varsigma$ is important here, for the Paraclete functions as a prosecuting attorney, rather than counsel for the defense, as the agent of the heavenly court who presses the case against the unbelieving world before the eschatological judge. By realizing the future eschatological judgment, the Paraclete reproves or exposes the unbelieving world.

Paul's discussion of prophecy at Corinth does not directly state that rebuke and pronouncement of judgment are prophetic functions, but this is implied in I Cor. 14: 24–5. The hearer of the prophet's message responds as he does because he is addressed as one who already stands before the court of the eschatological judge, whose sentence he hears in the prophet's announcement. In the case of Paul himself, the living Christ who speaks through him will execute powerful judgment against the Corinthian sinners

(I Cor. 5: 3–5; II Cor. 13: 3). The secondary literature on Paul also portrays him as one who pronounces prophetic judgment (Acts 13: 11; 28: 25–8; I Tim. 1: 20). So also the prophetic oracles of Luke 1–2 contain the element of eschatological judgment (1: 51–3; 2: 34–5). Although Hermas is something of a pale literary reflection of his prophetic predecessors, both in Israel and the church, he does preserve this element of rebuking and judging immorality. In sum, the prophets appear to have been not moralizers but those who rebuked the sins of the eschatological community in the name of the judge who would shortly appear.

Revelation of men's hearts

Another characteristic of early Christian prophecy evidenced in our sources that seems to be an aspect of its eschatological nature is that extraordinary revelation of men's hearts described, for example, by Paul in I Cor. 14: 25. This has sometimes been called 'clairvoyance', which was one of the primary characteristics of Hellenistic prophets but is practically absent from descriptions of Jewish prophets.[19] In addition to I Cor. 14: 25, several references in our sources indicate that knowing the secrets of the human heart is a mark of the prophet (Mark 14: 65 par.; Luke 2: 35; 7: 39; John 2: 24–5; 4: 19; 6: 65; 13: 11, 21; 16: 19; Rev. 2: 23; 3: 1, 8, 14). It may be that some Christian prophets simply shared this characteristic with other θεῖος ἀνήρ types, or that the tradition process had imposed this common Hellenistic prophetic trait onto the image of the Christian prophet and that 'clairvoyance' is the proper designation for this phenomenon. But a better explanation may be found in terms of the eschatological nature of early Christian prophetic preaching, so that such references as I Cor. 14: 25 are to be explained not by 'thought reading', but by the kind of direct address in which the prophet, speaking in the person of the eschatological judge, brings the hearer proleptically before the judgment (cf. I Cor. 4: 5). As will happen on the Last Day, so already in the prophetic encounter, the heart's secrets are revealed and confessed. In particular, it is the Son of Man who will know the hearts at the Last Judgment, and it is especially the voice of the Risen One who speaks as Son of Man that is heard in the prophet's word, as we shall see.[20]

Concern of false prophets

Wherever the phenomenon of prophecy appears, the problem of distinguishing true from false prophets also emerges. Thus it is no surprise that the early church speaks of 'false prophets' as well as 'prophets'. The use of false-prophet vocabulary was encouraged by two other developments antecedent to the rise of prophecy in the church. First, since the time of the translation of the LXX, which used ψευδοπροφήτης for the prophets who opposed the canonical prophets, 'false prophet' had become a term of abuse for one's theological opponents. This represented a claim that the content of the teaching that was opposed was false, without indicating that the opponents in fact made claims to prophetic inspiration. We thus find ψευδοπροφήτης used as a polemical *Schimpfwort*, as a synonym for 'false teacher' (II Pet. 2: 1; Did. 11.3–6). Secondly, a common feature of the apocalyptic drama was the multiplication of false prophets just before the End, part of the furniture of apocalyptic. This meant that an apocalyptically-oriented community, such as early Christianity, would find talk of false prophecy to be a given part of its theological resources. Some references to false prophets in our literature may be simply a reflection of this apocalyptic milieu (e.g. Did. 16.3).

As in the Old Testament (Jer. 14: 13–16; 23: 9–32; 29: 8–9; Ezek. 13: 1–16; I Kings 22: 5–28; cf. Zech. 13: 2–6), those in the early church who themselves claim the gift of prophecy, or who are most sympathetic to the prophetic ministry of the church, are those who are most sensitive to the prophetic claims of others and most able to resist them. Deut. 13 and 18, and Did. 11–13, illustrate the difficulty the non-charismatic community had in dealing with prophetic claims. The prophet-author of Revelation is concerned with false prophets not merely as an apocalyptic *theologoumenon*, but because he is met by counter-claims in his own churches from prophets who present a different message from his own (2: 20; cf. 2: 14, 15). It is quite likely that the ψευδοπροφήτης of 16: 13; 19: 20 and 22: 10 represents not only the pagan priesthood promoting emperor-worship in Asia (cf. 13: 11–18), but also, or even primarily, the church prophets who encouraged sacrifice to the emperor by announcing this as the will of the exalted Lord. Likewise Matthew, who values the prophetic ministry very highly, is also concerned to point out the danger of false prophets within the church (7: 15–23), as is the Didache (11.8–12), the Johannine community (I John 4: 1–3) and Hermas (Mand. XI). Paul does not use the term ψευδοπροφήτης but as a charismatic himself is very concerned that the congregation which experiences inspired speech recognizes that the claim to inspiration itself is not sufficient to distinguish authentic from false prophecy (I Cor. 2: 6–16; 12: 1–11; 14: 1–39; II Cor. 10–13). Of our major sources, only Luke–Acts is unconcerned with the problem of false prophecy within the church, but this is readily explained by Luke's reluctance to describe *any* internal problems between Paul and his mission churches.

In this section I have not intended to pursue the question of what criteria were developed by the early church to aid it in distinguishing true

prophecy from false. This has been done by others.[21] I have intended
rather to point out that concern with false prophecy is itself characteristic
of prophetic speech and that this feature might be used as one material
criterion of prophetic speech in the synoptic tradition of Jesus' words.

(2) Historical prediction

All the material characteristics of prophetic speech so far considered have
been aspects of the eschatological nature of early Christian prophecy. Were
the prophets also predictors of historical, this-worldly events, as distinct
from the events associated with the End? In the popular mind, this kind of
prediction is so closely associated with 'prophecy' as to be practically
identical with it. In the Hellenistic world, this kind of mundane predictive
power was an integral part of the prophet's role, and, to a lesser degree,
this was also the case in first-century Jewish prophecy.[22]

The support in our sources for the view that Christian prophets predicted the historical future is extremely slight. The author of Revelation
does not predict the future in the normal sense of this expression because
in this sense the future did not exist for him. The series of catastrophes
that he announces are not predictions of events *in* history but those which
form the end *of* history. Even the predicted persecution that he announces
as about to fall upon the churches is an eschatological, not a purely
historical, event. So also Paul never uses προφητεύειν to mean 'predict',
nor is there any indication that forecasting historical events was a part of
Corinthian prophecy. Paul's 'predictions' (e.g. I Thess. 3: 4) were an
element of his eschatology, as we have seen. It is primarily from Acts that
the picture of the Christian prophet as predictor comes (11: 27–8; 20: 23,
29–30; 21: 10–11; 27: 10, 23–6), but this is due to Luke's modeling of
church prophets on the pattern of Old Testament prophets, whom he
understands to have been primarily predictors (1: 16–20; 2: 16, 25, 30–1;
3: 18, 21, 24; 4: 25; 8: 35; 10: 43; 11: 27–8; 13: 27, 33–41, 47; 15: 15).
The evidence of predictive prophecy in John may be more significant, in
that he names prediction of the future as one of the Paraclete–prophet's
functions (16: 13). This might be a clue to the role some Christian
prophets played in John's church, whose ministry is portrayed in the
description of the Paraclete, although the prophet-author himself is not at
all interested in the prediction of historical events. This might also account
for the emphasis on Jesus' ability to announce events before they happen
(13: 19; 14: 29; 16: 4; 18: 4, 32; 19: 28). Also in I Tim. 4: 1–3, prophecy
is remembered as the gift of predicting the mundane future, ὑστέροις
καιροῖς probably being intentionally set over against the more eschatological ἐσχάταις ἡμέραις.

(3) Concrete directions for church life

The prophet appears in several of our sources as that figure who is
empowered by the Spirit to declare to the community what it must do in
situations for which the tradition provided ambiguous guidance or none at
all, or when the church's life had outgrown its tradition. The Apocalypse is
such a prophetic word to a specific problem: how should the church
respond to the demand for emperor-worship? The book as a whole gives
one clear answer to this burning question, not by a direct appeal to
tradition (Mark 12: 17 is conspicuous by its absence) but by direct
revelation, in which elements of the old tradition are taken up and recast
as a new message from the exalted Lord. In the course of this prophetic
response to the primary issue, answers to other problems of church life are
also revealed: the 'Nicolaitans' are a heretical sect and are to be rejected
(2: 6, 15); food sacrificed to idols is not to be eaten by faithful Christians
(2: 14, 20).

Like John, Hermas also writes to deliver the prophetically-revealed
answer to a major issue of church life: is repentance for post-baptismal sin
possible? But *en route* Hermas too responds with prophetic decisions
regarding other concrete questions within the church: does a husband sin
if he continues to live with an adulterous wife (Mand. IV.1.4–6)? If one's
spouse dies, does the surviving partner sin if he or she remarries (Mand.
IV.4.1–4)? Thus not only the somewhat 'haggadic' disclosures of the
eschatological future, but the 'halachic' regulations of church order and
Christian life formed part of the substance of the prophetic message.

The author of the Fourth Gospel apparently knew that prophets in his
church dealt pastorally with problems of church life by giving prophetic
answers to particular problems, since he pictures the Paraclete as one who
will 'teach all things' (14: 26) and 'guide into all truth' (16: 13). The
author is aware that it is the function of the prophet to address himself to
disputed theological questions, especially those that affect practical church
life (4: 19–20).

In Acts 10 and 15, as in Eph. 2: 20 and 3: 5, the prophets are the
primary figures in the church's making the momentous decision to extend
the gospel to the Gentiles.[23] Here a question faced the church for which
the tradition had no answer, an unsatisfactory answer or contradictory
answers. Only a charismatic leap around and beyond the tradition or
charismatic insight into the tradition's current meaning, a fresh revelation
of the will of God for the present moment in the church's life, would have
sufficed to guide the church, and this is apparently what occurred. This
great new insight did not come only as a vague spiritual osmosis, but by

the leadership of those prophets who claimed to have a word from the risen Lord that transcended all previous tradition.

Not only major theological issues but sometimes the day-by-day life of the church appears as directed by the Spirit through the prophets. In Acts 13: 1–3 and I Tim. 1: 18 and 4: 14, Christian prophets designate certain persons for specific service in the church, and repeatedly in Acts directions that affect the mission of the church are given by Spirit-inspired spokesmen or by revelatory experiences of the prophetic figures in their dreams (8: 26, 29; 16: 6, 9; 18: 9–10; 21: 4; 22: 17–21). That this is not merely the legend-building thrust of the tradition nor Luke's romantic editorializing (though some of the latter is present) is confirmed by Paul's own reference to his call, which he describes in prophetic terms (Gal. 1: 12–17), and by Paul's claim to have gone to the Jerusalem conference κατὰ ἀποκάλυψιν (Gal. 2: 2). This latter reference shows clearly that as a Christian prophet Paul believed that his life was directed, at crucial points, for the sake of the church, by a revelation that was not merely a private experience but the Spirit's directing an individual for the purpose of facilitating the church's mission. Paul himself typically settles practical questions of church life (e.g. divorce, eating meat sacrificed to idols, *glossolalia* during worship) not on the basis of personal prophetic revelation but by an appeal to a 'word of the Lord' or by his apostolic authority (I Cor. 7: 10–40; 8: 1 – 11: 1; 14: 1–39). But too much should not be made of this – the line between traditional words of the Lord and words of the heavenly Lord is a thin one for Paul, as is the line between apostle and prophet. Paul too, as a Christian prophet, speaks to the practical problems of church life.

Since we know that rendering decisions on disputed issues of religious life was also understood to be a function of the prophet within Palestinian Judaism (e.g. I Macc. 4: 41–6; 14: 25–49; John 4: 19–20), we may assume that this characteristic, which appears in later Christian sources, was also an aspect of the ministry of early Christian prophets. In fact, if prophets continued to play such a role after the church had developed official structures, it is even more likely that this was the case in the earliest days of the church.

(4) Revelatory Spirit and angel

In Revelation, the prophetic state is described as being ἐν πνεύματι (1: 10; 4: 2; 17: 3; 21: 10), the prophetic mode of discourse is called πνευματικῶς (Rev. 11: 8) and πνεῦμα is frequently used in other expressions as the vehicle of revelation or the power at work in the revelatory event (2: 7, 11, 17, 29; 3: 6, 13, 22; 14: 13; 19: 10; 22: 6, 17; probably also 1: 4; 3: 1;

4: 5; 5: 6). Since apocalyptic thought in general includes revelation by angels as a common element, it is not unexpected to find many references to angels in Revelation as well. But it is striking that some of the Apocalypse's references to angels are not simply a part of the apocalyptic idiosyncrasy, but are found in a group of statements closely parallel to statements about the revelatory Spirit. To ἐν πνεύματι corresponds διὰ ἀγγέλου (1: 1); to πνευματικῶς corresponds μέτρον ἀνθρώπου ὅ ἐστιν ἀγγέλου (21: 17); and to the series of statements where the Spirit is the vehicle of revelation, there is an equally-long list in which the angel performs this function (5: 2, 11; 7: 2, 11−12; 10: 1−11; 14: 6, 8, 9, 15, 18; 17: 1, 7; 18: 2, 21; 19: 17; 22: 6, 16). In some of these, the Spirit and the angel are identified (17: 1−3; 22: 6). We see that the Spirit and angels are associated very closely in Revelation, that the prophetic ministry is associated closely with both, and that this has left its mark on the vocabulary of the prophet's message.

Acts associates the Spirit with the revelatory experiences of prophets, so that the utterances of prophets contain references of the Spirit (2: 33; 11: 28; 13: 2; 15: 28; 16: 6, 7; 20: 23; 21: 4, 11). Acts also associates angels with such revelatory experiences, sometimes using 'angel' and 'spirit' interchangeably (Acts 8: 26−9; 10: 3−19; 23: 8−9; 27: 23). The prophetic scenes of Luke 1−2 alternate between revelation by an angel (1: 8−22, 26−38) and by the Spirit (1: 41, 47, 67; 2: 25−7). Luke−Acts is thus a witness to the use of Spirit/angel terminology as an indication of Christian prophecy. This is also clearly the case in *Hermas* throughout, especially in Man. XI. In all of this there is nothing unique to Christian prophecy, for in several streams of heterodox Judaism the revelatory angel and revelatory Spirit were identified or closely associated.[24]

There are two items of negative evidence from the New Testament that are important for this discussion. Paul often speaks of revelation as coming to prophets by the Spirit (I Thess. 5: 19; I Cor. 2: 9−16; 12: 4−11; 14: 1, 31−2, 37) but never refers to angels as the vehicle of prophetic revelation. He does indicate clearly that others in the early church had this understanding, of which he himself is suspicious (Gal. 1: 8; I Cor. 13: 1; II Cor. 11: 14). So also the Fourth Gospel replaces the traditional angel in the revelatory event with the Paraclete, which is clearly defined as the Spirit. The Paraclete figure had probably previously been understood as an angel figure, which John is subtly demythologizing.[25] This shows that some in John's tradition and community had associated angels with prophetic speech, as had also been the case in Paul's.

I am not suggesting that all the references to angels in first-century Jewish and Christian literature should be related to the prophetic experience, nor is there any reason to explore here the various ways that angelology functioned theologically in the many streams of late-Judaism and Christianity. Rather, I am calling attention to the striking way in which angel/Spirit terminology appears in our sources for early Christian prophecy and suggesting that in the synoptic tradition an interest in the Spirit and/or angels as the media of revelation may be a mark of prophetic speech.

(5) Wisdom motifs

It is now a commonplace of Old Testament studies that the prophets and wise men of Israel are not simply to be contrasted with each other, but that Israel's prophets utilized themes, materials and forms from the wisdom tradition in the expression of their prophetic message.[26] Particularly after the exile, wisdom, which had formerly often been little more than common sense honed by community experience, assumed more and more the role of the divine call to men. This role has formerly been held primarily by prophecy, and this development brought wisdom and prophecy even closer together. Although von Rad has overstated the case in declaring that apocalyptic is not prophecy at all but is to be classified under the heading of 'wisdom',[27] it is true that in late-Jewish prophecy and apocalyptic, the categories of prophecy and wisdom had collapsed into each other. A wide spectrum of late-Jewish literature shows that not only did wise men sometimes feel themselves to be the heirs and successors of the prophets, writing with a consciousness of divine commission, but prophets were seen to be envoys of Wisdom (Wis. Sol. 1: 6–7; 7: 27; 9: 17; Sirach 24: 30–4; 39: 1–6; IV Ez. 14: 1–48; I En. 37.1–5; 42.1–2; 49.3; 63.2; 82.1*b*–3; 84.3; 92.1; Baba Bathra 12*a*; 1 QH 2.4–5; 11 QPs^a 1–4). It thus should come as no surprise that our sources for early Christian prophecy indicate that prophecy in the early church manifests some wisdom features.

The Apocalypse has the same wisdom heritage as apocalyptic in general. In particular may be noted the 'conquering' (ὁ νικῶν) sayings in chapters 2–3, which are a borrowing of wisdom formulae.[28] For Paul, too, wisdom and prophecy are correlative modes of discourse that blend into each other, as can be seen from the train of thought in I Cor. 1: 18 – 2: 16, where Paul's use of σοφία, in distinction from that of the Corinthians, is oriented to prophecy/apocalyptic, rather than to *Gnosis*. This Pauline affinity between wisdom and prophecy is preserved also in Ephesians, though in a somewhat more gnosticizing way, as is illustrated e.g. by the combination of σοφία and ἀποκάλυψις in 1: 17. Similarly, the λόγος concept lying behind the Johannine prologue has points of contact with both the late-Jewish wisdom speculations and the prophetic understanding of the Johannine community.[29] When we remember that in the wisdom tradition the heavenly, pre-existent Wisdom came upon selected recipients and made them 'friends of God and prophets' (Wis. Sol. 7: 27), we probably have a clue as to how the Johannine community understood John 13: 15*b*: 'I have called you friends, for all that I have heard from my father I have made known to you.' Not only does this sapiential context reveal the presence of prophecy in the Johannine community more clearly, it alerts us to look for wisdom motifs in the products of Christian prophecy.

Numerous scholars have pointed out the presence of wisdom forms and materials in the tradition of Jesus' sayings in the synoptic gospels.[30] Without yet raising the question of whether some of these sayings are from Christian prophets, this fact is also the primary evidence for the confluence of prophecy and wisdom in the early church, for Jesus himself was certainly primarily a prophetic figure, not a sapiential one. The discussion of wisdom materials in prophetic oracles has already introduced the issue of form, and to that I now turn directly.

9 FORMAL CHARACTERISTICS OF PROPHETIC SPEECH

The formal nature of prophetic speech

The rediscovery of the formal and often poetic nature of the prophetic speech of Israel's prophets is one of the achievements in which modern biblical scholarship can take justifiable pride.[1] It is now recognized that the initial revelatory experience was expressed and elaborated in the prophet's own words, and that traditional forms were available for this.[2] The Old Testament would teach us that formal structure, even a degree of formal rigidity, need not be incompatible with genuine prophetic inspiration. The same is true of what we know of prophecy in the Hellenistic world, both Jewish and pagan. Martin Hengel describes the prophecy of a Syrian soldier, Buplagus, who arose from the dead and prophesied – in hexameters – the vengeance of Zeus against Rome, and the oracle of a severed head that spoke – in verse – the message of Apollo against Rome.[3] It was considered unusual when the Pythia at Delphi spoke in prose rather than $\dot{\epsilon}\nu$ $\mu\dot{\epsilon}\tau\rho\omega$.[4] Josephus (*Wars*, VI.5.3) reports the constantly-repeated oracle of a Jewish prophet during the war of 66–70, which has a strikingly neat form, even in Greek, of two strophes of three stichs each:

> φωνὴ ἀπ᾿ ἀνατολῆς
> φωνὴ ἀπὸ δύσεως
> φωνὴ ἀπὸ τῶν τεσσάρων ἀνέμων
>
> φωνὴ ἐπὶ Ἱερουσόλυμα καὶ τὸν ναόν
> φωνὴ ἐπὶ νυμφίους καὶ νύμφας
> φωνὴ ἐπὶ τὸν λαὸν πάντα.

New Testament prophecy also manifests formal regularities. A considerable portion of the Apocalypse is presented as formally-structured units. Not only the hymns and other poetic passages, which are printed as poetry by the RSV, but briefer oracles such as 3: 5*b*, 10; 13: 10; 16: 6; 22: 12, 18–19 also exhibit recognizable formal patterns. Such translations as Heinrich Kraft's and Paul Minear's, which print the entire text in rhythmical, structured units, have perhaps pressed a valid point too far but are still closer to the linguistic form of the Apocalypse than those which regard it as primarily straight prose.[5] Incidentally, this formal characteristic serves to relate Revelation more closely to prophecy than to apocalyptic.

The oracular material of Luke (1: 14–17, 22–3, 35, 46*b*–55, 68–79; 2: 29–32, 34–5) is in strophic, metrical form, as is also the case to some extent in the Johannine discourses,[6] both bodies of material having been influenced by Christian prophets. It is less often noticed that Paul's prophetic oracles manifest formal structures, as is seen for example in I Cor. 15: 51–2:[7]

ἰδοὺ   μυστήριον   ὑμῖν   λέγω
πάντες   οὐ   κοιμηθησόμεθα
πάντες   δὲ   ἀλλαγησόμεθα
    ἐν   ἀτόμῳ
    ἐν   ῥιπῇ   ὀφθαλμοῦ
    ἐν   τῇ   ἐσχάτῃ   σάλπιγγι
σαλπίσει   γάρ
    καὶ   οἱ   νεκροὶ   ἐγερθήσονται   ἄφθαρτοι
    καὶ   ἡμεῖς   ἀλλαγησόμεθα

Rom. 11: 25–6 also manifests a schematization, one strophe of three members, past/present/future, in which the emphatic verb comes last in each line:[8]

πώρωσις   ἀπὸ   μέρους   τῷ   Ἰσραὴλ   γέγονεν
ἄχρις   οὗ   τὸ   πλήρωμα   τῶν   ἐθνῶν   εἰσέλθῃ
καὶ   οὕτως   πᾶς   Ἰσραὴλ   σωθήσεται.

Käsemann finds still other formalized oracles in Paul: I Cor. 3: 17; 14: 38; 16: 22; II Cor. 9: 16; Rom. 2: 12; Gal. 1: 9, and the most recent studies of Roetzel and especially Müller find even more.[9] The studies of Müller and Dautzenberg have shown that the roots of these prophetic formulae are found in the apocalyptic literature,[10] which reveals that it was the circles behind the production of such literature that kept alive Old Testament prophetic forms; these were then borrowed by early Palestinian Christian prophets, whence Paul himself derived them.

All of the preceding is to provide some support for the general thesis that when we speak of 'sayings of Christian prophets' we do not have in mind formless emotional outpourings or short staccato ejaculatory utterances, but sayings formed according to intentional patterns, some-times of considerable length. We may now ask what particular formal characteristics may inhere in the oracles of early Christian prophets. Since the discussion of criteria for identifying prophetic oracles in the synoptic tradition has for the most part centered on form-critical issues, I will not repeat that work here but only attempt to give a summary account of work done by others, supplementing it somewhat with evidence from primary sources.

Speaking for the risen Lord in the first person

Celsus gives an interesting description of the Christian prophets he encountered in the third century (Origen, *Contra Celsum*, VII.9):

> 'There are many who, although of no name, with the greatest facility and on the slightest occasion, whether within or without temples, assume the motions and gestures of inspired persons; while others do it in cities or among armies, for the purpose of attracting attention and exciting surprise. These are accustomed to say, each for himself, "I am God"; "I am the son of God" (παῖς θεοῦ); or, "I am the Divine Spirit"; "I have come because the world is perishing, and you, O men, are perishing for your iniquities. But I wish to save you, and you shall see me returning again with heavenly power. Blessed is he who now does me homage. On all the rest I will send eternal fire, both on cities and on countries. And those who know not the punishments which await them will grieve in vain; while those who are faithful to me I will preserve eternally."'

The prophets described are not the churchly figures we have discovered in earliest Christianity, but independent street-corner prophets whose prophecy has degenerated considerably from its earlier form. Yet characteristic features remain: the eschatological orientation, the pronouncement of blessing (see below, pp. 133–5), the claim to inspired, but intelligible, speech. But one important point is misunderstood by Celsus: the prophet is claiming nothing for himself, but the exalted language he uses ('I am the son (or 'servant') of God' etc.) is the prophetic mode of discourse by which the prophet speaks for the deity in the first person, either with or without the messenger-formula.[11] The fact that the prophet says 'You shall see me returning again in heavenly power' shows that he is not speaking of himself, but in the person of the heavenly Lord who speaks *through* him. Thus when Montanus says 'I am the Father and the Son and the Paraclete' and 'Neither angel, nor ambassador, but I, the Lord God the Father, am come', it is a matter of prophetic, not just personal, exaltation.[12] At Delphi, the god spoke through the Pythia always in the first person, never in the third.[13] The primitive prophets of Arabian paganism, the kahins, spoke of themselves in the third person, or to themselves in the second person, as the jinn-spirit spoke through them in the first person.[14] Moving closer in time to the early Christian prophets, we find that the Odes of Solomon manifest this characteristic in a way particularly relevant for the relationship of Christian prophets to the synoptic tradition. In Ode 42 for example, we have sayings of the risen Jesus, who speaks in the first person through the mouth of the inspired singer. This must have been a not-uncommon phenomenon in the time of the poet, according to the Ode itself: 'For I live and am resurrected, am with them and speak through their mouth.' (Odes Sol. 42.6) Such revelations of the deity spoken in the first person were quite common in the syncretistic Hellenistic religions of the first century.[15]

This prophetic mode of discourse appears in a significant way in some of our sources for early Christian prophecy. Its absence from others is also significant. The prophet of Revelation has no hesitation about speaking in the person of the risen Lord. The formula ἐγὼ Ἰησοῦς (22: 16) concludes a prophetic document that contains no less than sixty 'I-sayings'. The prophet can take material from the Old Testament, re-form it and present it as a first-person saying of the risen Jesus (e.g. 21: 6; cf. Is. 55: 1). The repeated use of the I-form is a recovery of the prophetic style of direct address by the deity, which had declined in apocalyptic in favor of third-person discourse. The formula with which Agabus begins his prophecy, τάδε λέγει τὸ πνεῦμα τὸ ἅγιον (= ὁ κύριος) (Acts 21: 10) may accurately represent one of the forms of Christian prophetic speech, or may be another example of Luke's casting church prophets in the same role as Old Testament prophets, for the LXX regularly rendered כה אמר יהוה as τάδε λέγει ὁ κύριος. Acts 13: 2 is direct evidence that the first-person form of prophetic speech was familiar in the Lukan tradition, for which indirect evidence is found in the ἐγώ εἰμι of the risen Jesus in 9: 5; 22: 8; 26: 15. The οὗτός ἐστιν of 8: 10 probably corresponds to the revelatory ἐγώ εἰμι of the false prophet Simon. This prophetic ἐγώ εἰμι is also a dominant feature of the discourses of the Fourth Gospel. This is to be expected, in view of the identification of (the risen) Jesus and the Paraclete—prophet who will not speak 'from himself' (16: 13). The many 'I-sayings' of the Fourth Gospel should not be accounted for as simply literary fiction, the retrojection into the mouth of the historical Jesus of *theologoumena* that he could not have said, nor by Mandean or other parallels, but are to be seen as prophetic utterance in which the risen Lord speaks through his prophet in the first person.[16] The repeated οὗτός ἐστιν with a christological predicate is the confessional response of the community to such prophetic declarations.

Our other sources do not evidence this form of prophetic speech. Hermas does not speak with the 'I' of the risen Christ but reports on visionary conversations with a Sybil-like woman, an angelic young man and the shepherd-angel of repentance. The Didache offers no indication of the speech-forms used by the prophets. The absence of this form in Paul is significant. He can hardly have been unaware of it, since it is so frequent in the Old Testament and in Jewish and Hellenistic prophecy. It was probably the danger of being misunderstood as a Hellenistic prophet, from within whom the god spoke, that caused Paul to avoid this form. Like other early Christian prophets, Paul understood his prophetic speaking to be 'in Christ's stead', commissioned by the risen Christ. But the prophetic oracles transmitted by him are spoken with the ego of the prophet, not in the first-person form of 'I-sayings' spoken with the ego of the risen Christ. This would have been too readily understood as a kind of Hellenistic mystical union with the deity, which Paul wished to avoid. Paul's own substitute for the prophetic messenger-formula seems to have been formulae such as $\dot{\epsilon}\nu\ \tau\hat{\omega}\ \dot{o}\nu\acute{o}\mu\alpha\tau\iota\ (\alpha\dot{\upsilon}\tauo\hat{\upsilon},\ X\rho\iota\sigma\tauo\hat{\upsilon},\ \kappa\upsilon\rho\acute{\iota}o\upsilon\ \kappa\tau\lambda)$; $\dot{\epsilon}\nu\ \lambda\acute{o}\gamma\omega\ \kappa\upsilon\rho\acute{\iota}o\upsilon$; $\kappa\upsilon\rho\acute{\iota}o\upsilon\ \dot{\epsilon}\sigma\tau\iota\nu\ \dot{\epsilon}\nu\tauo\lambda\acute{\eta}$ (I Thess. 4: 2, 15; II Thess. 3: 6, 12; I Cor. 1: 10; 5: 4; 9: 14; 14: 37), which both declared his message to be directly from the risen Lord and distinguished the person of the message-bearer from that of the message-giver. Other early Christian prophets also made use of these forms, especially $\dot{\epsilon}\nu\ \tau\hat{\omega}\ \dot{o}\nu\acute{o}\mu\alpha\tau\iota\ (\kappa\upsilon\rho\acute{\iota}o\upsilon\ \kappa\tau\lambda)$ (Matt. 7: 22; Mark 13: 6 par.; John 14: 26; Acts 9: 27, 29). Mark 13: 6 par. and John 14: 26 identify 'I-sayings' and speaking 'in the name of' the risen Lord as the same kind of (prophetic) speech.

The result is clear. One of the forms of speech used by early Christian prophets was the first-person speech of the risen Lord, including the revelatory $\dot{\epsilon}\gamma\acute{\omega}\ \epsilon\dot{\iota}\mu\iota$. But this was not the only style appropriate to the prophetic self-consciousness, and Christian prophecy should not be identified with the first-person form alone. Both types of sayings could later have been included within the pre-Easter framework as sayings of Jesus.

'Sentences of holy law'/'eschatological correlative'

The form 'sentence of holy law' is a statement marked by a legal style, eschatological fervor and the pairing of *lex talionis* and *chiasmus*, as found, for example, in I Cor. 3: 17 and 14: 38. Due to the influence of Ernst Käsemann, it has been widely accepted as an indicator of Christian prophetic speech. This view has also been severely criticized, especially in the writings of Klaus Berger, who has shown that the form is more closely related to the wisdom tradition than to the combination legal-apocalyptic genre posited by Käsemann.[17] But Berger did not sufficiently consider the fact that prophets used wisdom materials and that, though the 'sentences of holy law' are expressed according to wisdom *forms*, the *content* of such sayings is often of an eschatological nature impossible in the teaching of a sage. The 'sentences' seem to have survived the discussion and are to be regarded as one indication of prophetic speech.[18] The discussion has made clear, however, that Käsemann was too generous in the number of sayings he assigned to this formal category and too easily declared a saying to be prophetic on the basis of this form alone. Also, the discussion has mostly been methodologically unclear, in that it has primarily revolved around consideration of the synoptic sayings themselves, rather than inquiring whether this form is sufficiently documented in our sources for early Christian prophecy (apart from the synoptic sayings themselves) to be considered a characteristic indication of prophetic speech. This I will attempt briefly to do.

As defined by Käsemann, this prophetic form functions by bringing the hearer proleptically before the judgment of the Last Day, where he hears the legal verdict of the eschatological judge. Legal utterances presented in the power of the Spirit also correspond in general to this form. In our sources, then, we are seeking not only precise examples of the eschatological *lex talionis* chiastic form, but also indications of this function of the form. Both are in fact found in our primary example of Christian prophecy, the Apocalypse. Revelation does not simply predict the imminent coming of the Last Day, but brings the hearer before the eschatological judge as he hears the prophecy. 'Pure' examples of the form are found, such as 22: 18–19, which is in the chiastic ABB^1A^1 form, with the same verb in the protasis and apodosis, the protasis being introduced by ἐάν τις and the aorist subjunctive, the apodosis having the future indicative, the whole being eschatological in tone and legal in form. Other more-or-less pure examples of the form are found in 3: 5, 10; 11: 18; 13: 10; 16: 5–6; 22: 11. So also Paul's writings manifest the general function of prophetic speech to bring the hearer before the eschatological judge (e.g. I Cor. 5: 3–5; Rom. 11: 31, where the troublesome νῦν should be explained in terms of proleptic prophetic eschatology) and specific instances of the prophetic form (Rom. 2: 12, I Cor. 3: 17; 14: 38; 16: 22; II Cor. 9: 6; Gal. 1: 9). Likewise in the Fourth Gospel, the Spirit–Paraclete will convict the world by declaring the things to come as already operative; the final judgment is anticipated in the conviction of the world by the Paraclete (16: 30), and the post-Easter Jesus does in fact speak in the form of 'sentences of holy law' (20: 23). A closely-related form detected in the Q-material by Richard Edwards, the 'eschatological correlative', also is reflected in Pauline and Johannine materials.[19] All of this corresponds to a feature of prophecy from the sociological and history-of-religions point of view for which Weber even gives the *terminus technicus: aisymnete*, the type of prophecy in which law for the community is codified in the time of crisis.[20]

These converging lines of evidence are significant but not overwhelming. They suggest that 'sentences of holy law' and related forms were indeed used by Christian prophets, that there is much prophetic speech not in this form and that the form may be found elsewhere than among Christian prophets, as Berger has pointed out. Further, the form occurs only rarely in its 'pure' state. The conclusion must be that the form is somewhat characteristic of prophetic speech but is not unique to Christian prophets, that prophetic speech may occur in other recognizable forms and that no saying in the synoptic tradition may be attributed to a Christian prophet on the basis of this form alone.

Initial ἀμήν (λέγω ὑμῖν/σοι)

When Jesus of Nazareth *began* some solemn sayings with the Hebrew word אָמֵן (Greek transliteration ἀμήν), he apparently introduced a new usage of this word, which normally appeared in response to the words of another, meaning 'certainly', or as the affirmative response at the conclusion of a blessing or benediction.[21] Jeremias has examined the attempts to refute this and argues persuasively that this peculiar speech-form was first introduced by Jesus himself, and that we should continue to regard it as a characteristic mark of the *ipsissima vox Jesu.*[22] The form is an indication of Jesus' prophetic self-consciousness, a mark of received revelation, which is communicated to the hearers with the complementary form λέγω ὑμῖν/σοι, with which it is always found in the gospels.[23] But as Jeremias already saw, this situation of receiving revelation and delivering it to the community with formulae that claim revelatory authority is appropriate not only to the situation of the life of Jesus but also to the setting in the post-Easter church. 'Christian prophets ... spoke in the name of the exalted Lord *and with his words.*'[24] Thus though ἀμήν is a mark of the peculiar speech of Jesus himself, it is not peculiar to Jesus, is of itself no guarantee of the authenticity of any particular saying and is appropriate on the lips of a Christian bearer of revelation.[25]

Our sources suggest some use of this form by Christian prophets. Outside the gospels, the word is found more frequently in Revelation than in any other New Testament document. There are, however, no clear instances of a saying beginning with the formula ἀμήν λέγω ὑμῖν/σοι. This should not cause us to leap to the conclusion that all the instances of ἀμήν in Revelation are of the usual responsorial kind. Some of these (1: 6, 7; 5: 14; 22: 21) may represent the usual non-prophetic liturgical usage, and even those which precede the statement to which they are attached may in fact be a response to the preceding affirmations of praise (7: 12; 19: 14). But even so, it should not be overlooked that twice the ἀμήν is the prophet's response to revelation he receives (1: 7; 22: 20), and that the voices to which the ἀμήν respond are in every case heavenly voices, so that the frequent occurrence of ἀμήν in Revelation is to some extent an indication of prophetic speech. Both features have some similarity to the way ἀμήν is used in the synoptic tradition of Jesus' words and tend to link the introductory ἀμήν to Christian prophecy. Furthermore, the manner in which ναί and ἀμήν are equated in 1: 7 suggests that the ναί in 14: 13; 16: 7 and 22: 7 is analogous to the introductory ἀμήν. In addition, Victor Hasler's redaction-critical study of ἀμήν in the synoptic tradition, including those places where ἀμήν is obviously a secondary addition, indicates that in the church ἀμὴν λέγω ὑμῖν/σοι was used as an authority-formula to describe a word of the exalted κύριος.[26] Hasler also contends that the fact that a discussion of ἀμήν-saying emerges precisely in the discussion of Christian prophecy in I Cor. 14: 16 is a positive link between the two.[27] The repeated use of the formula in the Fourth Gospel's speech material, where it has been doubled for liturgical solemnity, is another point of contact between the formula and Christian prophecy. Obviously some occurrences of ἀμήν are only due to prosaic imitation in the development of the tradition, as a comparison of Matthew with Mark will immediately make clear, so that by no means is every occurrence of ἀμήν a guarantee that, if not Jesus, then a Christian prophet is the speaker. But the converging lines of evidence, fragile and indirect through some of them are, do seem to point backward to a time when ἀμὴν λέγω ὑμῖν/σοι was an indication of prophetic speech.

Blessing and curse

In the New Testament, the unconditional pronouncement of blessing and curse is almost entirely limited to the synoptic sayings of Jesus and to those who claim to speak by the inspiration of the risen Lord: Paul and the prophet John of Revelation.[28] Such a word-count as is found in note 28 is not convincing evidence in itself that blessing and curse are forms of early Christian prophetic speech, since one who makes no claim to inspiration could use the vocabulary of blessing and cursing as a part of ordinary conversation (e.g. Luke 14: 15). But the great majority of cases in which blessing and cursing are attributed to charismatic types, especially the high incidence found in Revelation, would suggest that this is one of the forms of prophetic speech. This impression is strengthened when one examines the passages separately; for as Käsemann has pointed out, many of them proceed from an awareness of God that goes beyond the realm of warning or exhortation and becomes the type of unconditional pronouncement, in which the word effects what it proclaims, and which only one conscious of prophetic authority could utter.[29]

The prophet-author of the Apocalypse, indeed with full awareness of what he is doing, makes use of the blessing-and-curse form as a vehicle of his prophetic message. He delivers exactly seven blessings (1:3; 14:13; 16:15; 19:9; 20:6; 22:7, 14), which resemble their synoptic counterparts in that blessing is pronounced on the poor, crying, persecuted congregations of Asia, and seven sentences announcing woes, containing a total of exactly fourteen occurrences of the word οὐαί (8:13; 9:12; 11: 14; 12:13; 18:10, 16, 19).[30] All these beatitudes and curses give proleptic voice to the eschatological blessing and curse. Some themes of the beatitudes in the synoptic gospels are also expressed in Revelation's beatitudes. This has sometimes been explained as the Seer's speech having been influenced by the synoptic gospels or the synoptic tradition. G. B. Caird, for example, declares 21:6—7 to be 'resonant with echoes of the [synoptic] beatitudes'.[31] But examination reveals that traditional words of Jesus are neither quoted nor alluded to. Rather, it is the case that the *themes* of the synoptic beatitudes are there (eschatological blessing for the hungering, thirsting, crying). This would argue that such pronouncements have their *Sitz* in the speech of Christian prophets but not necessarily that John here has a traditional saying of Jesus in mind.

Unless it is hinted at in I Cor. 14:25, there is no trace of the prophetic blessing/curse form in the speech of the Corinthian prophets. The ejaculatory curse of I Cor. 12:3 is doubtless to be associated with the kind of ecstasy opposed by Paul, rather than the prophecy that he encourages, but may be a gnosticizing version of the prophetic curse-form. The blessing-and-cursing form is not explicitly present in Paul's own prophetic speech. The one instance of his pronouncement of blessing (Rom. 14:22) is probably to be taken at the more prosaic 'conversational' level rather than as a pronouncement of eschatological prophecy. It may be that Paul deliberately avoided such terminology, which was perhaps being abused by his gnosticizing opponents, as James Robinson surmises.[32] More likely, the absence of explicit blessing-and-cursing formulae is simply accidental and related to the epistolary form and function, rather than a result of intentional disavowal of the form, since Paul does pronounce eschatological judgments, occasionally using explicit ἀνάθεμα formulae (I Cor. 5:3—5; 16:22; Gal. 1:8—9).

The speech of those figures in Acts explicitly named prophets by Luke does not contain the blessing/curse formulae, but the function of such forms may still be traced in the pronouncements of the prophetic figures in Acts 5: 9 and 13: 10—11. The speeches of Luke 1—2 relate the pronouncement of blessing to inspired prophetic speech (1: 42, 45, 67—8). When the above is taken with the fact that Old Testament prophecy and Jewish prophecy contemporary with early Christian prophecy also used blessing-and-curse forms, we may conclude that this was one of the characteristic forms of early Christian prophetic speech.[33]

10 SUMMARY

Without claiming that every early Christian prophet embodies all the features discussed above, I can now assemble a list of characteristics that, with more or less certainty from case to case, may be considered typical of early Christian prophets. Prophets were not uncommon figures but were widespread in early Christianity. The prophets functioned as a distinct group within the community but as an integral part of it, within the worship life of the congregation in close proximity to the teachers and the tradition process. Although the prophet was respected as a pneumatic whose words were permeated with a sense of call, authority and mission, the community knew that the true prophet is not possessed but retains his own responsibility for what he says, and that his words are not to be automatically accepted but to be tested by the community. The prophet frequently is associated with miracles and other pneumatic phenomena of the charismatic community. Like the Old Testament prophets, he may engage in symbolic acts and exhibits a peculiar life-style frequently marked by poverty and asceticism. The prophet does not fashion his oracles *ab ovo* but functions as an inspired interpreter of the community's history, of the Scriptures and of traditional sayings of Jesus. Since the rebirth of prophecy in the church is itself an eschatological phenomenon, the prophet's message has a dominant eschatological orientation, which is expressed from time to time in apocalyptic content, eschatological *paraclesis,* rebuke of immorality and pronouncement of proleptic judgment of the Last Day, references to persecution and suffering, the revelation of the secrets of men's hearts and a concern for false prophets. The prophet's message may involve historical prediction and may give concrete directions addressed to ambiguous or controversial issues in church life. Wisdom motifs and an interest in the modes of revelation (angels, Spirit) may appear in the prophet's sayings. Prophetic speech is not chaotic but may be characterized by particular forms: ἐγώ εἰμι and first-person address in the name of the risen Lord, 'sentences of holy law' and related forms, initial ἀμήν, the pronouncement of blessing and curse, and a characteristic vocabulary.

PART THREE

Christian prophecy in the synoptic tradition

11 CHRISTIAN PROPHECY IN Q

To this point I have rigidly excluded from my resources whatever sayings of Christian prophets may be contained in the sayings-tradition of the synoptic gospels themselves. We now turn to an examination of the streams of tradition in which the sayings of Jesus were handed on and the documents in which the deposit of these traditions was preserved. The oldest of these is Q. Although at some point(s) in its history the Q-materials were written into a document or series of documents, we should not regard Q simplicistically as a static, flat-surface entity. The Q-materials and the Q-community had a history, a trajectory, of expansion and modification. There are earlier and later sayings in Q. This is what Schulz has succeeded in showing, although he has not been convincing in his effort to distinguish two sharply-defined phases (and geographical locations) in the history of the Q-community and to assign each saying in Q to one or the other.[1] I shall assume that some sayings in Q reflect earliest Palestinian Christianity and that some sayings reflect later phases of the community's history, but that there was an identifiable community with a continuous history within which the Q-traditions were transmitted and shaped, and to some extent created.

My procedure will be to take the hypothesis that Christian prophecy existed in the early Palestinian–Syrian church as I have reconstructed it in the preceding pages and to proceed through the Q-materials saying by saying, in the Lukan order, comparing each saying with our profile of Christian prophecy. Those sayings will be discussed that seem to have significant points of contact with Christian prophecy and seem to be illuminated by being considered in the light of the hypothesis here explored. An effort will be made to come to a decision as to whether the saying originated as Christian prophecy (or was affected by Christian prophets in some other way) or whether the apparent points of contact are only coincidental. The results of such an investigation are as follows.

Luke 6: 22—3/Matt. 5: 11—12

In both Luke and Matthew this *logion* is the concluding element of a series of blessings, the *Traditionsgeschichte* of which is complicated and disputed at many points. The following outline of the development of the tradition is here regarded as the most coherent and enjoys a broad range of support.[2]

(1) Q originally contained four beatitudes, those in Luke 6: 20—4 par. The additional beatitudes in Matthew 5: 5, 7—10 are additions to Q in the Matthean stream of tradition (Q^{Mt}), or from Matthew himself, and will be discussed later.

(2) The first three beatitudes, Luke 6: 20*b*—21 par., are an original unity. The poor, hungry and crying who are pronounced blessed because of the coming eschatological reversal are not three different groups but three descriptions of the same group of pious עֲנָוִים , who will receive the same blessing at the *eschaton*. Their form and content are all identical, so that their separation in the Gospel of Thomas (Luke 6: 20*b* = GT 54; Luke 6: 21*a* = GT 69) represents the dissolution of an original unit.

(3) There is a sharp break between the third and fourth blessings. The differences are striking: the fourth saying is longer than the first three put together; the first three pronounce blessing on particular *persons* as such, while the fourth refers to persons in a particular *situation*; the first three promise eschatological reversal of present conditions, while the fourth simply promises heavenly reward; the first three address those whose condition is inherently distressing, while the fourth speaks to those who are in difficulty only because of their relation to the Son of Man; active participles describe the blessed in the first three beatitudes, while ὅταν ... ὑμᾶς and passive finite verbs are used in the fourth; the subordinate clause, which states the basis for the pronouncement, begins with ὅτι in the first three, but γάρ in the fourth. An additional important difference in form would be present if we could be sure, as is often argued, that the first three beatitudes were couched originally in the third person, as in Matthew, rather than all four being expressed in the second person, as in Luke. All this clearly indicates that the fourth beatitude was originally a saying independent of the others and only secondarily added to them by the Q-community.

(4) The three primary beatitudes derive from the historical Jesus, essentially in the form in which they are still preserved in Luke. To be sure, these sayings manifest some of the features of early Christian prophecy (pronouncement of blessing, eschatological content, παράκλησις termin-ology, poverty motif) and thus have sometimes been considered the products of church prophets.[3] However, since Jesus himself was a prophetic figure, marks of prophetic speech alone are not sufficient to identify a

saying as from the church rather than from Jesus. This must be argued on other grounds, and in this case there seem to be no convincing reasons to regard the sayings as secondary.

(5) Luke 6: 22–3/Matt. 5: 11–12 does not derive from Jesus but from the church. Unlike the first three beatitudes, this saying presupposes a church situation in which persons are suffering because of their faith in Jesus as the Son of Man. The references to the person of Jesus (ἕνεκεν ἐμοῦ, Matthew; ἕνεκα τοῦ υἱοῦ τοῦ ἀνθρώπου, Luke) point ineradicably to some reference to faith in the person of Jesus in the original saying and thus point to a post-Easter situation. It is difficult to know whether the references to persecution (Matthew) and exclusion from the synagogue (Luke) were in the original Q-form of the saying or not; if the saying originally included either or both of them, this is further evidence of the origin of the saying in a church *Sitz* rather than in the life of Jesus. Similarly with the phrase τοὺς πρὸ ὑμῶν at the end of the Matthean form: these words make clear that the saying comes from a time in which new prophets have arisen, i.e. after Easter. But even if they were not in the original Q-form of the saying, they only make explicit what was in any case already implied: that the hearers are in the succession of the prophets, which was a belief of the church but not of Jesus. Thus most scholars regard the saying as secondary, and even T. W. Manson was hard-pressed to defend it as belonging to the historical Jesus by assigning it to a different, later stage in Jesus' ministry than the older beatitudes.[4]

It is, of course, possible that this saying originated in the church but not as a saying of a Christian prophet. Additional beatitudes came into being in the course of the development of the tradition by the process of imitation of the beatitudes already in the tradition and by redactional activity. But there are indications that this saying was in fact spoken by a Christian prophet.

The saying speaks for Jesus in the first person, rather than being a general beatitude that could have been spoken by anyone and then attributed to Jesus. This beatitude makes sense only if it was originally conceived as coming from the mouth of Jesus; for the distress of those who are blessed is incurred precisely because of their commitment to the speaker, whether this be expressed as the ἕνεκεν ἐμοῦ of the Matthean form or, as is more likely, the Lukan ἕνεκα τοῦ υἱοῦ τοῦ ἀνθρώπου. The saying is formally a pronouncement of blessing, which, as we have seen, is a characteristic prophetic form. Such pronouncements originate either from wisdom settings or prophetic ones; the basis of this pronouncement is obviously not practical wisdom but prophetic revelation. The original wisdom-form is seen to be 'in the process of transformation into a revealer speech in which a divine mystery is disclosed'.[5] The saying is typical of Q in general, which is not to be seen as a collection of proverb-like catechetical materials for the moral instruction of the early church but as a setting-forth of a radical understanding of life, and a call to such a life, that can only be understood as *revelatory*.[6] Such forms of speech are at home in Jesus' own mouth, and in the mouths of his inspired post-Easter spokes-men, but are not particularly appropriate to teachers and non-charismatic transmitters of tradition.

'The declaring of well-being as a word of power and not simply as an observation leads to the cultic use of the form ... within a well-defined community.'[7] Beardsley's observation about beatitudes in general is especially appropriate as an indication of the prophetic origin of this beatitude, which cannot have been invented simply as a wise saw for general exhortation. The saying rather has the tone of a proclamation in the worship of the gathered, persecuted community, where Christian prophets speak οἰκοδομὴν καὶ παράκλησιν καὶ παραμύθιαν (I Cor. 14: 3) in the name of the risen Lord. The saying interprets the events that are happening to the persecuted community as part and parcel of *Heilsge-schichte*: thus it has always been with God's prophets, in whose succession the persecuted community now stands. The prophetic theme of persecution and the prophetic function of interpreting present events to the community in the perspective of God's saving plan for history are combined in this saying.

The above considerations are sufficient to indicate that the Q-saying probably derives from a post-Easter Christian prophet. There are two additional features of the saying that also point in this direction, but it is not certain that they were in the Q-form of the saying. First, the hearers seem to be addressed as members of a community that numbers prophets in its midst, but this is made explicit only in the Matthean form, which contains the clarifying words τοὺς πρὸ ὑμῶν at the end. If these words were in the Q-form of the saying, which was probably *not* the case, there would be no doubt that the saying comes from a community with a prophetic self-consciousness.[8] But even without these words, the saying expresses a relationship with the prophets of Israel and a sense of being their successors that is typical of the Q-community. This does not mean that every member of the community is addressed as a prophet, but that the pronouncement of blessing originally applied particularly to the prophetic messengers of the community, who were persecuted for propagating the message that Jesus was the Son of Man in the synagogues of Palestine—Syria and who were rejected just as were the earlier messengers to Israel, the prophets. The saying was only applied secondarily to the community as a whole when it was combined with the other beatitudes, which do address the community generally.

A final prophetic feature of this saying is its reference to the Son of Man, if indeed 'Son of Man' belonged to the Q-form. Although this is a disputed point, the recent study of Q has revealed a strong tendency to regard Luke's ἕνεκα τοῦ υἱοῦ τοῦ ἀνθρώπου as original and Matthew's ἕνεκεν ἐμοῦ as secondary, on the basis that Luke never adds the title to his Markan *Vorlage*, and Matthew does tend to substitute 'I' for 'Son of Man' in Markan passages.[9] We shall be showing that 'Son of Man' is a mark of earliest Christian prophetic speech, which strengthens the arguments both that the Q-version of the saying did contain 'Son of Man' and that this helps confirm the saying as coming from a Christian prophet.[10] In the early Palestinian church, confession of Jesus as the Son of Man, i.e. identifying him with the imminently-expected judge of the world, was a more radical statement, and a more important one, than is indicated by our New Testament documents, all of which are from the later Greek-speaking church. But 'Son of Man' is the only christological title found in Q and was both fundamental to the community's confession of Jesus and the cause of its persecution.

The saying Luke 6: 22–3/Matt. 5: 11–12, then, should be seen as having originated as the pronouncement of an early Christian prophet, addressed to missionary preachers of the Q-community, who were told to anticipate persecution and rejection because of their identification of Jesus and the exalted Son of Man in behalf of whom they preached in the Palestinian–Syrian synagogues. The saying was accepted by the Q-community as a saying of Jesus, the risen Lord, and transmitted by it within its stock of Jesus-sayings. When these were arranged into longer complexes, and finally into a written document, this saying was combined with the three beatitudes spoken by the historical Jesus, as the opening words to the Great Sermon of Luke 6: 20–49. The line between sayings of the pre-Easter Jesus and those of the risen Lord, if it ever existed at all in the Q-community, was blurred; the community was addressed by the same Lord in the whole series of pronouncements. And later on, when the whole series of sayings was incorporated within a pre-Easter framework, this saying too became a word of the historical Jesus.

Luke 10: 2–16/Matt. 9: 37 – 10: 40; 11: 20–4

In Q this missionary address was given neither to the Twelve nor to the Seventy(-two) at the time of their being sent out by Jesus, for these historicizing frameworks for the speech belong to the redactional work of Matthew and Luke respectively. But Q did contain a group of sayings that had been combined by the Q-community into one more-or-less unified address on the nature of the disciples' preaching mission, their conduct and equipment for it and their response to their anticipated reception or rejection. This cluster of sayings was not originally a unity.[11] We will examine the independent sayings separately in regard to their possible prophetic origin, before inquiring about the nature of the speech-complex as a whole as it functioned in the Q-community.

Luke 10: 2/Matt. 9: 37—8

The harvest was a common symbol for the eschatological judgment in both Jewish and Christian apocalyptic (Is. 27: 12; Joel 4: 13; IV Ez. 4: 28—32; 9: 17—21; II Baruch 70: 2; Rev. 14: 15—16; Matt. 3: 12 par.; 13: 24—30). The Lord of the harvest sending out laborers into his harvest is thus an eschatological scene. The work of gathering in, 'harvesting', men either for salvation or damnation was not simply a human, historical work but was part of the eschatological events, sometimes attributed to the angels who accompany the Son of Man at his *parousia* (Matt. 13: 41; 24: 31). In this saying Jesus instructs the disciples to pray for God to send $\dot{\epsilon}\rho\gamma\dot{\alpha}\tau\alpha\varsigma$ into the harvest work, participating in the eschatological work shared by angels. The strong verb $\dot{\epsilon}\kappa\beta\dot{\alpha}\lambda\eta$ indicates urgency almost to the point of violence. As in Matt. 10: 23, it is not the extent of the mission field that is the question but the shortness of the time before the end, which compels the believer to pray for God to send out workers quickly, before it is too late.

Did Jesus of Nazareth so instruct his disciples?

The crucial factor is the question of whether or not Jesus in fact did send out missioners during the course of his earthly ministry. If he did, then some of the sayings associated with this mission can probably be attributed to the historical Jesus. If he did not, then all of them should probably be assigned to the church. Both Dibelius and Bultmann consider the sayings to be primary and to have generated a narrative framework for themselves in the tradition, or to have been given one by the evangelists, so that neither the mission of the Twelve nor that of the Seventy was historical.[12] All the concrete evidence for a particular setting in the life of Jesus does seem to derive ultimately from Mark's editorial framework.[13] Yet skepticism concerning the historicity of the pre-Easter missionary trip of the disciples seems to be waning, so that the unhistoricality of the event cannot be used as an argument for the inauthenticity of any of the sayings associated with it.[14] These must be examined from case to case.

The evidence in the case of Luke 10: 2 turns out to be inconclusive. On the one hand, the saying manifests the kind of antithetic parallelism that

Jeremias has argued was characteristic of the sayings of the historical Jesus, which, along with its lack of christology, would argue for its authenticity.[15] On the other hand, ἐργάτας was a church word used of Christian missioners (II Cor. 11: 13; Phil. 3: 2; I Tim. 5: 18; II Tim. 2: 15), and the saying as a whole is quite appropriate in a Christian setting.

If the saying is post-Easter, as it may be, there are a few indications that it was first promulgated by a Christian prophet. The antithetic parallelism was characteristic of prophetic speech as well as of Jesus', and the eschatological urgency is prophetic. The situation pictured in Acts 13: 1–3, in which, in the context of prayer, the Lord responds by speaking through a prophet to call forth new laborers into his harvest, has obvious points of contact with this saying. Even the perspective from which this saying is expressed, in which men are seen as doing the eschatological work of angels, might be considered as a peculiarly prophetic point of view. Yet the prophetic characteristics are not in themselves strong enough to tip the balance in favor of the probability of the inauthenticity of this saying, and unless the inauthenticity can be made probable first, the saying should not be regarded as prophetic. In sum, we may say that the saying is possibly from the historical Jesus but also has some points of contact with Christian prophecy. If the saying did originate in the post-Easter church, then it was probably first spoken by a prophet rather than originating in some other manner.

Luke 10: 3/Matt. 10: 16

'Behold I send you out as sheep/lambs in the midst of wolves' seems to have been the independent saying that was taken up into the Q-discourse at this point. The saying can stand alone and has some tensions with its context in both Matthew and Luke: in Luke 10: 2 it was the 'Lord of the harvest', a third party from the speaker, Jesus, who sends the workers into the harvest; here, Jesus himself sends them. In Matthew 9: 36 and 10: 6, the hearers of the missioners are sheep; here, the missioners themselves are sheep, and their hearers are wolves. The saying must then be judged to have been an originally independent *logion*.

It is difficult to find a satisfactory setting for the saying in the life of Jesus. Even if the mission of the Twelve were historical, there is no evidence that the disciples were ever in peril because of their mission prior to Easter. On the other hand, the setting of hostility and persecution presupposed by the saying does fit the earliest decades of the church's life in Palestine.

Formally, the saying is a prophetic saying. Both the ἰδού and the ἀποστέλλω ὑμᾶς fit the speech-forms known to be characteristic of

Christian prophets.[16] The emphatic ἐγώ, unnecessary for Greek style and therefore probably dropped from the saying by Luke, represents more than the bringing over of the pronoun from the Aramaic; it represents the intense consciousness of the prophet who speaks authoritatively with the ἐγώ of the risen Christ, ἐγώ being relatively rare in the synoptic words of Jesus.

The saying also bears the imprint of motifs of Christian prophetic thought. The reference to sheep among the wolves, rather than indicating a distinctive prophetic dress, refers to the situation of the church (the true Israel) among the wolf-like Gentiles (whose place is now taken by the persecuting Jews).[17] Thus the Jewish people, who traditionally saw themselves as sheep among the Gentile nations of the world (Ps. Sol. 8.28; IV Ez. 5: 18; Tanchuma Toledoth 32*b*; En. 89.55), are here declared to be no better than Gentiles themselves. A prophetic pronouncement of judgment upon 'this generation' is implicit here, just as it was in the preaching of the prophet John the Baptist, whose preaching of repentance and call to baptism placed the Jews in the situation normally accorded to Gentiles (Luke 3: 3; 7: 8 par.). The saying also implies a thoroughly eschatological orientation, not only in the expected persecutions, which are a mark of the End Time and of prophetic speech, but in that the generation to which the missioners are sent is seen to be radically evil, the purported people of God having become themselves the persecuting wolves. As at Qumran, this evil generation is assumed to be the last.[18] There seem to be adequate formal and material grounds to support the assertions previously made by others, that this saying derives from early Christian prophets.[19]

Luke 10: 4/Matt. 10: 9–10

This saying, which has a later form in Mark, was originally in Q simply a series of prohibitions of purse, knapsack, sandals and staff for traveling missioners.[20] It is difficult to determine whether it ever existed independently, or only in connection with the sayings in Luke 10: 5–12. A judgment that the saying is authentic would require positing not only a mission of the disciples during the lifetime of Jesus, which is possible, but accepting Schweitzer's radically apocalyptic view of Jesus' message in conjunction with the mission of the disciples, which is not.[21]

Several features of Christian prophecy inhere in the saying. The radical series of prohibitions presupposes an intensely eschatological view of the mission. The missioners *can* 'travel light', without even the minimal equipment usually carried by the wandering Cynic–Stoic preachers, because they are freed from the normal cares of providing for themselves and the future by the near approach of the Kingdom. And the missioners *must* not be hindered in their journey by the usual traveler's gear, not even taking time for the usual courtesies of exchanging greetings on the road, because of the eschatological urgency of their message. The same tone that reverberates through Matt. 10: 23, a prophetic saying, is also heard here.[22] The radicality of these mission instructions was noticed by the earliest evangelists or their tradition, each of which came to terms with them in his own way: Mark by modifying them to be less radical, permitting sandals and the staff that Q had forbidden (Mark 6: 8–9), Matthew by inserting the consoling word about receiving provisions from people along the way into the list of prohibitions (Matt. 10: 10*b*, removed from its later context in Q), and Luke by indicating that these rigorous demands were only for the special period of Jesus' life but are rescinded for the post-Easter period of the church's mission (22: 35–8). But the radicality remains and is best seen as an expression of the eschatological faith of the early Christian prophets, for whom the End was already dawning, and as analogous to the radical symbolic actions of the prophets. To go barefoot on an extended mission without even the simplest means of provision or protection was a 'sign' that accompanied the missioners' verbal message and gave credibility to it. Further, there is probably an allusion, in the prophetic manner, to the Scriptures. Just as the prophet Elisha once commanded his servant to proceed with his mission in such haste that he must not greet anyone on the road, so also the Christian prophet urges the same rule upon his missioners. This is done not by citing the text and its fulfillment but by seeing the present in terms of the text and using the words of the text for the expression of the present 'fulfilled' reality. The legal form of the saying calls for no hesitation in attributing the saying to a Christian prophet, who functioned as promulgator of 'sentences of holy law'.

Luke 10: 5–12/Matt. 10: 7–15

In this section too we probably have a fusion of sayings that were originally independent units, but they have become so interwoven in the tradition that it is difficult to separate them.[23] As is the case with the above sayings, if there was a pre-Easter mission of the Twelve, then elements of these sayings may go back to the historical Jesus. But the sayings so correspond to the situation of the early church's mission that this section must be judged basically a post-Easter product; whatever authentic elements from Jesus may be contained in it can no longer be separated out.[24]

These instructions too are permeated with early Christian eschatology. The nearness of the Kingdom explicitly proclaimed in 10: 9, 11 as the substance of the missioners' message, the urgency implicit in the directions in 10: 10–11, the reference to ἡμέρα ἐκείνη (Luke 10: 12) or ἡμέρα κρίσεως (Matt. 10: 15) as the validating horizon within which the declaration is made, the pronouncement of blessing and curse that already anticipates and makes present the pronouncement of the final judge, all indicate that the speaker is imbued with the message of the early Christian prophets. The rejection anticipated for God's messengers (10: 6, 10–12) is also a part of the eschatological scenario for the prophets of the last generation.

Miracles accompany the charismatic word (10: 9) and further relate this passage to Christian prophecy. The dramatic act of shaking the dust of unreceptive cities from the feet of the missioners is reminiscent of the symbolic acts of the Old Testament prophets and of Agabus. This is more than the customary shaking of the dust off the feet when the Palestinian Jew returned to the sacred land, to prohibit the holy land from being profaned with soil from pagan countries; here, the customary ritual has become a sign against the cities of Israel herself. As in 10: 3 above, Israel is assigned the role usually reserved for Gentiles because all evil has been summed up in this 'last generation'. Thus not only the symbolic act but the judgmental message embodied in it is of prophetic character.[25]

There are no quotations from the Old Testament in this passage, nor even any allusive uses of Old Testament language. It may be, however, that the images of the hospitality due to the prophetic messenger from the Elijah–Elisha cycle of stories (I Kings 17: 8–16; II Kings 4: 8–10) have influenced the formation of those sayings as they seem to have done in the above cases. In view of the other prophetic features of this passage, Ernst Haenchen is probably correct in his conjecture that Luke 10: 7 is the response of an inspired prophet to the question 'How shall the missionaries be supported?'[26]

In addition to these material traits of Christian prophetic speech, these sayings also manifest the prophetic speech-form. The (ἀμὴν) λέγω ὑμῖν[27] may be properly regarded as an indication of prophetic speech in this *logion*; the *gründend* nature of the formula need not come at the very beginning of a speech to be characteristically prophetic.[28] But even more than the detailed particulars of prophetic speech, the form of the whole argues for the prophetic origin of these sayings: the speaker speaks for God/Jesus/Spirit, so that to accept the words of the speaker is to be encountered directly by the powerful word of God, and to reject the words of the speaker is to reject God/Jesus/Spirit himself. The self-consciousness is the same as in Luke 12: 10/Mark 3: 28–9, which is of prophetic origin.[29] The speaker delivers his message conscious that revelation has been given to him, imparting information about the future judgment that can only be delivered prophetically (10: 5–6, 10–12). This style of speech, if not from Jesus, is appropriate only to his post-Easter prophetic spokesmen.

Luke 10: 13–15/Matt. 11: 20–4

The woes pronounced on the Galilean cities of Bethsaida, Chorazin and Capernaum have often been considered to be of prophetic origin.[30] That they are independent of their present contexts is clear from their different settings in Matthew and Luke and the inappropriateness of pronouncements against Galilean cities delivered as part of a commissioning address to the disciples. This would suggest that the common denominator of these sayings is not their addressees but their source and *traditionsgeschichtlich* settings: Christian prophecy. This hypothesis is supported by the evidence, which suggests the sayings are post-Easter: they seem to look back on the ministry of Jesus as a whole; they regard miracle as a sufficient basis for faith; they refer to two cities that seem to have played no role in the life of Jesus as we otherwise know it. The sayings are thus widely regarded as post-Easter.[31]

The sayings correspond to the profile of prophetic speech both formally and materially. The antithetic parallelism and pronouncement of woe are properly regarded as prophetic forms; the λέγω ὑμῖν of Matthew, if original, is also prophetic. The oracle announces in advance the verdict of the judge of the Last Day, which functions as an implicit call to repentance, in the manner of the Christian prophets. The emphatic positive valuation of miracles, the allusive use of Old Testament words to express the message of the present (Is. 14: 13–15) and the eschatological reversal of roles, in which an oracle directed against the King of Babylon is now directed against Israel, are all characteristics of Christian prophecy. While not demonstrable, it thus seems that these words originated in an early Christian prophetic group whose mission to these Galilean towns had been rebuffed. Since their offer of salvation to these towns was seen as part of the eschatological event itself, and since this offer had been rejected, the prophets respond with the pronouncement of the eschatological doom, spoken from the mouth of the final judge himself through his prophets. Just as the pronouncements of blessing are not exhortations but contain an implied imperative, so the pronouncements of woe are not appeals to repent but still function as such; they are not simply vindictive responses of wounded pride but stand in the tradition of Old Testament prophetic preaching in this regard (e.g. Amos 6: 1–8).

Luke 10: 16/Matt. 10: 40

That this is an originally independent saying with a long and complicated
history in the tradition is seen from the fact that it has five contexts in
New Testament materials (Mark 9: 37; Q; Luke 10: 16; Matt. 10: 40
(= Mark + Q) and John 13: 20), as well as being cited as an independent
saying twice by Justin Martyr (Apol. I.16.10; 63.5). Neither the original
form nor the *Traditionsgeschichte* can any longer be recovered in detail,
though the general outlines of both are clear. For our purposes, all that is
important is that there was available to the Q-community a saying of the
Lord that declared that to receive/hear/reject his messenger was the same
as to receive/hear/reject the Lord himself, and that to receive/hear/reject
the Lord (Jesus) was to receive/hear/reject God.

Although there may have been a pre-Easter original form in which Jesus
asserted that to hear him was to hear God,[32] which would have been an
authentic expression of Jesus' own prophetic self-consciousness, the
present form, in which Jesus himself is the primary sender, is properly
regarded as a post-Easter (?re-) formulation of the church.[33]

The speaker is the risen Jesus, who has his place in the revelatory 'chain
of command' second only to God.[34] Even as the exalted one, he is still the
'sent one', who now sends forth his own missioners to speak his word. The
speaker is to declare his message with the ἐγώ of the exalted Lord, not
reporting what Jesus once said but speaking the word of the Lord in the
first person in the present, so that the hearer is addressed by the risen
Jesus, who speaks in behalf of God. Further prophetic traits are seen in
the rejection that the prophetic messenger anticipates, in the antithetic
parallelism, even in the *chiasmus* that inheres in some forms of the saying
and, even if it is not original, in the ἀμὴν ἀμὴν λέγω ὑμῖν introduction in
the Johannine form of the saying. This prophetic understanding of the
origin and background of the saying is superior to the frequent attempt to
understand the saying in terms of the Jewish institution of the שָׁלִיחַ.[35]
The latter part of the saying, in which Jesus is the 'sent one' from God,
must be understood in prophetic terms, and this is the key to the first part
of the saying, in which Jesus now stands in the place of the sending deity
himself, sending forth his own prophets.

The Address to Missioners in Q

The historicizing settings of this speech at the sending out of the Twelve
in Mark and Matthew, and at the sending out of the Seventy in Luke, are
all artificial, as is seen both from the variety of settings and from the fact
that the setting in each case is in the redaction, not the speech itself. The
instincts of the evangelists were good, however, for in Q the sayings were

not simply a collection of isolated *logia* but had already been gathered into a speech appropriate to the sending out of missioners. This speech probably began with Luke 10: 2 par. and ended with Luke 10: 16 par., containing essentially what is presently contained in Luke 10: 2–16.[36]

We have seen that several of the elements of this speech probably came into being as the utterances of Christian prophets. These individual sayings seem to have been preserved in the Q-community and formed into one speech, which was heard as the address of the risen Lord to the missioners whom he sends out. Not only the individual units but the speech as a whole is the present address of the exalted Lord in the Q-community. It is exegetically significant that items in the speech that originally may not have been heard eschatologically and prophetically are now, at this point in the trajectory, heard as the present eschatologically-oriented word of the risen Jesus. For example, 'the laborer is worthy of his hire' in Luke 10: 7, originally perhaps a proverb placed in Jesus' mouth, becomes in the context of this speech as a whole an affirmation that the eschatological laborers prayed for in 10: 2 are already present in the sending-out of the Q-missioners. The eschatology inherent in some of the prophetic elements that were put together to make this speech-complex now pervades it all. This community does indeed look back to Jesus, who was once sent by the Father, and forward to the return of Jesus as the Son of Man. But in the meantime, Jesus continues to speak to the community in the words of Christian prophets, who preserve the traditional words of Jesus and continue to declare them as the contemporary word of the Lord. Thus even the elements of this speech that may have had a pre-Easter or non-prophetic post-Easter origin are now heard as the present word of the exalted Lord who continues to send out his messengers. Some of these messengers may themselves have been prophets, but not necessarily all of them. The mission is seen from a prophetic point of view, but this is because the speaker is a prophet. In view of the frequent assertion that early Christian prophets were 'wandering', it should be noted here that it is those who are addressed who 'wander', not necessarily the prophet-speaker of this mission charge himself.

This speech implies a somewhat settled, structured community, from which wandering missioners are sent out and to which they return. The very existence of the Q-tradition that precipitated a Q-document also implies a settled community. We should probably think of a scene resembling Acts 13: 1–3 as a representative event in the life of this community and the setting for such a missionary charge as this speech.

Luke 10: 21–2/Matt. 11: 25–7

The once-popular view that Matt. 11: 25–30 was an original unit composed of three strophes, to be understood as originating in the context of Hellenistic Christianity, has been dissolved by more recent study. Although no consensus has emerged concerning this 'umstrittenester Textabschnitt in Q', the following positions are well supported in recent literature and are here adopted.[37] (1) Matthew 11: 28–30 was not an original part of this sayings-unit, nor was it included in the Q collection. (2) Luke 10: 21–2 par. was originally two independent sayings, which were already combined in Q. (3) Luke 10: 21 is an authentic saying of Jesus, at least in its original form. The hypothesis here argued for is that Luke 10: 22 is a post-Easter expansion of this original saying of Jesus made by a Christian prophet. The secondary nature of the saying is readily apparent: Jesus speaks of himself absolutely as the 'Son', a manifest post-Easter christology; he claims to possess a knowledge of God that others may possess only by his mediation; the saying itself is a different form from the saying to which it is joined (10: 21 is a thanksgiving prayer, addressed to God; 10: 22 is a revelatory declaration addressed to men). The union of the two sayings is secondary but not arbitrary; nor is it a matter simply of *Stichwortverbindung* (ἀπεκάλυψας, verse 21; ἀποκαλύψαι, verse 22). The second saying presupposes the first and is something of an interpretation of it, re-presenting it in a different light.[38]

There is some evidence that this interpretative expansion was made by a Christian prophet. It is characteristic of such prophets that they take up an earlier tradition and re-present it with their own interpretative expansions, so that a saying that might previously have been heard as the past message of the pre-Easter Jesus is heard in the prophet's re-presentation as the present word of the exalted Lord. The thanksgiving prayer as it circulated independently in the pre-Q tradition seems to have already had a historicizing introduction, reflected in different forms in both Matthew and Luke. But when the post-Easter saying of 10: 22, which mediates the present address of the risen Lord, is added to the traditional saying, 10: 21 is now heard in a new way, so that it too expresses the prophetic self-consciousness of the Q-community.[39]

This prophetic self-consciousness is also manifest in the way the saying presupposes a revelatory 'chain' as in Rev. 1: 1–3. The Father gives the revelation to the Son, who is the exclusive mediator of revelation to the community. The understanding of the 'Son' in this passage is not the content of the revelation but the presupposition of it, i.e. the Son is a constituent part of the revelatory configuration presupposed by Christian prophets. The 'Spirit' was also sometimes inserted as a link in this revelatory chain, as in Rev. 1: 1–3 and Matt. 28: 18–20, neither of which should be explained in terms of trinitarian speculation but in terms of the prophetic context from which they emerged.[40] The mutual and exclusive knowledge of the 'Father' and the 'Son' should thus no longer be explained as related to Hellenistic mysticism or the adaptation of a Jewish proverb.[41] The prevailing tendencies to interpret the saying against the background of Jewish prophecy and apocalyptic are given further support, and made more precise, by our seeing the saying as originating from Christian prophecy, which has the same background.[42] The wisdom motifs inherent in the saying, where the role of σοφία as the mediatrix of revelation is played by the exalted Lord (not the earthly Jesus), are also an indication of the prophetic character of this saying; for Christian prophecy, like apocalyptic generally, included a significant admixture of wisdom motifs and materials.[43]

Several recent interpreters of Q are agreed that the saying claims to reveal the eschatological significance of the events that have recently transpired and are presently transpiring in the Q-community: the advent and exaltation of Jesus, the sending of the Q-missioners (some of whom were prophets, the re-appearance of prophecy being understood eschatologically), the curses being pronounced on non-believing Israel. Here as elsewhere prophecy functions as interpreter of events. This is the meaning to the Q-community of the mysterious ταῦτα of verse 21.[44] This *heilsgeschichtlich*, eschatological kind of insight into the meaning of history (rather than gnostic or mystic 'knowledge') is what is meant by the key verb (ἐπι) γινώσκω.[45] The combined sayings have become a veritable manifesto of Christian prophecy, affirming that revelation continues as the risen Jesus (understood in terms both of the Son of Man and of the Wisdom traditions) interprets through his messengers the meaning of the history they are experiencing and have experienced. The worship setting that the saying presupposes is appropriate to Christian prophecy as seen in our reconstruction.[46]

Some further details confirm that the saying is from a Christian prophet. The saying has a carefully constructed form, verse 22 being a neat four-liner, which has rhythm and rhyme even when translated into Aramaic.[47] The clearest formal parallel in the literature of the first century is found in our prime example of Christian prophecy, Rev. 11: 17–18. The *Hodayoth* from Qumran, products of an inspired prophetic interpreter of the community's history and experience, is the next-nearest example.[48] The declaration with which verse 22 begins, πάντα μοι παρεδόθη ὑπὸ τοῦ πατρός μου, has obvious affinities in both form and content with Matt. 28: 18b, ἐδόθη μοι πᾶσα ἐξουσία ἐν οὐρανῷ καὶ ἐπὶ τῆς γῆς which is certainly post-Easter and probably prophetic, as will be argued below. The often-noticed similarities of 10: 21–2 to the Johannine sayings of Jesus and to I Cor. 2: 6–16 should, in the light of the above, be explained not in terms of a common gnosticizing or Hellenistic–mystical approach but in terms of their common denominator, Christian prophecy. The acknowledged prophetic connections of the Pauline and Johannine passages argue for prophetic connections of the synoptic passage as well. It is thus no surprise that Luke recognizes the prophetic nature of the saying, introducing it with the same phrases (πνεῦμα ἅγιον, ἠγαλλιάσατο) with which he introduces prophetic speech in 1: 14–15, 47, nor that contemporary scholars have suggested that the saying was of prophetic origin.[49] This understanding of the saying's origin also answers the objection of Stauffer that no one would have dared invent such a saying for Jesus and place it in his mouth, since the prophets regarded themselves as speaking for the risen Jesus and were heard as such.

Luke 10: 23–4/Matt. 13: 16–17

This isolated saying, placed by Matthew and Luke independently in their respective contexts, has been regarded as an authentic saying of Jesus by even the most skeptical critics.[50] Yet the saying, brief as it is, does exhibit several features of Christian prophecy: the form of a pronouncement of blessing, the (ἀμὴν) λέγω ὑμῖν formula, the eschatological orientation that sees the *eschaton* as already breaking in, the eschatological reversal in which the last generation obtains the privileges of the people of God from which the traditional chosen people are excluded. Thus examination of the saying in the light of our reconstruction of early Christian prophecy does give some support to the suggestion sometimes made that even here we have a saying of the exalted Jesus rather than a saying from the pre-Easter tradition.[51] If the saying is from a Christian prophet, the new things 'seen' and 'heard' would not be only the eschatological realities in general, which are seen to be breaking into the present in the working of miracles and gift of the Spirit, but would refer to the new revelations in particular, which Christian prophets 'see' and 'hear'. Even if the saying is pre-Easter, it would tend to be heard in this latter sense in a community that experienced the phenomenon of prophecy, such as the Q-community. But since there are no compelling reasons for denying the saying to Jesus of Nazareth, and since the features of Christian prophecy manifest in it were also characteristic of Jesus' own speech, or could have been impressed on the saying in the transmission process, it is probably better to continue to regard this saying as authentic. Even so, it is an excellent example of how a pre-Easter saying of Jesus would be heard in the early Christian prophetic community as a saying of the exalted Lord addressing the post-Easter situation.

Luke 11: 29–32/Matt. 12: 38–42
The Sign of Jonah

The original form of 11: 29*a* par., the absolute refusal to give a validating sign, goes back to Jesus himself, and had not been modified in the form of the saying that came to Mark (8: 12).[52] It also seems to me likely that 11: 31–2 par. is an independent saying that derives from Jesus himself, since the sayings do not point to the person of Jesus, but the neuter πλεῖον in each saying refers to the presence of the Kingdom. On this basis even Bultmann attributed them to Jesus, while Käsemann, who agrees that the content is appropriate to Jesus, attributes them to the church on the basis of their form.[53] The church may have taken the form from Jesus, however, or impressed a post-Easter form on original pronouncements of Jesus; so, owing to the christological reticence of the sayings, it is better to regard them as authentic. The saying regarding the sign of Jonah that binds the two sayings together is widely accepted as a secondary development.[54] The Q-form of this addition is best preserved by Luke, Matthew's addition being an allegorical elaboration of what was once a prophetic declaration. The two original sayings of Jesus (Luke 11: 29*a* par. and 11: 31–2 par.), now fused into a single sayings-unit by the prophetic addition of 11: 29*b*–30, were then re-presented as *in toto* the word of the exalted Lord to the situation of the Q-community.

The evidence that the key secondary material in this sayings-complex comes from a prophet rather than some other church figure is as follows: (1) its allusive use of the Old Testament, including its interest in an Old Testament prophet; (2) its eschatological perspective, including its use of τῇ γενεᾷ ταύτῃ to refer to the last generation; (3) its use of 'Son of Man' in the first person, at the same time identifying the earthly Jesus and the Son of Man;[55] and (4) the form 'eschatological correlative', which was used by the prophets of the Q-community. To these could be added the themes in the traditional sayings of Jesus that were particularly attractive to this anonymous Q-prophet and attracted him to them: the interest in the significance of miracles (which accompanied prophetic phenomena in the Q-community) and the pronouncement of proleptic eschatological judgment. In particular, the motif of the reversal of roles at the *eschaton*, when the traditional people of God will be so no longer, was a favorite theme of church prophets.

Luke 11: 39–52/Matt. 23
Against the Pharisees

The historical Jesus spoke against some forms of Pharisaic piety, so that some of his words may underlie, or be contained in, the series of Q-oracles against the Pharisees. The pronouncements against cleaning up the outside but not the inside, and tithing garden herbs while neglecting justice (11: 39, 42*a*), for instance, may be rooted in Jesus' own preaching. Even the form of these pronouncements might derive from Jesus; for in Aramaic the repeated ὅτι might represent ‫די‬ , which in Jesus' mouth would have meant 'who', (rather than ὅτι = 'because'), so that the sayings would not have been a blanket condemnation of the Pharisees *per se* (with some of whom Jesus was often in friendly conversation) but would have meant 'Woe to the Pharisees who ...'.[56] Such criticisms of Pharisees are found in their own writings. But these possibilities are the most that may be said concerning the authenticity of this series of sayings. The form of the discourse as it appears in both Matthew and Luke, and as it appeared in Q, represents a group that has marked itself off (or been marked off) completely from Pharisaic Judaism as such, against which it launches indiscriminate broadsides.

The present settings of this discourse are altogether the work of the evangelists. Matthew has combined these oracles with materials from his own tradition and inserted them into the life-of-Jesus framework provided by Jesus' warnings against the scribes in Mark 12: 38–40. Less happily, Luke has incorporated the woes into the table-talk at the house of a Pharisee (in Samaria?!). In Q, the speech appeared entirely without a narrative framework, as a series of seven woes followed by an oracle of doom.[57] The original order of these woes in Q has been jumbled in the tradition and by the editing of both Matthew and Luke, and can no longer be recovered. It appears, however, that Matthew has preserved the general pattern of Q, which consisted of seven woes, with the climactic seventh woe concerning the treatment of prophets having been elaborated by further prophetic material, an oracle of doom. The Lukan form of two groups of three woes, separated by a little dialogue, with the initial woe rewritten as a transitional piece, can then be seen as his effort to accommodate an inappropriate series of oracles to a dinner-party setting.

The more clearly the Q-form of the speech becomes visible, the more closely it is seen to be related to early Christian prophets. The woe-form itself is a prophetic form, and the sevenfold pronouncement of woe is characteristic of the Christian prophecy of the Apocalypse. But, as Bultmann and Schulz have noticed, the woe-form is sometimes fused with the law-form, both in the proclamation of definite legal decrees, as in 11: 42, and in the general radicalizing of the law's demand found throughout the series.[58] This proclamation of the divine law of the Last Days is the function of the prophet.

The series of oracles throughout presupposes this eschatological orientation of early Christian prophecy. The threat against τῆς [ἐσχάτης] γενεᾶς ταύτης with which the series ends makes explicit the eschatological tone of the whole. The prophetic—eschatological perspective from which the woes are spoken is manifest in the sharpening of the demands of the Torah as in 11: 39—40, for the near advent of the *eschaton* brings with it both the demand to keep the total intent of the law and the ability to do so, since this-worldly considerations no longer count. The criticisms of Pharisaic piety here found are thus analogous to those of the Zealots and Qumran covenanters, both of which were eschatological communities with prophets in their ranks. The latter-day prophetic revelation has made it clear to the community that the eschatological reversal of roles has occurred: the Pharisees, claiming to be the leaders of Israel, are in fact the false leaders of Israel. It is rather the rejected and persecuted Q-community that is the eschatological Israel, whose prophets pronounce judgments upon purported Israel, very much as the prophet of Revelation condemns those who 'say they are Jews but are not' (Rev. 2: 9; 3: 9). No attempt is made at converting the Pharisees; it is eschatologically 'too late' for that, as the proleptic verdict of condemnation of the judge of the Last Day is already pronounced by his prophetic spokesmen.[59] Such pronouncements could have been made only by those convinced of their charismatic authorization to speak for the Lord himself. That the supposed guardians of the purity of Israel are themselves hidden contaminators of Israel's purity, corrupting the unsuspecting, is not the carping grumbling of those who resent the Pharisaic piety or are repelled by it, but the pronouncement of those who claim a divinely-given ability to see beneath the surface of things, to interpret the present as it really is. The basis for such authoritative speaking can only be the revelation claimed by the prophetic band in the Q-community.

The prophetic nature of this series of woes becomes explicit in the climactic pronouncement, which deals with the relation of the Pharisees to prophets. Just as the final beatitude (Luke 6: 22 par.), which deals with prophets, is the most extensive, so also here. As in the beatitudes, the conviction of the Q-community that true prophets must suffer comes to expression here. The Pharisees attempt to disavow the deeds of their ancestors, who killed the prophets of Israel, by building memorial tombs for them, but in fact they show that they are no better than their fathers; for they honor only the prophets of the past and, like their fathers, reject the prophets of the present (11: 47—8). Here is the expression of a continuing conflict between the Pharisaic leaders of the Palestinian synagogues and the prophets of the Q-community. This is echoed in the declaration of 11: 52 par.: a dispute has been raging concerning who has the authority to open the Kingdom to men. The Pharisees claim this authority of the 'keys' by insisting on keeping the Law, oral and written. The Christian prophets claim this authority of the 'keys' by proclaiming Jesus as the coming Son of Man, the keeping of whose word will be the criterion of acceptance on the Last Day. The prophets were without political and religious power and received the worst of this conflict, interpreting their rejection in terms of that persecution which is always the mark of the true prophet.

This point of view is summed up in the final declaration of the Q series of woes, Luke 11: 49–51 par. Schulz's argument that this section is a separate oracle from a later community, only secondarily bound to the woe-oracle, is unconvincing; it is better to see it with Bultmann, Manson, Hoffmann and Suggs as having been an elaboration of the final woe already in Q.[60] While Matthew has made considerable redactional modifications, the saying as it appeared in Q has been preserved almost intact by Luke. The most debated point concerns whether ἀποστόλους appeared already in Q, or is to be attributed to Luke.[61] If Q already spoke of ἀπόστολοι being sent by Wisdom, which does not seem likely to me, the term would have been understood of traveling missioners generally, as in the Didache, not in the somewhat ecclesiastical sense of Luke. At only one point is it clear that Matthew has preserved the Q-saying better than Luke: ἀμήν stood in Q, and Luke has changed it to ναί. The reasons for this judgment are as follows. (1) Matthew has no demonstrable tendency to add ἀμήν to his sources; he inserts ἀμήν into a Markan context twice at most (24: 2/Mark 13: 2 and 19: 23/Mark 10: 23). Of the twelve Markan contexts containing ἀμήν incorporated by Matthew, he omits ἀμήν from three. (2) There is no instance where Matthew changes a ναί in his source to an ἀμήν. (3) There are eleven Q-sayings in which Matthew has ἀμήν and Luke does not. In fact, Luke never has ἀμήν in a Q-passage. On a purely mechanical reckoning of Q, one would therefore have to say that ἀμήν was not found in Q. Few have been willing to do this.[62] The more probable solution is that Luke has systematically suppressed ἀμήν when it did occur in his sources. He retains only three of Mark's thirteen instances, plus three from sources peculiar to him. Luke seems to be concerned to purge the tradition of foreign words not understandable by his Greek readers and entirely eliminates ὡσαννά, ἀββά, ἔλοι, ῥαββί etc., which we know appeared in his *Vorlagen*.

The saying concluded, then, with the solemn, prophetic formula ἀμὴν λέγω ὑμῖν. This clear indication of prophetic speech is augmented by other points of contact with Christian prophecy that suggest a prophetic origin for the *logion*: the concern with the sending of prophets, who alone certainly appeared in the Q-saying; the conviction that prophets suffer persecution; the view that the guilt of previous generations is summed up in the last generation (Rev. 18: 24); the pronouncement of judgment in the name of the risen Jesus who will shortly come as judge; the prophetic formula διὰ τοῦτο.[63] We have seen that all these features were characteristic of early Palestinian Christian prophecy. Their coherence in this one saying argues strongly for its prophetic origin.

In this regard, what are we to make of the unique formula that introduces this saying, διὰ τοῦτο ἡ σοφία τοῦ θεοῦ εἶπεν? This introduction has sometimes been taken to mean that the saying was taken from a lost wisdom book from which Jesus is pictured as quoting by Q.[64] In the light of such passages as Prov. 1: 20–31, it is possible that the saying was originally taken from such a wisdom writing, where the saying was given as an oracle of personified wisdom. But in the Q-context this should not be seen as placing this saying in the mouth of the earthly Jesus. The saying is the present address of the risen Lord, as the woe-oracle context and the concluding ἀμὴν λέγω ὑμῖν indicate, and we should think rather of a Christian prophet introducing the saying from the supposed wisdom document into his speech of the risen Jesus. On the hypothesis of a quotation from a wisdom document, the quotation should be regarded as forming part of the materials that the prophet uses to express the message of the exalted Lord. The context in Q has no pre-Easter narrative framework at all, so we should not think in terms of the Q-community's retrojecting these words into the earthly Jesus' situation.

The theory that a wisdom book is here quoted has not found general support. Already Plummer had noted that words from a written book would be likely to be introduced by λέγει rather than εἶπεν, and most recent students of Q have abandoned the hypothesis of a lost wisdom writing.[65] So efforts have been made to understand the phrase as equivalent to 'God in his wisdom says' or as 'a variant for the normal rabbinic "the Holy Spirit" says or "the divine righteousness" says, meaning "God says".'[66] Neither of these is convincing, especially since the content – the suffering of God's prophets – is not found in connection with personified wisdom. We do not seem to have a general *theologoumenon* that is here taken up by either Jesus or the prophets, but a saying the content of which suggests it first came into being among Christian prophets. This might lead us to ask whether the difficult introductory formula itself is an expression of the prophetic form of speech. Lührmann has observed that ἡ σοφία τοῦ θεοῦ εἶπεν is reminiscent of the prophetic formula כה אמר יהוה.[67] The analogy with this formula would also explain the presence of the aorist εἶπεν in the midst of the present-tense address. As an alternative possibility to the view that a Christian prophet here mediates the word of the risen Jesus by quoting a lost wisdom-apocalypse, serious consideration should be given to the view that the Q-prophet is here speaking directly for the risen Jesus, who is identified with pre-existent Wisdom. Suggs has shown convincingly that the Q-community did not identify the *earthly* Jesus as the incarnation of Wisdom but saw Jesus as a messenger of Wisdom.[68] Suggs says 'the *last* of Wisdom's messengers', (emphasis mine) but the view proposed here would see all the prophets — Old Testament, John, Jesus and the Q-prophets — as messengers of Wisdom, all standing in the same series. The earthly Jesus was not therefore the *last*, chronologically speaking, but the *decisive* messenger of Wisdom. The exalted Jesus is also interpreted by the Q-community in terms of the figure of Wisdom. The Q-community used both the figure of the Son of Man and the figure of Wisdom to interpret the exaltation of Jesus, but here the Wisdom image dominates. What is implied in other Q-sayings (e.g. 10: 22) becomes explicit here: the exalted Jesus is the pre-existent Wisdom of God (cf. I Cor. 1: 30), who foresaw the sweep of history in which she/he would send her/his prophets, who would be rejected in all generations, including this present final one.[69] Σοφία θεοῦ functions in the same role in the revelatory chain characteristic of prophetic thinking as υἱὸς [θεοῦ] in 10: 22 (cf. Rev. 1: 1–3) and παράκλητος in the Fourth Gospel. The revelatory event expressed in this oracle would then be as follows: at the climax of the series of woes, the Christian prophet delivers to the community the revelation of the ancient decrees of heavenly Wisdom, now identified with the exalted Jesus, which decreed the sending of prophets throughout the generations until their repeated rejection resulted in the culmination of guilt in the final generation, which has now arrived. Not only does this interpretation of the exalted Jesus in terms of personified Wisdom mesh with the other wisdom motifs sprinkled throughout the woe-pronouncements, the saying is somewhat related to apocalyptic modes of thought in that both have a kind of retrojection into the past of a speaker who 'predicts' what has actually already occurred in the author's present.[70] Apocalyptic and wisdom are fused in this saying, which, as we have seen, is characteristic of Christian prophecy.

Luke 12: 2–12/Matt. 10: 26–33
Exhortation to Fearless Confession

This section of Q is a complex unit with a complicated history in the tradition, which can be recovered only partially. There were at least five originally independent units: verses 2–3, 4–7, 8–9, 10, 11–12, some of which may themselves be composite.[71] Within the Q-community these sayings seem to have been fused into one speech-complex. Apart from the prophetic characteristics of the individual sayings to be examined below, the sayings-cluster as a whole is permeated with the themes of near-expectation of the End, persecution by Jewish opponents and the Christian's conduct in this eschatological situation – all of which is appropriate to Christian prophets. It is not unexpected that this group of sayings has been regarded *en bloc* and in each of its parts as sayings of the risen Jesus through church prophets.[72] The extent to which this general impression is true can only be tested in the examination of the individual sayings.

12: 10

I will begin with the saying that most clearly seems to have originated as Christian prophecy. The saying is an independent oracle that rests uncomfortably in all its contexts. The Q-setting, which is preserved in Luke, cannot have been its original context, for the Q-form declares that a word spoken against the Son of Man can be forgiven, which contradicts the immediately preceding saying. It was apparently attracted to this context in Q by the catchwords πᾶς ὅς and υἱὸς τοῦ ἀνθρώπου in verses 8–9 and 10 and, as we shall see, by the fact that it was derived from the same historical setting as other sayings in this cluster, i.e. a circle of early Christian prophets. In Matthew, the saying is preserved in the context of the Beelzebul controversy only because that is the setting in Mark (3: 20–30). But the Markan setting also turns out to be secondary, as is clear from the following observations. The subject matter of verses 28–9 is forgiveness, which has no point of contact with 24–7. In verses 24–7, the sayings attempt to include the hearer and reason with him, but the tone changes at verse 28: the hearer receives a pronouncement, over against him, not necessarily in the hostile sense, but the note of appeal and persuasion is replaced by that of authoritative declaration. The promise of παραβολαί to follow is made in verse 23, and verses 24–7 are somewhat parabolic, but not verses 28–9. The Holy Spirit is not discussed in verses 24–7 but is integral to 28–9. The lack of connection between verses 27 and 28 is also indicated by the introductory formula with which verse 28 begins: ἀμὴν λέγω ὑμῖν. The saying is thus to be interpreted apart from its context as originally an independent saying.

There are several reasons for doubting that the saying is from Jesus. First and most telling of these is that in all its forms the saying exalts the Spirit to a superlative degree and makes blasphemy against the Spirit the ultimate sin. Thus the saying comes from an environment and speaker that explicitly exalted the Spirit in a most radical degree. There can be little doubt that Jesus himself was something of a 'charismatic type'. But alongside this datum must be placed the equally-certain fact that references to the πνεῦμα are amazingly scarce in the synoptic tradition and practically absent from the tradition of Jesus' words.[73] Mark 3: 29/Luke 12: 10/ Matt. 12: 32 is the only saying in the synoptic gospels in which Jesus refers to himself as the bearer of the Spirit. It is therefore extremely unlikely that a saying that so exalts the Holy Spirit belongs among the authentic sayings of the historical Jesus. The earliest church, on the other hand, knew itself possessed of the Holy Spirit and, in the absence of Jesus, would tend to exalt the Spirit with which he was identified as the risen Lord.

The limitation of forgiveness pronounced so arbitrarily also makes the saying difficult to regard as authentic. Not only does the *logion* limit the divine forgiveness — in itself very inappropriate to Jesus, for whom the pronouncement of judgment rather than the limitation of forgiveness would seem more fitting — but the limitation is imposed for dogmatic reasons, i.e. is pronounced against those who are guilty of theological, and not just moral, error. The saying is easily intelligible as the answer to a charge that was raised against the early Christian community in its Jewish environment, a fundamental and blasphemous charge, a charge that not only denied that the power impelling the Christian movement was from God but described it in some way blasphemous to the Christian community: that it was from Satan or some such. As Norman Perrin has pointed out, 'Finally, the saying echoes the beginning of a consciousness of a problem that was to haunt the church for decades, the problem of the comparative failure of the Jewish mission.'[74] It is not easy to find such a suitable *Sitz im Leben Jesu*, and the saying should be regarded as having originated in the early church.

The saying is extant in several variations (Mark 3: 28–9; Luke 12: 10; Matt. 12: 31, 32; Did. 11.7, GT 44; GB 5.2), but these are all variations of the two basic forms, the Markan form and the Q-form. Of these, the Markan form is the more primitive.[75]

A part of this earliest pre-Markan saying may go back to Jesus himself: the initial declaration, staggering in its radicality, that all sins shall be forgiven to men, however much they may blaspheme. It is not difficult to imagine Jesus making such an announcement, since several independent streams of tradition clearly portray him as announcing forgiveness even to those considered blasphemous by the pious (Mark 2: 5–10; Matt. 11: 19/ Luke 7: 35; John 7: 53 – 8: 11; Luke 7: 47–9; 15: 1–32). This unconditional declaration of universal forgiveness might be a pre-Easter kernel that was taken up by an early Christian prophet and expanded into the following chiastic form, which is the ancestor of both the Markan and Q-forms of the saying:[76]

ἀφεθήσεται πάντα τὰ ἁμαρτήματα τοῖς υἱοῖς τῶν ἀνθρώπων
ὅσα ἐὰν βλασφημήσωσιν
ὃς δ᾽ ἂν βλασφημήσῃ εἰς τὸ πνεῦμα τὸ ἅγιον
οὐκ ἔχει ἄφεσιν ἀλλὰ ἔνοχός ἐστιν αἰωνίου ἁμαρτήματος

That this saying, whether or not it contains a saying of the historical Jesus as its kernel, is from a Christian prophet is probable for the following reasons. (1) The introductory formula ἀμὴν λέγω ὑμῖν is an indication of prophetic speech, if it originally belonged with the oracle and was not secondarily added in the tradition. (2) The saying is a *chiasmus*, in the particular form 'sentence of holy law' used by Christian prophets. (3) As such a sentence of holy law, it has a definite legal tone, formally akin to those rabbinic declarations of types of sins that may not be forgiven in the Age to Come. It is the divine law of the Last Day that is proleptically announced. (3) The eschatology inherent in such a pronouncement relates it to Christian prophets, who anticipated the Last Judgment and made it present. The divine verdict of the eschatological judge who is shortly to appear is already pronounced in advance by his servants the prophets.

It is to be noted in passing that this understanding of the origin of the *logion* clarifies an exegetical problem that has long burdened commentators.[77] The reason the sinner has no forgiveness εἰς τὸν αἰῶνα but is guilty of αἰωνίου ἁμαρτήματος is not that he has committed a sin that is beyond the scope of God's forgiveness or that he has entered into a state in which repentance, and therefore forgiveness, is impossible. Rather, the ultimate character of the sin derives from the fact that the judgment is pronounced in an ultimate situation from which there is no appeal: the Last Judgment.[78] In this respect the prophetic *logion* is like the pronouncement in Rev. 22: 11, 'Let the evildoer still do evil, and the filthy still be filthy, and the righteous still do right, and the holy still be holy.' There too it is not a matter of the sinner having entered into a *state* in which he can do no other, but the affirmation is surrounded by the words ὁ καιρὸς γὰρ ἐγγύς ἐστιν and Ἰδοὺ ἔρχομαι ταχύ.

We return to our list of reasons for considering the *logion* prophetic. (4) The nature of the authority claimed in this *logion* — an authority that does not hesitate to announce universal forgiveness coupled with the pronouncement of eternal judgment — is such that it could have been claimed only by a charismatic. (5) C. K. Barrett has suggested that the saying was formed as something of a pesher on Is. 63: 3–11.[79] This suggestion must not be rejected simply because the passage does not quote or allude to the Old Testament text directly, for this was not the manner in which Christian prophets dealt with Scripture. The Old Testament text portrays a divine figure with bloody garments, who comes both to judge

and to save. Following this is an exclamation of praise to God for his
mercy and then a lament that nevertheless some 'grieved his holy spirit',
which God 'had put in the midst of them', so that God 'turned to be their
enemy'. The possibility exists that to early Christian prophecy this passage
revealed the advent and suffering of Jesus, by virtue of which the church,
empowered by the Spirit, announced the eschatological day of forgiveness,
which is the day of judgment for those who do not believe and 'grieve his
holy spirit'. This possibility is strengthened by the fact that at least one
Christian prophet did later twice use the language of this Is. 63 passage
with reference to the Christ-event (Rev. 14: 20; 19: 15), but the connection
is fragile and little can be based on it alone.

(6) The saying's concern with the Spirit, which in wide circles of
Palestinian Judaism would mean the Spirit of Prophecy, indicates that the
saying, if secondary, more likely derives from a circle that claimed the
spirit of prophecy than from a non-charismatic setting, e.g. a scribal trans-
mitter and expander of the tradition. Furthermore, a prophetic group,
claiming by its very existence to have the Spirit, would be the most likely
to run foul of those Jews who held that the Spirit (of Prophecy) had ceased
since Ezra or Malachi; they would invite their derision and be provoked to
utter, in the name of the exalted Lord, just such a rejoinder as is found in
this saying.

(7) These considerations of form and content argue for the prophetic
origin of this saying. This would seem to be confirmed by the oldest
extant interpretation of the saying outside the New Testament, in Did.
11.7, which contains the injunction, 'While a prophet is speaking by the
Spirit, you must not test nor examine him. For "every sin will be forgiven,
but this sin will not be forgiven".' The prophet is here held to be inviolable,
and his word beyond question, a tenet also reflected in 11.11: 'Every
genuine prophet ... must not be judged by you. His judgment rests with
God.' Both these categorical injunctions against testing prophecy are
immediately qualified, and rule-of-thumb tests to determine whether a
prophet is true or false are in fact provided — which would suggest that the
injunctions against testing prophets, with their accompanying 'word of the
Lord', are authoritative traditional material taken up and modified. This
would mean that the connection between Mark 3: 28—9 par. and Christian
prophecy is very old indeed. In view of the various strands of evidence for
this connection presented above, it is not too much to suggest that the
tradition found in the Didache represents an actual memory of this
connection, and that this oldest extant interpretation of the saying is still
the correct one: the earliest form of the unforgivable-sin *logion* is to be
interpreted in terms of Christian prophecy and is, in fact, its product.

This prophetic saying was taken up by the Q-community and re-formed to speak to its situation. Since the Q-form of the saying is also in the form of a sentence of holy law, preserving the eschatological fervor of the original saying while modifying the form from ABB¹A¹ to ABA¹B¹, and since the saying has now become a Son-of-Man saying, this reformulation was probably done by a prophet of the Q-community, who takes up this traditional prophetic saying and re-presents it as the *au courant* word of the exalted Lord.[80] If the saying was still in circulation in Aramaic, the Q-prophet may have understood the לְבַר נָשָׁא of the first line, rendered τοῖς υἱοῖς τῶν ἀνθρώπων in the oldest Greek form, by κατὰ τοῦ υἱοῦ τοῦ ἀνθρώπου. A particular problem is in view as the Q-prophet deals with this text: that some have 'spoken against the Son of Man'. The Q-prophet wishes to declare that this is a forgivable offense – only speaking against the Holy Spirit is unforgivable. The second half of the saying has lost its cutting edge and has now become a *theologoumenon*, from which conclusions may now be drawn. The prophet's conclusion, the new 'sentence of holy law' that he is promulgating in the name of the risen Lord, is found in the reformulated first half of the saying, which now receives the emphasis: speaking against the Son of Man *can* be forgiven. The popular understanding of this emphasis has been that in the Q-community a kind of *heilsgeschichtlich* consciousness has developed that presupposes two periods: the pre-Easter incognito lowliness of the Son of Man and the post-Easter period of the Spirit. The 'speaking against the Son of Man' is thus often supposed to refer to those who rejected the ministry of the pre-Easter Jesus and who, this *logion* declares, can now be forgiven.[81] An alternative understanding has been that the saying is a ruling on those Christians who, under duress from non-Christian Jews, have (temporarily) renounced their faith in the Son of Man: they can in fact be forgiven. Since 'Son of Man' in Q rarely if ever refers to the lowly historical Jesus, but usually refers to the apocalyptic, exalted and coming Son of Man, this latter interpretation is preferable to the former one. But an even better interpretation has been proposed by Richard Edwards, who correctly perceives that the saying is entirely an eschatological statement, looking not back at the past history of Jesus but forward to the imminent coming of the Son of Man and outward to the mission, the eschatological harvest.[82] In the mission of the Q-community to the Jewish population of Palestine—Syria, forgiveness is announced not only to those who rejected the earthly Jesus but even to those who have reviled Jesus, the exalted Son of Man who is soon to come as judge. But those who reject this last offer of forgiveness mediated through the Spirit-inspired Q-prophets and revile them and it – for such there is no forgiveness, ever. The presupposition of the prophetic origin and reinterpretation of the saying thus seems to offer the most satisfactory explanation at every point in its trajectory.

Luke 12: 11–12/Matt. 10: 19–20

This too is an originally independent saying, which has found its way into the pre-Markan apocalypse (13: 11), at which point Luke uses it again in modified form (21: 14–15). The Johannine community seems to have recoined it as one of the Paraclete–prophet sayings in John 14: 26.

The present forms of the saying are certainly secondary. The persecutions presupposed by the saying are a post-Easter experience of the disciples. Talk of the Holy Spirit was rare for Jesus, or foreign to him altogether, as we have seen in the previous discussion. The terms ἀρχάς and ἐξουσίας in the Lukan version are certainly post-Easter, though they probably were not present in the Q-version. The παραδίδωμι terminology in the Markan/Matthean version reflects the post-Easter influence of the passion story on the description of the disciples' persecutions.[83] Due to the overlapping of Mark and Q, the Q-form of the saying is difficult to reconstruct, but there is no reason to believe it was free of all these secondary elements. It could be, as Werner Kümmel has argued, that there was a pre-Easter form of the saying, the ancestor of all our present forms, which predicted persecution for the disciples after Jesus' death, in the short interim before the coming of the Kingdom, and promised the disciples that God would give them what they needed to say in that hour.[84] Alternatively, the command μὴ μεριμνήσητε could be a pre-Easter word of Jesus that was developed in terms of the specific needs of the community after Easter. But whatever pre-Easter elements this saying might contain, the present forms of the saying are post-Easter, directed to a situation in the church.

The presupposition of persecution as the lot of the disciples, taken with the promise of inspired speech, already suggests a prophetic setting in the church for the origin or fundamental reformulation of the saying. The specific reference to the Holy Spirit as the one who gives the Christian what to say in the hour of crisis is also prophetic. (The Markan form of the saying has progressed further along this trajectory — the ἐγώ of the speaker being virtually displaced by that of the Spirit — than is the case in the Q-form, where prophecy is still a matter of the Spirit's giving the prophet what he is to say.) The saying is a *Trostwort*, an example of the παράκλησις, οἰκοδομή and παραμυθία that Christian prophets gave their congregations (I Cor. 14: 3). The fact that all the saying's contexts in the gospel tradition (Q; Mark 13; Matt. 10; John 14) have connections with Christian prophecy also indicates the origin of the saying in a prophetic circle. The Johannine context is especially revealing, for it is precisely the Paraclete-function that is emphasized in the saying as it circulated in the Q-community. It is this same aspect of the saying that is elaborated in the Johannine community as a description of Christian prophecy, using a developed form of this same saying. The saying in the Q-community, then, seems to have been the promise of the risen Lord through a Christian prophet that the prophetic charism, which was usually only associated with certain persons in the community and functioned primarily in worship, would come upon any member of the community who needed it in the hour of trial.

Luke 12: 8–9/Matt. 10: 32–3

This saying, especially in its Q-form, contains very old material that reflects the linguistic milieu of Palestine: ὁμολογεῖν ἐν + dative instead of the simple accusative and ἄγγελοι τοῦ θεοῦ is more primitive than either of the corresponding expressions in Mark or Matthew, indicating an Aramaic *Vorlage* for this saying.[85] The saying also seems to make a fundamental distinction between the Jesus who speaks and the Son of Man who is to come, a distinction which the post-Easter church would not have originated. Thus some of the most skeptical scholars have regarded this as an authentic saying of Jesus, and others have regarded a more primitive form of the saying as probably deriving from Jesus.[86] It should be conceded by all that if Jesus had not made declarations which distinguished between himself and the coming Son of Man, this distinction would not have originated in the church after Easter. There must have been stereotyped Son-of-Man sayings that made this distinction circulating in the church, which the church did not create. The pre-Easter Jesus did apparently assert that the coming Son of Man would vindicate those who were committed to him and his ministry. But such a view of the teaching of the historical Jesus is no guarantee that any particular saying is an authentic saying, nor is the evident antiquity and Aramaic background. In the case of this saying, the situation presupposed, in which the issue is confessing and denying Jesus, centered on the person of Jesus, indicates a church formulation. The disciples' situation of having to decide whether to confess or deny Jesus, in such a way that the verdict they would hear in the Last Judgment depended on their decision, is a situation that simply did not arise prior to the early Christian church's conflicts with Judaism in Palestine. Thus numerous scholars regard the saying as secondary.[87]

The saying is an independent unit secondarily added to this context by the Q-community, for it appears in another context in Mark 8: 38, where it is also only loosely connected to its context, and it has a fresh introduction within its Q-context. Considered by itself, the saying has a certain oracular quality appropriate to Christian prophets. Analysis of the saying reveals several points of contact with our profile of Christian prophecy. The introduction λέγω δὲ ὑμῖν, if, as is probable, it belonged to the Q-form, was characteristic of prophetic speech. Several have noted the form of the saying as a 'sentence of holy law', and on this basis alone have attributed it to Christian prophecy.[88] Ulrich Müller is more precise in pointing out that the form was originally a wisdom form, here taken over by a prophet.[89] The saying is permeated with eschatology, but not of a speculative kind. The tension between the confessors of Jesus and 'this generation' (the last) is inherent in all forms of the saying, though explicit only in the Markan form. The eschatology at work in this saying totally determines the present, so that the hearer is brought before the Last Judgment as he makes his present decision for or against Jesus. We have seen that this is the function of eschatology in early Christian prophecy. A kind of eschatological law is in fact proclaimed by the saying, for ὁμολογεῖν and ἀρνεῖσθαι both have forensic overtones. Tödt, who believes the saying is authentic, still repeatedly remarks that the saying has a legal character – which is more appropriate to Christian prophets than to Jesus.[90] The saying seems to have withstood a few recent attempts to prove that it was not originally a Son-of-Man saying; the careful work of Higgins and Kümmel has established that 'Son of Man' is integral to the original form of the saying.[91] As we shall see, the promulgation of Son-of-Man sayings in the name of the risen Jesus was the work of Christian prophets, so that the presence of 'Son of Man' in this saying is a bit of corroborative evidence for its prophetic origin. But particularly the way in which 'Son of Man' functions in this saying suggests a prophetic back-ground: the Son of Man is a παράκλητος before the heavenly court, as well as functioning as judge.[92] These indications of prophetic speech in this *logion* would seem to be confirmed by the presence of a very similar saying in the Apocalypse (3: 5). Even if the prophet-author of Revelation has taken up a saying from the synoptic tradition and re-presented it as a saying of the exalted Lord, it is significant that it was *this* saying, so in accord with Christian prophecy, that he chose.

As is the case with the other Son-of-Man saying in Q, the Son of Man in this saying is the exalted Son of Man who will shortly come as judge. But the 'I' that speaks is also that of the exalted Jesus as he speaks through his prophets. For the community that created this saying, there was no *heils-geschichtlich* distinction between the 'I' of the speaker and the Son of Man; to confess faith in the risen, exalted-and-present Jesus is to be acknowledged by the Son of Man when he comes.

Luke 12: 2–3/Matt. 10: 26–7

The Q-form has been more nearly preserved by Luke. Käsemann's view that this pair of sayings represents Christian prophecy's transformation of a secular proverb ('Don't tell secrets at all unless you want them to become public') has been developed by Schulz.[93] Prophecy turns the insight of secular wisdom into its opposite. Eschatologically, it is demanded to do just what otherwise would be avoided. The neatly structured form is in fact appropriate to Christian prophets, as are the themes of the eschatological reversal and the revelation of the secrets of men's hearts. However, there is nothing that clearly points to a post-Easter *Sitz*, nor is there sufficient evidence to compel a prophetic origin for the sayings, so in their original form they may have been part of the authentic teaching of Jesus. As taken up by the Q-community in conjunction with the other prophetic words of this sayings-cluster, however, the sayings would be a word of prophetic assurance (παράκλησις, οἰκοδομή and παραμυθία: I Cor. 14: 3) to the Q-community that the hardly-noticed beginnings of its proclamation will be revealed to the whole of Israel and the world, because God himself (divine passives ἀκουσθήσεται and κηρυχθήσεται) will bring it about.

Luke 12: 4–7/Matt. 10: 28–31

Such exhortations to fearlessness as are found in these sayings are rare in late Judaism, by no means a *topos* of Pharisaic exhortation or synagogue preaching. This could suggest that we have here either the authentic word of the pre-Easter Jesus or the prophetic preaching of the early church.[94] There are several points of contact with early Christian prophecy: the artful form; the repeated λέγω δὲ ὑμῖν and ναὶ (= ἀμήν?) λέγω ὑμῖν in verses 4 and 5 (the former of which at least was in Q, and probably the latter as well); Jesus' addressing his disciples as φίλοι, which might have the prophetic overtones that this word had in the Johannine community (John 15: 14–15 and cf. Wis. Sol. 7: 27); the similarity of 12: 4–5 to Rev. 2: 10, which may be better understood as an utterance of Christian prophecy that became a saying of Jesus in the synoptic tradition than vice versa.[95] In any case, the words concerning God's care for sparrows and numbering the hairs of our heads represent prophetic exhortation with the motifs of persecution and eschatological judgment in the background, not a romanticist view of nature. The words are prophetic declarations, but it is not clear whether they originated with the prophet Jesus of Nazareth or among his prophetic followers in the church. Some of the characteristics of church prophets discussed above may have been impressed on the sayings secondarily in the course of the tradition process. Even if the sayings, or some elements from them, derive from Jesus himself, these words would be heard in the Q-community as the address of the exalted Jesus to the current situation of the threatened Q-community.

Conclusion: the speech-complex in Luke 12: 2–12 par. has some sayings that probably originated as Christian prophecy, perhaps with a minimum of pre-Easter words of Jesus as their core (12: 8–9, 10, 11–12), which were combined by the Q-community with other sayings of Jesus from the tradition (12: 2–3, 4–7), some of which may have originated with the historical Jesus. But these sayings from the tradition were taken up, re-presented and sometimes reformulated in the forms of Christian prophetic speech as the message of the exalted Lord to the present of the Q-community, in immediate and undifferentiated union with sayings from Christian prophets. Rather than sayings of the risen Jesus being placed in the mouth of the historical Jesus by the Q-community, it appears that the tendency was the other way: traditional, even pre-Easter sayings of Jesus are claimed for the risen Lord.

Luke 12: 22–34/Matt. 6: 25–33; 19–21

This extensive section seems to be a redactional unit in Q.[96] It has generally been regarded as wisdom material, containing some authentic sayings of Jesus, but recently Schulz has argued that the whole is 'eindeutig eine prophetische Warnrede'.[97] He bases this judgment on the prophetic introductory formulae διὰ τοῦτο λέγω ὑμῖν (12: 25), τίς δὲ ἐξ ὑμῶν (12: 27) and λέγω δὲ ὑμῖν (12: 29), supposing that in Q there was also a λέγω ὑμῖν in verse 33, and the eschatological presupposition of the whole unit, of which the poverty motif in verses 33–4 is a part. While it is true enough that prophecy did take up wisdom materials, eschatologize them and incorporate them into its oracles, this is no ground for labeling all the wisdom materials in the synoptic tradition as prophetic without further evidence. In this case, the evidence seems to be insufficient. The traditional critical view is here better; we should continue to regard this material as traditional wisdom teaching, some of which goes back to Jesus himself. But the value of Schulz's argument is that he does enable us to hear these sayings with the ears of the Q-community: the risen Lord speaks words of assurance and command to this eschatological community that is attempting to put into practice the radical life of trust in its situation over against its Jewish environment. Schulz is correct that it is eschatological radicalism (not nature mysticism, interim ethic or the romanticizing of poverty) that comes to expression here. The prophetic introductory formulae were probably added to the traditional sayings by the Q-prophets as they re-presented the tradition as the word of the risen Lord. But there is no indication that we have material of prophetic origin in these sayings.[98]

Luke 12: 51–6/Matt. 10: 34–6; 16: 2–3

Due to the uncertain textual attestation of Matt. 16: 2–3 and its awkwardness in its present context, this text may be a later interpolation into the text of Matthew; if so, its presence in Q is very uncertain. The saying probably does go back to Jesus' own ministry, which itself was the 'sign' that his contemporaries could not interpret. Luke 12: 51 par. could also readily come from the historical Jesus, reflecting his own prophetic consciousness of having been sent. Of this Q-section then, only verses 52–3 are possibly secondary and they are often so regarded on the basis of their representing a common apocalyptic *topos* and reflecting the situation of the post-Easter Palestinian church.[99] There are a few indications that the expansion of the original saying of Jesus was made by a Christian prophet: the allusive way of re-presenting Scripture (Mic. 7: 6) as the interpretation of the present and, conversely, the interpretation of the present events happening to the Q-community as the eschatological events foretold in Scripture; the consciousness of persecution that called for the radical decisions that even divided families. There is hardly enough evidence to make a firm decision regarding the prophetic origin of verses 52–6, but one thing is certain: in the Q-community, this entire complex of verses 51–6 was proclaimed and heard as the present address of the exalted Lord to his distressed community. Even the difficult verse 56, though ambiguous in Jesus' situation, is clear in the Q-community. The persecution of the Q-community and the radical events happening in it (persecution, division of families) are the signs of the times. To understand them eschatologically, as the Q-community did with the interpretation of its prophets, is to experience them as signs of hope and salvation; to be blind to them is to receive judgment.

Luke 12: 57–9/Matt. 5: 25–6

There is nothing here to call into question the traditional view that the original saying was from Jesus. The sage advice not to go to court with a hopeless case has been transmuted by the eschatology presupposed into a warning to come to terms with the accuser before the imminent Last Day, but this eschatology is as appropriate to Jesus' situation as it is to that of the Q-community. Also, the prophetic formula ($\dot{\alpha}\mu\dot{\eta}\nu$) $\lambda\acute{\epsilon}\gamma\omega$ $\dot{\upsilon}\mu\hat{\iota}\nu$ could derive from the original saying in Jesus' ministry. But even if from the pre-Easter Jesus, the saying would be heard in the Q-community in the light of *its* expectation of the near End, as a word of the exalted Jesus speaking directly to its situation. Also, the ($\dot{\alpha}\mu\dot{\eta}\nu$) $\lambda\acute{\epsilon}\gamma\omega$ $\dot{\upsilon}\mu\hat{\iota}\nu$ could be the secondary addition of a Q-prophet to the original saying, but there is no way to determine this in a saying that itself originated from Jesus. Here we have

an excellent example of a probably-authentic saying of the pre-Easter
Jesus that was prophetically re-presented in the Q-community as the word
of the exalted Lord. Such sayings illustrate the fluidity between prophetic
and non-prophetic sayings. Even such non-prophetic and undoubtedly-
authentic sayings as the Parables of the Mustard Seed and the Leaven
(Luke 13: 18–21 par.) could be proclaimed and heard in the Q-community
as the direct expression of its own theology, as Schulz's instructive
discussion has shown.[100]

Luke 13: 23–30/Matt. 7: 13–14, 22–3; 8: 11–12

It is difficult to determine whether this complex of sayings was already a
unit in Q or whether Luke first composed them into a single speech. The
unit in its present form contains three independent sayings, each of which
has been assigned to Christian prophecy.

Bultmann designates 13: 24 as one of his 'characteristically prophetic'
logia, but offers no evidence.[101] Schulz refers unconvincingly to the neat-
ness of the form in Matthew, which he considers the more original, and the
'prophetic imperative' as evidence of prophetic origin.[102]

The saying in 13: 26–7 is rightly regarded as secondary because it looks
back on the ministry of Jesus as completed and views it from the perspective of the eschatological judgment.[103] Schweizer, Hahn and Schulz
declare the saying to be the oracle of a Christian prophet, but with a
minimum of evidence, and even this evidence comes from the Matthean
form, which cannot simply be identified with the Q-form.[104] The history
of the saying is complicated; it apparently was derived from some
parable,[105] and in its Q-form gives little indication of prophetic origin.

There is no reference to the person of Jesus in 13: 28–9 and no compelling evidence of a post-Easter origin of the saying, the original form of
which may well be genuine.[106] Yet, Käsemann and Zeller have labeled the
saying as Christian prophecy, and Schulz has supported their assertions
with some evidence: the λέγω ὑμῖν formula, the proleptic eschatology
inherent to the saying and its radicality, which calls for some charismatic
authority as the presupposition of its emergence, since no ordinary teacher
or apocalyptist would dare to utter it.[107]

I fail to find convincing evidence that any of the sayings in this group
originated as oracles of Christian prophets, but the considerations of the
scholars mentioned above, especially Schulz, show how traditional
materials did tend to take on prophetic features in the Q-community and
how fluid the line was in this community between traditional sayings of
Jesus and the contemporary address of the risen Lord.

Luke 13: 34–5/Matt. 23: 37–9
The Lament over Jerusalem

The speaker in this saying must be regarded as a transcendent being who, by sending prophets through the generations, has attempted without success to bring Jerusalem within the true people of God – for this is the meaning of the allusion to bringing Jerusalem 'under the wings'.[108] In this saying, the historical Jesus is one of the prophets sent by the transcendent Wisdom, not the sender of them, so it is fruitless to attempt to find a setting for it in the life of Jesus.[109] Whether the situation presupposed by the saying can be determined as precisely as is thought by Steck, who places it in the last years before the outbreak of the war in Jerusalem, is debatable, but the post-Easter, churchly origin of the saying is clear.[110] Since the saying appears in different contexts in Matthew and Luke, and since redactional explanations can readily be given for each, it is better to consider the Q-context of the saying as unknown and treat the saying as an independent *logion*.

It has been common simply to regard the saying as a quotation from Jewish wisdom that was secondarily attributed to Jesus by the church.[111] But the saying is also replete with the marks of Christian prophecy. We shall explore these first and then inquire whether the proposed wisdom and prophetic origins of the saying are mutually exclusive.

The saying belongs generally to the class of prophetic judgment pronouncements. Steck, who does not affirm the Christian prophetic origin of the saying, lists seven formally prophetic traits that place this saying in the tradition of the Old Testament prophets: introductory ἰδού (הִגֵּה), the combination reproach/threat (*Scheltwort/Gerichtswort*), the repeated naming of the addressees, the characteristic naming of the addressees with participles describing their rebellious conduct, the contrast-motif, the metaphorical comparison and the repetition of the introductory formula near the end of the oracle.[112] Of these, ἰδού and λέγω δὲ ὑμῖν are particularly associated with Christian prophets. Formally, the saying is a prophetic oracle.

Themes associated with, or even peculiar to, the Christian prophets permeate the saying. The characteristic eschatology of Christian prophetism provides the presupposition of the declaration: the hearers are addressed as the last generation, in whom guilt is summed up, and who are set over against the prophetic speaker as αὕτη ἡ γενεά, even though this expression is not used. The eschatological judgment is already spoken, 'Your house is abandoned [by God]', and is already effective. As in other prophetic sayings, the sentence of the judge of the Last Day is proleptically present. Whether this is a hopeless sentence, or one that still holds open the door of

repentance, depends in part on how one understands the concluding
εὐλογημένος ὁ ἐρχόμενος ἐν ὀνόματι κυρίου. This has traditionally been
understood in relation to the return of Jesus as the Son of Man, so that the
meaning is 'You will not see me [the earthly Jesus] until, at the *eschaton*,
you will say: "Blessed is the one who comes in the name of the Lord", but
then it will be too late.' This is the natural explanation if in fact what we
have here is a bit of wisdom tradition artificially placed in the mouth of
the pre-Easter Jesus by the church. In favor of it would be the formula
ὁ ἐρχόμενος, which was certainly used of the Messiah. But there are some
problems with this view. There is no evidence that Ps. 118: 26 was understood messianically in first-century Judaism. Indeed, the 'one who comes
in the name of the Lord' is the worshipper who comes to the temple, who
is pronounced blessed for having done so by the priests. The phrase ἐν
ὀνόματι κυρίου may in fact have been understood adverbially in connection
with εὐλογημένος, as argued by McNeile, with the resultant meaning:
'Blessing in the name of the Lord is pronounced upon the one coming [to
the temple to worship].'[113] The messianic use of the phrase is first broached
in Mark 11: 9 and then made explicit by the addition of βασιλεύς in Luke
19: 38 and John 12: 13. Even if it could be assumed that the one coming
in the name of the Lord is the Messiah at the *eschaton*, it has never been
clear why unbelieving Jews should be told that they will someday greet the
returning Jesus with this new messianic acclamation. Perhaps exegesis has
too quickly taken ὁ ἐρχόμενος as the clue that has led to a messianic
understanding of the statement, which is in fact a misunderstanding. It
may rather be the case that the significant element is the phrase ἐν ὀνόματι
κυρίου, which may be readily understood in terms of Christian prophecy.[114]
The saying would then have meant in the prophetic Q-community: 'You
who reject the exalted Lord who now speaks to you through his prophets,
will never "see" [= be accepted by, experience the blessed presence of] me
until and unless you say: "Blessed is the prophetic messenger of the risen
Lord." '[115] As in Hermas and Revelation, the prophet offers the exalted
Lord's last chance for repentance. Alternatively, if the traditional messianic
understanding of the blessing is correct, it still fits well into Christian prophecy, as an acclamation similar to Rev. 1: 7; Mark 9: 1; 13: 30; Matt. 10: 23;
all from Christian prophets. In either case, the eschatology of the saying
accords with Christian prophecy. Other prophetic traits are the exclusive
concern with prophets as the messengers of the Lord, the assumption that
prophets are always persecuted and the allusive way in which the Old
Testament is cited as the word of the presently-speaking Lord.[116] It should
further be noted that the form of Luke 13: 35/Matt. 23: 39 agrees with a
series of other sayings, which all seem to be of prophetic origin.[117]

I now return to the purported wisdom origin of the saying. The contacts with Christian prophecy pointed out above would seem to make improbable the older view that a piece of wisdom writing was simply attributed to the earthly Jesus in a literary manner. Yet, we have seen repeatedly that 'wisdom' and 'prophecy' are not alternatives. There was a profound interest in the transcendent figure of Wisdom in the prophetic Q-community, an interest fed by the community's concern for prophecy and its own prophetic self-understanding. The community adopted the view that it was the transcendent figure of Wisdom who had sent prophets to Israel through the generations, with John, Jesus and the prophets of the Q-community itself climaxing the series. Seen in terms of the series of prophets, the historical Jesus was simply one of the series, though the decisive one. As Suggs has argued, the Q-community did not identify the earthly Jesus as the incarnation of Wisdom. But the community conceived the exaltation of Jesus after his death in terms not only of identification with the coming Son of Man but also (in a manner not neatly worked out conceptually) in terms of an identification with the transcendent Wisdom who had inspired all the prophets and who now speaks through the Q-prophets.[118] It was Wisdom who spoke through the Jesus of history; it is the exalted Jesus, now identified with transcendent Wisdom, who speaks through the Q-prophets. This seems to me to be the most satisfactory way of regarding the saying under discussion: it is both the voice of Wisdom and the voice of the exalted Jesus speaking through a prophet in the Q-community. Although the Jewish community rejected Wisdom in rejecting the historical Jesus, they are now given a second and final chance to accept him, as he addresses them in the prophecy of the Q-community. This pattern of thinking corresponds exactly to the way the Q-community conceived the relation of the ministry of the historical Jesus and of the Son of Man: the one who is now identified as Son of Man was rejected when he appeared on earth but he now offers through his prophets absolutely the last chance of forgiveness (Luke 12: 10).

Luke 16: 17/Matt. 5: 18

This saying once circulated independently of both its Matthean and Lukan contexts; hence its setting in Q can no longer be determined. The saying is an absolute declaration of the validity of even the smallest bit of the Law until the *eschaton* and hence presupposes the debates about the Law in early Christianity. In view of Jesus' own relaxing of elements of the Law, it is difficult to find a setting in the life of Jesus for the saying, which should be regarded as a church product. There are some significant indications of prophetic speech: the introductory formula ἀμὴν λέγω ὑμῖν, if it was in Q and not added by the Matthean church or Matthew himself, would certainly be such an indication, as is the chiastic form and the declaration that something will not happen until (ἕως) some eschatological event happens.[119] Further, the apocalyptic orientation of the saying should be taken seriously. Ἕως πάντα (τὸν οὐρανὸν καὶ τὴν γῆν) γένηται (παρελθεῖν) is not a folk-expression for 'for ever', but is meant the way the early Christian prophets intended it: the end of history when the Son of Man returns. We have here, then, a response that was given to an early church question: 'Since the Kingdom has already started to come in the ministry of Jesus and his post-Easter followers, is the Law abolished, as some of our traditions say will happen at the *eschaton*?' The reply is given in an authoritative, legal-sounding declaration: 'For the time being the Law remains totally in effect; it will not pass away until the end of history, which is shortly to occur when the Son of Man returns.'

It is difficult to imagine a teacher or scribe in early Palestinian Christianity who could have promulgated such a saying of Jesus and had it accepted on his own authority. Although the marks of Christian prophecy in this saying are relatively few, such indications as are present point to a prophet as the most probable source for the saying.

Luke 17: 22–37/Matt. 24: 26–8, 37–41; 10: 39
The Day of the Son of Man

The introduction to this composite speech (17: 22) is widely held to be from Luke, and correctly so.[120] The reference to the earthly fate of the Son of Man in 17: 25 is also the work of Lukan redaction.[121] The materials in verses 28–9 and 32, none of which have Matthean parallels, are also frequently considered to be from Luke, but Manson has made a good case that they originally belonged to Q.[122] Verse 37a is a typically Lukan conversational insertion.[123] With the editorial framework and insertions removed, we have a speech that, though composed of originally independent sayings, has been secondarily arranged into a somewhat unified declaration on the coming of the Son of Man. Verses 23–4 declare that the advent of the Son of Man will be not a local but a universal event. In Q this was probably followed by 17: 37, the point of which is not the certainty and quickness of the *eschaton* but, in confirmation of verses 23–4, the fact that it cannot be hidden. This was followed in Q by verses 26–7 (28–9), 30, which assert that the Son of Man will arrive without warning. Since in Matthew these verses are separated from Matt. 24: 26–8/ Luke 17: 23–4, 37 only by Matthew's insertion of Markan material, it appears that in Q Luke 17: 23–4, 37, 26–7 (28–9), 30 was a continuous unit. To this should be added Luke 17: 31, another isolated saying that was independently incorporated by Q in this context and by Mark in 13: 15.[124] Probably 17: 32 also belonged in this Q-context. The Q-speech continued with the saying about gaining and losing one's life, 17: 33 – an independent *logion* that Mark and Matthew have incorporated in different contexts (Mark 8: 35; Matt. 10: 39), which in the Q-context is a call for unreserved commitment to the eschatological future that will vindicate the lives of the members of the Q-community, who now seem to be 'lost' in the eyes of their Jewish opponents. The speech concludes with the picture of the separation that will occur at the unexpected arrival of the Son of Man (17: 34–5; verse 36 is a gloss).

The speech is almost universally regarded as secondarily composed of originally disparate elements, with considerable variation existing in the evaluations of how many, if any, of these elements derive from the pre-Easter Jesus. Taken as a whole, however, the speech is unquestionably a secondary composition of someone in the early church, although it may contain some authentic words of Jesus. I use the word 'composition' advisedly here, because the speech is far from a haphazard conglomeration of individual sayings. Although the originally independent elements are still apparent, the speech is now a unified whole. It has no historical framework, nor any reference to the historical Jesus. As a whole, it belongs to the genre of 'prophetic and apocalyptic' sayings, as Bultmann recognized.[125] It has one main thrust, to which all else is subordinated: the Son of Man will certainly arrive as the judge of the Last Day; he will make an ultimate separation between those whom he accepts and those whom he rejects, so that it is this eschatological future that is to be the orientation point of all of life in the present, for it is worth any sacrifice. One gains and loses life in reference to this and nothing else (17: 33).

There is no apocalyptic calculating of the times in this speech. Even 17: 31 is not, as commonly interpreted, a fragment of apocalyptic advice about when to flee to avoid the terrors of the *eschaton* – the 'flight' motif is not present in the Q-version and is falsely read into it from the Markan apocalypse. Rather, like verse 33, verse 31 is a warning not to be attached to earthly things; even in the last moment one can, like Lot's wife, forfeit participation in eschatological salvation by turning toward material possessions. The present poverty and other-worldly orientation of the Q-community must be maintained until the very end in order to obtain salvation. This kind of eschatology, which functions as parenesis, is appropriate to Christian prophets and raises the question whether it was a prophet of the Q-community who compiled this speech.

In favor of the suggestion that the speech is a prophetic composition is the fact that, when the editorial framework is removed, the speech does indeed have the general form of a prophetic oracle. The use of traditional sayings, some of which may derive from the historical Jesus, is no argument against prophetic origin. There are a few indications of specifically prophetic speech: the 'eschatological correlatives' in verses 24, 26 and 30, and the λέγω ὑμῖν of verse 34, if it belonged to Q and is not a Lukan addition.[126] In addition, one might mention the use of the Old Testament in verses 26–7, although this is a more direct reference to Old Testament events than is the typical allusive use of the Old Testament by Christian prophets. The specific evidence of the work of Christian prophets in this speech is not impressive. The most that we should say is that someone in the Q-community, influenced by the prophetic eschatology of the community, combined traditional sayings of Jesus into a unified eschatological speech that would have been heard as the contemporary word of the exalted Lord urging the community to be prepared for the sudden coming of the Son of Man, and that he incorporated a few of the forms of prophetic speech that were current in the community. I would tend to think of the composer of this speech as himself a Christian prophet who consciously re-presents these words as the address of the risen Lord, but there is not enough evidence to make this a compelling conclusion.

Luke 22: 28–30/Matt. 19: 28

The verbal agreements between Luke 22: 28–30 and Matt. 19: 28 indicate that they are two forms of the same saying that appeared in Q, which each evangelist has rewritten and inserted into his own context. The variations between the Matthean and Lukan forms of this saying have caused some scholars to question whether it was in Q, but recent students of Q are virtually unanimous that the saying was in fact a part of the Q-document.[127] Our investigation below will show that the *logion* is appropriate to the life and self-understanding of the Q-community.

While it is clear that the original form of the saying declared that at the *eschaton* those addressed would participate in the judgment of the twelve tribes of Israel, the exact Q-form of the saying is difficult to reconstruct. The saying had no historicizing introduction in Q; the εἶπεν αὐτοῖς of Matthew has no parallel in Luke in this context and was formulated by Matthew in order to insert the saying into his narrative context taken from Mark. There was already an ἀμὴν λέγω ὑμῖν in the Markan context introducing another saying, and the phrase is absent from the Lukan parallel, so it is sometimes argued that the Q-saying had no introductory formula.[128] However, ἀμὴν λέγω ὑμῖν was a common formula in the Q-sayings and would readily have been omitted by Luke in the considerable rewriting of the saying that he did in order to adapt it to his context, so the introductory formula may be preserved in Matthew. The emphatic ὑμεῖς of direct address with which the *logion* begins was certainly in Q, followed perhaps by some sort of descriptive phrase indicating the hearers' relation to Jesus, but since both οἱ ἀκολουθήσαντες (Matthew) and οἱ διαμεμενηκότες (Luke) fit the theologies of their respective evangelists so well, it cannot be decided which is original, if either; probably both are redactional, and Q contained no historicizing description of the hearers. It is generally agreed that the Hellenistic term παλιγγενεσία is from Matthew and could not have stood in Q, but that Matthew's substitution of the Hellenistic term is an accurate 'translation' of the Q-original, which spoke of the eschatological renewal of the world, a common idea in Jewish apocalyptic. Thus, even though Luke's βασιλεία is a part of the Q-vocabulary, it is also congenial to Luke's redactional interests, and it is better to see Matthew as representing Q here, in essence though not in word.[129] The tendency for Son-of-Man sayings to become 'I-sayings' is here manifest, so that on this point Matthew will be the more original. An objection to this is that since Matt. 19: 28, ὅταν καθίσῃ ὁ υἱὸς τοῦ ἀνθρώπου ἐπὶ θρόνου δόξης αὐτοῦ, seems to be so similar to the 25: 31, ὅταν δὲ ἔλθῃ ὁ υἱὸς τοῦ ἀνθρώπου ἐν τῇ δόξῃ αὐτοῦ ... τότε καθίσει ἐπὶ θρόνου δόξης αὐτοῦ, and since these are the only two passages in the New Testament in which the Son of Man sits on the judgment-throne, both are redactional phrases of Matthew. However, it should be noticed that the structure of the saying under consideration calls for a statement about the Son of Man sitting on his throne in the first clause, for this is presupposed by the parallel statement in the second clause, καὶ καθήσεσθε ἐπὶ θρόνους κρίνοντες τὰς δώδεκα φυλὰς τοῦ Ἰσραήλ. It would thus seem more likely that the original Q-saying contained a reference to the Son of Man sitting on his throne of judgment, which Matthew has preserved, and in imitation of which he composed 25: 31. The Q-saying certainly contained a reference to the future twelve tribes of Israel, but did it also refer to the twelve thrones upon which Jesus' disciples would sit? The more general form in Luke is sometimes seen as a later 'democratizing' of the specific reference to the twelve disciples that the original saying is supposed to have contained.[130] But at least as good a case can be made for Matthew, or his tradition, having added the reference to twelve thrones, as for Luke, or his tradition, having omitted it. Matthew had an undeniable interest in the Twelve, and once the historicizing introduction to the saying, εἶπεν αὐτοῖς, was added, it would naturally be supposed that the saying was addressed to the pre-Easter Twelve. But this idea of the Twelve was in fact a fairly late development within the church. And Q certainly knows of no special role played by the Twelve; if this saying contained a reference to the Twelve, it would be the only such reference in Q. The Q-saying, then, will have been addressed not to the Twelve but to the disciples generally and may be reconstructed, with appropriate tentativeness, as follows:

[ἀμὴν λέγω ὑμῖν]
ὑμεῖς [οἱ   ]
ἐν τῇ [παλιγγενεσία], ὅταν καθίσῃ ὁ υἱὸς τοῦ ἀνθρώτου
        ἐπὶ θρόνου δόξης αὐτοῦ
καὶ καθήσεσθε ἐπὶ θρόνους
κρίνοντες τὰς δώδεκα φυλὰς τοῦ Ἰσραήλ

Both the Matthean and Lukan contexts are demonstrably secondary, as is the historicizing introduction. The saying's Q-context is no longer recognizable, so that it must be regarded as an independent saying. The saying is oracular in quality and requires no narrative setting to be coherent.

The *logion* describes what will happen at the *eschaton*. The Son of Man is portrayed as not only 'coming' or 'appearing' at the End but as sitting on his throne, apparently for the purpose of judging, as in Matt. 25: 31–46. The saying also pictures the eschatological reconstitution of the twelve tribes of Israel. In the typical apocalyptic scenario, this eschatological regathering of all Israel is thought of as a blessing,[131] but here the twelve tribes are judged by the Son of Man — a fate usually reserved for the Gentiles. Those who now believe in Jesus as the Son of Man will share his function of judging the twelve tribes of Israel. This 'judging' is sometimes understood, in the Semitic sense of שָׁפַט, to mean 'rule', with the result that the disciples are promised the ruling seats within the blessed eschatological Israel. But the Greek word κρίνω does not mean 'govern', except in semitizing Greek such as the LXX where κρίνω translates שָׁפַט, and the New Testament nowhere else adopts this usage. The familiar apocalyptic picture of the saints participating in the judgment of the world (I En. 108. 12; 61.8; 62.2; 69.27; 45.3; I Cor. 6: 2; cf. Rev. 20: 4, 11) suggests that judgment in the critical, condemnatory sense is intended. The oracle thus affirms the reversal of eschatological expectations: all Israel will in fact be regathered at the *eschaton* — for judgment. The saying thus presupposes a historical setting in which 'all Israel' can be juxtaposed to the followers of Jesus, a setting in which blanket condemnation can be pronounced upon Israel, presumably for her consistent rejection of the prophets of past and present, as in Luke 11: 49–51 par. This, along with the apocalyptic detail, indicates that the saying is from the early church rather than from the pre-Easter Jesus. Dupont thinks that this saying reflects the situation of the historical Jesus, who promises a judgment limited to Israel to correspond to the mission of the Twelve, which was likewise limited to Israel, the rejected disciples getting to participate in the judgment of those who had rejected them.[132] But not only is this *lex talionis* uncharacteristic of the historical Jesus, the whole situation he describes should be transferred to the post-Easter Q-community, whose messengers did carry on an unsuccessful mission to Israel and who are promised by the word of the exalted Son of Man that they will participate with him in meting out judgment to all Israel for her rejection of the prophets, culminating in the rejection by this last generation of Israel of the prophetic messengers of the Q-community.

Our investigation so far indicates that the saying was promulgated by a Christian prophet in the name of the exalted Lord. Some further considerations strengthen this probability. The Apocalypse also declares that the believers who are presently persecuted will share the judgment-throne of the returning Lord (3: 21 and cf. 20: 4), as does Paul (I Cor. 6: 2). Thus the only two other references similar to the saying under consideration are from Christian prophetic figures, one of them being in the form of a declaration of the risen Lord through prophetic speech. The saying functions within the congregation of suffering eschatological saints as a word of consolation (παράκλησις, οἰκοδομή, καὶ παραμυθία: I Cor. 14: 3) by picturing the reversal of roles that will take place at the near *eschaton*. The elaboration of apocalyptic detail then functions not speculatively but as parenesis. In all these features the saying corresponds to the Christian prophecy of the Apocalypse. Formally, the saying is similar to Luke 12: 8–9 par. and 12: 10 par., both of which, as we have seen, are from Christian prophets. The introductory formula, ἀμὴν λέγω ὑμῖν, if it belonged to the Q-form of the saying, is likewise a prophetic form. The saying does not quote Scripture but is obviously inspired by the images of Dan. 7: 9–10, 13, 21–2 and is best understood as an oracle promulgated on the basis of charismatic interpretation of this passage, which has also played an important subliminal role in the formation of the Book of Revelation.[133] In the Q-community, which had attempted to prepare Israel for the imminent encounter with Jesus the Son of Man and had been rebuffed, 'judged' and persecuted, some anonymous prophet, on the basis of his inspired interpretation of Dan. 7, announced the consoling word of the exalted Lord: contrary to present surface appearances, it is you, the suffering disciples, who will be the judges of those who now reject you, in the great renewal of the world that is about to take place. This is the origin of the saying and the way it was heard in the Q-community.

Christian prophecy in the Q-community: a summary

My study indicates that, with varying degrees of probability, we can designate a considerable number of sayings in the Q-tradition that originated as the oracles of Christian prophets: Luke 6: 22–3; 10: 3; 10: 4; 10: 5–12; 10: 13–15; 10: 16; 10: 21–2; 11: 29b–30; 11: 39–52; 12: 8–9; 12: 10; 12: 11–12; 13: 34–5; 16: 17; 22: 28–30. An additional impressive number of sayings has been identified, which, while probably not originally created by Christian prophets, do bear the marks of the reformulation and/or re-presentation by Christian prophets of traditional material that originated from the historical Jesus and non-prophetic sources in and outside the church: Luke 6: 20b–21; 10: 2 (–16); 10: 23–4; 11: 14–23; 11: 29a, 31–2; 12: 2–3, 4–7 (12: 2–12); 12: 22–34; 12: 51–6; 12: 57–9; 13: 23–30; 17: 22–37. There are also numerous prophetic touches to the non-prophetic forms within the Q-tradition, such as the λέγω ὑμῖν conclusions to the parables in Luke 14: 24; 15: 7 and 19: 26. There is a considerable amount of other material in Q, not discussed in the above, such as Luke 6: 27–49, which, though probably from Jesus and non-prophetic sources in the church, could readily have been heard in the Q-community not as the remembered voice of the historical Jesus but as the word of the exalted Son of Man. The preceding analysis offers concrete support for the often-made assertion that Q is a prophetic document from a charismatic community.[134]

This does not mean that the Q-sayings were entirely transformed into the prophetic mode. As sayings circulated singly or in clusters, there was a tendency for them to create a historicizing frame for themselves, whether this was some brief introductory formula, such as καὶ εἶπεν αὐτοῖς, or a miniature narrative of which the apothegmic saying was the point and generating core. The Q-community never severed the exalted Son of Man from the figure of its recent historical past, Jesus of Nazareth, and thus felt no compelling need to purge the tradition of all historicizing elements. The document began with the appearance of John the Baptist, possibly told of Jesus' baptism and related the temptation of Jesus in the wilderness, none of which were transformed into present-tense messages from the risen Lord. A very few apothegm-like sayings such as Luke 7: 1–10 and 10: 21–2 are preserved with their historicizing framework. But this is not the central thrust of the Q-material. The sayings are not those that were once said by a rabbi of a past generation; their validity does not rest on the authority of a past figure. To picture Q as intending simply to preserve the teaching of a historical figure is to miss the point.[135]

Likewise, the Q-materials are not well described by the term 'Words of the Wise' (ΛΟΓΟΙ ΣΟΦΩΝ).[136] While it is true that Q has many points of contact with the wisdom tradition in both form and content, Q is in no sense a 'Christian Book of Proverbs'.[137] Over against those who claim to live by traditional wisdom, the Q-community knows itself to live by revelation (Luke 10: 21—2). The manner of address of wisdom materials is that of a 'timeless truth', which speaks to the hearer because of its inherent validity, although it may be incidentally attached to a figure of the past: Solomon, Ahikar, Sirach. We have seen that Q does contain expressions of what was once gnomic wisdom, just as it contains teachings appropriate to a rabbi but, as proclaimed and heard in the Q-community, these tend to be transformed into the prophetic address of the exalted Jesus who is imminently expected as the Son of Man and judge of the world. Two basic tendencies are present in the Q-materials: (1) the historicizing tendency, represented by the introductory formula καὶ εἶπεν αὐτοῖς, places wisdom and prophetic sayings into a past-narrative setting and opens up the way to regard them as sayings of the pre-Easter Jesus; (2) the contemporizing tendency, represented by the prophetic λέγω ὑμῖν, takes historical sayings and sayings that have already been historicized and re-presents them as contemporary address. More than one mode of address is thus still present in Q, representing the literary remains of struggles to perceive Jesus as rabbi or teacher of wisdom, as well as exalted Lord, but the fundamental orientation of the Q-sayings as they came to Matthew and Luke is neither the timeless mode of wisdom nor the traditional mode of rabbinica but the present/future mode of prophecy.

In addition to the analysis of particular sayings, there are some general features of the Q-complex of materials that relate it to Christian prophecy. Streeter has pointed out that the form of the 'book' itself is prophetic, beginning with the baptism and temptation stories analogous to a prophetic 'call' and continuing with a collection of oracles and a minimum of narrative, somewhat like Jeremiah.[138] While the point may not be pressed, Q is probably closer to Jeremiah than to Proverbs, related more to traditional prophetic forms than to wisdom.

The view that prophets are persecuted seems to be an over-arching concern of the document, not just of individual pericopae, so that the whole document can be described as a 'Persecution Code' formulated by prophets and teachers.[139] Similarly, the perspective of the Q-materials on miracles corresponds to that of the prophets. Jesus and his post-Easter followers work miracles, but not by virtue of their divine 'essence', as the pre-Markan miracle stories tended to portray Jesus (Mark 3: 10; 5: 25ff; 6: 56). Rather, Jesus (and his disciples in the Q-community) perform as (prophetic) agents of God, who alone works miracles, in carrying out their mission of eschatological proclamation.[140] As in the prophetic books, the center of gravity is on the proclamation itself. The manner of using the Old Testament is also more closely related to the prophetic use of Scripture than to other styles of interpretation. Although there are many allusions to Scripture, in which the present proclamation is couched in images and phrases from Scripture, exactly as in Revelation, there is only one direct quotation in the whole of Q (Luke 7: 27 par.).[141] In conjunction with this charismatic—eschatological interpretation of Scripture, the Q-community knew itself to be charismatically enabled to interpret the events through which it had lived and was living as the eschatological act of God.[142] It had the revealed mystery of the meaning of the appearance of John and Jesus and the meaning of the struggles of its own time. This is the prophetic self-consciousness.

The historical Jesus was indispensable for the theological understanding of the Q-community. He had been the decisive prophetic messenger of transcendent Wisdom and had been exalted to become the Son of Man. His words, and a few of his deeds, had formed the original nucleus of the Q-materials. But the prophetic understanding of the Q-community tended more and more to focus on the post-Easter exalted Jesus. What Jesus of Nazareth had said became dissolved in what the post-Easter Jesus said through his prophets. If these two categories of material were ever distinguished, they had ceased to be by the time of the redaction of the Q-materials. While the dissolution of the word of the historical Jesus into the word of the heavenly Jesus had not yet occurred in Q, the center of gravity had shifted, so that Q was moving in the direction of a collection of 'sayings of the living Jesus' such as the Gospel of Thomas.[143] The preceding analysis also brings to light data bearing on the relation of Christian prophets to the generation of Son-of-Man sayings and the origin of christology, which is developed below in the Appendix, pp. 239–50.

12 CHRISTIAN PROPHECY IN MARK

(1) Son-of-Man sayings

Since the analysis of the Q-materials indicates that Christian prophets were one of the primary sources of the promulgation of Son-of-Man sayings in the name of the risen Jesus, we may first examine this group of sayings in Mark to determine whether any of them appear to be of prophetic origin.[1]

Mark contains fourteen instances of 'Son of Man' in thirteen sayings: 2: 10; 2: 28; 8: 31; 8: 38; 9: 9; 9: 12; 9: 31; 10: 33–4; 10: 45; 13: 26; 14: 21 (twice); 14: 41; 14: 62. Of these, we must exclude from consideration those sayings that cannot stand alone as independent oracles but require the narrative context of the life of Jesus in order to be meaningful. Although such sayings are not from Jesus as Son-of-Man sayings, they are to be accounted for by non-charismatic development of the tradition and by the composition of Mark. We thus exclude 8: 31; 9: 9; 9: 12; 9: 31; 10: 33–4; 14: 21 and 14: 41, all of which look *forward* to the cross and therefore, even though they probably originated after Easter, were not intended originally to be heard as the voice of the *risen* Lord. The situation is only slightly more complicated in the case of 14: 62, which theoretically could stand alone as an independent saying (with some prophetic characteristics: ἐγώ εἰμι, pesher style of Old Testament interpretation, eschatology) but on closer examination is seen to be thoroughly integrated into its narrative context, which it never existed apart from.[2] The remaining sayings need to be examined for possible prophetic origin.

8: 38

This saying comes to Mark from the tradition and has been rewritten by him in a more apocalyptic form. We have seen above that the more original form of the saying derives from a Christian prophet.[3]

13: 26

This saying is part of the Markan apocalypse 13: 5–31, which as a whole is of prophetic origin, as we shall argue below.[4]

183

2: 10

As it presently stands, the declaration ἐξουσίαν ἔχει ὁ υἱὸς τοῦ ἀνθρώπου ἀφιέναι ἁμαρτίας ἐπὶ τῆς γῆς appears to be an integral part of the narrative. But that 2: 1–12 is composite has long been argued and is accepted by as conservative a critic as Vincent Taylor.[5] The inserted section 5b–10 on forgiveness has as its heart the saying of verse 10, which may have been primary and may have generated the controversy scene as a framework for itself.[6] This possibility is strengthened by the introductory ὅτι, if it is taken as *recitativus*, and by the awkward gap as the narrative is resumed, which tends to set the saying off as an independent unit. This is a definite possibility, but no more than that. If the saying is an independent *logion*, it could have been first spoken by a Christian prophet. It can be appropriately heard as a declaration in early Christian worship that the church's Lord, the exalted Jesus/Son of Man, forgives sins. But the brevity and lack of distinguishing marks prohibits either the substantiation or the denial of this possibility.

2: 28

Κύριός ἐστιν ὁ υἱὸς τοῦ ἀνθρώπου καὶ τοῦ σαββάτου is readily separable from its context and is regarded by even the most cautious critics as an additional comment to the preceding narrative.[7] It is not clear whether the evangelist himself composes this comment or draws it from tradition. That the subject is ὁ υἱὸς τοῦ ἀνθρώπου, and not simply ἄνθρωπος, which one expects as a parallel to the preceding statement, suggests that this is an independent, traditional *logion*. In this case, it could have originated from a Christian prophet. But aside from the Son-of-Man reference itself, and the presumed function of settling a disputed point in the church's life by a pronouncement from heaven, the *logion* has no particularly prophetic characteristics, and its prophetic origin must remain only a possibility.

10: 42–5

The tradition-history of this sayings-cluster is complex and cannot be recovered with confidence. The cluster is composed of sayings that were originally independent but had been joined into one parenetic unit in the pre-Markan tradition.[8] This unit traveled by an independent path into the Lukan context, being modified *en route*. Thus both the Markan and Lukan forms of the sayings-unit bear the marks of church development; neither is the 'primitive' form from which the other developed. Both have 'primitive' and 'developed' features.[9] The original core of the sayings may go back to Jesus, without the references to Son of Man and the λύτρον terminology, but the saying in its present Markan form is definitely a church product.[10]

The final form of the sayings-complex as found in Mark manifests a surprising number of contacts with Christian prophecy. Formally, the parallelism already present in verses 42−4 has been impressed on verse 45, so that the whole has an oracular ring.[11] When the sayings were combined, some care was taken to maintain the formal structure inherent in the original saying, which probably came from Jesus. A hortatory, parenetic outlook, reminiscent of the 'sentences of holy law', pervades the whole, although that particular form is not present. It is significant that Bultmann classifies the saying under 'Legal Sayings and Church Rules'.[12] The replacement of an original 'I' by 'Son of Man' might be only an instance of this general tendency of the tradition, or it could be a point of contact with the prophetic stream that identified Jesus and the Son of Man and continued to express both its eschatology and christology in Son-of-Man terms. The understanding of the death of Jesus as λύτρον ἀντὶ πολλῶν may also reflect the charismatic interpretation of event by Scripture characteristic of Christian prophets.[13] The *Sitz im Leben* of the saying was the worship life of the community, centered in the eucharist, where Christian prophets were active.[14] If this cluster of sayings gradually received these characteristics via an accumulation of individual changes to the saying over an extended period of development in the pre-Markan tradition, then there is no reason to consider it as particularly related to Christian prophecy. However, if all the secondary features characteristic of the Markan form of the saying were impressed upon it at one point, on one occasion, we have an instance in which (i) a traditional saying of Jesus is taken up, (ii) given oracular form throughout, (iii) expanded by a free application of the Old Testament to interpret a recent historical event, the advent and death of Jesus (ἦλθον, λύτρον ἀντὶ πολλῶν) as the saving act of God, (iv) re-presented to the community as a saying of Jesus himself in the present tense (v) in the name of the exalted Son of Man, who is understood to come to speech in the saying as now delivered, (vi) to form a hortatory, edifying rule for church life, (vii) all of which transpires in the worship setting. If this all happened at once, it is best to attribute the saying to a Christian prophet.

We may now summarize our findings. Of the thirteen Son-of-Man sayings in Mark, two probably derive from Christian prophets (8: 38; 13: 26). Three more could have such an origin (2: 10; 2: 28; 10: 45), but only for 10: 45 is there any real reason to believe so, and the evidence here is far from compelling. Eight sayings certainly did not originate from Christian prophets (8: 31; 9: 9; 9: 12; 9: 31; 10: 33; 14: 21; 14: 41; 14: 62). Our analysis seems to uncover a peculiar fact: although there was a close relation between Christian prophets and Son-of-Man sayings in earliest

Christianity and in Q, there is not a high incidence of prophetic sayings among the Son-of-Man sayings in Mark. We must keep this in mind as we investigate further the extent of prophetic sayings among the remainder of Mark's sayings of Jesus.

(2) The Unforgivable Sin saying (Mark 3: 28—9)

We have seen above, in the discussion of the Q-form of this saying, that it was probably originally formulated as an oracle of a Christian prophet, the more primitive form of which is preserved in Mark.[15]

(3) The Missionary Commission (Mark 6: 8—11)

Here Mark has sayings similar to, and partly identical with, the Q Missionary Address (Luke 10: 2—16 par.). It is difficult to say whether this is excerpted from Q, as Bultmann thinks,[16] or represents independent tradition, just as it is difficult to be sure whether the historicizing framework is first supplied by Mark,[17] or was already traditional.[18] In any case, Mark here includes a brief collection of sayings that, as we have already seen, derive from, and have been formed by, Christian prophecy.[19]

(4) The Imminence of the *Parousia* (Mark 9: 1)

This saying seems to be an independent *logion* because of its own introductory formula and its lack of connection to its context. The primary reason for regarding it as secondary is that it seems to reflect a concern over the delay of the *parousia* and offers an encouraging word to a post-Easter community in which some members have already died, reaffirming that the *parousia will* come anyway. *Some* (even if not all) will live to see it. The saying has often been regarded as a product of Christian prophecy.[20] There is some evidence for this judgment in the saying: the eschatological certainty of the coming of the Lord, the authority to make a declaration about its date, the ἀμὴν λέγω ὑμῖν introductory formula, the function of οἰκοδομὴ καὶ παράκλησις καὶ παραμύθια, which the saying would have performed in the anxious post-Easter community, the similarity in form and function to I Cor. 15: 51 and I Thess. 4: 15—17 (prophetic oracles that speak to the same problem in the same way) and the formal similarity to Matt. 10: 23, which, as we shall see, is a product of Christian prophecy. This evidence is probably sufficient to justify the conclusion that Mark 9: 1 was originally spoken by a Christian prophet.

(5) The Markan 'Apocalypse' (Mark 13: 5—31)

This is the most extensive and significant unit in Mark related to Christian prophecy, and calls for an extended discussion. The proposal first made by

Timothy Colani in 1864, that Mark 13 contains an independent apocalypse by an unknown Jewish-Christian author, was widely adopted by the end of the century and was still considered by many to be 'assured results' of synoptic criticism as late as 1954.[21] Suggestions that the author of this 'apocalypse' was a Christian prophet were accompanied by efforts to identify the occasion of its promulgation, with the Caligula crisis of 40 and the war of 66–70 being the chief candidates. Recently, however, the 'Little Apocalypse' theory has fallen on hard times. On the one hand, there are efforts to argue that the discourse should be regarded as mainly a redactional composition of Mark.[22] But still more recently, the magisterial work of Rudolf Pesch has reaffirmed the existence of the post-Jesus, pre-Markan apocalyptic core that was reworked by Mark.[23] Study of Mark 13 may be regarded as at something of an *impasse*. The time is ripe for a reconsideration of the question from the point of view of the hypothesis being proposed in this study. I shall not duplicate the thorough analyses and exegetical work that have been done in the major recent monographs on Mark 13. Rather, I shall approach the material with only one question: what points of contact with early Christian prophecy, as reconstructed in Part Two above, are found there? We will then be in a position to ask whether phenomena that were problematic for earlier versions of the 'Little Apocalypse' theory find a more satisfactory explanation.

I need waste no space demonstrating the secondary nature of the discourse. Although numerous scholars regard the discourse as containing varying degrees of authentic sayings of Jesus – a view not incompatible with the hypothesis of Christian prophetic origin – no one, not even Beasley-Murray, regards the discourse in its present form as from Jesus. The usual reasons need not be detailed here: composite nature, conflicts with the unquestioned teaching of Jesus, reflections of post-Easter church life etc. Even though the discourse contains some elements from the pre-Easter Jesus, someone in the church is the author of the present form of the discourse. On the other hand, the redactional activity of Mark need not be denied. If Mark did incorporate a 'Little Apocalypse' into his eschatological discourse, it has been at least semi-digested and integrated with Mark's other sources, partially rewritten in Mark's own style and formed into a speech-complex that now bears something of a Markan stamp throughout. Thus the work of such scholars as Beasley-Murray, on the one hand, and Lambrecht, on the other, has weakened the traditional form of the 'Little Apocalypse' theory, but has not demolished it. We may now ask whether the theory of a pre-Markan apocalyptic document can be reasserted and strengthened by seeing it as Christian prophecy. Since verses 1–4 are a Markan introduction, verses 32–7 are an obvious appendix and verse 31 forms a proper conclusion, I shall consider 13: 5–31 as the unit to be examined.

(1) The most obvious prophetic feature of Mark 13 is its claim to reveal the events of the End Time and of the eschatological future. The general eschatological themes found in this passage are of course present throughout broad streams of early Christianity and were shared by many who did not function as prophets. There is a difference between this general eschatological perspective that permeated the early church, which came to expression mainly as *theologoumena* declared on the basis of Christian tradition (e.g. Acts 1: 11; II Pet. 3: 8–13), and the explicit revelations about the eschatological future that occur as the oracles of Christian prophets (e.g. I Thess. 4: 15–17; I Cor. 15: 51–2 and Revelation *passim*). The general content of the chapter is most closely akin to the other material in the New Testament that we know was from Christian prophets. It will not do, however, simply to designate this eschatological character as 'apocalyptic'. The discourse does share some features with Jewish apocalyptic literature,[24] but also lacks many typical features. There is no calculation of the times, no description of the final wickedness of the world, no last battle, no judgment scene, no national Messiah and 'days of the Messiah', no description of the anti-Christ, no portrayal of the delights of the saved and the woes of the damned. And above all, the discourse, though not from the historical Jesus, is not pseudepigraphical and should not be described as such.

(2) A related feature that distinguishes Mark 13 from Jewish apocalyptic and associates it with Christian prophecy is its hortatory character. Nineteen imperatives are found in the discourse, fifteen of them within the unit we are considering, verses 5–31. This parenesis is not tacked on to an 'apocalyptic fly-sheet' but comprises the fundamental structure of the discourse itself.[25] Nor is the hortatory element Markan redaction, for there is no evidence at all that Mark was accustomed to transform his tradition into a hortatory form.[26] The structure of eschatologically-motivated parenesis already characterized the pre-Markan unit. The difference from Jewish apocalyptic on this point is clear and has often been documented. The only real parallels to the hortatory apocalyptic of Mark 13 are found in Christian prophecy, above all in the Book of Revelation. This must be taken as a solid link with Christian prophecy.

(3) The Christian prophet could speak directly to his hearers/readers, using second-person imperatives, because he spoke with the ego of the risen Christ, not pseudonymously in the name of some ancient figure. If Mark 13 is regarded as Christian prophecy, this must not be called pseudonymity, for it is precisely here that there is another characteristic

feature in which Jewish apocalypse and Christian prophecy differ. Not only does Mark 13 not appeal to some ancient worthy such as Enoch, Noah or Elijah, it does not appeal to *Jesus* in the sense of claiming the authorship of a figure of the *past*. The difference between Christian prophecy and Jewish apocalypse in this regard is more than a difference in the length of *time* that elapsed between the writing and its purported author, though that difference too is significant. It is a difference in *nature*. If Mark 13 contains Christian prophecy, this was never conceived as the words of Jesus spoken in the past — even the recent past — and handed down to the Christian situation, but always as the message of the con-temporary Christ. On the other hand, no writer of Jewish apocalypse considered himself to be the 'mouthpiece of the exalted Enoch' or any such. As we shall see below, this is not at all changed by the fact that Mark has placed the discourse within the pre-Easter narrative framework.

The consciousness of speaking with the ἐγώ of the exalted Christ is present throughout the discourse, especially in the forms of the first-person pronoun found in verses 6, 9, 13, 23, 30 and 31. The author is acquainted with the revelatory formulae ἐγώ εἰμι and ἐπὶ τῷ ὀνόματί μου used by Christian prophets but does not use them himself because they have been appropriated by his opponents. The ἐγώ εἰμι of 13: 6 is not a claim to be the returned Jesus Christ but is the prophetic formula by which the Christian prophets opposed by the author authenticated their oracles and is itself an indication that the discourse derives from a situation where the phenomenon of Christian prophecy was very much alive.

(4) This concern with false prophets is very important to the author of the discourse. He begins with it (verses 5b—6) and comes back to it in verses 21—2. The deceivers against whom the author warns his readers have been understood to be Jewish messianic pretenders, false Christian teachers, those claiming to be the returned Jesus himself, or a group of gnostic-like pneumatic θεῖοι ἄνδρες.[27] There are difficulties with all these explanations, a primary one being that the persons named will both speak ἐπὶ τῷ ὀνόματί μου and will characteristically say ἐγώ εἰμι. Taylor and Klostermann are typical of commentators in general who have squirmed under the difficulty of accounting for both phrases; both finally decide that ἐγώ εἰμι is a quasi-messianic claim and that ἐπὶ τῷ ὀνόματί μου is a Christian addition. But both phrases are comprehensible in terms of Christian prophecy (and only there, I think), for only Christian prophets speak both in the name of Jesus (ἐπὶ τῷ ὀνόματί μου = with and under his authority) and in his person (saying ἐγώ εἰμι). This is an important ex-egetical point: the phenomenon of Christian prophecy clarifies the meaning of the problematic verse 6. But it is also a point for regarding the discourse

as the product of Christian prophecy, for, as we have seen, it is characteristically the prophets themselves who raise the cry against 'false' prophets.

(5) The editors of the Nestle text have indicated numerous points at which phrases from the Old Testament, especially Daniel, have been woven into the eschatological discourse. Close study reveals even more such points of contact with the Hebrew Scriptures, as the works of Haenchen, Hartmann and Pesch make clear.[28] *Yet there are no explicit quotations as such*; the Old Testament material is re-presented as an integral part of the present address of the prophet's speech, exactly as in the Book of Revelation. We have seen that this style of interpretation is characteristic of Christian prophets. Hartmann has argued convincingly that the discourse not only contains Old Testament material but is based on it, derived from it — considering the whole a 'meditation' or 'midrash' on Daniel texts.[29] This, coupled with his argument that the parenetic sections originated at the same time as the 'apocalyptic', makes unnecessary the hypothesis, which he adopts rather casually, that at the core of our discourse is a 'miniature apocalypse taken over from Judaism'.[30] In other words, the eschatological discourse, or its core, can readily be seen as having come into being as a charismatic interpretation of Scripture predicting the eschatological future as the basis for hortatory admonitions. One need not posit an 'apocalyptic fragment' that was 'supplemented' with Christian exhortations. Hartmann has been helpful in showing how the subconscious mind puts together Scripture material into new constellations and how these erupt as new revelations into the conscious mind,[31] but is quite incorrect and misleading in referring to its product as 'midrash' and in limiting its reference to Daniel. Again, what we have seems to be accounted for better on the hypothesis of Christian prophecy.

(6) In 13: 11 we find a text that circulated independently, which I have already argued was the product of Christian prophecy.[32] Its presence in this discourse is of course another point of contact with prophetic circles. It should also be noticed here that the saying expresses a 'prophetic' understanding of the way the Spirit functions. This saying conceives of the Spirit not as a general gift 'immanent' in the church but as the occasional gift to particular persons in times of crisis, a charisma that confers supernatural speech abilities. This testifies to an understanding of the Spirit that would not have been at home in every *Sitz im Leben der Kirche* but would have been very appropriate among Christian prophets. This promise of the risen Christ of pneumatic speech in crisis situations was also transmitted in the prophetic circles of the Johannine community, where it was generalized and made the subject of theological reflection, to emerge as the Paraclete-doctrine of the Fourth Gospel.

(7) The Christian prophets spoke with an authoritative tone, and their oracles were delivered with the exalted feeling characteristic of those who are aware of speaking and acting with more than their normal conscious-ness. This is a difficult criterion to apply in this case, for the discourse could be seen as characterized by the calculating bookishness characteristic of some late-Jewish apocalyptic. I would regard this as an error, however, for the mode of direct address already discussed, the lack of the speculative, calculating aspect and the concluding words in verses 30–1 do seem to express the direct authority of the one who knows himself to speak with the voice of the risen Lord.

(8) The note to 'the reader' in verse 14, ὁ ἀναγινώσκων νοείτω, has been understood in the sense that the private reader is to attend to the veiled meaning of the document in hand. This is of course possible, just as it is possible that Mark added the phrase at the final stage of redaction. But the only parallel in early Christian literature to the absolute ὁ ἀναγινώσκων is found in Christian prophecy, Rev. 1: 3, which refers to the lector who reads aloud in public worship a prophetic document written for that purpose. Ordinarily the prophets would deliver their own oracles in the setting of the worship service but in the case of Revelation the message concerned a present crisis of history that involved many churches, so the revelation was committed to writing and provision made for it to be read by others to the congregations gathered for worship. The numerous second-person plural imperatives suggest this as the setting for the delivery of the 'Little Apocalypse', as does the expression ὁ ἀναγινώσκων νοείτω and the other points of contact with Revelation discussed below.

(9) The document originates from a setting in which persecution was the expected lot of both author and hearers, the theme appearing in verses 8, 9–13 and 14–19. These sufferings bear the dual aspect of the eschatol-ogical sufferings that the faithful must undergo as the prelude to the End and the suffering that is the lot of the true prophet, both of which are characteristic prophetic themes. Related to this is the pronouncement of eschatological blessing for those who endure, so that 13: 13*b* finds its closest parallels in the promises of Rev. 2: 7, 10, 11, 17, 26–7; 3: 5, 10, 12, 21.

(10) There are points of contact between Mark 13 and the forms associated with Christian prophets: the first-person speech for the risen Lord, the reflection of ἐγώ εἰμι as a prophetic formula, the plethora of parenetic second-person plural imperatives, the abundance of prophetic–eschatological vocabulary such as ἡ γενεὰ αὕτη, the announcement of οὐαί (13: 17) and the ἀμὴν λέγω ὑμῖν formula in verse 30, which comes in the final, *gründend* position as it does in several of the prophetic

speeches in Q. The discourse as a whole has a rhythmical formal structure as well. Although this is variously reconstructed [33] (the uncertainties as to the precise form being due in part to materials taken over by the prophet that were not completely digested and in part to Markan rewriting), it is clear that the discourse as a whole was not a formless jumble, nor the characteristic prose of Jewish apocalyptic, but reflects the formally-structured speech of Christian prophecy.

We have seen that several features of Christian prophecy are to be found in the unit 13: 5–31. Further, some of the key objections to the usual form of the 'Little Apocalypse' theory are not valid against the hypothesis of Christian prophetic origin. The composite nature of the discourse is not necessarily evidence of *Markan* redaction, since Christian prophets did not create their oracles *ex nihilo* but incorporated and re-presented previous tradition. The presence of authentic sayings of Jesus, such as the parable of verse 28, is likewise no argument against prophetic origin, for the prophets of the church re-presented sayings of the historical Jesus in their revelations of the word of the risen Jesus.

It is striking that the peculiarly Christian prophetic characteristics discussed above practically all occur outside the verses that are most frequently assigned to the 'Little Apocalypse': verses 7–8, 14–20, 24–7. The parenetic admonitions are in verses 5–6, 9–10, 23, 28–9; the Christ-ego consciousness is expressed in verses 5–6, 9, 13, 23, 30–1; the concern for false prophets in verses 5–6, 22; the concern for speaking by the Holy Spirit in verse 11; the theme of persecution and promise of eschatological blessing principally in verses 9–13. The other characteristics of Scripture interpretation and concern with eschatological themes are shared by Christian prophets and Jewish apocalypse. This concentration of Christian prophetic traits outside the traditional 'Little Apocalypse' may indicate that an apocalyptic fragment was in fact taken over by the Christian prophet, which he re-issued with his characteristic formulations. This would indeed account for the phenomena. It is more likely, it seems to me, that the history of the investigation of Mark 13 has simply played a trick on us. In searching for the (Jewish) apocalyptic 'core', all was excluded from consideration except what was specifically apocalyptic in the Jewish sense. When this process was carried through, all the peculiarly prophetic elements were naturally excluded, being considered secondary accretions, and the 'Little Apocalypse' was reduced to the minimal section, verses 7–8, 14–20, 24–7. This reconstruction is then open to all the objections leveled against it by Beasley-Murray and others. But on the hypothesis of Christian prophecy this reduction is unnecessary; for verses 5–6, 9–13, 21–3, 28–30 need not be excised, and the discourse retains its coherence, which it has admittedly lost in the reductionism of the 'Little Apocalypse' theory. In view of the work of Hartmann, I would regard also the apocalyptic 'core' (verses 7–8, 14–20, 24–7) as the work of the Christian prophet on the basis of his own interpretation of the Old Testament, and I would consider these verses and the remainder of verses 5*b*–31 to be one unit, though containing pre-existing traditions. This does not exclude the fact that *Mark* later reworked this unit, making additions and modifications of his own. But there came to Mark a coherent unit of Christian prophecy containing the bulk of Mark 13: 5*b*–31.

(11) To what situation was this oracle directed? We have seen that prophecy and interpretation of event are closely related, so that the indications that we are dealing with Christian prophetic speech already discussed would lead us to expect that the discourse was the interpretation of the meaning of some event. The discourse itself clearly indicates that it is not free-wheeling speculation about the End, but is related to a particular crisis (verses 6, 7–8, 9, 11–13, 14, 19, 24). But which?

Colani's original suggestion that the prophecy is to be seen in relation to the imminent fall of Jerusalem, probably identical to the 'oracle' that Eusebius says commanded the Jerusalem Christians to flee, has been adopted by others, most recently by Ferdinand Hahn and Rudolf Pesch.[34] Others have seen the years immediately preceding 70 as the best setting for the Gospel of Mark itself and have therefore postulated an earlier origin for the source Mark used. The argument to be presented below concerning Mark's own relation to the tradition of Jesus' sayings, and especially to the prophetic tradition, is additional support for this latter view.

An excellent setting for this prophecy is provided in the threat of Caligula to place his image in the temple in Jerusalem in the year 39–40, a threat that would certainly have been carried out but for his death. While in the nature of the case the connection cannot be proven, the argument is so compelling that even Beasley-Murray must admit that 'the suitability of the occasion for such an oracle cannot be contested'.[35] My present concern, however, is only to point out that the hypothesis of Christian prophecy makes it all the more understandable that in the year of crisis 40 C.E. a church prophet might declare the word of the risen Lord to give eschatological meaning to this situation, precisely as in Revelation.

(12) In the preceding discussion of eleven points of contact between this discourse and Christian prophecy, Revelation has been frequently mentioned. In concluding this argument, I should like to summarize the numerous parallels between Mark 13 and Revelation that illustrate that the Markan discourse is more like our one clear example of Christian prophecy than anything else in early Christian literature:

13: 5–8 – the same four woes, in the same order, are found in Rev. 6.

13: 5 – the warning against false prophets who will deceive ($\pi\lambda\alpha\nu\acute{\alpha}\omega$) the faithful if possible; cf. Rev. 2: 20; 13: 14; 19: 20.

13: 7 – the prediction of $\pi o\lambda\acute{\epsilon}\mu o\upsilon\varsigma$ as part of the prelude to the End. Of the thirteen occurrences of $\pi\acute{o}\lambda\epsilon\mu o\varsigma$ outside Mark 13 and its synoptic parallels, nine are in Revelation, always in an eschatological context.

13: 7 – the expression $\delta\epsilon\hat{\iota}$ $\gamma\epsilon\nu\acute{\epsilon}\sigma\theta\alpha\iota$ is found in the New Testament only here and in Rev. 1: 1; 4: 1 and 22: 6.

13: 7 – $\tau\acute{\epsilon}\lambda o\varsigma$ as the expression for the eschatological End (Rev. 2: 26; 21: 6, 13).

13: 7–8 – as in Revelation, these terrors are only signs of the beginning of the End, not of the End itself.

13: 9 – the suffering of the prophetic community is $\epsilon\grave{\iota}\varsigma$ $\mu\alpha\rho\tau\acute{\upsilon}\rho\iota o\nu$. Cf. Rev. 6: 9; 11: 7; 12: 11, 17; 19: 10.

13: 10 – unless this verse is entirely redactional, which may well be the case, the preaching of the gospel to all the world may not have been, in the original prophetic oracle, an exhortation to the hearers to evangelism but the apocalyptic event described also in Rev. 14: 6 (but nowhere else in the New Testament).

13: 11–13 – the general situation of being persecuted $\delta\iota\grave{\alpha}$ $\tau\grave{o}$ $\ddot{o}\nu o\mu\alpha$ $\mu o\upsilon$ corresponds to the general situation of Revelation and verbally to 2: 3, 13.

13: 13 – $\acute{\upsilon}\pi o\mu o\nu\acute{\eta}$ as *the* Christian virtue under persecution; cf. Rev. 1: 9; 2: 2 etc.

13: 13 – salvation promised to the one who holds fast until the end; cf. Rev. 2: 10*c*.

13: 14 – the interpretation of the present historical crisis as full of eschatological meaning corresponds to the *raison d'être* of Revelation. Both documents use the terminology of $\beta\delta\acute{\epsilon}\lambda\upsilon\gamma\mu\alpha$, which with one exception (Luke 16: 15) is used only in Mark 13 and its synoptic parallels and three times in Revelation in the New Testament.

13: 14 – the expression $\acute{o}$ $\grave{\alpha}\nu\alpha\gamma\iota\nu\acute{\omega}\sigma\kappa\omega\nu$ is used only in Mark 13 par. and in Revelation in the New Testament, having the same function in each instance.

13: 14 – $\phi\epsilon\upsilon\gamma\acute{\epsilon}\tau\omega\sigma\alpha\nu$ $\epsilon\grave{\iota}\varsigma$ $\tau\grave{\alpha}$ $\ddot{o}\rho\eta$; cf. Rev. 6: 15–16; 12: 6.

13: 17 – $o\grave{\upsilon}\alpha\acute{\iota}$. Revelation has fourteen announcements of $o\grave{\upsilon}\alpha\acute{\iota}$ in seven passages. Rev. 8: 13 has the same grammatical construction as the Mark passage.

13: 19 – the great $\theta\lambda\hat{\iota}\psi\iota\varsigma$ is also a part of the eschatological drama in Rev. 1: 9; 2: 9, 10, 22 and especially 7: 14.

13: 20 – in the Markan apocalypse, God himself is not *bound* by the apocalyptic scheme (as in e.g. II Esdras) but is sovereign over it and can change his mind, as in the dynamic understanding of God's relation to history in the prophets of both Israel and the church, illustrated in Rev. 2: 5, 16, 22.

13: 21–2 – both the Markan apocalypse and Revelation respond to false prophets for whom earthly σημεῖα are validating credentials; cf. 13: 14–15; 16: 14; 19: 20. For both Revelation and the Markan apocalypse, the only sign to be expected is the sign from heaven at the End.

13: 24–7 – both the Markan apocalypse and Revelation have the same general scheme of historical troubles, final tribulation, cosmic dissolution, and then the coming of the Son of Man on the clouds.

13: 30 – for the writers of both the Markan apocalypse and Revelation, their generation is the last; the End will come soon. Cf. Rev. 1: 1, 3; 2: 16, 25; 3: 11, 20; 6: 11; 10: 6–7; 11: 2; 12: 6, 12; 17: 10; 22: 6, 7, 10, 12, 20.

The above list is by no means exhaustive but is a fair sample of the similarity between the Markan apocalypse and Revelation. Especially, the similarity of the vocabularies could be further illustrated, for the vocabulary not only sets off 13: 5–31 from the rest of Mark but binds it closely to Revelation.[36] But enough has been done to document the close resemblance between Mark 13 and our prime example of Christian prophecy, and this serves as a concluding point in the argument here offered that the pre-redactional form of Mark 13: 5*b*–31 is itself the product of Christian prophecy.

Mark, Christian prophecy and the origin of the gospel form

The study of the sayings of the risen Jesus in Q and Mark respectively has revealed an important difference that is fundamental to understanding the relation of Christian prophecy to the canonical gospels. Whereas Q contains a considerable number of prophetic sayings, is tending to be understood as a whole as sayings of the risen Jesus and by its nature is open to continued expansion by the addition of new revelatory sayings, Mark contains only a few prophetic sayings, which are entirely contained within the historicizing pre-Easter framework, closing the door to further prophetic expansion. This is seen in the following two sets of data:

Q

Q contains 79 sayings-units, containing 3652 words, which could have circulated independently of a narrative context.

Of these 79 sayings-units, 42 sayings-units, containing 1803 words, are from Christian prophets or have been significantly reshaped by them. (22 sayings (28%), containing 802 words (22%) originated from Christian prophets; 20 sayings (25%) containing 1001 words (27%), bear the marks of prophetic expansion, reshaping and/or transmission.)

Of the sayings-units in Q, 53% are prophetic, representing 49% of the words in the Q sayings-units.

Mark

Mark contains 77 sayings-units, containing 3089 words, which could have circulated independently of a narrative context.

Of these 77 sayings-units, at the most 11 sayings-units, containing 611 words, are probably from Christian prophets.

Of the sayings-units in Mark, 14% are prophetic, representing 20% of the words in the Markan sayings-units.

(Even these figures are inflated by the fact that 13: 5*b*–31, comprising 6 sayings-units and 434 words, is substantially composed of prophetic material. Apart from this one prophetic discourse, which Mark may have included as a major exception to his usual practice,[37] only 8% of Mark's sayings-units, representing a bare 6% of their words, is of prophetic origin.)

Why is it that Mark contains only five sayings, plus the eschatological discourse, that may be attributed to Christian prophets? This question is related to the problem of why there is such a dearth of sayings-material in Mark at all. It might be assumed that Mark has few prophetic sayings as a result of including only a few of *any* kind of sayings. The hypothesis being proposed here is that precisely the opposite relation obtains: the paucity of sayings in Mark is to be explained on the basis of Mark's view of the prophetic sayings.

The data themselves need first to be presented more precisely. Mark has 77 sayings-units containing 3089 words. Matthew has 177 sayings-units containing 9385 words, 3.03 times as much as Mark. By a coincidence, Luke also contains 177 sayings-units, containing 8092 words, 2.6 times as much as Mark. Mark's sayings-material is 27.5% of his gospel, while Matthew's is 55.2% of that part of his material that corresponds to Mark, and Luke's is 48.5%.[38] These data indicate that both absolutely and relatively, and in terms of both number of sayings and number of words, and irrespective of whether 'saying' is defined narrowly or broadly, Mark has only a little more than half as much sayings-material in his gospel as either Matthew or Luke. Why this is so has been an unresolved problem in the literature on Mark since the rise of critical study of the gospels.

The problem is magnified when one considers that Mark seems to be interested in Jesus as a teacher. Διδάσκαλος is by far the most common 'title' given to Jesus by others in the gospel and is used by Jesus of himself (14: 14). Διδάσκω and διδαχή are used with reference to Jesus more than they are in either Matthew or Luke, despite Mark's smaller size. Likewise, Mark has an interest in the sayings of Jesus, as is seen not only by his including seventy-nine of them but also by his repeatedly including such statements as 8: 32: καὶ παρρησίᾳ τὸν λόγον ἐλάλει (cf. also 2: 2, 4: 14ff, 33). These considerations would lead one to expect more sayings of Jesus to be included in Mark and only make their paucity more noticeable and in need of an explanation.

Within the framework of the two-source theory, this problem has usually been expressed by the question: 'Did Mark know Q?', with numerous scholars standing on each side of this debate.[39] The dilemma is clear: if Mark did not know Q, then how can we account for the several places where he seems not only to overlap Q and Q-like materials but to be excerpting from them (e.g. 6: 7–13)? If he did know Q, then how can we account for his using so little of it and for his selection? The chief argument, in fact, in favor of the theory that Mark did *not* know Q has been that he would surely have included more of it had he known it.[40] Source criticism *per se* has not been able to present such an explanation.

The form critics have had no better success in attempting to offer a *traditionsgeschichtlich* solution and left the problem on the agenda of the redaction critics.[41] Redaction criticism looks within Mark's own purpose for an explanation for the paucity of sayings in his gospel and has presented four main types of explanation.

(1) Mark presupposes the sayings-material as well-known and writes to supplement it and be supplemented by it.[42] The value of this view is that it recognizes that Q, or a similar sayings-collection, played a significant role in the Markan community. But this explanation fails to explain why Mark used any of a tradition that he presupposed and affirmed.

(2) Some students have seen Mark as historicizing the sayings-tradition, that is, including sayings of Jesus only incidentally in a document intended primarily to ground the *kerygma* in history by presenting narratives of the pre-Easter Jesus. This cluster of explanations frequently ascribes an anti-Gnostic *Tendenz* to Mark, as already in the work of F. C. Burkitt.[43] Burkitt thought that in Mark's situation the *kerygma* was in danger of being swamped by the multiplication of material dealing with the resurrected Jesus. Mark is pictured as witnessing to the Risen One by presenting the words, but especially the deeds, of the pre-Easter Jesus. It is an incidental by-product of this process that relatively few sayings of Jesus are included. A significant insight is here, but the specific issue of why, having included

seventy-seven sayings of Jesus, Mark declined to include others, remains unanswered.

(3) This lack is somewhat remedied by the third group of explanations, which point to Mark's emphasis on the passion–resurrection *kerygma* as the key to his sparing use of sayings-material. Morton Scott Enslin, for example, argued that Mark included only those sayings that developed the conflict that led to the cross.[44] R. H. Lightfoot attempts to explain the two large blocks of sayings-material, chapters 4 and 13, by their appropriateness to the secrecy and suffering motifs that are bound up with Mark's passion *kerygma.*[45] But sayings are included that would be difficult to relate to the passion theme (4: 1–34; 7: 20–3; 10: 14–16 etc.), and sayings in Q are excluded that would have strengthened the conflict theme that leads to the passion: Luke 3: 7–9 and 11: 42–52, for example.

(4) A fourth type of explanation is represented by Eduard Schweizer and Étienne Trocmé.[46] While differing on many other points, Schweizer and Trocmé agree that Mark has so little of Q and Q-like material because he is basically opposed to this *kind* of material, that is, to the kind of Christianity it represents. Trocmé regards Mark's opponents as representing 'A Christianity contaminated by *rabbinic tradition* in the matter of moral teaching and by somewhat naively apocalyptic eschatology'.[47] This is Jerusalem Christianity, he says, with its legalistic scruples, presenting the sayings-tradition as the historical legacy of Jesus now binding on the church. Schweizer's version of this approach agrees that Mark is hesitant about using Q-material, because he opposes the theology implicit in it, but Schweizer sees the objectionable element as being Q's tendency to 'historicize' Jesus, in the sense that Q binds Jesus' word to the past by repeating his words as the authoritative message of a past historical figure. Mark, says Schweizer, wants the Jesus of his gospel to address the hearer/reader in the present.[48]

These four types of redaction-critical explanation for the paucity of sayings in Mark may be summarized thus: (1) Mark *presupposes* the existence of Q or a Q-like collection as a factor in his situation to be reckoned with; (2) Mark *historicizes* his material, relating it to the story of the pre-Easter Jesus; (3) Mark *selects* his material to correspond to his emphasis on the cross–resurrection *kerygma*; (4) Mark *opposes* some kind of Christianity represented by the Q-materials. The hypothesis I would like to propose here draws together and extends these elements in previous hypotheses and sees them all in terms of the phenomenon of Christian prophecy. My hypothesis may be briefly stated: *Mark has so few sayings of Jesus because he is suspicious of Christian prophecy as it is present in his community and expressed in the sayings-tradition. He creates a new prophetic form intended as an alternative.*

We have seen that Q contained substantial prophetic materials and was coming to be regarded as altogether 'sayings of the risen Jesus'. It was not a *rabbinic* Q against which Mark was reacting but a *prophetic* Q. This prophetic aspect of Mark's opponents is an interpretative key to Mark's gospel that should be followed up. Only a few comments can be given here. A number of recent authors consider the opposition party in Mark's church to be θεῖοι ἄνδρες types who advocate a θεῖος ἀνήρ christology.[49] While this thesis has proven to be a helpful approach to Mark's theology, the term θεῖος ἀνήρ, as well as the figure denoted by it, has turned out to be somewhat difficult to pin down. Some students of Mark who understand Mark to be struggling against a θεῖος ἀνήρ christology have noted points of contact between the figure of the θεῖος ἀνήρ and the prophet. I would suggest that these prophetic aspects of Mark's opponents should be investigated more carefully. It is of the utmost importance to note that the only opponents of the church specifically named in the gospel itself are called ψευδόχριστοι καὶ ψευδοπροφῆται (13: 22). The troublesome ψευδόχριστοί may be best understood if the καί is regarded as epexegetical. One category of opponents is described, who speak as Χριστός (ἐγώ εἰμι: 13: 6!), who call themselves προφῆται and are so called by others, and whose trademark is that they come ἐπὶ τῷ ὀνόματί μου (13: 6), as do the prophets of Matt. 7: 22. The ἐπὶ τῷ ὀνόματί μου is a revelatory, but not messianic, claim, meaning that the claimants come in the authority of Jesus' name, as the prophets did, but not claiming to *be* the Messiah or the already-returned Jesus. Mark's opponents are inner-church prophetic figures, not extra-church messianic claimants.

There seems to be an anti-prophet motif in Mark. It comes to expression, for instance, in the fact that, except for the proverb in 6: 4,[50] Jesus is only twice called 'prophet' in Mark, 6: 15 and 8: 28, and in each case this is clearly to be taken as a misunderstanding. While Matthew and Luke modify these passages to indicate only that Jesus is one of the Old Testament prophets who has risen, Mark alone denies categorically that Jesus is εἰς τῶν προφητῶν, period. Mark seems to be an opponent of prophecy as it is expressed in his environment. The most probable reason for Mark's hesitating use of the Q-material is to be found in his suspicion of the genre that it represents, the post-Easter revelations of the risen Lord.

Now comes a peculiar, but equally important, point. Mark is not only anti-prophet, he is also pro-prophet and is in fact something of a Christian prophet himself. In his hands Christian prophecy becomes a dramatic new form, so that he no longer quite fits the definition of Christian prophecy with which I have been working. Mark is indeed a spokesman for the risen Lord, and he mediates the address of the risen Lord to the community, but he is not 'immediately-inspired' in the same way as his predecessors. In the Gospel of Mark, it is the risen Lord who addresses the hearer/reader's own present, not merely a historical figure whose words are reported and repeated. But the message of the risen Lord is now bound to, and contained within, the tradition of Jesus of Nazareth as this is contained within a narrative presented entirely in a pre-Easter framework. In short, one important factor in Mark's creation of the gospel form was his response to the challenge of Christian prophecy in his time by developing an alternative form to mediate the address of the risen and present Lord.

To establish in any convincing way the point that Mark functions as a prophet who sees himself as mediating the word of the risen Lord in his gospel would require a thorough redaction-critical analysis of the whole of Mark, which is impossible here. I will only mark out the main lines of evidence that such an investigation might follow, and cite the works of redaction critics who do understand Mark to be a Christian prophet.

(1) Mark's formulae for introducing direct discourse may be divided into two categories, 'historical' (e.g. ἀπεκρίθη καὶ εἶπεν αὐτοῖς) and 'present' (e.g. λέγει ὁ Ἰησοῦς). There are a total of 260 instances of direct discourse in Mark, of which 143 are from Jesus. The non-Jesus quotations (disciples, Pharisees etc.) contain 24.8% 'present' forms, while the introductory formulae to the words of Jesus are 39.1% 'present'. Both Matthew and Luke reduce this use of the present tense, Luke almost to the vanishing-point. While a thorough redaction-critical study would require distinguishing tradition from redaction, attention to 'mixed' forms and a more precise presentation of the evidence, this general phenomenon suggests that when Mark lets Jesus speak he thinks in terms of present address contained within the narrative framework. The difference between the way words of Jesus and words of others in the story are handled suggests that this is more than simply the 'historical present', its usual designation.

(2) Sometimes within the narrative framework Mark lets the Jesus in the story explicitly address the hearer/reader's own present (e.g. 13: 37; 8: 27 – 9: 1). In such scenes, what is told as an encounter between Jesus and his disciples 'back there' in history is patently an encounter between the risen Christ and his church. In 8: 27 – 9: 1, for example, the calling of the crowd in verse 34 is a strange feature of the story within the past-narrative framework; it is a means of extending Jesus' address from the disciples to a broader audience. Already in verse 30, Peter is only the spokesman for the disciples – Jesus rebuked αὐτοῖς, plural. And verse 33 καὶ ἰδὼν τοὺς μαθητὰς αὐτοῦ ἐπετίμησεν Πέτρῳ καὶ λέγει is another expression of the same point: Jesus addresses Peter, but with his eye on the disciples and in the present tense. Examples could be multiplied.

(3) Related to this is the fact that Jesus is portrayed as himself the one who proclaims τὸν λόγον, and that ὁ λόγος is a technical term for the Christian message in Mark (1: 45; 2: 2; 4: 14–20, 33; 8: 32; cf. 8: 38; 10: 22; 13: 31). An interesting variant reading occurs in 8: 32. Both the Sinaitic Syriac and Tatian apparently read λαλήσει in their *Vorlagen* and the Old Latin MS k reads *loqui*, thus connecting these words with the preceding infinitives so that the reference is to a speaking by the resurrected Lord after Easter. This was considered the original reading by F. C. Burkitt and Ernst Lohmeyer.[51] Original or not, when so read this verse does express the Markan theology as it comes to expression elsewhere. The prophetic connotations of παρρησία should also be noted.

(4) The impersonal tone, lack of quotation of sources, the author's receding anonymously behind his writing, were taken by the *formgeschichtliche Schule* to mean that the writer is completely subservient to his tradition, borne along by his material. But Mark is an author, not just a recorder of tradition. Yet these features remain, and it should be asked if they are not better explained by the consciousness of the prophet who is aware that he speaks for the risen Christ.

(5) Mark's use of εὐαγγέλιον in 1: 1; 8: 35 and 10: 29 may indicate that it is (the risen) Jesus himself who preaches the gospel contained in Mark's writing. Ἐυαγγέλιον Ἰησοῦ Χριστοῦ in 1: 1 is probably both subjective genitive and objective genitive, as in the parallel εὐαγγέλιον τοῦ θεοῦ in 1: 15. Willi Marxsen's development of this case should be pursued,[52] as well as the oracular associations of the word εὐαγγέλιον.[53]

(6) The study of Alfred Suhl, a pupil of Marxsen's, contends that Mark's use of the Old Testament compares to that of the Christian prophets as illustrated in Revelation.[54] According to Suhl, Mark's handling of the Old Testament does not use the promise/fulfillment scheme used by both Matthew and Luke, which historicizes the Christ-event in such a way that it remains an event of the past. Mark rather lets both the Old Testament and Jesus speak through his writing directly to the present, as in Revelation.

These are the kinds of considerations that should be pursued in a redaction-critical study of the prophetic nature of Mark's composition. To date we have no complete study of Mark from this point of view, but numerous redaction critics have indicated that in Mark's view it is the risen Christ who speaks through his composition.[55]

The anti-prophetic note in Mark is sounded by one who himself functions as a prophet. Mark's anti-prophetism is a part of his own prophetism. Mark does not oppose the view that the risen Lord still speaks — he is an exponent of this view. What he opposes is the view that the risen Lord comes to speech in the collections of sayings such as Q that were so open to being considered the post-Easter address of the exalted Lord, an address no longer grounded in history. Such collections were not only composed of material much of which did in fact come into being after Easter, they were open to this interpretation *in toto* and to continued growth and expansion by the risen Lord.

To counteract this tendency, Mark took a step at once paradoxical and radical: he presented the message of the living Lord in a narrative form in which the post-Easter Jesus, in the narrative story-line, says nothing. His message is confined entirely to the pre-Easter framework of the gospel form that Mark devised for this purpose. There is an intentional dialectic here. It is no accident that Mark ends at 16: 8 with the announcement that Jesus is risen, but without his having appeared. To tell an appearance story is to have the risen Lord speak in an undialectical way and to open the door to a flood of post-Easter revelations of which Mark is very critical. If Pesch is correct in arguing that Mark re-edited his gospel, inserting the apocalyptic discourse into his already-constructed outline, as a kind of contemporizing, immediately-relevant appendix, the question arises: 'Why not at the end?'[56] Perrin's analysis of the Markan outline, though he addresses the question from a different direction than Pesch, tends to confirm the unusual location of chapter 13,[57] and Trocmé's argument from a still different angle also emphasizes the strange fact of the gospel's continuing after 13: 37.[58] The hypothesis proposed here offers an answer to this troublesome problem: Mark is absolutely unwilling to tell the story in such a way that the risen Lord continues to speak in the story-line after Easter.

This dialectic may also be helpful in understanding Mark's view of the presence and absence of Jesus with his church. Of late numerous scholars have pointed to the absence of Jesus from the resurrection to the *parousia* as an important Markan theme.[59] The argument is well supported by evidence from the Empty Tomb and Lord's Supper pericopae. But there seems to be another, equally important emphasis in Mark, which portrays the Jesus of the gospel as present, dealing with his disciples in Mark's own day. The story of 6: 45–52, for example, pictures the disciples alone in the boat in the midst of the sea, in great trouble, βασανιζομένους, a picture in which the Markan church could see itself reflected. It is impossible that Jesus can come to them; yet he comes, even though they disbelieve and misunderstand, and makes himself known with his revelatory, prophetic ἐγώ εἰμι.[60] Although the absence of Jesus is 'a presiding feature in the Markan gospel', still 'the gospel (itself) functions in such a way as to extend Jesus into the Markan present'.[61] Jesus is not present physically, nor in terms of resurrection appearances, nor mystically, nor sacramentally.

And he is not only absent, he is silent. He does not speak directly, as Christian prophets deliver new post-Easter revelations in his name, nor is the word of the post-Easter Jesus mediated by prophetic sayings-collections such as Q. Mark avoids Q and has few Q-type sayings for this very reason. But neither is Jesus absolutely absent or mute. He is present and speaks prophetically in the new prophetic form, the Markan gospel.

Mark is thus Christian prophecy, but prophecy in a new idiom. He speaks with the voice of the exalted Lord but at the same time wishes to curb the uncontrolled increase of prophetic revelations. In this respect he is like Paul, who is a prophet himself, yet is opposed to the wild enthusiasm that strays too far from the tradition, and asserts his own writing as of prophetic authority (I Cor. 14: 37–8), thereby putting a restraint on others. If one accepts the idea of charismatic authority, as both Paul and Mark in their respective churches do, then only one who himself wields charismatic authority can effectively limit charismatic excesses. But the counter-charismatic authority must be expressed in a new form. This is what both Paul and Mark, each in his own way, attempt to do. The fact that they *write* their προφητεία at all is already something of a limitation of the free sway of the Spirit. The wind of the Spirit still blows, but no longer 'where it wills'. When Mark and his contemporary Paul put pen to paper, we already have the nucleus of 'Gospel and Epistle': the New Testament canon.

13 CHRISTIAN PROPHECY IN MATTHEW

In an earlier section I have dealt with the general relationship of Matthew to the Christian prophets in his church. I now wish to attempt to identify the materials from Christian prophets that are peculiar to Matthew's Gospel (those he takes over from Q and Mark having already been discussed) and to investigate Matthew's own stance *vis-à-vis* the phenomenon of the expansion of the sayings of Jesus through Christian prophets.

Matt. 28: 18*b*–20

This commissioning-speech of the risen Jesus is the most obvious place to begin, for as it is a post-Easter saying of the risen Lord in the first person, the possibility of prophetic origin is immediately suggested. But did the saying originate as the oracle of a Christian prophet in the strict sense, or is it a literary composition of Matthew or one of his predecessors, or some combination of the two?

The recent thorough study by Benjamin Hubbard reveals that there are striking Matthean elements in the passage ($\dot{\epsilon}\nu$ $o\dot{\upsilon}\rho\alpha\nu\tilde{\omega}$ $\kappa\alpha\dot{\iota}$ $\dot{\epsilon}\pi\dot{\iota}$ $\tau\tilde{\eta}\varsigma$ $\gamma\tilde{\eta}\varsigma$, $o\tilde{\upsilon}\nu$, $\mu\alpha\theta\eta\tau\epsilon\dot{\upsilon}\sigma\alpha\tau\epsilon$, $\delta\iota\delta\dot{\alpha}\sigma\kappa\sigma\nu\tau\epsilon\varsigma$, $\dot{\epsilon}\omega\varsigma$ $\tau\tilde{\eta}\varsigma$ $\sigma\upsilon\nu\tau\epsilon\lambda\epsilon\dot{\iota}\alpha\varsigma$ $\tau\sigma\tilde{\upsilon}$ $\alpha\dot{\iota}\tilde{\omega}\nu\sigma\varsigma$) and that the present form of the passage represents considerable redactional activity on Matthew's part.[1] But Hubbard's research also confirms the conclusion reached by others that Matthew is not composing from whole cloth but is rewriting a traditional commissioning saying.[2] When this saying is compared to the profile of Christian prophecy, several common features are apparent.

(1) In addition to the obvious overall form as a post-Easter saying of the risen Lord delivered in the first person, there are other features of form and vocabulary that relate the saying to Christian prophets. The saying is neatly composed of three elements: a declaration of authority, a commissioning charge and a promise of the abiding presence of Jesus. Even prior to Hubbard's research, it has been noted that this schema corresponds to the Old Testament schema in which Yahweh commissioned prophets, and the prophets reported their own commissioning (Ezek. 1: 1 – 3: 15; Is. 6; Jer. 1: 10; cf. Is. 49: 1–6),[3] except that here Jesus plays the role of

Yahweh, precisely as in Christian prophecy. This form is paralleled in the only first-hand report of the call of a Christian prophet in the New Testament, Rev. 1: 12–20: declaration of authority (1: 17*b*–18), commissioning (1: 19), promise of presence (1: 20, taken with 1: 13, is a declaration that the risen Christ is present in his churches in Asia). In addition, the οὖν of verse 20 is a characteristic prophetic word (though it is also characteristic of Matthew), and the ἐγὼ μεθ᾽ ὑμῶν εἰμί is reminiscent of the prophetic ἐγώ εἰμι not only in form but in its function here.[4]

(2) Related to this is the prophetic 'chain of command' from God the Father through the risen Jesus and his prophet to the church and the world, which we have found in Revelation and the Fourth Gospel, as well as in the Q prophetic *logion* Luke 10: 22/Matt. 11: 27. The saying in Matt. 28: 18*b*–20 is conceived in terms of that pattern, which corresponds to Christian prophecy.

(3) The emphatic note of authority with which a pronouncement on a disputed point (the carrying of the gospel to Gentiles) is made is appropriate to Christian prophets.

(4) It has long been a commonplace of exegesis that the text is composed as a kind of midrash on Dan. 7: 14.[5] The parallels are clear:

καὶ ἐδόθη αὐτῷ	ἐδόθη μοι
ἐξουσία	πᾶσα ἐξουσία
καὶ πάντα τὰ ἔθνη	ἐν οὐρανῷ καὶ
τῆς γῆς κατὰ γένη	ἐπὶ [τῆς] γῆς
καὶ πᾶσα δόξα	πορευθέντες οὖν μαθητεύσατε
αὐτῷ λατρεύουσα	πάντα τὰ ἔθνη

Yet Scripture is not directly quoted in the promise/fulfillment scheme characteristic of Matthew himself but is allusively peshered and re-presented as the word of the exalted Jesus, as in Revelation and Christian prophecy generally.[6]

(5) This relation to Dan. 7: 14 involves an implicit claim to be the exalted Son of Man. The speaker knows himself to speak with the authority of the heavenly Son of Man. We have seen that this self-consciousness was characteristic of Christian prophets.[7]

(6) The reference to the End of the age represents the eschatological perspective that was characteristic of Christian prophecy, though the saying itself is not aflame with *Naherwartung*. But there seems to be another kind of polemic that comes to expression in this declaration that the risen Jesus who speaks in the *logion* will be with the church until the End of the age: the prophetic gift is not to pass away but is to last as long as the church does. This corresponds to the kind of polemic in which Christian prophets sometimes engaged.[8]

(7) Thoroughly prophetic is the way in which the word of the Lord is given to bring the church the message appropriate to its post-Easter situation and to resolve a disputed issue (the validity of the mission to Gentiles). The prophetic speaker knows that the pre-Easter Jesus did not carry on a mission to Gentiles nor command his disciples to do so. Yet he believes that it is the will of the exalted Lord, who is present in the mission of the church, to carry out a universal mission and expresses this not in the form of his own exegetical theological reasoning but as a revelation of the risen Lord. We have seen above that there is considerable evidence that the Christian prophets played a major role in the broadening out of the church's mission to include Gentiles;[9] here we seem to have one of their oracles that played a part in this important transition in the history of the church.[10]

5: 3–12

We have seen that the Q-form of the beatitudes contains both original pronouncements of Jesus and an expansion from Christian prophets. As the beatitudes appear in Matthew, they have been expanded by the peculiarly Matthean tradition and/or by Matthew himself. The additions bear the marks of prophetic origin and reshaping. Phrases from Scripture are re-presented as the word of Jesus (5: 5 = Ps. 37: 11; 5: 8 = Ps. 24: 4; 51: 12; 73: 1). The persecution motif is elaborated (5: 10). The eschatological makarism is itself a prophetic form. A neat 'sentence of holy law' is found in 5: 7. In 5: 11–12 the Q-beatitude has been reformulated to make the persecution motif more explicit (διώξωσιν, verse 11, and ἐδίωξαν, verse 12). Ἀγαλλιᾶσθε is introduced, which has overtones of the prophetic exaltation of the spirit (Luke 1: 47; 10: 21; Rev. 19: 7; cf. ἀγαλλιάσει in Acts 2: 46). The addition of τοὺς πρὸ ὑμῶν makes it explicit that the hearers are considered prophets themselves. There can be no certainty concerning the allocation of these elements to the original Q (which were then omitted by Q^{Lk} or Luke), the pre-Matthean tradition (Q^{Mt}) and the redactional work of Matthew. What is clear is that the beatitudes, already formed by Christian prophets in Q, are even more prophetic in their Matthean form, which strongly suggests the influence of the Christian prophets of the Matthean community.[11]

Matt. 5: 18

We have already discussed the evidence that the Q-form of this saying is from a church prophet. If the introductory ἀμὴν λέγω ὑμῖν was not already present in the Q-form, the Matthean tradition, or Matthew, assimilates the saying to this prophetic form. The saying is also reformulated into a declaration that something will not take place until something else (of an eschatological nature) takes place, a form characteristic of prophets.[12] This prophetic saying that had circulated in Q is taken up by the Matthean community and assimilated more closely to typical prophetic forms.[13]

Matt. 5: 19

This saying is certainly a post-Easter creation of the church, in a situation where the continuing validity of the individual prescriptions of the Law was debated. It purports to settle this disputed point by a first-person saying of Jesus, in the form of a 'sentence of holy law'. On this basis Käsemann, Grundmann and Schweizer assign it to early Christian prophecy.[14] But there seems to be no other evidence linking the saying to Christian prophets, and, while it could have originated as prophecy, it could also be a scribal expansion of the tradition using the prophetic form that had apparently become familiar in the Matthean community.

Matt. 6: 14—15

Here we have a saying found also in Mark 11: 25, but the Matthean version is in the form of a 'sentence of holy law'. Käsemann was inclined to explain such cases as though the Matthean form was original, which Mark later 'dismantled'.[15] While this is not impossible, it is *a priori* more likely that sayings from Mark and floating sayings were taken up by the Matthean community and assimilated to the prophetic form of 'sentences of holy law'. This would account for the preponderance of this form in Matthew and would relieve Käsemann of his forced explanation that Matthew included a plethora of charismatic sayings although he was anti-charismatic himself. This saying may have been re-formed by a prophet in the Matthean community who re-presented it as a word of the exalted Lord. Alternatively, Matthew himself may have rewritten it, conforming it to the style of the prophets of his church with which he was familiar in order to give it a particularly solemn tone. In the latter case, the *form* of a 'sentence of holy law' alone is not adequate to establish a saying as prophetic, since non-prophets such as Matthew could utilize the form under the influence of prophets in their situation.

Matt. 7: 2

As in 6: 14—15, a non-prophetic saying circulating in the Matthean church has been tautened and recast in a form resembling the sayings of Christian prophets, but this is no proof that this was done by a Christian prophet.

Matt. 7: 13—23

The concern of Matthew and his community with the problem posed by Christian prophets is apparent in the reworking of these sayings from the Q-tradition in Luke 13: 24. To the general exhortation to disciples to struggle to enter through the narrow gate is added a specific warning against false prophets in verse 15. Although concern for the danger of false prophets was characteristic of Christian prophets, there is not enough evidence here to identify this saying as of prophetic origin. To this is then added the general Q-material concerning recognizing good disciples by their fruits, which is here made to apply specifically to the problem of false prophecy (verses 16—20). Then the Q-materials from Luke 13: 25—7 are resumed, but rewritten and augmented to bring out more clearly their reference to Christian prophets. There is some evidence that verses 20—3 contain material promulgated by a Christian prophet as the word of the risen Lord: the eschatological orientation, the law-form that declares who shall enter the kingdom on the Last Day, the concern with false prophecy, the allusive re-presentation of Scripture (verse 22 = Jer. 14: 14; verse 23 = Ps. 6: 8),[16] the menacing, authoritative tone of the *Gerichtswort*. Here we probably have more than the incidental influence of prophets on the way things get said in the Matthean community; a prophet has taken a traditional saying and reformulated it as a more precise word of the risen Lord to his contemporary situation.[17]

Matt. 10: 5*b*—42

In this extensive composition, Matthew takes the Q commissioning-speech, which had already been created and formulated by Christian prophets, and elaborates it with material drawn partly from Mark but mostly from his own sources. As the materials from Q and elsewhere developed in the Matthean community and in Matthew's own hands, they took on an even more prophetic character, partly by the addition of oracles formulated by Christian prophets in the Matthean stream of tradition, partly by editorial changes made by Matthew and his predecessors under the influence of Christian prophets.

The prohibition of a mission to Gentiles in 10: 5*b*—6 is probably a post-Easter assertion from within the Palestinian church opposing the Gentile mission, rather than Matthew's own composition.[18] Although Käsemann characteristically labels the saying a product of prophecy, and Dunn, usually quite cautious in this respect, considers this saying a 'plausible' example of prophetic speech transformed into a saying of the historical Jesus,[19] it lacks any specifically prophetic traits. If the saying was originally connected with 10: 23 in the history of the tradition and originated in the same *Sitz im Leben*, then this connection may be evidence for its prophetic origin, for 10: 23 is from Christian prophecy, as we shall see below. The only other evidence of prophetic origin would be the evident authority of the saying, which prevented Matthew from simply ignoring it, although it conflicted with the post-Easter commission of Jesus in 28: 16–20.

In 10: 7–16, Matthew adapts Q-material to the speech he is composing. This material was already prophetic, and Matthew adds no further prophetic characteristics, with the possible exception of inserting ἀμήν into the introductory formula of verse 15, if this was not already present in the Q-form.

The section of verses 17–22 agrees almost verbatim with Mark 13: 9–13, which is commonly taken to be Matthew's source. This would seem to be supported by the fact that Matthew fails to repeat most of this Markan segment in his own apocalyptic discourse in 24: 9–13. But since the unit is coherent in itself, and in view of the awkwardness of imagining Matthew rolling his scroll of Mark forward at this point to copy these verses, it may be that Matthew is quoting the 'Little Apocalypse' as it circulated independently of Mark or that the Q-material Matthew is interpreting also contained these sayings.[20] In any case, these verses were originally Christian prophecy before being placed in their present context. Matthew has not made any changes that make the Matthean form more prophetic than its predecessor.

Matthew then adds verse 23, which has been interpreted in so many ways. If the saying originated as the pronouncement of a Christian prophet, some of the exegetical mystery connected with this text would be clarified. The following evidence indicates that this is indeed the case.

(1) The form of the saying is strikingly similar to that of four other synoptic sayings (Mark 9: 1; 13: 30; Matt. 5: 18; 23: 39): a solemn introduction with ἀμὴν λέγω ὑμῖν (ἀμήν is now absent from Matt. 23: 39), an emphatic (οὐ μή) declaration that something will not happen until (four times ἕως ἄν as here, once μέχρις οὗ) before the *eschaton*, which in at least four of the cases is assumed to be near. This form is appropriate to Christian prophets but not to others. In addition to the prophetic introductory formula, a declaration that the *eschaton* will occur before some present state of affairs ceases to be is the kind of statement that can only be made *ab ovo* by one who knows himself authorized by charismatic power. Later scribes may repeat it but not invent it. The remarkably close similarity in form between the five sayings suggests the same *Sitz im Leben*. All four of the other sayings seem to be from Christian prophets,[21] which suggests the same origin for this saying.

(2) The *logion* presupposes a setting in which bands of Christian

missioners go from city to city, thus expressing a concern for the mission typical of, but of course not limited to, Christian prophets. The speaker of this saying is not one of the missioners but is among those who send them forth, instructing them for their mission by means of a 'word of the Lord'. While it is notoriously difficult to fit this saying into the pre-Easter ministry of Jesus, a most appropriate *Sitz im Leben* for the origin of such a saying would be a 'commissioning service' in which the church sends forth its missioners, as in Acts 13: 1–3. In the Acts scene, not only are Christian prophets among the missioners but the prophetic voice is heard among those who send the missioners forth, as someone speaking by the power of the Spirit gives instructions for the mission. So also in this case. Matt. 10: 23 can be readily understood as the pronouncement of a Christian prophet made in the Spirit during a worship service in which missioners are commissioned and instructed for their task.

(3) The saying reflects not only mission but persecution. Such explicit references to persecution are evidence not only of post-Easter origin but of prophetic speech. The expectation that the missionaries would be persecuted is especially appropriate to Christian prophets, who would tend to see the church's mission in prophetic terms.

(4) The saying fits the function of Christian prophecy of supplying a word of the risen Lord to settle an ambiguous situation for which there was no clear or satisfactory dominical saying in the tradition. There was a clear tradition that the Christian missionary should stand firm in the face of opposition. Some of this tradition was from sayings of Jesus and some was from Christian prophets, as Revelation, for example, shows. But what if standing fast in the face of persecution endangers the mission with which the missionaries have been charged by the risen Lord himself? Should the missionaries stand fast, even at the risk of their lives (and of the mission), or flee? The latter course seemed not only to accept defeat but to concede that the mission itself was illegitimate, since the true prophet does not retreat at the threat of suffering. It appears that it was to just such a situation that the oracle of 10: 23 was directed. Belief in the Spirit could legitimize breaks with the tradition. Flight in the face of persecution was not cowardice or strategy but obedience to the exalted Lord, authorized by a word from his prophet.

(5) The saying represents the eschatological-apocalyptic *paraclesis* typical of Christian prophets. However Matthew himself may have understood the saying, the reference to the coming of the Son of Man that is the motivating power for the *paraclesis* was originally a fervently eschatological declaration. The coming of the Son of Man can be understood as the *parousia* at the (near) End of history, but other explanations were at least

possible for Matthew: a meeting of Jesus and the Twelve during the course
of their mission, Jesus' death and/or resurrection, the crisis of the Jewish
war 66–70.[22] Such explanations may help a later generation – Matthew's
or ours – to make acceptable sense of a saying that in its obvious meaning
has become an embarrassment. But no one who wanted to speak of a
rendezvous between Jesus and the Twelve, or the resurrection, or the
Jewish war, would choose to express any one of these meanings in the
form in which Matt. 10: 23 now stands. The original meaning of this
oracle must refer to the *parousia* at the End of history. The inner logic of
the saying is this: 'When you are persecuted, the heavenly Lord authorizes
you to flee to another town. This is not cowardice but is made necessary
by the shortness of the time before the *eschaton* and by the missionary
imperative. Do not remain in an inhospitable town, because you will not
have completed the assigned task of preaching in every city in Israel before
the End.' It is on the basis of their claimed insight into the eschatological
Heilsplan Gottes that the Christian prophets offer their word of command
for the present situation. The command is not arbitrary, nor based on its
authority as an inspired oracle alone, nor is the eschatological content
simply speculative. Eschatological insight functions pastorally; pastoral
'advice' is more than that, it is command grounded in a revealed eschatological mystery. The Apocalypse is similar in form and function, though
the resulting command is different.

(6) A corroborative bit of evidence is that the saying is formulative as a
Son-of-Man saying, which was characteristic of Christian prophets.[23]

(7) The saying expresses a consciousness of superlative authority on the
part of the speaker. One of the most frequent arguments for the authenticity of this saying is that it would not have been preserved after its
erroneous prediction became obvious unless, as Carsten Colpe states, 'it
really was a saying of the Lord'.[24] But we must not fall into the trap of
supposing that all the sayings that the early church considered to be 'really'
from the Lord were from the pre-Easter Jesus. It is of the nature of
genuinely prophetic sayings that their authority remains, and the materials
themselves are preserved, even when their predictions fail of fulfillment.[25]
Again, Revelation is 'Exhibit *A*' in this regard.

(8) The *traditionsgeschichtlich* associations of this saying in its various
settings in the history of the tradition (Mark 9: 1; 13: 30; Matt. 5: 18; 23:
39/Luke 12: 2–12/Matt. 10 speech-complex) are all with materials that
have themselves numerous contacts with Christian prophecy. This is further
evidence for the prophetic origin of this saying. The cumulative effect of
this evidence permits us to conclude with some confidence that Matt. 10:
23 originated as the oracle of a Christian prophet.

In 10: 24, Matthew or his tradition has taken a saying from another Q-context and refashioned it into a more prophetic *logion*. The addition of the δοῦλος/κύριος metaphor suggests the Old Testament understanding of the prophets as servants of Yahweh and may be related to the servant = prophet terminology of Revelation. The addition of the reference to Beelzebul in verse 25 may also be an echo of the anti-prophet polemic to which prophets responded.

The Q-materials found in Luke 12: 2–9, 51–3, which we have seen to be influenced by Christian prophets and to a large extent created by them, are taken over by Matthew or his tradition in 10: 26–36. At one point, verse 27, the Matthean version is decidedly more prophetic. A general exhortation to fearless confession has been accommodated to fit the prophetic experience of reception of revelation and its proclamation.

In 10: 40–2, Matthew or his tradition takes over a prophetic Q-saying found in Luke 10: 16 and elaborates it with a saying from his own tradition, which specifically refers to Christian prophets, and a saying also found in Mark 9: 41, which is also appropriate to Christian prophets, concluding the whole speech with the prophetic promise of eschatological reward, couched in a saying introduced by ἀμὴν λέγω ὑμῖν. The saying in verse 41 may have been influenced by the prophetic form 'sentence of holy law'. The προφήτης and δίκαιος of verse 40 are not two different terms for the same person but indicate that the missioners of the Matthean community included both prophets and non-prophets.

Thus we see that at almost every point the selection and editing of the missionary discourse to the disciples in Matt. 10 shows the influence of Christian prophets, and the impression of Bultmann seems to be confirmed: 'it was the risen (or ascended) Lord who spoke'.[26] That this is not just owing to Matthew's editing but represents something in the formative process of a pre-Matthean tradition-complex that developed in Matthew's church, may be seen from the numerous contacts between the prophetic speeches of the Fourth Gospel and the discourse of Matt. 10.[27]

Matt. 11: 28–30

This Matthean addition to the prophetic Q-*logion* may also be from a Christian prophet, as Beare and Dunn suggest,[28] but there is little evidence in the saying itself to support this. None of the distinctive characteristics of Christian prophets are expressed in the saying, except for the strong consciousness of speaking with the ἐγώ of the risen Christ and the allusive re-presentation of Jer. 6: 16 as the word of Jesus.[29] Prophetic influence may be considered no more than a possibility here.

Matt. 12: 33–5

This Q-material, though not of prophetic origin, is again brought into conjunction with traditions that have prophetic contacts by Matthew or someone in the Matthean church, as in 7: 17–20 above. In verses 34, 36 and 37, the general criterion of 'knowing them by their fruits' is made to apply directly to recognizing authentic Christian speech, i.e. is related more closely to the issues at the heart of Christian prophecy.

Matt. 13: 35

This citation from the Old Testament by Matthew is not the word of a Christian prophet but Matthew's own editorializing. But its selection and interpretation is probably influenced by the Christian prophets in Matthew's church, for it embodies several themes of Christian prophecy: the disclosure of what has been hidden, the revelation of contemporary events as part of the eschatological plan of God, the similarity to I Pet. 1: 10–12, the awareness of interpreting Scripture with divinely-given insight, as in the Qumran community, and the selection of a text from Scripture in which Jesus could speak in the first person, are all appropriate to Christian prophecy. Though Matthew is not a prophet himself, his use of the Old Testament is influenced by the prophets.

Matt. 16: 17–19; 18: 18

The declaration in 18: 18 could hardly be from the historical Jesus, since it presupposes a post-Easter church that functions institutionally, needing some rabbinic-like procedures and structures for settling disputed issues. The saying has several indications of prophetic origin: (1) the introductory formula ἀμὴν λέγω ὑμῖν, (2) the legal-sounding declaration that settles a disputed issue in the community's life, expressed in (3) antithetic parallelism, similar to 'sentences of holy law', and (4) the relation to John 20: 23, where the saying is a post-Easter saying of the exalted Christ, from the prophetic Johannine community.

The saying in 18: 18 has an obvious connection with 16: 17–19. This connection, the references to revelation from the Father and the assumed originally-post-Easter setting of the story of Peter's confession have led some scholars to regard 16: 17–19 as also having originated in Christian prophecy.[30] But the matter needs to be stated more precisely. The form of 16: 17–19 is not appropriate to a prophetic saying, despite the material connections with Christian prophecy: the saying pictures Jesus addressing a third party (Peter), rather than the hearer/reader. Prophets do not narrate incidents in which Jesus addressed a revered leader of the past but allow the risen Jesus to speak directly to the present. Yet the prophetic

characteristics of the passage call for explanation. I would propose the
following history of the tradition. (1) The tradition originated with the
prophetic declaration 18: 18 to the early Palestinian church, giving to the
community (through its leaders) the power to bind and loose, i.e. regulatory power comparable to that exercised by the rabbis in the Jewish
community, although its decisions were based on the charismatic utterance
of prophetic figures in the community, rather than on scribal tradition.
(2) At a later date this *logion* was combined with a story narrating the
risen Lord's appearance to Peter and establishing him as the foundational
leader of the eschatological congregation. This accounts for both the post-
Easter prophetic characteristics of 16: 17–19 and the un-prophetic
objectifying and historicizing third-person style.[31] (3) Matthew then
combined this material with the narrative of Peter's confession in Mark,
which also may have originally been a resurrection story.

The common opinion is that 16: 17–19 is primary and 18: 18 secondary
to it.[32] If that were the case, we should think of an early tradition reporting Jesus' words to Peter as having been taken up, generalized to address
the whole community and re-presented as the word of the exalted Lord
using prophetic forms.

Matt. 18: 19–20

This saying is certainly a post-Easter creation, for it gives a rule for prayer
in the Christian community and represents Jesus as the cultically-present
Lord of the community, who takes the place of the Torah as the mediator
of God's presence (cf. Aboth III.2). The saying, or at least verse 20, is
often considered to be the word of a Christian prophet.[33] This may be the
case, even though there are few specific indications of prophetic origin.
The ἀμήν of verse 19 is of doubtful attestation, and otherwise the only
indication of prophetic speech is the first-person form of a saying that is
obviously post-Easter. But this could also readily be the literary product of
a scribe or teacher who created a saying of Jesus in imitation of the Jewish
saying about the Torah. The presence of prophets in Matthew's church
would have made this more acceptable, but not every such expansion of
the tradition is prophetic.

Matt. 19: 12

This saying is not from a Christian prophet; it may even be from the
historical Jesus.[34] But its preservation in the Matthean church, and its
inclusion by Matthew alone, may reflect the ascetic life-style of the
Christian prophets, so that Matt. 19: 12 is a 'prophetic confession'.[35]

Matt. 17: 20; 19: 23*b*

In these two passages, material from Q and Mark respectively has the prophetic formula ἀμὴν λέγω ὑμῖν added by the Matthean community or by Matthew himself. This does not mean that these two passages thereby become sayings of Christian prophets but it does mean that prophetic formulae are known and respected in the Matthean community and find their way into the tradition as it is handed on and around, and by literary imitation.

Matt. 22: 3

It is generally agreed that the Parable of the Great Supper, which was probably transmitted in the Q-materials, has been allegorized in the Matthean community or by Matthew. The 'servants' of verses 3–6 are usually taken as intended to represent the Old Testament prophets. But Jack Kingsbury has pointed out that the 'son' is already on the scene when the story opens, so these cannot be Israel's prophets.[36] He might have taken the observation one step further and noted that since all the figures in the story belong 'to the eschatological age he [the 'son'] has inaugurated', the 'servants' must be the Christian messengers who were rejected and persecuted, i.e. Christian prophets. The parable seems to have been re-shaped in a community where prophecy was alive and respected.

Matt. 23: 1–39

In this long speech against the Pharisees, Matthew incorporates the entirety of the prophetic Q-speech against the Pharisees, preserving its original sevenfold pattern, appends the prophetic lamentation against Jerusalem from another context in Q and expands the speech with material from his own tradition. What was already basically a collection of sayings from Christian prophets is amplified with other material from prophets in Matthew's own community, while the traditional material receives even more pronounced prophetic characteristics.

In verses 8–12 we clearly have expansions to traditional *logia* made within the Matthean community, as J. Ramsey Michaels has shown.[37] Whether the expansions were made by Christian prophets, as argued by Käsemann, Haenchen and Schniewind, is not so clear.[38] The sayings would be appropriate to Christian prophets, for they represent the voice of charismatic enthusiasm against the development of a Christian rabbinate and this is expressed in legal terms that include the re-formation of traditional materials into a 'sentence of holy law' in verses 11–12. There is not enough evidence to indicate whether this expansion was done by Christian prophets themselves or only by people in a community acquainted with prophetic forms. Even if only the latter is the case, these verses testify to the influence of Christian prophets on the developing tradition in the Matthean community.

In verses 29–33, Matthew or his community has reformulated the saying in order to obtain another προφῆται/δίκαιοι pair, which represents his whole community, has increased the references to the suffering of the prophets and has made it more explicit that, just as the opponents stand in the succession of those who persecuted the true prophets of old, so he and his community stand in the succession of the true prophets themselves. The ironic imperative of verse 32, and the charge in verse 33 resemble the prophetic preaching of John the Baptist. In all of this, an intensification of the prophetic consciousness of Matthew's community *vis-à-vis* the tradition that came to it is manifest.

The Matthean editing of the concluding oracles in verses 34–6 and 37–9 makes them refer all the more clearly to the persecution of *Christian* prophets (and wise men and scribes), intensifying the references to persecution and replacing the ambiguous reference to the Wisdom of God with the prophetic ἰδοὺ ἐγὼ ἀποστέλλω. The addition of υἱοῦ βαραχίου in verse 35 is best seen not as a mistake, a marginal gloss, or a reference to the Zechariah who was killed in the temple by the Zealots in 70 C.E., but as Matthew's intent to make clear that this Zechariah is a *prophet*, in order to obtain yet another of his προφήτης/δίκαιος pairs (cf. Ἀβελ τοῦ δικαίου in verse 35). The tendency of the prophetic characteristics of the tradition to become more explicit in the Matthean community and in Matthew's redaction of this discourse is vividly illustrated in these closing lines.[39]

In the great eschatological discourse of 24: 4 – 25: 46, Matthew edits his sources himself without apparent influence from the Christian prophets in his community. The only possible exceptions are 24: 10–12, which might reflect the concerns of Christian prophets,[40] and 24: 30, which has the same conflation of Old Testament texts as Rev. 1: 7.[41]

The relation of Matthew's Gospel to sayings of the risen Jesus

We have seen that Matthew's church and tradition are directly influenced by the presence of Christian prophets and that Matthew himself is open to the reception of sayings from Christian prophets. Matthew is suspicious of miraculous, charismatic phenomena when they are used to buttress a faulty theology or ethic, but not of charismatic speech as such (7: 15–22). Thus Matthew re-incorporates the Q-tradition that had been rejected by Mark and strengthens and elaborates the prophetic motifs and materials in it. Unlike Mark, he has no hesitancy about allowing the risen Jesus to appear after Easter and to deliver a post-Easter speech that forms the climax of the book (28: 16–20). Matthew throughout has a programmatic emphasis on the continuing presence of God with the community by means of the continuing presence of Jesus (1: 23; 13: 37–8; 18: 18–20; 28: 18–20). Unlike Luke, Matthew does not neatly contain Jesus within the framework of birth and ascension. The risen/exalted Christ remains on this earth with his church, so that the 'life of Jesus' is not a 'midst of time', nor a distinct *heilsgeschichtlich*, epoch.[42] All of this would tend to suggest that Matthew himself intends the discourses and sayings of Jesus in his gospel to be heard as the direct address of the exalted Lord, and the Matthean emphasis on the title 'Lord' would seem to confirm this.[43] Some have even considered Matthew himself to be a Christian prophet.[44]

On the other hand, a number of items in Matthew indicate that the sayings of Jesus that he records are intended to be heard as the teaching of a historical figure of the past. Matthew adopts the Markan pre-Easter framework for his sayings, which he certainly understands in a historicizing manner, as is proven by his frequent addition of temporal connectives to Mark's rather 'timeless' narrative style (e.g., τότε in 3: 13; 4: 1, 17; 9: 14, 37; 15: 1, 12, 28; 16: 21, 24), showing conclusively that Matthew thinks of the narrative he is relating in a there-and-then rather than here-and-now perspective. The five great discourses are specifically set off from the present as part of the historicizing narrative by the repeated formula καὶ ἐγένετο ὅτε ἐτέλεσεν [ὁ Ιησοῦς] τοὺς λόγους τούτους (7: 28; 11: 1; 13: 53; 19: 1; 26: 1). The teaching of Jesus that is to be taught to disciples of all nations is that which the pre-Easter Jesus commanded, a given body of material delivered in the past (28: 18–20). The contemporizing final word of Mark's eschatological discourse (13: 37) is conspicuously absent in Matt. 24: 42. There is no place in the Matthean narrative, in fact, where Jesus addresses the reader directly – unlike the prophetically-oriented narratives of Mark and John. The teaching of the historical Jesus is generalized to include the reader *in*directly, by such formulae as ὃς ἐάν and πᾶς ὁ + participle.[45] Jesus is not presented to the reader as a prophet who addresses him immediately but as the supreme rabbi/teacher for the community (23: 8–10), whose teaching is contained in the document before him. This does not mean that the teaching of Jesus is a rigid new law, for the community has within it both prophetic and scribal leaders whose function it is to interpret and make relevant the teaching of Jesus (23: 34; 13: 52; 18: 18).

Matthew seems to have both a historicizing and a contemporizing orientation to the sayings-material he presents in his gospel. How should we understand this dual thrust in Matthew? Is it an intentional dialectic, as in Mark and later, in another form, in John?[46] Is the Markan form of direct address of the risen Lord via the traditional materials maintained in the speeches but not in the narrative, so that Matthew *contains* the direct address of the Lord in the five great discourses but *is* not direct address through the Matthean narrative as such?[47] Is this an unintentional ambiguity or inconsistency on Matthew's part, a result of his never having thought about the issue in this way or, rather, a result of our imposing an alien issue upon his work? I must leave this question open to future redaction-critical studies of Matthew. I offer my own tentative solution as a suggestion for further research: Matthew regards the sayings of Jesus that he transmits as the words of the historical Jesus, which have been preserved, amplified and interpreted by the prophetic and scribal leaders of his community, of which he himself is one (scribe, not prophet: 13: 52). The teaching of Jesus in the Gospel of Matthew is thus for Matthew basically report, not address: the word of the historicized Jesus in the narrative past, not the present word of the exalted Lord. But the sayings of Jesus are not a dead letter. The living Lord is present with his church as it transmits and interprets the teaching of its historical Lord (18: 18–20; 28: 18–20). The word of the exalted Lord heard in the preaching of church prophets, and the contemporizing interpretation of Jesus' teaching done by church scribes, must stand in historical continuity with the teaching of Jesus in the gospel narrative and must responsibly interpret its content, though not necessarily repeat it. The prophetic phenomenon is affirmed by Matthew, but not uncritically, and all is seen through the rabbinic eyes of that scribe who has been trained for the Kingdom of Heaven and who brings out of his treasure things both new and old.

14 CHRISTIAN PROPHECY AND THE GOSPEL OF LUKE

In discussing the value of Luke—Acts as a source for the reconstruction of early Christian prophecy, I presented the general relationships between Luke and Christian prophecy. I now turn to inquire whether Luke contains sayings of Christian prophets within the tradition of Jesus' words that he includes in his gospel. Obviously, Luke takes over some sayings that originated as, or were shaped by, Christian prophets by virtue of using Mark and Q-materials that included such sayings. But there is no indication that Luke understood these sources to contain sayings of the risen Jesus (cf. Luke 1: 1—4; Acts 1: 1—2). And it is a striking fact that Luke never contains the more prophetic form of a saying that he has taken from Mark or Q. This indicates that, unlike the Matthean tradition of Jesus' words, Luke's material from Mark and Q has not been reshaped in his immediate community by Christian prophets. I will now examine the peculiarly Lukan traditions, including those inserted into Markan and Q-contexts, to determine whether they contain expansions to the tradition made by Christian prophets.

Luke 4: 24—7

Although Luke certainly has Mark 6: 1—6 before him as he composes his programmatic scene of Jesus' rejection at Nazareth, it appears that he also has independent traditions, which he works into his presentation. Luke 4: 24 is not directly from Mark 6: 4, as is seen not only in the variations in wording but especially in the presence of ἀμὴν λέγω ὑμῖν in Luke. Luke usually omits or paraphrases this formula when it is found in Mark; there is no reason to think of his having added it to a Markan saying here. This saying, so obviously appropriate as a motto among prophetic circles in the church, appears to have picked up the prophetic introductory formula in the course of the tradition.

Since verses 25—6 are defending the Gentile mission against Jewish-Christian objections, they come from the church's post-Easter situation. There are some reasons for regarding these verses as a pre-Lukan independent tradition created by a Christian prophet. The Lukan ἐπ' ἀληθείας δὲ λέγω ὑμῖν probably replaces an original ἀμὴν λέγω ὑμῖν. The designation of the drought as having lasted three-and-a-half years could be a prophetic–apocalyptic replacement for the less-than-three-years of the Old Testament text (I Kings 18: 1; cf. Dan. 7: 25; 8: 14; 9: 27; 12: 11–12; Rev. 11: 2, 3; 12: 6, 14; 13: 5). The general motif of the rejection of the prophet by those who suppose themselves to be the people of God comes to expression in this saying, as does the awareness that the extension of the gospel to the Gentiles was a result of prophetic revelation. Thus a case can be made to support Bultmann's assertion that verses 25–6 are Christian prophecy.[1] But this is not a very persuasive case. The three-and-a-half-years motif is not specifically prophetic but is a Jewish-Christian *theologoumenon*, as James 5: 17 proves. Israel's rejection of her prophets is a traditional theme made into a programmatic structuring principle of Luke's presentation, as is made clear by Acts 7: 35–53; 28: 25–9 and by his placing of the scene of Nazareth's rejection of the true prophet Jesus at the very beginning of his narrative of Jesus' ministry, despite the chronological problems this causes (cf. 4: 23, 31). Likewise the theme that God's Spirit has always led his prophets beyond Israel to the Gentiles is a programmatic Lukan principle, as the structure of Acts 1–15 makes clear. Although the sayings may initially seem to represent that fresh interpretation of Scripture characteristic of Christian prophets, there is no contemporizing re-presentation of Scripture in the prophetic style, but allusions to Elijah and Elisha as figures of the past from whom lessons for the present may be drawn. All this is more in accord with Luke's own handling of Scripture, just as casting Jesus in the role of Elijah and Elisha is a Lukan motif (e.g. Luke 7: 11–17; 9: 51).

It thus appears that what we have is a Lukan composition portraying Jesus in a prophetic role, attributing appropriate sayings to him based on Luke's understanding of Jesus as the prophet *par excellence* on the Old Testament model, rather than sayings from a Christian prophet incorporated by Luke. At the most, we have a pre-Lukan tradition, possibly shaped by Christian prophets, which Luke has rewritten in the light of his understanding of the prophetic ministry of Jesus. The prophetic aspect of the sayings is thus more redactional than traditional, more closely related to the prophets of Israel than to those of the church. We shall find that this first instance of the phenomenon is typical of Luke.

Luke 6: 24–6

The history of the tradition of this unit is a very complicated issue, which cannot be discussed in detail here. The three major positions are (1) that the unit was originally in Q, which Matthew has then omitted, as advocated for example by Heinz Schürmann,[2] (2) that the unit was not in Q but was added to the tradition between Q and Luke, therefore in Q^{Lk} or in an independent tradition connected to the beatitudes as argued by Otto Steck,[3] and (3) that the unit is the composition of Luke on the basis of the Q-beatitudes, as argued by Dupont.[4] The detailed study of Dupont has made clear that the unit could never have existed independently of the beatitudes, and that it is permeated with Luke's vocabulary and style. Yet the points of contact pointed out by Steck between the Lukan 'woes' and the peculiarly Matthean beatitudes argue for some kind of interplay between the woes and the Matthean beatitudes in the pre-Lukan tradition. Thus we seem to have basically a Lukan composition, not *ex nihilo* but representing the thorough rewriting of a tradition, so that it now represents Lukan style, vocabulary and theology, as the complement to the Lukan beatitudes.

The four sayings manifest some features of early Christian prophecy. The woe-form itself is basically prophetic. The negative reference to παράκλησις in verse 24 reflects the prophetic vocabulary. The eschatological orientation, including the motif of the reversal of status at the End Time, is appropriate to prophets, as is the reference to false prophets in verse 26. One could thus readily imagine that at some point in the developing tradition between Q and Luke, the four beatitudes were taken up by a Christian prophet and expanded by his adding the corresponding woes. Yet there is probably a better explanation. Luke himself, on the basis of some traditional elements, expands the beatitudes in his tradition, placing four 'woes' in the mouth of Jesus in order to underscore dramatically the meaning of the beatitudes. He does this not as a Christian prophet but as an author who exercises the right to make a literary expansion of the historicized speech of Jesus, just as he did with the speeches of his characters in Acts, and just as Josephus did in his histories. This would better account for the precise correspondence between woes and blessings; the author had the blessings before him in written form and composes the woes accordingly. This would also account for their prophetic form, for there are no features of the woes that are not readily explained on the basis of *Old* Testament prophecy. The content of the woes accords with the peculiarly Lukan blessing of the poor and the admonition of the rich (1: 46–55; 2: 8–14, 22–4 (cf. Lev. 12: 2–8); 3: 11–14; 4: 18; 12: 13–21; 16: 14, 19–31). The prophetic features of this text can then be seen more readily as redactional than traditional, and we have a second case of the peculiarly Lukan sayings of Jesus sounding the prophetic note because of Luke's interest in portraying Jesus as a prophet.

Luke 10: 18

This saying is unrelated to its context and appears to be a detached fragment, perhaps from some larger sayings-complex now lost to us. The brevity of the saying precludes any firm decision as to its authenticity. It could derive from Jesus' own report of some visionary experience, analogous to his baptismal experience and the call-vision of a prophet, or it could represent some occasion of elation in Jesus' ministry in which he expressed his certainty of the defeat of Satan, similar to Mark 3: 27. Some scholars have seen it as offering an important insight into Jesus' own self-consciousness.[5] If the saying is from Jesus, it expresses his prophetic insight into the ultimate, behind-the-scenes meaning of his own ministry, as a response to the healings and exorcisms that he (and his disciples?) performed, rather than reporting some Miltonian fall of Satan observed by Jesus in his pre-existence, as Origen already interpreted.[6] If the saying is not from Jesus, it is probably from a Christian prophet, for the nearest parallel is Rev. 12: 8–9, where the Seer expresses the divinely-given insight that Satan has already been defeated in the heavenly world, so that the beleaguered disciples on earth can take courage. Since the saying reports a visionary experience, using eschatological language, to interpret the meaning of the present, it is more probable that the saying is of prophetic origin than from some other setting in the life of the church, if it is not from Jesus himself.

Luke 10: 19–20

If the sending-out of the Twelve and/or Seventy was an actual event in the pre-Easter ministry of Jesus, then possibly this text represents authentic words of Jesus. But we have seen reasons for doubting that this was the case with the Twelve, so that the mission of the Seventy is even less likely to be historical. The circumstance of an exaltation of the spiritual powers that needed to be dampened was certainly present in the early church (e.g. I Cor. 12–14; II Cor. 10–13); whether this was also true during Jesus' ministry is debatable, though possible. The sayings are quite appropriate to a post-Easter setting, as their similarity to the spurious ending of Mark indicates, for the reference to Jesus' ἐξουσία reminds one of Matt. 28: 18. The issue of the authenticity of these verses may be a borderline case, in which the relation to Christian prophecy might tip the scales in the direction of a church product.

There are points of contact with Christian prophecy in the vocabulary: ἰδού, πατέω, ὄφις, σκορπίος, all occur frequently in Revelation. The saying in verse 19 was originally intended eschatologically, declaring that in the *eschaton*, which is already dawning, the disciples will triumph over the

demonic powers that are defeated at the *eschaton.* The saying was not,
then, intended as a promise that the disciples would survive snake-bites
(Acts 28: 3–6; Mark 16: 18); its horizon is eschatological, not historical.
There is probably an allusive re-presentation of Scripture as the word of
the exalted Jesus in the reference to treading on snakes and scorpions (Ps.
91: 13; cf. Deut. 8: 15), exhibiting the prophetic interpretation of
Scripture in eschatological terms. The general perspective of the saying is
appropriate to Christian prophets, in that it is readily understood as a post-
Easter commissioning declaration, in which the exalted Lord confers
authority on his missioners, as in Matt. 28: 16–20; Acts 13: 1–3. Verse 20
would then fit a church setting in which charismatic phenomena were in
danger of being over-rated and would be the appropriate response of a
Christian prophet who exhorts the Spirit-filled community not to be too
impressed by signs and wonders but rather to be impressed by their
election to the eschatological covenant-community made known to them
in the prophetic word, as in Paul (I Cor. 12–14), Revelation (e.g. 13: 8–
14), Mark 13: 22–3 and Matt. 28: 16–20.[7] The evidence is not compelling
either for the inauthenticity or for the prophetic origin of these sayings,
but the similarity to prophetic oracles does strongly suggest that if these
two sayings are not from the historical Jesus, they most likely were
originally spoken by Christian prophets.

Luke 12: 32

This isolated saying was apparently not in Q but added to the tradition in
the Q^{Lk} tradition, on the basis of the catchword $\beta \alpha \sigma \iota \lambda \epsilon \iota \alpha$.[8] Joachim
Jeremias points out several features that indicate that the saying had an
Aramaic original.[9] This would mean that the saying is probably early and
Palestinian but not necessarily that it is from Jesus. This point is argued by
Rudolf Pesch, who attempts to find a suitable pre-Easter setting in Jesus'
life for the saying.[10] But the saying would also fit well into a post-Easter
situation in which the church knows itself to be the threatened 'little flock'
in need of assurance. The brevity of the saying makes it almost impossible
to be confident of either its authenticity or its secondary origin. The
context in which the saying is presently found has been shaped by Christian
prophets. The introductory formula $\mu \dot{\eta} \; \phi o \beta o \tilde{v}$ is a form of prophetic
reassurance in Rev. 1: 17; 2: 10; is the address of the risen Lord in Matt.
28: 5, 10; Acts 18: 9; is the address of an angel in the context of prophetic
revelation in Matt. 1: 20; Luke 1: 13, 30; 2: 10; is combined with the
prophetic revelatory formula $\dot{\epsilon} \gamma \dot{\omega} \; \epsilon \dot{\iota} \mu \iota$ in Mark 6: 50 par.; Matt. 14: 27;
John 6: 20; occurs in Christian prophetic material in Matt. 10: 26, 28, 31
and Luke 12: 4, 7; and occurs elsewhere in the New Testament only as a

word of Jesus. Μὴ φοβοῦ is thus clearly a prophetic form. The saying reflects the eschatological orientation of Christian prophecy, expressing the tension between the troubled present and the happy future that will soon be brought about by the eschatological reversal that was a theme of Christian prophecy. The behind-the-scenes decision of God, not apparent to anyone except the prophet who has divinely-given insight, comes to expression in this saying, which as a whole resembles the *Heilsorakel* of the Old Testament prophets.[11] Thus, if the saying is not from Jesus, it is probably from a Christian prophet or from Luke, who composes such prophetic sayings for the prophet Jesus in his narrative. A firm decision between these three is not possible.

Luke 12: 35–8

These sayings were probably not in Q, nor are they a Lukan composition, but represent a small independent cluster of traditions taken over by Luke and included without editing or rewriting.[12] The passage is similar to early Christian parenesis found in the epistles (e.g. I Pet. 1: 13; I Thess. 5: 6; Eph. 5: 14), seems to reflect the waning hope of the *parousia* and is thus probably a church formulation, though perhaps preserving some echoes of authentic teaching of Jesus. There are some points of contact with Christian prophecy: the twofold pronouncement of blessing (verses 37, 38), the ἀμὴν λέγω ὑμῖν formula, eschatological parenesis as the substance of the saying. There is, then, at least a minimal basis for the judgment of Bultmann and O'Neill that these sayings are from Christian prophets.[13] But one receives the impression from the sayings as a whole of a disparate collection of fragments that have incidentally accumulated some prophetic forms in the tradition, rather than of a unified prophetic oracle.

Luke 19: 42–4/(21: 20–44)/23: 28*b*–31

Walter Bundy considers 19: 42–4 a church product and describes it as 'a lyrical composition, a typical prophetic oracle or elegy', thus expressing the opinion of Bultmann and others that the saying is from a Christian prophet.[14] The saying does seem to represent the prophetic insight as to what is really transpiring in history as seen from God's point of view (although the masses are unperceptive), and to express this in prophetic–predictive form, using the language of Scripture (Is. 29: 1–4; Jer. 6: 6–21; 52: 4–5; Ezek. 4: 1–3; Hos. 13: 16; Hag. 2: 15; Ps. 137: 9), which is re-presented as the word of the exalted Jesus. Thus the saying could have been a prophetic oracle rewritten by Luke. But 19: 42–4; 21: 20–44 and 23: 28*b*–31 should all be considered together. In the Lukan narrative, these are three prophetic predictions by Jesus of the coming destruction of

Jerusalem: the first given just before he enters the city, the second during the course of his teaching there and the third as he leaves the city for the last time. Luke seems to have a definite interest in portraying Jesus as the last prophet to announce God's word in Jerusalem and be rejected, a prophet who gives the final announcement that God has rejected the city, which now faces the inevitable doom. The three oracles are related not only in general subject matter but in vocabulary, which suggests that they all have the same author. There is considerable peculiarly Lukan vocabulary, which has many contacts with the LXX. This suggests Lukan composition on the basis of his knowledge of the LXX; the supposed Aramaisms are most likely Septuagintisms. Peculiarly Lukan motifs occur, e.g. the resemblance of Jesus to Elisha, who also wept for the coming destruction of his people, using the identical verb from II Kings 8: 11: ἔκλαυσεν. In Luke 21: 20–4 we can see Luke himself rewriting the eschatological prediction of Mark 13: 14–19, transforming it into the historicized *vaticinium ex eventu* that makes Jesus appear to be a prophet predicting the great historical crisis of the siege of Jerusalem during the Jewish war with Rome. This is all that is necessary to explain all three oracles of 19: 42–4/21: 20–4/23: 28b–31. Although the possibility that Luke is rewriting material that had originally been created by Christian prophets cannot be excluded, the more likely possibility seems to be that once more Luke is himself composing prophetic-sounding sayings to place on the lips of the last great prophet, Jesus.

Luke 21: 34–6

The Lukan ending of the eschatological discourse may embody pre-Lukan tradition. If so, the nature of the material as eschatological parenesis, its allusive use of the Old Testament and the reference to the Son of Man all suggest a connection with Christian prophecy. However, the Lukan vocabulary indicates that Luke is here probably composing a suitable ending to the discourse himself, based on the Markan ending and common traditional themes.

Summary

As is the case in other streams of the synoptic tradition, so also in Luke, sayings of Christian prophets have made their way into the tradition of Jesus' words. But this has happened only to a small extent in the traditions peculiar to Luke. Christian prophets do not seem to have played a major role in the development of the sayings-tradition in Luke's context. The more influential factor seems to have been the Lukan picture of Jesus as a prophet on the Old Testament model, which encouraged Luke to modify the sayings-tradition redactionally so that Jesus speaks more like a prophet (of the Old Testament) in Luke than in his sources.

Luke—Acts and the sayings of the risen Jesus

Luke pictures the early church as in frequent communication with heaven. The church's mission unfolds on the stage of history as it receives promptings from the heavenly world by a variety of means. Sometimes a heavenly voice, not otherwise identified, is the vehicle of the divine revelation (10: 9–16; 11: 7–10). Frequently the agent who instructs the church concerning the next steps in its mission is simply called 'the Spirit', or 'the Holy Spirit', without further description of the revelatory process (8: 29; 10: 19; 13: 2; 16: 6; 19: 21; 20: 22 (cf. 21: 4)); once this Spirit is identified as the 'Spirit of Jesus' (16: 7). Divine instruction is sometimes given through an 'angel' (10: 7, 22; 11: 13), called also an 'angel of the Lord' (5: 19; 8: 26; 12: 7–11) or an 'angel of God' (10: 3; 27: 23). The angel sometimes appears in a vision (10: 3) and appears in scenes inter-changeably with 'the Spirit' (8: 26/9; 11: 12/13/15). Sometimes the various media of revelation are effected through a 'vision' (9: 10; 10: 3, 17; 18: 9; 26: 19), and sometimes the vision alone is the means of revelation (16: 9). Occasionally, the revelation is simply attributed to 'God' (10: 28) or 'the Lord', in the sense of 'God' not the 'Lord Jesus' (10: 33). It is thus clear that Luke intends the reader to see that the expansion of the early church, both geographically from Jerusalem to Rome and theologically from a Jewish sect to an inclusive world-wide religion, was directed by God himself from heaven, by means of heavenly voices, visions, angels and his word mediated by persons inspired by his Spirit.

It is striking that in all this the exalted *Jesus* plays a minor role, and then only in the case of one person, Paul. Jesus himself speaks from heaven after the ascension only in 9: 4–16; 22: 6–10; 26: 12–18, all referring to the one occasion of Paul's call to be an apostle/prophet, and in 18: 9; 22: 17–21 and 23: 11. Paul is made a special case in this regard in order to authenticate him as a *witness* (26: 16), since he does not qualify to be a full apostle in the Lukan understanding of the term.[15] The exalted Jesus appears amidst the plethora of heavenly communication in Acts in only this relatively modest role and for this special purpose in connection with Paul's ministry.

A second remarkable fact is that the multitude of heavenly communi-cations in Acts is primarily for revealing the divine strategy for the con-tinuation of the church's mission, and for encouragement and consolation, rather than for the revelation of new information concerning the will of God of the type made known in the teaching of the pre-Easter Jesus.

Post-Easter revelations by voice, angel, vision, Spirit or the word of the exalted Jesus himself do not add to the content of the revelation given in the word and ministry of Jesus of Nazareth. This is not the case even in the crucial account of Peter's extension of the gospel to the Gentiles in chapters 10—11 and the report of the Apostolic Council in chapter 15. In the first of these scenes, the church is led by an overwhelming display of divine revelations to include those who were formerly excluded. But this only makes effective what was already revealed by Jesus prior to his ascension (Luke 7: 1—10; 13: 22—30; 20: 9—16; 21: 24; 24: 44—8) and was implicit in the Pentecost events and the preaching of Peter on the first day of the church's existence (Acts 2: 5—11, 17, 21, 39). Neither the risen Jesus nor any other heavenly messenger reveals new increments of information concerning the divine will in Acts 10—11. Rather, the divine Spirit leads Peter and the others to realize in practice in their new situation the will of God that had already been revealed. The new insights in this regard are mediated by divine revelations and confirmed by the decision of the community that contains apostles (11: 1, 18). So also in Acts 15 — on the basis of reports of what God has done in the community by the Holy Spirit — the apostles and elders decide what God's will is for the present mission of the church (15: 6—12, 22, 25), and the result is described as what 'seemed good to the Holy Spirit and to us' (15: 28). This is radically different from picturing the post-Easter community as receiving qualitatively new revelations from the risen Jesus.

By the power of the Spirit at work within it, the church continues to preach the 'word of God', just as Jesus did during his earthly ministry (Luke 4: 1; 8: 11, 21; 11: 28; Acts 4: 31; 6: 2; 8: 14; 11: 1; 13: 5, 7, 44, 46, 48; 17: 13; 18: 11). But the 'word of God' proclaimed by the church is not a continuation of, or supplement to, the preaching of the pre-ascension Jesus; Jesus himself, his life, ministry, death, resurrection and future role as judge, is the content of the preaching of the 'word of God' by the church. This identification is clearly made in 8: 12—14; 13: 44—9, for example. The latter instance also makes clear that 'word of the Lord' is simply a synonym for 'word of God', rather than 'word of the (risen) Lord (Jesus)' understood as a subjective genitive. The church's inspired preaching of the word of God is not for Luke a repetition of the teaching of the historical Jesus. Only in 11: 16 and 20: 35 is there reference to sayings of Jesus. The church's message is entirely a message *about* Jesus (= what God had done through him) rather than a continuation or repetition of his message. The word of Jesus is thus strictly confined by Luke to the historical past, to the 'midst of time' in which Jesus appeared and delivered his message.[16] The sayings of Jesus are authoritative in that they were spoken by a past authority, introduced by the Lukan historicizing formula adapted from Mark (Acts 11: 16; 20: 35; cf. Luke 22: 61 = Mark 14: 72). In this the words of Jesus are not different in kind from the words of the Old Testament prophets, who are constantly cited as an authoritative word from the past. Luke intends his portrayal of Jesus as a prophet (Luke 4: 16—21; 7: 16; 24: 19; Acts 3: 22; 7: 37) to be taken seriously, filling in his picture of Jesus with details and allusions from the prophets Moses, Elijah and Elisha (e.g. 4: 25—7; 7: 11—17; 8: 49—56; 9: 31 (9: 36 omits the Markan *John* = Elijah equation), 9: 51, 54, 57—61).[17] In 9: 8, 19, Luke twice adds the word 'old' to the traditional saying, to indicate that, while Jesus is not one of the 'old' prophets, the identification of him as a 'prophet' is not to be rejected. But the ministry of the prophet Jesus is firmly restricted to the historical past, the time before 'the day when he was taken up', the time recorded in the $\pi\rho\tilde{\omega}\tau o\varsigma$ $\lambda\acute{o}\gamma o\varsigma$ of the Gospel of Luke, specifically dated as the fifteenth year of Tiberius Caesar (3: 1—2). The $\mathring{\eta}\rho\xi\alpha\tau o$ of Acts 1: 1 is strictly pleonastic and does not imply that Acts relates what the risen Jesus *continued* to do and teach.[18] The relation of the power of God to the unfolding mission of the church in Acts is conceived by Luke in a different way than as the continuing ministry of Jesus, as we have seen above. The point may be seen by comparing Luke to Mark in this regard. In Mark, the 'then' of Jesus' ministry is dialectically represented in the 'now' of Mark's and his reader's own time. For Luke, Jesus' word and ministry are past history; but all revelations of the Spirit, all new communications from heaven, must be judged by the recollection of the life, teaching, death and resurrection of Jesus. God leads his community forward, but not along a line contrary to his definitive revelation in Jesus. As expressed by Norman Perrin:

> 'Where Mark involves his readers directly in his story — addressing them out of it, reflecting their situation in it, and so on — Luke separates his readers from the story of Jesus and then provides a new and more formal way of relating them to it. Mark's gospel is open ended so that the reader relates directly to it; Luke's is closed off so that the reader relates to it more formally.'[19]

This is clearly illustrated, for example, in the ways in which Mark and Luke respectively handle the missionary charge of Jesus to his disciples. Mark 6: 8—11 changes the original radicality of the instructions to make them more realistically applicable to Mark's own day, because he intends them to be heard as the present address of the risen Lord. The missioners are thus permitted to take a staff and to wear sandals. In Luke, on the other hand, the original radicality of the Q-form of the saying is preserved in the instructions to the disciples during Jesus' ministry (9: 3; 10: 4) but is 'corrected' by Jesus at the end of his ministry (22: 35–6). The teaching of Jesus is *directly* applicable only during the 'midst of time', the historical time when Jesus was on the earth. The teaching of Jesus is still authoritative but no longer addressed the reader directly as the word of the living Lord.

We are thus faced with the conclusion that Luke, who pictures the church as guided by the Spirit and frequently addressed by Christian prophets, does not understand these prophets to have produced new words of *Jesus*. Speeches inspired by the Holy Spirit do not result in sayings of Jesus (2: 1–36; 4: 8–12; 7: 2–56), but proclaim the gospel about Jesus, reinterpreting the Scriptures in the process, in accord with the post-Easter ministry of Jesus in Luke 24: 25–7, 44–7. The form of Christian prophecy in Acts is not that of 'sayings of the risen Jesus' (11: 28; 21: 11). We have seen that this is not a result of accurate historical tradition but of Lukan *Tendenz*. Although Luke refers several times to 'speaking in the name of Jesus' in the early church (4: 17–20; 5: 28; 5: 40–2; 9: 27–9), it is everywhere clear that for Luke this is not a description of speaking *for* the risen Jesus but describes the authority with which the disciples preached *about* Jesus and his soteriological significance (cf., e.g., 9: 20–2 and 9: 27–9; 4: 7–12 and 4: 17–18). Luke does not expect Jesus to speak through the Christian prophets of his own church. One has the distinct impression that Luke not only looked back upon the ministry of Jesus, when Jesus *said* what he had to say, but, like the author of Ephesians (2: 20), also looked back to the ideal early days of the church, when Christian apostles and prophets under the sway of the Spirit led the church into new missionary paths.

15 SUMMARY AND CONCLUSIONS

The influence of Christian prophets on the synoptic tradition

Has it been demonstrated in the preceding pages that sayings of Christian prophets can be identified within the synoptic tradition? No. If the reader has persevered with more or less patience through the preceding pages and wishes to say at the end: 'I am still not convinced. You have not proven that Christian prophets added to the sayings of Jesus in the gospels', nothing can prevent him or her from doing so. But the study itself may have shown that this is not the appropriate way to frame the issue. If one begins with a particular saying in the gospels and asks for proof that it is from a Christian prophet, in the nature of the case this proof can never be forthcoming. All such historical judgments are matters of probability, including the historical judgment that *Jesus* said any given saying in the gospels. If one asks for evidence that conclusively demonstrates that any particular saying is from the historical Jesus, there will always be a margin of doubt and here too one must accept the verdict 'not proven'. When the issue is argued in this way, the conclusion is built into the starting-point: if one begins with the assumption that every saying in the gospels is from Jesus until proven otherwise, one will be able to salvage most (in principle, all) of the sayings for the historical Jesus; if one begins with the assumption that the materials are from the church and the evangelists, placing the burden of proof on those who assert that any given saying comes from Jesus, a minimal number (in principle, none) of the gospel sayings can be attributed to Jesus. That students of the gospels rarely arrive at these extreme results on either side of the issue is sufficient evidence that all of us in fact work with degrees of probability for our historical judgments, requiring 'proof' neither of ourselves nor our colleagues. So long as those who deny that Christian prophets contributed to the synoptic tradition require 'proof', and so long as those of us who affirm it are willing to assume the burden of proof, so long will the argument remain a stalemate, and our approaches will remain somewhat defensive and will allow the questioner to say at the end: 'I'm still not convinced.'

230

The preceding study has given a new shape to the question and a new standpoint from which to ask it. If we begin with the question: 'Do all the sayings of Jesus in our gospels come from the pre-Easter Jesus exactly as they now stand?', all except the most naive fundamentalist will readily answer with a clear 'no'. Then the question may be pressed: 'How do we separate primary (pre-Easter) from secondary (post-Easter) elements in the tradition of Jesus' words?' This process itself is far from clear, but it is a task that does not belong only to those who affirm that Christian prophets added to the tradition of Jesus' words. It is a continuing problem with which all are involved who work historically with New Testament materials. Sayings and elements within sayings can be isolated that, with varying degrees of probability, can be attributed to Jesus, the post-Easter church and the evangelists. This is simply a 'given' for all concerned. If one then looks at the 'middle' layer of the tradition, which seems to come neither from the pre-Easter Jesus nor from the evangelist, the question arises: 'How are these additions to, and transformations of, traditional sayings of Jesus to be accounted for?' This question too does not only belong to those who are inclined to believe that Christian prophets had something to do with the expansion of the tradition. But neither arbitrary affirmations nor wholesale denials of this possibility are helpful. Appropriate arguments can be marshaled to show that there is a probability that Christian prophets were active in the process of the transmission and expansion of Jesus' words. The preceding chapters have shown that this can never be demonstrated but can be affirmed with a fairly high degree of probability. With varying degrees of probability, individual sayings can be shown to have been created by, or influenced by, Christian prophets.

The preceding study has also shown that 'Is saying X from a Christian prophet or not?' in many cases poses the question in too simplistic a way. Our study has shown that it is likely that Christian prophets contributed to the tradition of Jesus' words in a variety of ways: both primarily (creating new sayings) and secondarily (modifying traditional sayings), both directly (by contributing to it) and indirectly (by influencing the ways others contributed to it), and at more than one moment in the trajectory of a saying. Christian prophets were apparently related to the developing tradition of Jesus' words in a number of ways, of which the following may be listed:

(1) A traditional saying of the historical Jesus could be taken up by a Christian prophet and re-presented in exactly the same form as a saying of the risen Jesus. Such a saying would have been proclaimed by the prophet as the present address of the exalted Lord and heard by the community as such, with a meaning appropriate to the new post-Easter situation. When

this happens, there are no formal or material means of identifying the saying in our gospels as 'from' a Christian prophet.

(2) A traditional saying of Jesus could be taken up by a Christian prophet, modified in ways that make it more relevant to the post-Easter church situation and re-presented to the community as a saying of the risen Lord. This could happen without any characteristic traits of Christian prophetic speech being impressed on the saying. In this case, the saying belongs both to Jesus and to Christian prophecy, but we would not be able to identify it as related to Christian prophets, though we might be able to detect post-Easter elements in the saying.

(3) A traditional saying of Jesus could be taken up by a Christian prophet, re-formed in ways characteristic of prophetic speech and re-presented as a saying of the risen Jesus. Here, we might be able to identify the saying as 'from' a Christian prophet but without denying that an earlier form of the saying originated with Jesus. In such sayings, 'Jesus *or* Christian prophet?' is the wrong way of putting the question.

(4) One or more traditional sayings of Jesus could be taken up by a Christian prophet, re-presented as the word of the exalted Lord, with or without modification in senses (2) and (3) above, and expanded by adding an additional saying or sayings, which the prophet had created. When this happens, we might be able to identify the additions as from Christian prophets, without claiming that the whole sayings-complex of which it is a part originated *ex nihilo* from Christian prophecy.

(5) Without beginning with a saying of Jesus from the tradition, a prophet could deliver a new word of Jesus as an oracle from the risen Lord. Such oracles need not be seen as *creatio ex nihilo* and could use pre-existing materials from the Old Testament and Christian tradition, but such traditional elements in the prophet's oracle would not have been heard previously as a saying of *Jesus*, pre- or post-Easter. If there are characteristic items of form or content present in such sayings, they can be identified as from Christian prophets. We should not expect that this will always be the case. Christian prophets may well have contributed sayings to the tradition of Jesus' words of any of the above types, which did not contain sufficient typical prophetic traits of form and/or content to allow them to be identified by us. But my study has shown that a relatively large number can in fact be identified with some degree of probability.

(6) Non-prophetic transmitters and shapers of the tradition between Jesus and the evangelists could have been influenced by the presence of Christian prophets in their community. Christian prophets might thus influence the tradition indirectly, as non-charismatic tradents modify the

tradition in response to the presence of prophets in their community. This response could be either positive, where non-prophets reshape elements of the tradition into forms that prophets have made common, or negative, where traditional material is reshaped to oppose a certain kind of Christian prophecy.

(7) The redactor could himself be a Christian prophet who includes his own oracles (of any of the above varieties) in his gospel. In such cases, redactional features of a saying are not arguments against prophetic origin, for 'Christian prophecy *or* redactional composition' is a false alternative.

(8) Sayings that originated from Christian prophets in any of the above senses could be retouched by the (prophet or non-prophet) redactor, with the result, again, that Christian prophetic oracles would also contain redactional features.

In sum: Christian prophets influenced the synoptic tradition of Jesus' words in a variety of ways in addition to coining new sayings of the risen Jesus, and this influence can frequently be detected with a reasonable degree of probability.

A history of the interaction of Christian prophecy and the gospel form

We have seen that the influence of Christian prophets can be detected in each of the synoptic gospels and all their sources. Sayings of the risen Jesus appear in Q, Mark, 'M' and 'L' materials. But neither the number of sayings of the risen Jesus nor other influences of Christian prophets are randomly or equally distributed across the various layers and streams of the synoptic tradition and the gospels into which they flowed. This is the result of the tension inherent between the prophetic form of 'sayings of the risen Jesus' and the historicizing narrative form of the gospels being resolved in different ways in the history of the development of the synoptic gospels. In bold strokes that history may be charted as follows:

(1) In the earliest Palestinian church, disciples who believed that Jesus had been exalted to the presence of God, and that this risen Jesus spoke through them, delivered pronouncements in his name in which he addressed the community as the exalted (and soon-to-reappear) Son of Man. These prophetic pronouncements were a significant factor in the development of christology.[1]

(2) The Palestinian—Syrian church handed on the tradition of Jesus' words but made no sharp distinction between them and the new words of the exalted Lord that came into being through the Christian prophets in its midst. This collection of sayings, containing sayings of both the historical and the exalted Jesus, later crystallized into one or more editions of the document Q. The community that produced Q was led primarily by

prophetic figures and tended to develop a prophetic understanding of the entire tradition of sayings of Jesus, so that even the sayings of the pre-Easter Jesus were heard more and more as the word of the exalted Lord, and Q began to take on the character of 'sayings of the risen Jesus' *in toto*. Q contains a relatively large number of sayings originating from, and influenced by, Christian prophets.

(3) One factor in Mark's creation of the gospel form was his wariness of the genre of sayings-collections represented by Q, in which the sayings of Jesus threatened to float free from the Jesus of history. Mark's suspicion of the Q-genre accounts for the paucity of sayings of Jesus in Mark in general and the small number of sayings of Christian prophets in particular. Mark created a narrative form, 'gospel', in which the risen Jesus addresses the community only from within the framework of the pre-Easter life of Jesus. Prophecy receives a new form in the hands of Mark. But after Mark, the word of Jesus seemed to be expressed in the church in two contrary forms: 'sayings of the risen Jesus', in which the living Lord of the church addressed the community directly, as one always contemporary with it (even if sayings of the historical Jesus were taken up into such an address), and the gospel form, which was understood more and more in a histor-icizing manner, tending to contain the word of Jesus within a narrative anchored in the past.

(4) Christian prophets similar to those of the Q-community continued to be active parallel to the circulation of Mark in the church. In the stream of tradition in which Matthew was located, traditional sayings of Jesus were reshaped by Christian prophets and their influence, and new sayings were created. Adopting the historicizing framework of Mark as fundamen-tal, Matthew had no hesitation about accepting the prophetic Q-materials back into the tradition. But by the including of Q *within* the gospel framework, the danger Mark feared was still avoided, though no longer with the sharpness and intentionality of Mark. Matthew finds the prophetic form 'sayings of the risen Jesus' congenial, so that we find a relatively large number of sayings of Christian prophets in Matthew, but he has followed Mark in enclosing these within the life-of-Jesus framework. It is not clear that he has maintained the Markan dialectic between the historical and the exalted Jesus, and the sayings are probably all to be understood from a rabbinic rather than from a prophetic point of view, in Matthew's own eyes.

(5) The peculiarly Lukan traditions contain a minimum of sayings of Christian prophets. This corresponds to Luke's own point of view, for he clearly transforms the Markan gospel form into a life of Jesus. The Jesus of Luke's second volume still lives in heaven but he no longer speaks to his

church on earth; the Jesus of the first volume is the definitive figure of the past, but past nonetheless. For Luke, 'sayings of the risen Jesus' has ceased to function as a category that has any relation to the tradition of the historical Jesus. Whatever sayings of Christian prophets appear in the Gospel of Luke as sayings of Jesus are accidental and incidental. Direct address has become report; prophecy has become history.

Theological struggles with Christian prophecy are apparent in the variety of ways that the New Testament relates the Jesus of history to 'sayings of the risen Jesus'. These struggles have not ceased.

A concluding quasi-theological postscript

In the spring of 1966 the German news magazine *Der Spiegel* published a series of articles by Werner Harenberg on the struggles in the German university and church between critical Bible scholars and conservative non-critics. The author located a text (Matt. 11: 28–30) that Bultmann, the preacher, proclaimed from a Marburg pulpit as 'the word of Jesus' but which his critical studies of the gospels had led him to believe was a saying placed on Jesus' lips by the post-Easter community.[2] It is not entirely clear whether the reporter considered this legitimate theology, double talk or duplicity on Bultmann's part. The incident brings into sharp focus several issues that the preceding study has raised: can post-Easter sayings of Christian prophets be legitimately considered to be words of *Jesus*? Can the preacher in good conscience proclaim the gospel from a text he does not consider 'authentic'? What is the relation of the text of *Scripture* to the word of *Jesus*?

The historical and theological issues here are inseparably related but they are not indistinguishable. Bultmann himself indicated that even when one's concern is restricted entirely to the historical question of reconstructing the message of Jesus, the secondary accretions to the authentic sayings of Jesus cannot simply be excluded from consideration. The secondary and tertiary layers of tradition that accumulated around the central core of authentic sayings of Jesus, must themselves be viewed as the historical results of this center and are necessary for recovering its shape and mass, for they are a result of Jesus' historical impact.[3] This is the minimum that must be said. A saying that must be regarded as having originated from the church or the evangelist may still accurately represent the historical Jesus, perhaps even more accurately than any extant 'authentic' saying, even when the matter is regarded in altogether historical terms. Mark 1: 15 would be one such example (not an example used by Bultmann) of a saying that is almost certainly from Mark himself, yet it would be difficult to locate a saying among the 'authentic' *logia* that more accurately summarizes the message of the historical Jesus.

For Bultmann, however, this is not simply a historical point but a theological one, a matter of faith. I agree with Bultmann that in the post-Easter proclamation of the church that generated sayings of the risen Jesus we obtain increments not only to our knowledge of the historical Jesus but also to our knowledge of Jesus-as-he-was-interpreted-in-the-earliest-church, and that therefore the church is inextricably involved in the Christ-event toward which the Christian's faith is directed.[4] A doctrine of the church is implicit in the Christian's confession of faith in Christ. The 'decision for Christ' (the A.D. 30 event) includes a 'decision for the church', especially for the church's function in the first crucial decades (30–100) that produced our gospels. We receive Jesus from the hands of the church, not vice versa. This point is repeatedly developed in the works of John Knox, one instance of which it may be helpful to quote here in full:

'The words which are of greatest and deepest concern to us as Christians are not the words of Jesus but the words of Christ, and the authenticity of these words is not established and cannot be impugned by criticism higher or lower. The words of Christ are the words which truly and at firsthand set forth the meaning of the event, which is Christ, and therefore the meaning of the church's true life. Those words attributed to Jesus in the gospels which set this meaning forth are authentic words; those which do not set it forth truly or are not concerned with it are *not* words of Christ.

The words of Christ in this most important sense are the words of God — or better, formulations of the Word of God. This Word of God is not a word at all but a deed. The Word of God is what God did in and through the event of which Jesus was the centre. Since this event was the eschatological event, since this act of God was the final saving act, Jesus is the Christ; and we can speak of what God did "through Christ" and can call the event itself or the act itself by his name. Thus Paul writes, "In Christ God was reconciling the world unto himself." The event culminated in a new community through which this reconciliation is mediated and conveyed and in which therefore the event itself is continued and perpetuated, not simply as something remembered, but as a living, present, and creative reality. This living, present, and creative reality — sometimes called the Spirit in the New Testament, sometimes Christ — is continuous with Jesus of Nazareth, but is not to be simply identified with him. The words of the Spirit are as certainly the words of Christ as are the words of Jesus. To deny this is to deny the reality and significance of the resurrection. If Christ still lives, we have no right to limit his authentic utterances to words actually spoken by human lips in Galilee.'[5]

To be sure, Bultmann and Knox express the point with different nuances appropriate to the general theological framework within which they are working — though they are not so far apart on *this* point as one might at first suppose a Lutheran and an Episcopalian to be.[6] They are fundamentally in agreement with the view, which is the view of the gospels themselves, that the risen Jesus of Nazareth is authentically present in the post-Easter sayings attributed to him by church prophets (and others). A number of theologians, from a broad segment of the theological spectrum, affirm this same point, to which I myself subscribe.[7] One simply cannot have Christian faith without, consciously or unconsciously, affirming the interpretation of the significance of Jesus made by the early church. This proposition, generally true with regard to all the secondary material attributed to Jesus or his Spirit in the New Testament, receives a particular importance when seen in terms of the prophetic phenomenon. For here it is represented not only that the revelatory *Gestalt* was 'historical Jesus/church interpretation' but that 'church interpretation' was done in first-person terms in the name and person of Jesus himself, so that 'Jesus' appears on both sides of the equation, on both sides of Easter, in inseparable continuity and unity.

The preacher, then, can be both historically honest and theologically legitimate when he proclaims the present-day meaning of a gospel text as being from Jesus, even though he judges the saying to have originated after Easter. The risen Christ continued to speak in the church. But the proper extension of this point of view is that the exalted Lord did not continue to speak only in the *early* church and in the *New Testament* documents but continued to speak in the proclamation of the church through the ages and continues to speak in and through the church's proclamation today. I would hold to that theology of preaching which understands the church's proclamation in any generation to be the vehicle of the address of the risen Lord, that Christ may speak in the sermon of any country priest.[8] Does this mean that the Christian minister today is, or should be, a Christian prophet? No. Not in the sense in which 'prophet' is used in this book. Once again and finally, definition of terms is important. The Christian minister has the responsibility inherent in his or her calling to be prophetic in the common sense of that term: to oppose unjust power structures in the name of Christ who is champion of the poor and the oppressed, to proclaim justice and righteousness as the will of God even at the cost of personal sacrifice, to stand against the cultural enslavement of the faith in the name of the living God, to be a voice to the culture rather than an echo of its values. Ministry in the name of Jesus Christ is inherently prophetic in this sense. Every minister has a prophetic vocation in this sense. But that is very different from claiming to be, or aspiring to be, a prophet in the same sense as those immediately-inspired spokesmen for the risen Lord of earliest Christianity who spoke in the first person for the risen Christ, and whose oracles were sometimes included in the synoptic tradition of Jesus' words. The Sunday-morning sermon, however 'prophetic' it may be in terms of content, is a different genre from 'sayings of the risen Jesus', just as the twentieth-century pastor and the first-century Christian prophet, *religionsgeschichtlich gesehen*, represent two different types of religious leader. Just as the modern minister's task is not to be an *apostle* but to be *apostolic*, i.e. to be committed to the apostolic faith rather than to a heretical alternative to it, so the minister's task today is not to be a prophet but to let the canonical prophets of the Old and New Testament be heard in such a way that they address the real world of the contemporary hearer, in the confidence that the risen Lord of the church founded on apostles and prophets is able thereby to make his own voice heard.

APPENDIX: CHRISTIAN PROPHECY AND THE ORIGIN OF CHRISTOLOGY

The study of Christian prophecy in Q above, pp. 137–82, brings to light an interesting phenomenon with regard to the tradition of Son-of-Man sayings in the gospels: in five of the fourteen sayings that appear to have originated from Christian prophets, the Jesus who speaks is identified by the Q-community as the Son of Man (Luke 6: 22; 11: 29b–30; 12: 8; 12: 10; 22: 30/Matt. 19: 28). In three additional instances among those sayings that are clearly influenced by the prophetism of the Q-community, the speaker is identified as the Son of Man (17: 24, 26, 30). In Q, only Jesus speaks the word 'Son of Man', and he uses no other christological title. In fact, Q's repertoire of christological titles is practically limited to 'Son of Man'.[1] Since the Q-community was led primarily, if not exclusively, by charismatic prophets, the possible connection between Christian prophecy and Son-of-Man sayings needs to be pursued beyond the question of whether particular Son-of-Man sayings originated as Christian prophecy to the more fundamental issue: is there a relationship between Christian prophecy and the identification of Jesus as Son of Man?

This calls for a venture into the contested territory of research on the relationship of Jesus and the whole tradition of Son-of-Man sayings, which is today a veritable mine field. It was already ambitious of Tödt to speak of a 'consensus' of a majority of scholars concerning the relationship of the Son-of-Man sayings to Jesus, and the divisions within the ranks of New Testament scholars on this subject have become even wider and deeper in the intervening twenty-five years.[2] No effort will be made here to argue a particular position within that debate, but anyone entering the discussion needs to declare where he or she stands, if only provisionally, on the disputed issues, in order to facilitate communication. I will list below my own positions, with a minimum of comment and documentation of those who have argued the position and those who oppose it.

(1) 'Son of Man' was available in first-century Judaism as a category of eschatological thought. Norman Perrin and Ragnar Leivestad[3] have properly chastened us for uncritically assuming that there was a

widespread, unified, Son-of-Man *concept* upon which Jesus and/or the early church could draw, but have not diminished the probability that there was already a tradition of interpreting Dan. 7: 13 in terms of an eschatological figure and that this tradition was a resource for the thought of Jesus and the early church.

(2) In the synoptic gospels, 'Son of Man' is always a title. Whatever may have been the case in first-century Aramaic, the sayings handed on in the church never use 'Son of Man' simply as the equivalent for 'I', 'man', or 'one'.[4] Even in the later strata of the tradition, where an original 'I' is replaced by 'Son of Man' (e.g. Matt. 16: 13/Mark 8: 27), this is not simply a periphrasis for 'I' but identifies Jesus with that One entitled Son of Man.

(3) Jesus did in fact use the title 'Son of Man'. The objections cited by Vielhauer, Käsemann and Conzelmann relating to the alleged incompatibility of 'Son of Man' and 'Kingdom of God' in the teaching of Jesus, and the resemblance of even those sayings purportedly most authentic to the oracles of Christian prophets, have been effectively answered.[5] But even if all our extant Son-of-Man sayings should turn out to be church products in their present forms, the historical probability is still that the coming of the Son of Man formed a part of Jesus' own proclamation, as will be argued below.

(4) But not all the categories of sayings go back to Jesus. Since the days of Bultmann and Kirsopp Lake, the Son-of-Man sayings have often been divided into the three categories of the present activity of the Son of Man; the suffering, dying and rising of the Son of Man; and the future eschatological coming of the Son of Man.[6] Not every saying fits neatly into these three categories, and the hypothesis presented here raises additional questions about this categorization, but the grouping remains essentially valid. Despite the repeated efforts to regard Jesus as the source of all three types of sayings,[7] the phenomena of the history of the tradition of the sayings, not to mention studies of the individual sayings themselves, makes this utterly unlikely. In the tradition, the sayings exist in separate categories that cohere as to both content (suffering–rising sayings never mentioned the *parousia* and vice versa, for example) and source (suffering–rising sayings never found in Q but only in Mark and passages in Matthew and Luke dependent on Mark, for example). This compels us to regard the sayings as having entered the tradition at different points from different sources.

(5) The sayings that speak of the present activity of the Son of Man are all secondary as Son-of-Man sayings.[8] Jesus did not speak of himself as the Son of Man, though he may have made some of the statements in which 'Son of Man' now appears as a secondary element, or possibly used בר אנש as a non-titular reference to himself, as at Matt. 11: 19 par.[9] If, as is argued

below, Jesus distinguished himself from the future Son of Man, he could not also have identified himself with the Son of Man in the present. This is an argument which was not overcome by the view, formerly championed by Reginald Fuller, that Jesus saw himself as Son of Man *designatus* — a view that stems ultimately from Rudolf Otto's (mistaken) perception of the 'hidden' Son of Man in Enoch.[10] Nor does Borsch's attempt to see Jesus as both distinguishing himself from and identifying himself with the Son of Man cohere, for the parallels he cites from the Odes of Solomon are better understood as Christian prophetic phenomena.[11]

(6) The predictions of the suffering and rising of the Son of Man are secondary as Son-of-Man sayings. Jesus may have foreseen his suffering and believed in his vindication afterwards, and expressed this to his disciples, but that he spoke of this in terms of what was to happen to the Son of Man is precluded by the same arguments that indicate that the 'present' sayings are secondary, by their late emergence in the history of the tradition (altogether absent from Q!) and by examination of the sayings themselves.[12]

(7) Jesus did speak of the Son of Man who was to come in the future, a transcendent, eschatological figure with whom he did not identify himself, yet with whom he did associate himself very closely. It is only within this category of sayings that we may look for authentic sayings of Jesus. I am myself unable to account for the distinction between the Jesus who speaks in these sayings and the Son of Man who is to come in the future (Mark 8: 38 par.; Luke 12: 8—9 par.; 17: 22, 24, 26, 30 par.; 18: 8; Matt. 19: 28; 25: 31) on any other basis than that it (the distinction, not necessarily these sayings) goes back to Jesus himself.[13] As Tödt so succinctly states: 'What is stated here is constructed as a soteriological correlation, not at all as a Christological continuity.'[14] The fact that Jesus did speak of the Son of Man as someone other than himself, who, in the eschatological drama, would vindicate discipleship to Jesus, does not mean that all sayings that evince this distinction are from Jesus. The genuineness of any particular saying must be settled from case to case, not *a priori* because it belongs in a particular formally-defined group. Käsemann, Vielhauer, Conzelmann, Perrin *et al.*, have at least shown that there is a substantial secondary element even among sayings of this category, as have our own analyses of the Q-materials above.

(8) The earliest Palestinian church identified the Son of Man who is to come and the Jesus who had come. They thought of Jesus as the one who had, after his death, been exalted by God and who was now the heavenly Son of Man, who would soon return in glory as the judge of mankind. This was the earliest christology.

(9) This opened the door for the title 'Son of Man' to be used of Jesus in his earthly life, both of his earthly authority in word and deed and of his suffering, death and resurrection. Sayings in which Jesus spoke of himself as already the Son of Man on earth thus came into being in the community — sometimes as the recoining of traditional sayings as Son-of-Man sayings, sometimes as fresh creations of the community.

(10) The application of 'Son of Man' to Jesus thus opened the door for other christological titles to be used of him, in both his pre-Easter ministry and his exalted status.

This ten-point sketch of the development of christology represents the position of one wing of the Bultmann school, which has been essentially adopted by others outside it[15] and appears to me to be the most cogent solution to this many-sided problem.

With regard to the Son-of-Man sayings, all of this means that of the sixty-seven sayings in the synoptic gospels in which 'Son of Man' occurs (thirty-nine not counting parallels), the great majority are secondary. The implications of this statement are not to be accepted casually. Frederick Borsch is perfectly correct in asserting that 'Son of Man' is not just another of the 'names of Jesus', one title among many, but is *the* designation which, in the synoptic tradition, Jesus *himself* uses as most revelatory of himself. A number of observations need to be viewed together: (i) 'Son of Man' is the only title that has serious claim to have been used by Jesus, though he did not refer to himself by this title; (ii) the oldest elements in Q derive from the earliest Palestinian church and represent the christology of that church;[16] (iii) practically the whole of the christology of Q is expressed in terms of the Son of Man; (iv) most of the Son-of-Man sayings in Q are secondary; (v) several Son-of-Man sayings in Q appear to be from Christian prophets; (vi) 'Son of Man' is the only christological title found on Jesus' lips in Q; (vii) it is found only there — no one but Jesus uses the term 'Son of Man'. In sum, the oldest christology is a Son-of-Man christology which is declared exclusively by the word of Jesus, but not by the historical Jesus. In the light of our hypothesis, an apparent explanation for this constellation of phenomena immediately suggests itself: not only did Christian prophets contribute sayings to the developing synoptic tradition of Jesus' words by promulgating individual sayings in the name of the exalted Son of Man, but they stand at the transition-point between the sayings of the historical Jesus *about* the Son of Man and the sayings of the post-Easter Jesus who speaks through his prophets *as* the Son of Man. If this hypothesis is true, there is a sense in which explicit (titular) christology, and therefore Christian theology, began in the immediately post-Easter revelations of Christian prophets; these experiences may have been very closely related to the Easter experiences of the first disciples, or even identical with them.

I say, there is a *sense* in which, on this hypothesis, Christian prophets should be thought of as the originators of christology, and, before exploring the evidence to support this possibility, the precise nature of the *sense* in which this may be true should be explicated. The sense in which I intend post-Easter Christian prophecy as the origination of christology has to do entirely with the application of christological titles to Jesus of Nazareth. Whatever titles may have been proffered to Jesus by others during his earthly ministry, the evidence is that he adopted none of them as an expression of his own self-understanding. But we should not define christology entirely in terms of titles, and perhaps not even primarily so. Especially, the use of christological titles of Jesus by his post-Easter disciples should not be represented as the foisting of a series of official 'messianic' designations on an essentially 'unmessianic' Jesus. The minimum that must be affirmed is that Jesus' word and deeds — not only his 'call to decision' — implied a christology, and the line between 'implicit' (non-titular) and 'explicit' christology should not be drawn as crisply as has sometimes been the case. Christology is more than applying titles to Jesus. There is continuity, as well as discontinuity, between the life and claim to ultimacy *of* the pre-Easter Jesus and the claim *about* him by the post-Easter community. The discontinuity is primarily expressed in the use of titles. It is in the origination of this explicitly titular christology that Christian prophets may have played a key role.

Since Bultmann, the transition from the preaching of Jesus to the preaching of the earliest church has often been expressed as the proclaimer's having become the proclaimed.[17] The one who had proclaimed not himself but the coming Kingdom of God as the saving event, was himself proclaimed as the saving event (the Son of Man, the Christ, the Lord, the Son of God etc.) by the early church. It is clear from our outline above that point (8) is the crucial, transitional point. 'Son of Man' is the gateway through which all the other supernatural titles were applied to Jesus, so that whoever first proclaimed Jesus to be the Son of Man opened the door that leads through Paul and John to Nicaea and Chalcedon.

How did this transition take place? This is the key question. The typical response, from Bousset on, has been in terms of a deductive process that is supposed to have taken place among the followers of Jesus as a result of the Easter experiences.[18] It was only a short step from Jesus' proclamation of the coming Son of Man to the conviction, based on the resurrection experiences, that Jesus himself was the Son of Man. Pannenberg states in thetical form what he supposes must have been the logic of the earliest

Christian community: 'Through his resurrection from the dead, Jesus moved so close to the Son of Man that the insight (*Einsicht*) became obvious: the Son of Man is none other than the man Jesus who will come again.'[19] It can hardly be doubted that something like this chain of reasoning was at work, however unconsciously, in the church's attribution of the title 'Son of Man' to Jesus. But this explanation only shows conceptually how it could be thought that Jesus was Son of Man, at the most could account for confessional declarations that Jesus was the Son of Man (which declarations are conspicuously absent from the tradition), and falls short of accounting for the actual event of the transition from the Jesus who spoke *about* the Son of Man to the Jesus who spoke *as* the Son of Man.

A more recent answer to the question of how the proclaimer became the proclaimed has been in terms of the exegetical work of the earliest Christian community.[20] This approach argues that the Easter appearances gave the disciples a fresh impetus to study the Scriptures, which provided the categories and content for their confession of faith in the exalted Jesus, with Ps. 110 and Dan. 7 providing the basis for the confession of Jesus as Lord and Son of Man respectively. There can be no doubt that the Easter faith provided the disciples with a new impetus to study the Scriptures and new eyes with which to perceive the eschatological truths that were revealed to them there. But, like the process of logical inference described above, this explanation of the origin of christological confession of Jesus does not account for the *form* in which this christology first emerges (sayings of Jesus) but at the most accounts for how materials from the Scriptures could be appropriated as the means for confessing faith in Jesus. Both the logical and exegetical processes envisioned in these theories portray the origin of christology as a two-stage process: first the Easter experiences, which are then used as data from which logical or exegetical inferences are made. The result should be a series of third-person affirmations: Jesus is the Kurios, Jesus is the Son of Man, and such. But what we have, at the beginning-point of christology, is a series of first-person statements in which Jesus speaks as the Son of Man. This is an altogether remarkable fact, often noticed, but the significance of it has not often been appreciated. The community does not begin to make this affirmation on its own, but hears it, receives it, from the risen Jesus who speaks as the Son of Man. I would take this striking phenomenon, that the identification of Jesus and the Son of Man is made only in words attributed to Jesus, as evidence for my hypothesis that it was Christian prophets who first identified Jesus as the exalted Son of Man. They did this in association with the first Easter experiences, as the risen Jesus addressed the community through them. Their sayings from the risen Jesus formed the transition-point from the proclaimer to the proclaimed.

I have now fully explicated what my hypothesis is. If it is true, it is extremely important for the understanding of the role played by Christian prophets in the beginning of Christian theology. The hypothesis is at least inherently plausible and provides a way of making sense of the phenomena of the tradition. But plausibility is no reason for accepting the hypothesis. Is there any specific evidence in favor of it? Any inquiry for evidence enters the misty, legend-laden realm of Christian origins for which there are no direct sources that have not already been incorporated in traditions and documents bearing later understandings. But even so, it may be possible to uncover enough strands of evidence which, taken together, offer substantial support for the hypothesis. To this task I now turn.

There is an *a priori* likelihood that if the identification of Jesus and the Son of Man was first made by Christian prophets, some of their characteristics would be impressed upon the tradition of the Son-of-Man sayings taken as a whole. That is to say, that even if our extant corpus of Son-of-Man sayings is derived mostly from non-charismatics, it may still bear the impress of those Christian prophets who initiated the whole tradition.

We may first mention two points already introduced. First, the frequency with which 'Son of Man' occurs in the body of sayings in Q identified as prophetic on other grounds, which suggested this hypothesis in the first place, is also evidence for the correctness of it. Secondly, that 'Son of Man' is found only within a saying of Jesus in the synoptic tradition is indicative of the prophetic origin of the whole stream of Son-of-Man sayings. Teeple, following Bousset, considers this 'a literary device to promote the acceptance of the concept through repetition'.[21] This cannot be allowed as an explanation, for Teeple's referring to this as 'the Gospels' technique, as though 'the Gospels' were one entity that could formulate and execute a literary purpose, is obviously incorrect. Rather, what we have is several successive layers of tradition, *each* of which preserves the peculiarity that 'Son of Man' occurs only as a word of Jesus, a formal characteristic also preserved in the Johannine stream of tradition and the Gospel of John. There is no possibility of speaking of a 'device' here. A more satisfying explanation would be that some precedent-forming power at the earliest stages of the tradition was so authoritative that it dominated even the later stages of tradition, even though these were independent of one another, causing them to adhere to the originally impressive form. This would in the first instance be Jesus' own usage, for the fact that of all the Church's christological vocabulary only 'Son of Man' had been Jesus' own word could not have been an insignificant factor.

But this alone would not account for the phenomenon, for though 'Son of Man' was Jesus' word, he did not use it of himself as a title. The authority given the Son-of-Man sayings by Jesus' own usage was reinforced by the word of the exalted Jesus who spoke through his prophets and did identify himself with the Son of Man. This happened, it should be noted, not by any direct statements such as 'I am the Son of Man', but indirectly, as the exalted Jesus speaks *as* the Son of Man, though still in the third person as in Jesus' speech. With these two precedents, the historical Jesus and the exalted Jesus, both authoritative, later tradition would hesitate to use the term *of* him, for it was understood to be Jesus' (both pre-Easter and exalted) term for himself.[22] This datum points back prior to our extant sayings to those who spoke authoritatively in the name of the risen Lord as the source for this stream of tradition.

We have seen previously that the prophet functions as interpreter of event in conjunction with interpretation of Scripture. The beginning of christology was the interpretation of the event of Jesus of Nazareth as the Christ-event. This happened initially in conjunction with the interpretation of Scripture, for it was Scripture that provided the categories and content for the interpretation of the Jesus-event, and the Son-of-Man-sayings tradition as a whole is permeated with the allusive interpretation of the Old Testament characteristic of Christian prophets. This has been well-argued and documented in the studies of Tödt, Higgins, Lindars, Perrin, Teeple, Walker and Boers.[23] The difficulty that I have with their theories is the separation of the process of Scripture interpretation into a separate, later (in the case of Teeple and Walker, much later) event distinct from the process of identifying Jesus as the Christ (that is, Son of Man) in the first place. The evidence seems to point to a series of experiences, closely connected in time, shortly after the death of Jesus, which combine the reception of the eschatological Spirit (the Spirit of Prophecy), which bestows the gift of prophetic speech, the identifying of this Spirit as from Jesus, who did not remain in death but is now experienced as present in this charismatic speech, the renewed searching of the Scriptures and their reinterpretation in the light of Jesus' history and the Easter experiences, and the re-understanding of the identity of Jesus in the light of all this. Since Jesus had spoken of the Son of Man, immediately after his death his disciples were occupied in the study of Dan. 7; they were prepared to interpret the spiritual experiences of Easter as the exaltation of Jesus as Son of Man, and to identify the one who spoke to and through them in those experiences as the Son of Man. Although both Luke and John portrayed the resurrection and the giving of the Spirit in terms of their own theology, John (inadvertently) gave us the more historical picture:

Easter and Pentecost were the same day, resurrection and the disciples receiving the Spirit were two aspects of the same event. This interpretation is not intended to reduce the resurrection to the subjectivity of the disciples, to transform *kerygma* into psychology. The point being made here is simply that christology originated with the identification of Jesus and the Son of Man, that this occurred in the earliest Easter and post-Easter experiences of the church when those who had received the Spirit interpreted the Jesus-event in terms of their charismatic reinterpretation of Scripture, and that this is simply another way of saying it was done by early Christian prophets.

The point being made here would be reinforced by an examination of the resurrection narratives of the gospels, which, I believe, would show that they still bear traces of the prophetic character of the original event that has been recast into a variety of narrative forms. There is not space here for an extended treatment of this subject; this Appendix does not need its own Appendix. Suggestions along this line have been made by others.[24] I would only add, by way of example, the role that the angel plays in the resurrection drama. He is very similar to the *angelus interpres* of Christian prophecy,[25] interpreting the meaning of the event to the hearers, who do not perceive it in the event itself but only by means of the interpreting word. This is the revelatory paradigm of Christian prophecy. And it should not be forgotten that the one primary source of a witness to the appearance of the risen Christ describes the event in language and imagery taken from the call of a prophet.[26] Since Son-of-Man christology emerged from the Easter experience of the community, I would take the numerous points of contact between Easter and Christian prophecy as evidence relating Christian prophets very closely to the origination of christology.

The Son-of-Man tradition is thoroughly imbued with eschatological motifs, and that not only in the 'coming' sayings. The tradition as a whole seems to emanate from within an eschatological frame of reference. While some of the eschatological references simply refer to, or presuppose, the eschatological coming of the Son of Man in a way which would be appropriate to Christian prophets but not exclusively appropriate to them (e.g. Mark 14: 62 par.; Matt. 16: 28), the greater number seem to express the peculiarly prophetic aspects of eschatology. In contrast to Jewish apocalyptic, there is a minimum of detail about the coming of the Son of Man and the concentration is on the meaning of his future advent for the present life of the disciple (Matt. 16: 28; 19: 28 par.; 25: 31ff; Luke 18: 8; 17: 24 par.; 17: 26 par.; 17: 30 par.; 12: 40 par.; 21: 36). Thus, as in Revelation, eschatology functions not as speculation but as parenesis.

Even the note of 'mustness' or 'oughtness' (Mark 9: 12; 8: 31; 14: 21), though it derives from the milieu of apocalyptic, where the events of the End of history are predetermined, is not introduced as a speculative element. Rather, the understanding of predestination functions pastorally, putting the sufferings of the prophetic community in a transcendent context — again as in Revelation.

The feature that we have noted in several prophetic sayings in Q, that the Son of Man and the speaker of the Son-of-Man sayings is contrasted with this (last) generation in a self-conscious way, is also a characteristic of Christian prophecy. This trait permeates the whole Son-of-Man tradition (Luke 9: 58 par.; 6: 22 par.; 7: 34 par.; 11: 29*b*–30 par.; 16: 13; Mark 8: 38 par.; 9: 31 par.; Luke 19: 10; 24: 7; Mark 14: 41 par.) and is a contrast that expresses a 'rein ... eschatologisch(er) Gesichtspunkt',[27] the self-consciousness of Christian prophets. This sense of separation from the world of 'men' is radicalized in the sayings that anticipate rejection, suffering and death — which is characteristic not only of the 'suffering' sayings but is implicit in some sayings from the other groups as well (Luke 9: 58 par.; Matt. 10: 23; Luke 6: 22 par.; 17: 25; 22: 48; 24: 7; Mark 8: 31 par.; 9: 12 par.; 9: 31 par.; 10: 33 par.; Matt. 26: 2). Although it is Mark who has stylized the suffering-Son-of-Man sayings and has made them into a structural element of his theology and his gospel, the motif of rejection and suffering seems to have been impressed on the body of Son-of-Man sayings at the source of the stream itself. The explanation for this is not that Jesus saw himself as the Son of Man who was destined to suffer but that the stream of Son-of-Man sayings originated within the group of early Christian prophets who saw themselves as filling the role of the prophets of the last generation, for whom suffering was appointed as part of their prophetic calling.[28]

Also related to the eschatology of the prophets was their sense of authority, and this motif too is integral to the body of Son-of-Man sayings. It is manifest not only in their eschatological declarations but in the 'present' sayings, such as Mark 2: 10 and 2: 28, where the authority of the eschatological Son of Man is already manifest as he declares the forgiveness of sins and the relativization of Sabbath laws. Such sayings are not scribal applications of tradition, or simply the preserving of the authoritative words of Jesus, but are pronouncements that address church situations in the name of the Son of Man and resolve the issue by his proleptic eschatological authority. Whatever the origin of individual sayings in the tradition, the Son-of-Man stream of tradition as a whole bears the imprint of this prophetic authority, which suggests that prophets stand at the source of this stream.

Not only material connections but history-of-tradition considerations suggest that Christian prophets originated the tradition of sayings in which Jesus speaks as the Son of Man. It is surely not without significance that the only reference to the Son of Man preserved in Acts (7: 56) portrays one filled with the Holy Spirit, who in a vision sees the risen Jesus whom he identifies as the Son of Man, for which he is killed and his comrades are persecuted and driven out, all of which is reminiscent of Christian prophets. In Revelation, the risen Christ from whom the whole revelation proceeds is described as the Son of Man (1: 13) and is later pictured as the one who will come with clouds as the judge (14: 14), but 'Son of Man' is not a major christological category for the prophet-author. John does verify the connection between Christian prophecy and Son of Man, but is of minimal help in tracing the source and trajectory of Son-of-Man sayings of the synoptic type. In the late first century, the Seer seems not to have preserved the traditional type of sayings but to have transferred Son-of-Man sayings to the Son of God.[29] Another writing from the prophetic Johannine circle, the Fourth Gospel, is more illuminating in this regard. It is a strange fact that 'Son of Man', unlike 'Kingdom of God', is retained as one of the key theological terms of the gospel. This should not be explained only in terms of its amenability to John's own theology,[30] but also probably represents the result of old Son-of-Man material within the group of Christian prophets from which the Fourth Gospel emerged. In the Johannine community, confession of Jesus as the Son of Man is a crucial issue (9: 35), and in the Fourth Gospel, Jesus himself bridges the gap between himself and the Son of Man by speaking of his own exaltation as the Son of Man.[31] Precisely here is the missing link, absent from the synoptics, between Jesus' own use of 'Son of Man' and the earliest church's usage. Is the appearance of this late 'missing link' to be explained only in terms of John's own theology? Or is it more probable that the oldest prophetic sayings in which the exalted Christ first made this identification are reflected in the Johannine speeches? This is not to suggest that John preserves these earliest sayings intact; his Son-of-Man sayings, like his other traditions, have been re-melted and coined afresh in the idiom of the Johannine community. But the Johannine sayings, which are in some kind of continuity with early Palestinian prophecy, seem to have preserved the results of this group's initial creativity in identifying Jesus and the Son of Man.

This method of investigation has been pressed as far as it can helpfully take us. We may now summarize the argument. It is likely that Christian prophets, in continuity with the Easter experiences, first identified the risen Jesus with the Son of Man of which the historical Jesus had spoken, and did so with his (the exalted Jesus') own voice, for the following reasons: (1) a number of sayings from Christian prophets are spoken in the name of the exalted Son of Man; (2) 'Son of Man' is found only in sayings of Jesus; (3) the transition from Jesus' preaching to christology was a matter of interpreting the event of Jesus' appearance in conjunction with the interpretation of Scripture, and this is the *modus operandi* of Christian prophecy; (4) the narratives of encounters with the risen Christ in the gospels and Paul resemble prophetic experiences; (5) the eschatological motifs characteristic of Christian prophecy permeate the Son-of-Man tradition: judgment, contrast of the speaker with the last generation, the expectation of rejection and suffering, the function of eschatology as parenesis, the ring of eschatological authority; (6) the use of 'Son of Man' in Acts 7: 56, Revelation and the Fourth Gospel also supports the hypothesis.

The significance of this hypothesis is far-ranging. Here, in the Son-of-Man sayings delivered by Christian prophets, we stand at the transition-point from the teaching of Jesus to early Christian theology, from the proclaimer to the proclaimed. The transition is made by (the exalted) Jesus himself. It is made with Jesus' own words, reinterpreted, re-formed and re-presented. *Thus a third category emerges between 'proclaimer' and 'proclaimed': the proclaimer of the Kingdom becomes the self-proclaimed Son of Man by his Easter and post-Easter spokesmen.* The earliest church maintained both continuity and discontinuity with the word of the pre-Easter Jesus. There is indeed a gap between Jesus of Nazareth and the theology of the New Testament: Jesus did not teach christology. Yet the gap is not a void. It is bridged by those earliest prophetic men who speak in Jesus' own name and with his own word, a word now transformed by the pneumatic Easter experience.

Christian prophets indeed stand at 'the beginning of Christian theology'. Käsemann is right in this.[32] But he has erred in denying that this prophetic word has a point of contact in Jesus' own word, and in not seeing that this theology is principally a christology. It is not the case that Christian prophets simply reintroduce 'apocalyptic',[33] for it had not disappeared from Jesus' own message. This is not their contribution, and their importance is not appreciated so long as they are seen only as those who express the church's faith in the Christ-event in eschatological terms. Rather, they are those who first allow the Jesus-event to be seen as the Christ-event, and they do so by speaking in his name one word: Son of Man.

NOTES

1 INTRODUCTION

1 *The History of the Synoptic Tradition* (New York: Harper and Row, 1963), pp. 5, 105, 205; 'The New Approach to the Synoptic Problem', in *Existence and Faith*, ed. Schubert Ogden (New York: Meridian Books, 1960), p. 38; 'The Study of the Synoptic Gospels', in *Form Criticism* (New York: Harper, 1934/62), p. 60; *Jesus and the Word* (New York: Scribners, 1934), p. 13.

2 'Study', pp. 61–3, lists a total of forty-one verses of sayings-material that Bultmann considered authentic. He never made an exhaustive list. *Jesus and the Word* used considerably more than these forty-one verses as the basis for reconstructing the message of Jesus. Bultmann lacked precision here.

3 *Synoptic Tradition*, pp. 40, 56, 368.

4 The earliest specific suggestion known to me that a synoptic saying originated as Christian prophecy is that of Timothy Colani (*Jésus Christ et les croyances messianiques de son temps* (Strasbourg: Treuttel and Wurtz, 1864²), pp. 202–3), who suggested that Mark 13: 5–30 was identical with that oracle which, according to Eusebius, *Hist. Ecc.*, 3.5, warned the church to flee from Jerusalem in 65 C.E. A few similar suggestions can be found in the works of H. J. Holtzmann, Hermann Gunkel, Hermann von Soden and especially Alfred Loisy. None of these were developed.

5 'Study', pp. 56–8; *Theology of the New Testament* (New York: Scribners, 1951, 1955), 1: 47–8; *Synoptic Tradition*, pp. 37, 115, 122 *et passim.*

6 *Ibid.* pp. 127–8, 143; *Theology*, 2: 124.

7 *Synoptic Tradition*, p. 102. David Dungan's characterization of the form critics' view as being that 'new sayings of the Lord were constantly being created and *surreptitiously or accidentally* included with older authentic sayings', (emphasis his) is thus, to say the least, overdrawn (*The Sayings of Jesus in the Churches of Paul* (Philadelphia: Fortress, 1971), p. 142).

8 David Aune, 'Christian Prophets and the Sayings of Jesus: An Index to Synoptic Pericopae Ostensibly Influenced by Early Christian Prophets', in *SBL 1975 Seminar Papers* (Missoula: Scholars Press, 1975), pp. 131–42, lists a total of 113 different synoptic sayings considered prophetic by one or more of 28 scholars. A 1977 mimeographed supplement lists 69 passages and 19 scholars.

9 'Zur Synoptiker-Exegese', *TR* (new series) 2 (1930), 152, 171–3; *Das Evangelium nach Markus*, NTD (Göttingen: Vandenhoeck and Ruprecht, 1960⁹), pp. 3–5, 132.

10 'Das Sprachereignis in der Verkündigung Jesu, in der Theologie des Paulus und im Ostergeschehen', *Zum hermeneutischen Problem in der Theologie: Die existentiale Interpretation* (Tübingen: J. C. B. Mohr, 1965²), pp. 302–3. See also *Studies of the Historical Jesus*, SBT (London: SCM Press, 1964), pp. 67–8.

11 *Ibid.* pp. 225–6.

12 'Das Sprachereignis', p. 304.

13 The thesis was developed and defended in a series of essays now printed together in *New Testament Questions of Today* (London: SCM Press, 1969): 'Sentences of Holy Law in the New Testament' (1954); 'The Beginnings of Christian Theology' (1960); and 'On the Subject of Primitive Christian Apocalyptic' (1962).

14 *From Tradition to Gospel* (New York: Scribners, 1935), pp. 241–2.

15 Some examples of the kinds of expansion Dibelius sees: the prophetic proclamations of the historical Jesus were elaborated into casuistic applications for practical situations in the church, such as adding the 'excepting clause' in Jesus' teaching on divorce (Matt. 5: 32) (*The Sermon on the Mount* (New York: Scribners, 1940), p. 19). Jesus' general teaching on reconciliation in Luke 17: 3 was elaborated into the more detailed instructions for church discipline in Matt. 18: 15–17 (*A Fresh Approach to the New Testament and Early Christian Literature* (New York: Scribners, 1956), p. 34). Hortatory additions such as Luke 16: 8–13 were made to parables (*Tradition to Gospel*, p. 248).

16 Like the *halacha*, Jesus' words were more rigidly fixed than the 'haggadic' narrative material (*ibid.* pp. 27–9). This fixation occurred in the forties of the first century, under the control of eyewitnesses, thus setting the traditional words of Jesus apart from the 'inspirational' sayings (*ibid.* pp. 242, 293, 295, 298).

17 *Botschaft und Geschichte: Gesammelte Aufsätze von Martin Dibelius*, vol. 1: 'Zur Evangelienforschung' (Tübingen: J. C. B. Mohr, 1953), p. 221.

18 *Tradition to Gospel*, p. 241.

19 See below, ch. 12.

20 *Tradition to Gospel*, pp. 27, 240, 259.

21 *Ibid.* p. 61.

22 Harald Riesenfeld, *The Gospel Tradition and Its Beginnings* (London: A. R. Mowbray and Co., 1961), p. 19; Birger Gerhardsson, *Memory and Manuscript* (Uppsala: Almquist and Wiksells, 1961), p. 289.

23 Dungan, *Sayings of Jesus*, pp. 142–3.

24 É. Cothonet, 'Prophétisme dans le Nouveau Testament', *DBS* 8 (Paris: Ceffonds, 1972), pp. 1285–6; G. Delling, 'Geprägte Jesus-Tradition im Urchristentum', *Communio Viatorum* 4 (1961), 59–71; Thorleif Boman, *Die Jesus-Überlieferung im Lichte der neueren Volkskunde* (Göttingen: Vandenhoeck and Ruprecht, 1967), pp. 10, 35, 60–1, 112, 142.

25 For two critical reviews by scholars thoroughly competent in rabbinica, see Morton Smith, 'A Comparison of Early Christian and Early Rabbinic Tradition', *JBL* 82 (1963), 169–76, who demolishes the foundations of Gerhardsson's approach; and W. D. Davies, 'Reflections on a Scandinavian Approach to "the Gospel Tradition"', Appendix 15 of *The Setting of the Sermon on the Mount* (Cambridge University Press, 1966), pp. 464–80,

who is more sympathetic to the gains made by a theory that he still regards as untenable in the form proposed by Riesenfeld and Gerhardsson.

26 Gerhardsson, *Memory*, p. 178, who documents this and gives further literature.

27 *Tradition to Gospel*, pp. 279–84.

28 *Fresh Approach*, p. 110.

29 *Tradition to Gospel*, p. 298.

30 David Hill, 'On the Evidence for the Creative Role of Christian Prophets', *NTS* 20 (1974), 273.

31 *Ibid.* pp. 265–6. So also Gerhard Dautzenberg, *Urchristliche Prophetie: Ihre Erforschung, ihre Voraussetzungen im Judentum und ihre Struktur im ersten Korintherbrief*, BWANT (Stuttgart: Kohlhammer, 1975), pp. 27–8.

32 'Geistsprüche und Jesuslogien', *ZNW* 53 (1962), 218–28.

33 Hill, 'Creative Role', p. 274.

34 *Ibid.* p. 264.

35 Cothonet, 'Prophétisme', pp. 1285–6.

36 He speaks of those who would '... perceive at once, by the very turn of phrase, whether any given utterance was really in character. No saying would find its way into the record unless it bore the intrinsic marks of the language of Jesus ... Some one would certainly be present at every meeting who would know the facts and would protest against any statement that was plainly wrong' (*The Validity of the Gospel Record* (London: Nicholson and Watson, 1938), pp. 142, 161).

37 *The Formation of the Gospel Tradition* (London: Macmillan, 1933), p. 38.

38 Hill, 'Creative Role', p. 264; James Moffatt, *The First Epistle of Paul to the Corinthians*, MNTC (New York: Harper, n.d.), p. 80; Cothonet, 'Prophétisme', pp. 1285–6, and more explicitly in 'Les prophètes chrétiens comme exégètes charismatiques de l'écriture', in *Prophetic Vocation in the New Testament and Today* (Leiden: Brill, 1978), pp. 77–107.

39 'Geistsprüche', pp. 224–5.

40 This is the favorite text in support of the view that the early church kept the historical tradition of Jesus' words and the post-Easter revelations strictly separate. A typical comment is from Scott, *Validity*, p. 73: 'A line was drawn from the first between the interpretations given by the Spirit and ... the tradition which had been received from the Lord Jesus ... This was the position of Paul, and it was shared, we may be sure, by the whole church.'

On the other hand, some scholars argue that all the sayings referred to in I Cor. 7 are from the risen Lord, not from the historical Jesus, e.g. Werner Kramer, *Christ, Lord, Son of God*, SBT (Naperville: Allenson, 1966), p. 160; Ernst Benz, *Paulus als Visionär* (Wiesbaden: Steiner Verlag, 1952), pp. 37, 113. Dungan, *Sayings of Jesus*, p. 100, presents a curiously mixed view. After insisting that it is Paul who inserts the qualifying clause into the midst of the traditional saying in verse 11*a*, he continues: 'it is most interesting to observe Paul's scrupulous concern with the difference between *halakoth* of the Lord and his own, his conservatism as to "expanding" existing sayings of the Lord to fit new situations'.

Further discussion of the bearing of this text on the relation between Christian prophecy and the synoptic tradition should keep in mind:

(1) there is no consensus on the extent to which, if at all, Paul is 'quoting' a traditional saying of the historical Jesus; (2) there is no agreement on how Paul sees this text – as a word of a past authority-figure, as the exalted Lord speaking through a traditional saying or as a combination of these; (3) the relation of the traditional element to the element added by Paul remains unclear; (4) the extent to which we can generalize from this text to the purported practice of 'the early church' in maintaining a strict separation between traditional and prophetic words is minimal. Who would be willing to generalize from Paul's treatment of the miracle stories about Jesus to 'the practice of the early church'? See below, pp. 71–8.

41 A balanced discussion of the various possibilities is found in Ernest Best, *The First and Second Epistles to the Thessalonians*, HNTC (New York: Harper, 1972), p. 193.

42 Kramer, *Christ, Lord, Son of God*, p. 160; H. Lietzmann, *An die Korinther* (Tübingen: J. C. B. Mohr, 1949[4]), p. 57; Wilhelm Bousset, *Kyrios Christos* (Nashville: Abingdon, 1970), p. 154; Benz, *Paulus als Visionär*, pp. 37, 113; Howard M. Teeple, 'The Oral Tradition that Never Existed', *JBL* 89 (1970), p. 65.

43 Bultmann, *Synoptic Tradition*, pp. 62–9.

44 For the dual nature of the tradition as representing at once the historical Jesus and the exalted Lord, see Oscar Cullmann, 'The Tradition', in *The Early Church*, ed. A. J. B. Higgins (London: SCM Press, 1956), pp. 57–99, and ' "Kyrios" as Designation for the Oral Tradition Concerning Jesus' in *Scottish Journal of Theology* 3 (1950), 180–97.

45 Hill, 'Creative Role', pp. 268f; 'Prophecy and Prophets in the Revelation of St. John', *NTS* 18 (1972), 401–18.

46 'Geprägte Jesus-Tradition', p. 67; Neugebauer makes a similar point, 'Geist-sprüche', p. 224.

47 Delling, 'Geprägte Jesus-Tradition', p. 67; Hill, 'Creative Role', p. 267.

48 Neugebauer, 'Geistsprüche', pp. 222f.

49 Hill, 'Creative Role', p. 269.

50 Hill, 'Prophecy and Prophets', pp. 410, 415.

51 Delling, 'Geprägte Jesus-Tradition', pp. 66f.

52 Hill, 'Creative Role', p. 271; Neugebauer, 'Geistsprüche', p. 219; Cothonet, 'Prophétisme', p.1285; James D. G. Dunn, *Jesus and the Spirit* (Philadelphia: Westminster Press, 1975), p. 173.

2 DEFINITIONS

1 Erich Fascher, Προφήτης: *Eine sprach- und religionsgeschichtliche Untersuchung* (Giessen: Alfred Töpelmann, 1927), pp. 12, 22–7, 32–40, 44–7, 51–5, 98–9, 161–4.

2 Hill, 'Prophecy and Prophets', p. 410.

3 For an earlier, but in some respects more detailed, discussion of this definition, see my essay 'What Are We Looking For? Toward a Definition of the Term "Christian Prophet" ', in *SBL 1973 Seminar Papers* (Missoula: Scholars Press, 1973), 2: 142–54.

4 *De Pythiae Oraculis* c. 7 = 397c (cf. Fascher, Προφήτης, p. 21).

5 Fascher, Προφήτης, pp. 21, 52.

6 B. H. Streeter, *The Four Gospels: A Study of Origins*, rev. ed. (London: Macmillan, 1930), pp. 369–74.

7   Sigmund Mowinckel, *Prophecy and Tradition: The Prophetic Books in the Light of the Study of the Growth and History of the Tradition* (Oslo: I Kommisjon Hos Jacob Dybwad, 1946), *passim*, esp. pp. 67—77; *He That Cometh* (Nashville: Abingdon, 1954), pp. 252—3.

8   H. J. Kraus, *Worship in Israel: A Cultic History of the Old Testament* (Richmond: John Knox Press, 1966), p. 109.

9   Gerhard Friedrich, 'προφήτης', *TDNT*, 6: 848—9.

10 Eduard Schweizer, 'Observance of the Law and Charismatic Activity in Matthew', *NTS* 16 (April 1970), 226.

11 Dibelius, *Tradition to Gospel*, pp. 279—80; Bultmann, *Synoptic Tradition*, pp. 127, 142—3, 348; Cullmann, 'The Tradition'; and '*Kyrios*'.

12 Dietrich Bonhoeffer, *Act and Being* (New York: Harper and Row, 1956), p. 142; Karl Barth, *Church Dogmatics* (Edinburgh: T. and T. Clark, 1936—69), 1: 91, 205—6, 235, 320; Karl Adam, *The Spirit of Catholicism* (New York: Doubleday, 1935), pp. 22—3, 58, 159.

13 *Ibid.* p. 22.

14 C. K. Barrett, *The Gospel According to St. John* (London: SPCK, 1956), p. 406.

15 Bultmann, *Theology*, 2: 88—90; Eduard Schweizer, 'πνεῦμα', *TDNT*, 6: 443; Siegfried Schulz, *Komposition und Herkunft der Johanneischen Reden* (Stuttgart: Kohlhammer, 1960), p. 147.

3 SOURCES

1   E.g. H. B. Swete, *The Holy Spirit in the New Testament: A Study of Primitive Christian Teaching* (London: Macmillan, 1910), pp. 1—10; H. A. Guy, *New Testament Prophecy: Its Origin and Significance* (London: Epworth Press, 1947), pp. 1—27, 146—7; Oscar Cullmann, *The Christology of the New Testament*, rev. ed. (Philadelphia: Westminster, 1963), pp. 13—14.

2   Song of Songs Rabba 8.9*f*; Numbers Rabba 15.10; Qohel. Rabba 12.7 (106*a*); Deut. Rabba 8.6; T. b. Yoma 9*b*, 21*b*; T. b. Sukkah 48*a*; T. b. Sanh. 7*a*, 11*a*; T. b. Meg. 17*b*; Sota 13.2, 48*b*; Baba Mezi'a 59*b*; Baba Bathra 12*a*; Aboth I; Aboth de R. Nathan (A) 16*b*; Josephus, *Contra Apion*, 1.8, 38—42; Apoc. Baruch 85.3. Cf. Rudolf Meyer, 'προφήτης', *TDNT*, 6: 812—28; Bernhard J. Bamberger, 'The Changing Image of the Prophet in Jewish Thought', in *Interpreting the Prophetic Tradition*, ed. Harry Orlinski (Cincinnati: Hebrew Union College Press, 1969) and the literature there given.

3   E.g. Streeter, *Four Gospels*, p. 367; Charles H. H. Scobie, *John the Baptist* (London: SCM, 1964), p. 118; Joachim Jeremias, *New Testament Theology*, vol. 1: 'The Proclamation of Jesus' (New York: Scribners, 1971), pp. 78—80.

4   Geza Vermes, *Jesus the Jew* (New York: Macmillan, 1973), p. 92; W. C. Klein, 'Broad Survey of Prophetism', *ATR* (October 1960), p. 290.

5   Wilhelm Bousset, *Die Religion des Judentums im späthellenistischen Zeit-alter*, HzNT (Tübingen: J. C. B. Mohr, 1966), Appendix to ch. 19, pp. 465—8; Johannes Lindblom, *Gesichte und Offenbarungen: Vorstellungen von göttlichen Weisungen und übernatürlichen Erscheinungen im ältesten Christentum* (Lund: Gleerup, 1968), pp. 167ff; Joseph Blenkinsopp,

'Prophecy and Priesthood in Josephus', *JJS* 25 (summer 1974), 239–62; and cf. R. Leivestad, 'Das Dogma von der Prophetenlosen Zeit', *NTS* 19 (April 1973), 288–99.

6 Tosephta, Sota 13.2; T. b. Baba Mezi'a 59*b*.

7 Cf. the data given in Blenkinsopp, 'Josephus', esp. p. 257.

8 Ulrich B. Müller, *Prophetie und Predigt im Neuen Testament: Formgeschichtliche Untersuchungen zur urchristlichen Prophetie* (Gütersloh: Gütersloher Verlagshaus Mohn, 1975), pp. 168–9, 215–20.

9 In addition to Meyer and Blenkinsopp above, cf. Werner Foerster, 'Der Heilige Geist im Spätjudentum', *NTS* 8 (1961–2), 117–34, and in *Neutestamentliche Zeitgeschichte* (Hamburg: Furche Verlag, 1955), 1: 93.

10 The latter objection is elaborated by Lindblom, *Gesichte und Offenbarungen*, p. 169. The former objection is raised by Millar Burrows, 'Prophecy and Prophets at Qumran', in *Israel's Prophetic Heritage: Essays in Honor of James Muilenburg*, ed. B. W. Anderson and Walter Harrelson (New York: Harper and Row, 1962), pp. 223–4.

11 Millar Burrows, *More Light on the Dead Sea Scrolls* (New York: Viking, 1958), p. 381.

12 The most thorough presentation of this point is by Gert Jeremias, *Der Lehrer der Gerechtigkeit*, SUNT (Göttingen: Vandenhoeck and Ruprecht, 1963), esp. pp. 141–66, 324–5. Cf. also Otto Betz, *Offenbarung und Schriftforschung in der Qumransekte*, WUNT 6 (Tübingen: J. C. B. Mohr, 1960), pp. 64–108; Walter Grundmann, *Das Evangelium nach Matthäus*, THNT 1 (Berlin: Evangelische Verlagsanstalt, 1972), Excursus, 'Der Lehrer der Gerechtigkeit', pp. 115–18.

13 Hans Leisegang, *Der Heilige Geist: Das Wesen und Werden der mystischintuitiven Erkenntnis in der Philosophie und Religion der Griechen*, vol. 1 (Leipzig: Verlag B. G. Teubner, 1919), pp. 120–236, offered the most vigorous argument that Philo understood and experienced prophecy entirely in the Greek ecstatic sense. 'Wir stehen mitten in den Anschauungen des alten Dionysoskultes' (p. 236). This is disputed by Fascher, Προφήτης, p. 160, and Meyer, 'προφήτης', *TDNT*, 6: 823, who consider Philo's understanding of prophecy to be materially in line with that of the Old Testament, LXX and Palestinian Judaism, and only terminologically in agreement with Greek ecstatic prophecy.

14 For a helpful discussion of the Sibyllines, which relates their Jewish elements to the prophecy and oracle-mongering of the Hellenistic world, see John J. Collins, *The Sibylline Oracles of Egyptian Judaism*, SBLDS (Missoula: Scholars Press, 1974).

15 Fascher, Προφήτης, pp. 52–99; Richard Reitzenstein, *Die hellenistischen Mysterienreligionen: Nach ihren Grundgedanken und Wirkungen* (Leipzig: B. G. Teubner, 1927), p. 240; J. Reiling, *Hermas and Christian Prophecy: A Study of the Eleventh Mandate*, NovTSupp (Leiden: E. J. Brill, 1973), pp. 114–20.

16 Prior to Leisegang's work, Hermann Gunkel in *Die Wirkungen des heiligen Geistes: Nach der populären Anschauung der apostolischen Zeit und nach der Lehre des Apostels Paulus* (Göttingen: Vandenhoeck and Ruprecht, 1888) had already made a convincing case that earliest Christianity was pneumatic before it ever adapted itself to the Hellenistic world. C. K.

Barrett later refuted Leisegang point by point in *The Holy Spirit and the Gospel Tradition* (New York: Macmillan, 1947).

17   The phrase is from Fred O. Francis and Wayne Meeks, *Conflict at Colossae* (Missoula: Scholars Press, 1973), p. 8. Schmithals' views are argued in *The Office of Apostle in the Early Church* (Nashville: Abingdon, 1969), pp. 51–3, 226–7. For an effective alternative to Schmithals' excesses, see Robert McL. Wilson, *The Gnostic Problem* (London: Mowbray, 1958), pp. 76–85, and *Gnosis and the New Testament* (Philadelphia: Fortress, 1968), *passim*.

18   This is the opposite of the procedure of Lindblom, *Gesichte und Offenbarungen*, pp. 163–4, who wants to construct a general 'prophetic type' from extra-biblical sources as the basis for the study of Christian prophets.

19   E.g. Walter Wink, *John the Baptist in the Gospel Tradition*, SNTS 7 (Cambridge University Press, 1968); Dunn, *Jesus and the Spirit*, pp. 41–92, esp. pp. 82–94.

20   Ernst Lohmeyer, *Die Offenbarung des Johannes*, HzNT (Tübingen: J. B. C. Mohr, 1926), p. 133: 'Christus spricht nicht in der Apc. 4: 1 – 21: 5.'

21   R. H. Charles, *A Critical and Exegetical Commentary on the Revelation of St. John*, ICC (New York: Scribners, 1920), 1: xxi, cxvii–clix.

22   Angelo Lancelotti, *Sintassi Ebraica nel Greco dell' Apocalisse*, (Assisi, 1964), as summarized by Heinrich Kraft, 'Zur Offenbarung des Johannes', *TR* (September 1973), 93; for Kraft's own view, see *Die Offenbarung des Johannes*, HzNT (Tübingen: J. C. B. Mohr, 1974), p. 15.

23   Akira Satake, *Die Gemeindeordnung in der Johannesapokalypse*, WMANT (Neukirchen-Vluyn: Neukirchener Verlag, 1966). For a generally supportive review, see Mathias Rissi in *JBL* 86 (September 1967), 355–6; Satake's thesis is criticized on exegetical and historical grounds by Traugott Holz in *TLZ* 93 (1969), 262–4.

24   J. A. T. Robinson, *Redating the New Testament* (Philadelphia: Westminster, 1976), pp. 221–53.

25   This is argued by Kraft, *Offenbarung*, pp. 10, 176, 218–25.

26   Walter Bauer, *Orthodoxy and Heresy in Early Christianity* (Philadelphia: Fortress Press, 1971), pp. 77, 84–6; Ferdinand Hahn, *The Titles of Jesus in Christology* (London: SCM Press, 1969), pp. 94, 243–4, 267; Elizabeth Schüssler Fiorenza, 'The Quest for the Johannine School: The Apocalypse and the Fourth Gospel', *NTS* 23 (1977), 424; Kraft, *Offenbarung, passim*; Müller, *Prophetie und Predigt*, pp. 50, 92, 102.

27   David Hill, 'Prophecy', pp. 415–17.

28   For a more detailed discussion, see my 'The Apocalypse as Christian Prophecy', *SBL 1974 Seminar Papers* (Missoula: Scholars Press, 1974), 43–62.

29   *Gesichte und Offenbarungen*, p. 176.

30   Cf. Hill, 'Creative Role', p. 270.

31   Samuel Sandmel, *The Genius of Paul* (New York: Schocken Books, 1970), p. 75; John Gager, *Kingdom and Community: The Social World of Early Christianity* (Englewood Cliffs: Prentice-Hall, 1975), p. 69; Dunn, *Jesus and the Spirit*, p. 230; Benz, *Paulus als Visionär*, pp. 39, 115; J. M. Meyers and E. D. Freed, 'Is Paul Also Among the Prophets?', *Int* 20 (1966), 40–53; Käsemann, *New Testament Questions*, pp. 66–75; and, programatically,

Hans Windisch, *Paulus und Christus: Ein Biblisch-religionsgeschichtlicher Vergleich*, UNT (Leipzig: Hinrichs'sche Buchhandlung, 1934), pp. 143, 150—1, *et passim*.

32 Robert Funk, *Language, Hermeneutic, and Word of God* (New York: Harper and Row, 1966), p. 302.

33 J. Ramsey Michaels, 'The Johannine Words of Jesus and Christian Prophecy', in *SBL 1975 Seminar Papers* (Missoula: Scholars Press, 1975), p. 248.

34 Albrecht Oepke, *Der Brief des Paulus an die Galater*, THNT (Berlin: Evangelische Verlagsanstalt, 1973), p. 101.

35 Moffatt, *First Corinthians*, p. 34; Dautzenberg, *Urchristliche Prophetie*, pp. 138—40, 152, 236, *et passim*; T. W. Gillespie, 'Prophecy and Tongues: The Concept of Christian Prophecy in the Pauline Theology' (Ph.D. dissertation, Claremont Graduate School, 1971), pp. 155—70; E. Cothonet, 'Prophétisme', pp. 1287—8.

36 Hans Conzelmann, *First Corinthians: A Commentary on the First Epistle to the Corinthians*, Hermeneia (Philadelphia: Fortress Press, 1975) considers this passage to be not from Paul himself but from a Pauline 'school' contemporary with Paul, which sees itself as a group of prophets but in a more Hellenistic sense than Paul's own view of prophecy.

37 Calvin Roetzel, 'The Judgment Form in Paul's Letters', *JBL* 88 (1969), 305—12; Käsemann, *New Testament Questions*, pp. 66—76; Müller, *Prophetie und Predigt*.

38 *Ibid.* pp. 43—5, 138—9, 165, 211—12.

39 As a sample of scholars who have so argued, see Müller, *Prophetie und Predigt*, pp. 225—32; Michel, *Der Brief an die Römer*, KEK (Göttingen: Vandenhoeck and Ruprecht, 1966), pp. 249—50, and Dautzenberg, *Urchristliche Prophetie*; David Hill, 'Christian Prophets as Teachers', in *Prophetic Vocation in the New Testament and Today*, ed. J. Panagopoulos, NovTSupp (Leiden: Brill, 1977), pp. 117—18, and Delling, 'Geprägte Jesus-Tradition', pp. 66—7, are particularly significant in that they are both reluctant to regard New Testament material as having originated from Christian prophets.

40 A sample of scholars who have so argued: Martin Dibelius, *Paul*, ed. W. G. Kümmel (Philadelphia: Westminster Press, 1953), p. 110; Müller, *Prophetie und Predigt*, p. 224; Johannes Weiss, *Der erste Korintherbrief*, KEK (Göttingen: Vandenhoeck and Ruprecht, 1925), p. 378; Bartholomäus Henneken, *Verkündigung und Prophetie im 1. Thessalonicherbrief*, SBS (Stuttgart: Verlag Katholisches Bibelwerk, 1969), pp. 95—7, and Dautzenberg, *Urchristliche Prophetie*, p. 152.

41 A sample of scholars who have so argued: Hans Conzelmann, *An Outline of the Theology of the New Testament* (London: SCM Press, 1969), p. 38; Willi Marxsen, 'Auslegung von I Thess. 4: 13—18'. *ZThK* 66 (1969), 22—34; Henneken, *Verkündigung und Prophetie*, pp. 73—98; Best, *Thessalonians*, p. 193.

42 The classic statement of this tenet of the *religionsgeschichtliche Schule* is Reitzenstein's chapter, 'Paulus als Pneumatiker', in *Die hellenistischen Mysterienreligionen*, pp. 333—93, now reprinted in *Das Paulusbild in der neueren deutschen Forschung*, ed. Karl H. Rengstorf, WDF (Darmstadt: Wissenschaftliche Buchgesellschaft, 1969), pp. 246—303.

43 Hans Leisegang, *Pneuma Hagion: Der Ursprung des Geistbegriffs der synoptischen Evangelien aus der griechischen Mystik* (Leipzig: J. C. Hinrichs'sche Buchhandlung, 1922), pp. 115–20.

44 So Windisch, *Paulus und Christus*, p. 196, and Bultmann, *Theology*, 1: 188, both of whom cautiously suggest I Thess. 4: 15–17 as an example, although neither is inclined to exaggerate the connections of Paul to Palestinian Christianity. Cf. notes 39–41 above.

45 Müller, *Prophetie und Predigt*, pp. 37–42, 101 *et passim*; Dautzenberg's thorough work on I Cor. 12–14, *Urchristliche Prophetie*, which has this as one of its primary conclusions (p. 303); Heinrich Kraft, 'Vom Ende der Urchristlichen Prophetie', in *Prophetic Vocation*, p. 169; Cothonet, 'Prophétisme', pp. 1295–7.

46 Gustav Stählin, τὸ πνεῦμα 'Ιησοῦ (Apostelgeschichte 16: 7)', in *Christ and Spirit in the New Testament*, ed. Barnabas Lindars and Stephen Smalley (Cambridge University Press, 1973), pp. 229–52.

47 Friedrich, 'προφήτης', *TDNT*, 6: 849, cites H. J. Holtzmann and Adolf Harnack as arguing that the use of τε in 13: 1 identifies Barnabas, Simeon and Lucius as prophets and Manaen and Saul as teachers, an understanding adopted by Dunn, *Jesus and the Spirit*, p. 171. This purported distinction is rejected or ignored in the standard commentaries, lexica and grammars. That at any rate Luke considers Barnabas a prophet indicates that the puzzling equation in 4: 36 (βαρναβᾶς = υἰὸς παρακλήσεως) is intended to refer to Barnabas' prophetic preaching.

48 E. Earle Ellis, 'The Role of the Christian Prophet in Acts', in *Apostolic History and the Gospel: Biblical and Historical Essays Presented to F. F. Bruce on His Sixtieth Birthday*, ed. Ward Gasque and Ralph P. Martin (Grand Rapids: Eerdmans, 1970), is probably too uncritical in taking Luke's portrayal as accurately representing in detail the prophets whom he describes. But even Ernst Haenchen, *The Acts of the Apostles* (Philadelphia: Westminster Press, 1971), who is inclined to see considerable creativity on Luke's part, regards Luke as working with a tradition in the pericopae that concern church prophets. That Luke's Agabus-materials rest on tradition is argued by H. Patsch, 'Die Prophetie des Agabus', *TZ* 28 (1972), 228–32, and by Müller, *Prophetie und Predigt*, pp. 124f.

49 Hans Conzelmann, *The Theology of St. Luke* (New York: Harper and Row, 1960), pp. 95–136.

50 That παράκλησις, ἀποκάλυψις/διάκρισις and charismatic interpretation of the Scriptures to apply to contemporary issues are all aspects of Christian prophecy will be documented in Part Two below.

51 Note the equation μάγος = ψευδοπροφήτης in 13: 6, of Bar-Jesus; μάγος and μαγεία of Simon Magus in 8: 9–11; the inspired slave girl of 16: 16–18 who is described as having a πνεῦμα πύθωνα, and her conduct as μαντεύειν; all of which Luke is loath to call προφητεία.

52 Cf. the interplay of church prophecy and Luke's picture of Jesus as prophet in the discussions of Paul Minear in *I Saw a New Earth* (Washington: Corpus Books, 1968), pp. 286–98, and in *To Heal and To Reveal: The Prophetic Vocation according to Luke* (New York: Seabury Press, 1976), chs. 5 and 6.

53 See my elaboration of this point in 'Christian Prophecy and Matthew 23:

34–6: A Text [*sic*] Exegesis', in *SBL 1977 Seminar Papers* (Missoula: Scholars Press, 1977), pp. 117–26.

54   'Sentences of Holy Law', 'The Beginnings of Christian Theology', in *New Testament Questions*, pp. 66–107.

55   'Observance of the Law', pp. 213–30, esp. p. 226; *Matthäus und seine Gemeinde*, SBS (Stuttgart: KBW Verlag, 1974), esp. pp. 140–7.

56   'Observance of the Law', p. 228. Schweizer's 1974 *Matthäus und seine Gemeinde*, pp. 140–51, does however distinguish prophet and scribe.

57   Cothonet, 'Les prophètes chrétiens dans l'Évangile selon saint Matthieu', in *L'Évangile selon Matthieu; rédaction et théologie*, ed. M. Didier (Duculot: Gembloux, 1972), pp. 281–308; G. D. Kilpatrick, *The Origins of the Gospel according to Matthew* (London: Oxford University Press, 1946), pp. 110–11, 126; M. Jack Suggs, *Wisdom, Christology and Law in Matthew's Gospel* (Cambridge, Mass.: Harvard University Press, 1970), pp. 23–4.

58   David Hill, 'Δίκαιοι as a Quasi-Technical Term', *NTS* 11 (1965), 296–302; Cothonet, 'Prophétisme', pp. 1272–3.

59   Alexander Sand, 'Propheten, Weise, und Schriftkundige in der Gemeinde des Matthäusevangeliums', in *Kirche im Werden: Studien zum Thema Amt und Gemeinde im Neuen Testament*, ed. Josef Hainz (Munich: Verlag Ferdinand Schöningh, 1976), pp. 167–85; *Das Gesetz und die Propheten: Untersuchungen zur Theologie des Evangeliums nach Matthäus*, BU (Regensburg: Verlag Friedrich Pustet, 1974), pp. 168–77.

60   F. W. Beare, 'The Mission of the Disciples and the Mission Charge: Matthew 10 and Parallels', *JBL* 89 (March 1970), 1–13; cf. Joachim Jeremias, *New Testament Theology*, 1: 236–40.

61   Birger Gerhardsson, 'Die Boten Gottes und die Apostel Christi', *Svensk Exegetisk Arsbok* 27 (1962), 110–15; Cothonet, 'Prophétisme et ministère d'après le Nouveau Testament', *Maison-Dieu* 107 (1971), 36.

62   Benjamin Hubbard, *The Matthean Redaction of a Primitive Apostolic Commissioning: An Exegesis of Matt. 28: 16–20*, SBLDS (Missoula: Scholars Press, 1974), pp. 128–34.

63   Jean-Paul Audet, *La Didachè: Instructions des Apôtres* (Paris: Gabalda, 1958).

64   Cyril C. Richardson, *Early Christian Fathers*, LCC (Philadelphia: Westminster, 1953), pp. 161–6; Massey H. Shepherd, Jr, 'Didache', *IDB* (Nashville: Abingdon, 1962), 1: 842; Eduard Schweizer, *Jesus* (Richmond: John Knox Press, 1971), p. 56 (A.D. 80–90); Jeremias, *New Testament Theology*, p. 195 ('by A.D. 75').

65   Ernst Käsemann, *The Testament of Jesus* (London: SCM Press, 1968), p. 38; Streeter, *Four Gospels*, p. 367.

66   Charles, *Revelation*, pp. xxxii–xxxiv, who lists the points of contact.

67   I have elaborated this argument in my article 'The Influence of Christian Prophecy on the Johannine Portrayal of the Paraclete and Jesus', *NTS* 25 (1978), 113–22.

68   E.g. Hermann Sasse, 'Der Paraklet im Johannesevangelium', *ZNW* 24 (1925), 260–77; H. Weinel, *Biblische Theologie des Neuen Testaments: Die Religion Jesu und des Urchristentums* (Tübingen: J. C. B. Mohr, 1928), pp. 470–1; Hans Windisch, 'The Five Paraclete Sayings' in *The Spirit–*

Paraclete in the Fourth Gospel, ed. John Reumann (Philadelphia: Fortress Press, 1968), p. 21.

69 Streeter, *Four Gospels*, pp. 365–74, 383–9, 397.

70 David Aune, *The Cultic Setting of Realized Eschatology*, NovTSupp (Leiden: Brill, 1972), pp. 15, 89, 96–9.

71 *Ibid.* p. 101. Cf., e.g., Jeremias, *New Testament Theology*, p. 2; J. Ramsey Michaels in *The New Testament Speaks* (New York: Harper, 1969), pp. 393–7; Lloyd Gaston, *No Stone on Another: Studies in the Significance of the Fall of Jerusalem in the Synoptic Gospels*, NovTSupp (Leiden: E. J. Brill, 1970), p. 60; Wilhelm Wilkens, *Die Entstehungsgeschichte des vierten Evangeliums* (Zollikon: Evangelischer Verlag, 1958), pp. 169–74; Herbert Leroy, *Rätsel und Missverständnis: Ein Beitrag zur Formgeschichte des Johannesevangeliums*, BBB (Bonn: Peter Hanstein Verlag, 1968), pp. 180–2.

72 Practically all work on the Gospel of John now regards this as axiomatic, but see especially C. H. Dodd, *Historical Tradition in the Fourth Gospel* (Cambridge University Press, 1963); Raymond Brown, *The Gospel According to John*, AB (New York: Doubleday, 1966/70), esp. 1: xxiv–li; and D. Moody Smith, 'Johannine Christianity: Some Reflections on its Character and Delineation', *NTS* 21 (1975), 222–48.

73 'Affinités littéraires et doctrinales du Manuel de Discipline', *Revue Biblique* 60 (1953), 41–82.

74 Reiling, *Hermas*, pp. 173–4.

75 Müller, *Prophetie und Predigt*, p. 175, finds evidence of early prophetic forms preserved in Hermas.

76 If the Odes of Solomon came from a Jewish-Christian community in Palestine or Syria of the late first century, as is believed by some students, they would be a helpful resource for our reconstruction. But since their date and provenance remain very disputed, the Odes will not be used except to illustrate points established on other grounds.

4 METHOD

1 Hans von Campenhausen, *Ecclesiastical Authority and Spiritual Power in the Church of the First Three Centuries* (London: Adam and Charles Black, 1969), pp. 12–14.

2 David L. Tiede, *The Charismatic Figure as Miracle Worker*, SBLDS 1 (Missoula: Scholars Press, 1972), p. 246.

3 Kraus, *Worship in Israel*, p. 20.

4 Klaus Koch, *The Rediscovery of Apocalyptic*, SBT (London: SCM, 1972), p. 33; Alan Culpepper, *The Johannine School* (Missoula: Scholars Press, 1975), pp. 250–60; Rolf Rendtorff, 'Reflections on the Early History of Prophecy in Israel', in *History and Hermeneutic*, JThCh 4 (New York: Harper, 1967), p. 16.

5 Bultmann, *Synoptic Tradition*, pp. 11–12, 21, 47.

5 THE PROPHET AS A CHURCH FIGURE

1 Adolf Harnack, *The Mission and Expansion of Christianity in the First Three Centuries* (New York: Putnam, 1904), pp. 419–27.

2 In Acts 13: 6; II Pet. 2: 1; Rev. 16: 13; 19: 20; 20: 10, ψευδοπροφῆται

is used as a general pejorative term for deceivers and heretics without indicating that these opponents are προφῆται in the strict sense.

3 Satake, *Gemeindeordnung*, p. 168; Dunn, *Jesus and the Spirit*, p. 171; Gillespie, 'Prophecy and Tongues', pp. 5–6; Müller, *Prophetie und Predigt*, p. 113, regards the prophets in Luke's tradition as 'settled', but those in Luke's composition as 'wandering'.

4 Raymond Brown, ' "Other Sheep Not of this Fold": the Johannine Perspective on Christian Diversity in the Late First Century', *JBL* 98 (March 1978), 5–22; Reiling, *Hermas*, p. 9.

5 The view here argued is challenged by the recent work of Gerd Theissen, *Sociology of Early Palestinian Christianity* (Philadelphia: Fortress, 1978), ch. 2: 'The Role of Wandering Charismatics', which bases its view of 'wandering' prophets too much on inferences from the sayings of Jesus in the synoptic gospels.

6 Eduard Schweizer, *Church Order in the New Testament*, SBT (Naperville: Allenson, 1961), p. 135.

7 *Ibid.* Cf. Otto Michel, *Prophet und Märtyrer* (Gütersloh: Verlag Bertelsmann, 1932), p. 47; Cothonet, 'Prophétisme', pp. 1329–31; Michaels, 'Johannine Words of Jesus', pp. 233–64, who draws materials from both the Fourth Gospel and Revelation to portray the 'prophethood of all believers' in the Johannine community.

8 Schweizer, *Church Order*, p. 135. For a careful argument that the prophets in Revelation are a distinct group within the congregation, see Hill, *NTS* (1972), 409–10; and Kraft, *Offenbarung*, p. 21.

9 Sand, *Das Gesetz*, pp. 168–77.

10 Heinrich Schlier, 'Zum Begriff des Geistes nach dem Johannesevangelium', in *Besinnung auf das Neue Testament* (Freiburg: Herder, 1964), p. 269; Boring, 'Johannine Portrayal of the Paraclete', p. 114; Michaels, 'Johannine Words of Jesus', pp. 233–64.

11 Dautzenberg, *Urchristliche Prophetie*, p. 214.

12 Above, pp. 58–9, 63–4.

13 Minear, *I saw a New Earth*, p. 189; cf. Kraft, *Offenbarung*, p. 56.

14 E.g. Dautzenberg, *Urchristliche Prophetie*, pp. 138–40, 152, 225, 236–7; Gillespie, 'Prophecy and Tongues', pp. 168–70; Cothonet, 'Prophétisme', pp. 1287–8; Dunn, *Jesus and the Spirit*, p. 235.

15 Funk, *Language, Hermeneutic, and Word of God*, p. 293.

16 Dautzenberg, *Urchristliche Prophetie*, pp. 147 *et passim*, and in 'Zum religionsgeschichtlichen Hintergrund der διάκρισις πνευμάτων (I Kor. 12, 10)', *BZ* 15 (1971), 93–104, has made a carefully-argued case that this phrase refers to the *interpretation* of the mysterious speech of the prophets of the congregation and not to the *evaluation* of prophetic speech. The response by Müller, *Prophetie und Predigt*, pp. 27–8, confirms the validity of the traditional interpretation taken above. Dunn, *Jesus and the Spirit*, pp. 233–4, attempts a mediating view.

17 The older critical view, that the prophet was urged to prophesy according to the strength of his own faith (*fides qua creditur*), was advocated e.g. by Gunkel, *Wirkungen*, pp. 8, 26. Among those who have returned to the patristic view (*fides quae creditur*) are Lindblom, *Gesichte und Offenbarungen*, p. 195; Ernst Käsemann, *An die Römer*, HZnT (Tübingen:

J. C. B. Mohr, 1974²), p. 326; and von Campenhausen, *Ecclesiastical Authority*, p. 62.

18   James D. G. Dunn, 'Prophetic "I-Sayings" and the Jesus Tradition: The Importance of Testing Prophetic Utterances Within Early Christianity', *NTS* 24 (January 1978), rightly insists on this point, but, in the particular case he discusses in response to my 1972 *JBL* article, he arrives at the somewhat peculiar conclusion that Mark 3: 28–9 must be from the historical Jesus, because if it were from a Christian prophet it would not have passed the tests that he believes the early community applied to such sayings. That is, the saying must be from Jesus because the early church would have considered it to be from a false prophet if they had had opportunity to examine it!

19   Cf. L. Thompson, 'Cult and Eschatology in the Apocalypse of John', *JR* 49 (October 1969), 330–50; Otto Piper, 'The Apocalypse of John and the Liturgy of the Ancient Church', *CH* (1951), 10–22; G. Delling, 'Zum gottesdienstlichen Stil der Johannes Apokalypse', *NovT* 3 (1959), 107–37.

20   ἀναστάς is comparable to ἀνέστη in Luke 4: 16 and indicates a liturgical setting.

21   For John as the representative of individualistic piety, see C. F. D. Moule, 'The Individualism of the Fourth Gospel', *NovT* 5 (1962), 171–90; Dunn, *Jesus and the Spirit*, pp. 350–5, and the literature he gives. For John as the representative of a worshipping community, see for example Oscar Cullmann, *Early Christian Worship*, SBT (London: SCM, 1953), pp. 37–116, and Wilkens, *Entstehungsgeschichte des vierten Evangeliums*, pp. 169–74.

22   E.g. Brown, *Gospel According to John*, 1: xxiv–xl, cv–cxiv *et passim*; Aune, *Cultic Setting*, esp. pp. 15, 68–72, 93–129.

23   Boring, 'Johannine Portrayal of the Paraclete', pp. 113–20.

24   For Israel and Judaism, cf. Sigmund Mowinckel, *The Psalms in Israel's Worship* (Nashville: Abingdon, 1962), 2: 53–73. Both Reitzenstein, *Die hellenistischen Mysterienreligionen*, pp. 228 and 337, and Fascher, Προφήτης, p. 51, indicate that Hellenistic prophets were sometimes attached to a cult.

25   Friedrich, 'προφήτης', p. 853.

26   Leonhard Goppelt, *Apostolic and Post-Apostolic Times* (New York: Harper, 1962), p. 45.

27   Henneken, *Verkündigung und Prophetie*, p. 113.

28   Joseph Schmidt, 'Propheten, (b.) P. im NT', *Lexikon für Theologie und Kirche* (Freiburg: Herder, 1957–65²), 8: 799.

29   For this general subject see Sigmund Mowinckel, *Prophecy and Tradition*; for a good treatment of a particular example, see Hans Walter Wolff, *Joel and Amos*, Hermeneia (Philadelphia: Fortress Press, 1977), where Joel is revealed as one who, as a prophet, operated in relationship to the cult and its transmission of materials, and was himself immersed in the transmission process, including taking up the words of older prophets and re-presenting them without directly quoting them, in a manner genuinely new – all of which is similar to what early Christian prophets did, as we shall see.

30   D. S. Russell, *The Method and Message of Jewish Apocalyptic*, OTL (Philadelphia: Westminster Press, 1964), pp. 173–5.

31   Aboth I.2 shows that for Tannaitic Judaism, the prophets stand in a line of

tradition, which they both hand on and expand. Thus Rabbi Hillel's saying preserved in Aboth I.13: 'Who adds not makes to cease.' But this 'adding' was understood to express only what was implicitly already there.

32 Krister Stendahl, *The School of St. Matthew and Its Use of the Old Testament* (Uppsala: Gleerup, 1954), p. 33.

33 Hans von Campenhausen, 'Tradition und Geist im Urchristentum', *Studium Generale* 4 (June 1951), 351−7; *Ecclesiastical Authority*, pp. 151−2.

34 Kraft, *Offenbarung*, pp. 9, 11; Eduard Lohse, *Die Offenbarung des Johannes*, NTD (Göttingen: Vandenhoeck and Ruprecht, 1971), p. 3.

35 The original suggestion of Wellhausen that 11: 1−13 was a fragment of Zealot prophecy taken over by John has recently been argued by Martin Hengel, *Die Zeloten: Untersuchungen zur jüdischen Freiheitsbewegung in der Zeit von Herodes I. bis 70 nach Christi*, AGSU (Leiden: E. J. Brill, 1961), p. 249. Jeremias, *New Testament Theology*, p. 126, and Phillip Carrington, *The First Christian Century* (London: Cambridge University Press, 1957), p. 73, are among those who see this text as the Johannine reworking of an earlier Christian prophetic oracle.

36 Cf. Bauckham, 'Synoptic Parousia Parables and the Apocalypse', *NTS* 23 (January 1977), 162−76; Hill, in *Prophetic Vocation*, p. 121. See above, extended note 40 in ch. 1.

37 Cf. e.g. A. M. Hunter, *Paul and His Predecessors*, rev. ed. (Philadelphia: Westminster, 1961); Hans Conzelmann, 'Current Problems in Pauline Research', in *New Testament Issues*, ed. Richard Batey (New York: Harper and Row, 1970), pp. 136−8.

38 Victor Furnish, *The Jesus−Paul Debate: From Baur to Bultmann* (Manchester: The John Rylands Library, 1965), surveys the variety of results of the attempts to discover allusions to Jesus' sayings in Paul's letters.

39 Cf. above, pp. 9−12, and ch. 1, note 40.

40 Hawthorne, 'Christian Prophecy and the Sayings of Jesus: Evidence of and Criteria for', *SBL 1975 Seminar Papers* (Missoula: Scholars Press, 1975), p. 113.

41 Conzelmann, *Theology of St. Luke*, pp. 170−206; Ernst Käsemann, *Essays on New Testament Themes*, SBT (London: SCM Press, 1960), pp. 28−9.

42 For further discussion of prophecy and tradition in the Johannine writings see Windisch, *Spirit-Paraclete*, p. 17; Franz Mussner, 'Die joh. Paraklet-sprüche und die apostolische Tradition', *BZ* 5 (1961), 56−70, and George Johnston, *The Spirit-Paraclete in the Fourth Gospel*, SNTS (Cambridge University Press, 1970), p. 139.

43 See John Gager, *Kingdom and Community*, 'Charisma, Office, and Tradition', pp. 69−74, and the literature there given.

44 Gerd Theissen, 'Wanderradikalismus: Literatursoziologische Aspekte der Überlieferung von Worten Jesu im Urchristentum', *ZThK* 70 (1973), 245−71.

45 Bornkamm, *Jesus of Nazareth* (New York: Harper and Row, 1960), pp. 17−21, 174.

46 E.g. Dunn, *Jesus and the Spirit*, p. 186; Johnston, *Spirit-Paraclete*, p. 138; Ellis, 'The Role of the Christian Prophet in Acts', pp. 64−5; cf. most of the authors of *Prophetic Vocation*, esp. David Hill's study 'Christian Prophets as Teachers or Instructors in the Church', pp. 108−30.

47 Johnston, *Spirit-Paraclete*, pp. 128–35; Ulrich Müller, 'Die Parakleten-vorstellung im Johannesevangelium', *ZThK* 71 (March 1974), 77–8; cf. above pp. 49–50.

6 THE PROPHET AS 'HOMO RELIGIOSUS'

1 Lindblom, *Gesichte und Offenbarungen*, p. 164.
2 Reiling, *Hermas*, p. 9.
3 Dunn, *Jesus and the Spirit*, p. 84.
4 *Timaeus*, 71. English translation by R. G. Bury, from *Plato*, LCL (Cambbridge, Mass.: Harvard University Press, 1952) 7: 186–7.
5 *Pharsalia*, 5.161ff.
6 Lucian, *Alexander the False Prophet, passim*, and Vergil, *Aeneid*, 6.45–51.
7 *Quis Rerum Divinarum Heres*, 259–66, quoted in Dunn, *Jesus and the Spirit*, p. 304.
8 *Quis Rerum Divinarum Heres*, 264, quoted in Abraham Heschel, *The Prophets* (New York: Harper, 1962/9), 2: 112.
9 Quoted from Leisegang, *Der Heilige Geist*, p. 120.
10 *Ibid.* p. 121.
11 *Spec. Leg.*, 1.65; cf. Müller, *Prophetie und Predigt*, p. 32–4. Barrett, *Holy Spirit*, p. 112, interprets Philo's understanding of prophecy as less ecstatic.
12 Cf. my definition above, p. 16.
13 Cf. Thomas W. Gillespie, 'A Pattern of Prophetic Speech in I Corinthians', *JBL* 97 (March 1978), 80–5.
14 For this interpretation of the 'Christ party' see Walter Schmithals, *Gnosticism in Corinth: An Investigation of the Letters to the Corinthians* (Nashville: Abingdon, 1971), pp. 124–41; A. D. Nock, *St. Paul* (New York: Harper, 1938), p. 173; for the relation of this group to 12: 3, see Bousset, *Kyrios Christos*, p. 133; James L. Price, *Interpreting the New Testament* (New York: Holt, Rinehart and Winston, 1971[2]), p. 376; Gillespie, 'Prophecy and Tongues', pp. 39–45.
15 H. G. Liddell and Robert Scott, *Greek-English Lexicon* (Oxford: Clarendon Press, 1940), 2: 1073, document the use of this term in Bacchic frenzy in the sense of 'inspired by a god'. Cf. Gerhard Delling, *Worship in the New Testament* (London: Darton, Longman and Todd, 1962), p. 27.
16 Cf. Josephine Ford's comments on 'Ecstatic Prophecy as the Possible Background to the Stress on Sobriety in the Epistles', in 'Proto-Montanism in the Pastorals', *NTS* 17 (April 1971), 342–3.
17 Max Weber, *The Sociology of Religion* (Boston: Beacon Press, 1963[4]), p. 47; Johannes Lindblom, *Prophecy in Ancient Israel* (Philadelphia: Fortress Press, 1962), pp. 17, 50; Michel, *Prophet und Märtyrer*, p. 11.
18 Lindblom, *Prophecy*, pp. 2, 46; Weber, *Sociology of Religion*, p. 46.
19 Joachim Jeremias, *Der Schlüssel zur Theologie des Apostels Paulus* (Stuttgart: Calver Verlag, 1971), p. 23; Krister Stendahl, *Paul Among Jews and Gentiles* (Philadelphia: Fortress Press, 1977), pp. 7–23.
20 E.g. Rengstorf, 'ἀπόστολος', *TDNT*, 1: 425; Walther Grundmann, *Das Evangelium nach Lukas*, THNT (Berlin: Evangelische Verlagsanstalt, 1971), p. 137.
21 Cothenet, 'Prophétisme et ministère', p. 36; Gerhardsson, 'Die Boten Gottes', pp. 110–21.

22 Georg Fohrer, *Die symbolische Handlungen der Propheten*, ATANT (Zürich: Zwingli Verlag, 1953).

23 Kirsopp Lake and H. J. Cadbury, 'English Translation and Commentary', vol. 4 of *The Beginnings of Christianity*, ed. F. J. Foakes-Jackson and Kirsopp Lake (London: Macmillan, 1920—33), p. 268; Lindblom, *Gesichte und Offenbarungen*, p. 191.

24 Sand, *Das Gesetz*, pp. 173—4; Theissen, 'Wanderradikalismus', pp. 250—8; 'Legitimation und Lebensunterhalt: Ein Beitrag zur Soziologie urchristlicher Missionäre', *NTS* (January 1975), 192—221; G. Kretschmar, 'Ein Beitrag zur Frage nach dem Ursprung frühchristlicher Askese', *ZThK* 61 (1964), 27—67.

25 Weber, *Sociology of Religion*, p. 47; Père Ganne, *Le Pauvre et le Prophète*, CF (Paris: Cerf, 1977).

26 Vermes, *Jesus the Jew*, pp. 100—1.

27 See Lindblom, *Gesichte und Offenbarungen*, p. 191, note 51; cf. also II Clem. 14.2; I Cor. 7: 36—8 and commentaries thereto.

7 THE PROPHET AS HERMENEUT

1 George F. Moore, *Judaism in the First Centuries of the Christian Era* (Cambridge, Mass.: Harvard University Press, 1927), 1: 24—50; 2: 243; Müller, *Prophetie und Predigt*, p. 239, shows this approach was also present in the Hellenistic synagogue.

2 See Wolff, *Joel and Amos*, pp. 1—86, esp. pp. 10—11.

3 Friedrich, 'προφήτης', p. 819; Dautzenberg, *Urchristliche Prophetie*, pp. 91, 97; Russell, *Method and Message*, pp. 178—202; Gaston, *No Stone*, pp. 434—41 and the literature he gives.

4 Cf. Gaston, *No Stone*, pp. 458—68.

5 Cf. above, pp. 24—5; Otto Betz, *Der Paraklet: Fürsprecher im häretischen Spätjudentum, im Johannes-evangelium und in neugefundenen Gnostischen Schriften*, AGSU (Leiden: Brill, 1963), p. 132; *Offenbarung und Schriftforschung*, pp. 89—92, 99; Gert Jeremias, *Lehrer*, p. 141; IQH 2.13; 4.27; 5.25; 7.27; 9.23; 11.16; 12.11—12.

6 Cf. Blenkinsopp, 'Josephus', p. 258, and the literature given there.

7 *Ibid.* pp. 240, 247, and Gunkel, *Wirkungen*, p. 37; Josephus, *Wars*, III.352; Philo, *Som.*, 2.252; Friedrich, 'Προφήτης', p. 823.

8 Fascher, Προφήτης, pp. 22—7, 85—8.

9 C. H. Dodd, *According to the Scriptures: The Sub-structure of New Testament Theology* (New York: Scribners, 1953).

10 *Ibid.* p. 110.

11 This is the fundamental thesis of Käsemann's famous essay 'The Beginnings of Christian Theology', in *New Testament Questions*, in which he declared that 'Apocalyptic is the mother of all Christian theology' (p. 100).

12 E. C. Selwyn, *The Christian Prophets and the Prophetic Apocalypse* (London: Macmillan, 1900), p. 59.

13 Kraft, *Offenbarung*, p. 112. Kraft's commentary documents this statement admirably.

14 Kurt Aland, Matthew Black, Carlo M. Martini, Bruce M. Metzger, Allen Wikgren (eds.), *The Greek New Testament* (New York: American Bible Society, 1975³), p. ix. Nestle—Aland²⁶ has attempted to adopt a mediating

approach in Revelation but without success. The phenomenon calls for the either/or approach of Nestle[25] and *The Greek New Testament*[3].

15 Cf. Satake, *Gemeindeordnung*, p. 159.

16 Cothonet, 'Exégètes charismatiques', p. 79–81; F. Rousseau, *L'Apocalypse et le milieu prophétique du Nouveau Testament: Structure et préhistoire du texte* (Paris: Tournai, 1971), p. 138.

17 This insight, often expressed in the works on Christian prophecy by E. C. Selwyn, is somewhat smothered by his uncritical and hyper-imaginative expression of it. Cf. *The Christian Prophets*, pp. 4–6 *et passim*, and *The Oracles in the New Testament*, pp. 230, 291–6. More sober grounds for regarding Paul as an example of prophetic exegesis are given by Joseph Bonsirven, *Exégèse rabbinique et exégèse paulinienne* (Paris: Beauchesene, 1939), p. 307.

18 E. Earle Ellis, *Paul's Use of the Old Testament* (Grand Rapids: Eerdmans, 1957), pp. 107–13. The Pauline passages are Rom. 12: 19 and I Cor. 14: 21, where γέγραπται is used by Paul to introduce an Old Testament quotation to which λέγει κύριος has already been added. In II Cor. 6: 16–18, εἶπεν ὁ θεός introduces the quotation that in the Old Testament already contained the phrase λέγει κύριος, to which another has been subsequently added. In Rom. 14: 11 the λέγει κύριος was already in the Old Testament text.

Ellis claims to find six occasions where λέγει κύριος is a New Testament addition to the text. Of the eleven occurrences of this phrase (in eight passages), I only find three where it is added to the Old Testament, all of which are in Paul, showing that only Paul may be used for the argument here advanced. (The following passages contain the phrase; those where λέγει κύριος has been added are italicized: Acts 7: 49 (though printed as a New Testament addition in Nestle[25] and adopted as an instance of the phenomenon by Ellis, the LXX does in fact contain the formula at the *beginning* of the passage; this has been corrected in Nestle–Aland[26]); Acts 15: 16; *Rom. 12: 19*; 14: 11; *I Cor. 14: 21*; II Cor. 6: 17, 18; Heb. 8: 8, 9, 10; 10: 16. The occurrence in Heb. 10: 30 in Alexandrinus and some late MSS is secondary to Rom. 12: 19.)

19 *Ibid.* p. 109.

20 I have not seen this study (*Le langage de l'annonce missionnaire*), but it is cited favorably by Cothonet, 'Exégètes charismatiques', pp. 91–2, notes 54, 55, 57, 61, 90. Hill, 'Prophets in the Revelation of St. John', p. 417, and Ellis, 'Role of the Christian Prophet in Acts', pp. 58–9, also regard this text as an example of prophetic exegesis. I am inclined to see it as reflecting more of the redactional work of Luke, but this still might contain a tradition, via Luke, of how Christian prophet-teachers functioned.

21 Haenchen, *Acts*, p. 105; Hans Dieter Betz, 'Ursprung und Wesen christlichen Glaubens nach der Emmauslegende (Luke 24: 13–22)', *ZThK* 66 (1969), 7–21.

22 Brown, *Gospel According to John*, 1: lx; C. K. Barrett, 'The Old Testament in the Fourth Gospel', *JTS* 48 (1947), 155–69.

23 This is seen throughout the opening chapters of the Didache, particularly in the Two Ways section, chs. 1–5. In 14.3 the κύριος who speaks there (in the Old Testament) is probably intended to be the Lord Jesus, in view of

the fact that of the other seventeen usages of κύριος in the Didache, sixteen probably refer to Jesus, the only exception being the κύριε in the prayer of 10.5, which could also, of course, refer to Jesus.

24 Cf. Barnabas Lindars, *New Testament Apologetic* (London: SCM, 1961), *passim*; Lars Hartmann, *Prophecy Interpreted* (Lund: Gleerup, 1966); and John Donahue's comments in *Are You the Christ?*, SBLDS (Missoula: Scholars Press, 1973), pp. 15, 173.

25 Gerhard von Rad in *Essays in Old Testament Hermeneutics*, ed. Klaus Westermann (Richmond: John Knox Press, 1963), p. 25; *Old Testament Theology* (New York: Harper, 1962–65), 2: 59, 99–116.

26 'Ecstasy' is used here quite apart from its psychological and emotional connotations, to refer to the non-rational aspect of the reception of revelation, as in Paul Tillich, *Systematic Theology* (Chicago: University of Chicago Press, 1951), 1: 111–18.

27 Cf. Heschel, *Prophets*, 2: 252; Martin Noth, *The History of Israel* (London: A. and C. Black, 1960), p. 256.

28 Charles, *Revelation*, 2: 130; Martin Rist, 'Introduction and Exegesis of Revelation', *IB*, ed. George Buttrick (Nashville: Abingdon, 1957), p. 510.

29 G. B. Caird, *A Commentary on the Revelation of St. John the Divine*, HNTC (New York: Harper, 1966), p. 236; Martin Kiddle, *The Revelation of St. John*, MNTC (New York: Harper, n.d.), p. 383.

30 Gillespie, 'Prophecy and Tongues', p. 197, on I Cor. 12: 3.

31 Cf. πρόθεσις (9: 11) and τέλος (10: 4); and Michel, *Der Brief an die Römer*, p. 77.

32 Ellis, 'The Role of the Christian Prophet in Acts', pp. 64–5; Hawthorne, 'Christian Prophecy and the Sayings of Jesus', pp. 112–14; Dunn, *Jesus and the Spirit*, pp. 172, 174; cf. Cothonet, 'Les prophètes chrétiens dans l'Évangile selon saint Matthieu', p. 306.

33 Joachim Jeremias, *The Parables of Jesus*, rev. ed. (New York: Scribners, 1963), pp. 23–114.

8 MATERIAL CHARACTERISTICS OF EARLY CHRISTIAN PROPHETIC SPEECH

1 Otto Michel, 'Spätjüdisches Prophetentum', in *Neutestamentliche Studien für Rudolf Bultmann zu seinem siebzigsten Geburtstag am 20. August 1954*, ed. Walther Eltester (Berlin: Alfred Töpelmann, 1954), pp. 62–3; Scobie, *John the Baptist*, pp. 123–4.

2 Cf. Kraft, *Offenbarung*, p. 78.

3 Käsemann, *New Testament Questions*, pp. 125–30.

4 Henneken, *Verkündigung und Prophetie*, pp. 105–11.

5 According to Plutarch, *De Pyth. Orac.*, 21, the oracle οὔτε λέγει, οὔτε κρύπτει, ἀλλὰ σημαίνει. Quoted in Walter Bauer, *A Greek–English Lexicon of the New Testament and Other Early Christian Literature*, ed. William F. Arndt and F. Wilbur Ginrich (University of Chicago Press, 1957[4]), pp. 355.

6 Although there is nothing inherently apocalyptic about the word μέλλω, it is noteworthy that Revelation uses it twelve times to refer to the imminent apocalyptic events, including the use of stock phrases such as ἃ μέλλει γενέσθαι μετὰ ταῦτα (1: 19). The phrase λιμός μεγάλη is used in the New Testament besides Acts 11: 28 only in Luke 4: 25, where it is part of a *logion* that has been shaped by apocalyptic traditions, as the change from

the three years of I Kings 18: 1 has become the standard three-and-a-half
years of apocalyptic lore. The combination οἰκουμένη + ὅλη is found in
the New Testament besides Acts 11: 28 only in Rev. 3: 10; 12: 9; 16: 14
and Matt. 24: 14, all of them apocalyptic passages.

7   Cf. above pp. 36–7, 40–1, 109.

8   Koch, *Rediscovery*, pp. 20–4; John Gammie, 'The Classification, Stages
    of Growth, and Changing Intentions in the Book of Daniel', *JBL* 95 (1976),
    193–4; Russell, *Method and Message*, pp. 100–1.

9   Minear, *New Earth*, pp. 213–27.

10 It is not clear how this rendering is derived. Some have seen בְּרִינְבוּ
    as the original, which would contain the name of a pagan god that Luke
    has attempted to camouflage (Gustaf Dalman, *The Words of Jesus:
    Considered in the Light of Post-Biblical Jewish Writings and the Aramaic
    Language* (Edinburgh: T. and T. Clark, 1909), pp. 187–8, 310; Maurice
    Goguel, *The Birth of Christianity* (New York: Macmillan, 1954), p. 190.)
    But more probably Luke (?mis-)understood -ναβᾶς to be related to the Old
    Testament נָבִיא so that βαρναβᾶς = 'son of prophecy' = 'son of
    consolation', so that here too προφητεία = παράκλησις. Cf. H. H. Wendt,
    Die Apostelgeschichte, KEK (Göttingen: Vandenhoeck and Ruprecht,
    1913), *ad loc.*

11 Above, pp. 40–1.

12 Cf. pp. 49–50 above, and Barrett, *St. John*, pp. 385–6.

13 Mart. Is. 5.1; C. C. Torrey, *The Lives of the Prophets: Greek Text and
    Translation*, JBLMS (Philadelphia: SBL, 1946), pp. 20, 34. The latter
    document is particularly important in documenting late-Judaism's view of
    the prophet as a suffering figure. Acts 7: 52; Heb. 11: 32–8 also reflect
    this development. For further examples and elaboration of this point, see
    H. J. Schoeps, 'Die jüdischen Prophetenmorde', in *Aus frühchristlicher
    Zeit: Religionsgeschichtliche Untersuchungen* (Tübingen: J. C. B. Mohr,
    1950), pp. 126ff.

14 Leander Keck, in *Interpreter's One-Volume Commentary on the Bible*
    (Nashville: Abingdon, 1970), pp. 868–9, who points out several non-
    Pauline features of this section.

15 Kirsopp Lake, *The Earlier Epistles of Paul* (London: Rivingtons, 1911),
    pp. 87–8, though recent interpreters have not favored this view. Cf. Ernst
    Bammel, 'Judenverfolgung und Naherwartung. Zur Eschatologie des ersten
    Thessalonicherbriefs', *ZThK* 56 (1959), 294–315, and O. H. Steck, *Israel
    und das gewaltsame Geschick der Propheten*, WMANT (Neukirchen-Vluyn:
    Neukirchener Verlag, 1967), p. 274.

16 Müller, *Prophetie und Predigt*, p. 177.

17 Cf. Waldemar Schmeichel, 'Christian Prophecy in Lukan Thought: Luke 4:
    16–30 as a Point of Departure', *SBL 1976 Seminar Papers* (Missoula:
    Scholars Press, 1976), pp. 294–301.

18 Reinhold Niebuhr, *The Nature and Destiny of Man* (New York: Scribners,
    1943), 2: 28.

19 Reitzenstein, *Die hellenistische Mysterienreligionen*, pp. 240–1, gives a
    sample of the Hellenistic evidence.

20 See Appendix, pp. 239–50.

21 Heinrich Bacht, 'Wahres und falsches Prophetentum', *Biblica* 32 (1951),

260–2; Reiling, *Hermas*, pp. 67–72; von Campenhausen, *Ecclesiastical Authority*, ch. 8.

22 Bacht, 'Wahres und falsches Prophetentum', pp. 250–8; Martin Hengel, *Judaism and Hellenism: Studies in their Encounter in Palestine during the Early Hellenistic Period* (London: SCM Press, 1974), 1: 186, 240; Fascher, Προφήτης, pp. 66–8; Blenkinsopp, 'Josephus', pp. 241–4; Reiling, *Hermas*, p. 75, and the literature there given.

23 Cf. above, 36–7, 40–1.

24 II Baruch 55: 3; IQM 13.10–11; Test. Jud. 20.5; Jub. 1.25; 15.31–2; I En. 15.4–6; II En. (Slav.) 16.7; Mart. Is. 1.7–8 *et passim*.

25 Cf. Boring, 'Johannine Portrayal of the Paraclete', pp. 114–17.

26 Cf. e.g. Wolff, *Joel and Amos, passim*; William J. Whedbee, *Isaiah and Wisdom* (Nashville: Abingdon, 1971); William McKane, *Prophets and Wise Men*, SBT (London: SCM Press, 1965), pp. 65–130.

27 Von Rad, *Old Testament Theology*, 2: 301–8.

28 Cf. Müller, *Urchristliche Prophetie*, pp. 105, 179–80.

29 Rudolf Bultmann, *The Gospel of John: A Commentary* (Philadelphia: Westminster, 1971), pp. 22–3; Walter Eltester, 'Der Logos und sein Prophet', in *Apophoreta: Festschrift für Ernst Haenchen*, BZNW (Berlin: Topelmann, 1964).

30 Bultmann, *Synoptic Tradition*, pp. 69–108; Norman Perrin, *Jesus and the Language of the Kingdom* (Philadelphia: Fortress Press, 1976), pp. 48–56; W. A. Beardslee, 'The Use of the Proverb in the Synoptic Gospels', *Int* 24 (1970), 61–76; *Literary Criticism of the New Testament* (Philadelphia: Fortress Press, 1976), ch. 5 and pp. 129, 144; Paul Hoffmann, *Studien zur Theologie der Logienquelle* (Münster: Verlag Aschendorff, 1972), pp. 102, 136–7, 158–90, esp. pp. 176, 182.

9 FORMAL CHARACTERISTICS OF PROPHETIC SPEECH

1 Claus Westermann, *Basic Forms of Prophetic Speech* (Philadelphia: Westminster Press, 1967); David Noel Freedman, 'Pottery, Poetry, and Prophecy: An Essay on Biblical Poetry', *JBL* 96 (March 1977), 5–26; Norman Gottwald, 'Poetry, Hebrew', *IDB*, 3: 829–38.

2 Von Rad, *Old Testament Theology*, 2: 36–7, 72–3; Lindblom, *Prophecy*, p. 125.

3 Hengel, *Judaism and Hellenism*, 1: 186.

4 Fascher, Προφήτης, p. 23.

5 Minear, *New Earth*, pp. 300–65; Kraft, *Offenbarung, passim*. Kraft believes it is occasionally even possible to explain the Seer's choice of words and constructions as having *rein rhythmische Gründe* (pp. 193, 194, *passim*).

6 W. H. Raney, *The Relation of the Fourth Gospel to the Christian Cultus* (Giessen: Töpelmann, 1933), claims to have 'restored' the Johannine discourses to their original metrical arrangement.

7 Weiss, *Der erste Korintherbrief*, p. 378, has pointed out the changing of the normal word order in the second line, placing the οὐ after πάντες, in order to achieve parallelism.

8 For this form as an indication of prophetic speech, see W. C. van Unnik, 'A Formula Describing Prophecy', *NTS* 9 (1963), 86–94.

9 Käsemann, *New Testament Questions*, pp. 66–81; Müller, *Prophetie und Predigt*, pp. 140–233; Calvin Roetzel, 'The Judgment Form in Paul's Letters', *JBL* 88 (1969), 305–12.

10 Müller, *Prophetie und Predigt*, pp. 132–3, 215–16; Dautzenberg, *Urchristliche Prophetie*, pp. 43–121.

11 Von Rad, *Old Testament Theology*, 2: 37; Klaus Koch, *The Growth of the Biblical Tradition: The Form Critical Method* (New York: Scribner, 1969), pp. 189–90. The Psalms offer numerous examples of the prophet speaking for God in the first person, without an introductory messenger formula. Cf. Mowinckel, *Psalms*, 2: 52–73.

12 Quoted in Edgar Hennecke, *New Testament Apocrypha*, ed. Wilhelm Schneemelcher (Philadelphia: Westminster Press, 1963–5), 2: 686.

13 Dunn, *Jesus and the Spirit*, p. 305, who refers to the more-than-600 examples in H. W. Parke and D. E. W. Wormell, *The Delphic Oracle*, vol. 2, 'The Oracular Responses' (Oxford: Blackwell, 1956).

14 Lindblom, *Prophecy*, p. 17, cf. pp. 34–5.

15 Reitzenstein, *Die hellenistische Mysterienreligionen*, pp. 18ff.

16 Cf. Karl Kundsin, 'Zur Diskussion über die Ego-eimi-Sprüche des Johannesevangeliums', in *Charisteria Iohanni Kopp: Octogenario Oblata* ed. J. Aunver and A. Vööbus (Holmiae, 1954), pp. 95–107; Dunn, *Jesus and the Spirit*, p. 173; Eduard Schweizer, ΕΓΩ ΕΙΜΙ: *Die religionsgeschichtliche Herkunft und theologische Bedeutung der johanneischen Bildreden, zugleich ein Beitrag zur Quellenfrage des vierten Evangeliums* (Göttingen: Vandenhoeck and Ruprecht, 1939); Heinrich Zimmermann, 'Das absolute Ἐγώ εἰμι als die neutestamentliche Offenbarungsformel', *BZ* (new series) 4 (1960), 54–69, 266–76.

17 Klaus Berger, 'Zu den sogenannten Sätzen heiligen Rechts', *NTS* 17 (October 1970), 10–40; 'Die sogenannten "Sätze heiligen Rechts": Ihre Funktion und ihr Sitz im Leben', *TZ* 28 (1972), 305–30.

18 Schweizer, 'Observance of the Law', pp. 226–7; *Jesus*, p. 61; Müller, *Prophetie und Predigt*, pp. 179–81.

19 Cf. Richard Edwards, *The Sign of Jonah*, SBT 2: 18 (Naperville: Allenson, n.d.), pp. 47–52.

20 Weber, *Sociology of Religion*, p. 50.

21 Dalman, *Words of Jesus*, pp. 226–9; Heinrich Schlier, 'ἀμήν', *TDNT*, 1: 335–8; Joachim Jeremias has made the point in numerous places, most recently in *New Testament Theology*, pp. 35–8.

22 *Ibid.* p. 36; 'Zum nicht-responsorischen Amen', *ZNW* 64 (1973), 122–3.

23 Joachim Jeremias, *New Testament Theology*, p. 79; Walter Grundmann, *Das Evangelium nach Markus*, THNT (Berlin: Evangelische Verlagsanstalt, 1965), pp. 85–6; Bornkamm, *Jesus of Nazareth*, p. 99; Käsemann, *Essays on New Testament Themes*, pp. 41–2; Cothonet, 'Prophétisme', pp. 1268.

24 Joachim Jeremias, *The Prayers of Jesus*, SBT (Naperville: Allenson, 1967), p. 34.

25 Fuchs, *Historical Jesus*, p. 106.

26 Victor Hasler, *Amen. Redaktionsgeschichtliche Untersuchung zur Einführungsformel der Herrenworte 'Wahrlich ich sage euch'* (Zürich: Gotthelf-Verlag, 1969), pp. 162–7, *et passim*.

27 *Ibid.* pp. 168–73.

28 Of the fifty occurrences of μακάριος, thirty-nine are unconditional pronouncements. Of these, thirty-four are attributed to Jesus or prophets. Of the twenty-six occurrences of εὐλογέω, only five are pronouncements (excluding the four occurrences of εὐλογημένος ὁ ἐρχόμενος ἐν ὀνόματι κυρίου, an Old Testament quotation chanted by the crowd at Jesus' entry into Jerusalem) and all of these are spoken by prophets or by the *risen* Jesus. Εὐλόγητος is spoken only of God in the New Testament. Of the seven occurrences of ἀνάθεμα, four are pronouncements, three from Paul and one from a Corinthian πνευματικός. Of thirty-seven occurrences of οὐαί, thirty-one are pronouncements. All but two of these are from the synoptic Jesus or from Christian prophecy, i.e. the Apocalypse.

29 Käsemann, *New Testament Questions*, pp. 70–1, 100–1.

30 Cf. Lohse, *Offenbarung*, pp. 13–14; Minear, *New Earth*, pp. 149, 187, 214, 219.

31 Caird, *Revelation*, p. 267.

32 So James Robinson, 'Kerygma and History in the New Testament', in *The Bible and Modern Scholarship*, ed. J. Philip Hyatt (Nashville: Abingdon, 1965), p. 130.

33 For Old Testament prophecy, cf. Hans-Peter Müller, *Ursprünge und Strukturen alttestamentlicher Eschatologie* (Berlin: Verlag A. Töpelmann, 1969), part 2, chs. 1–2; for Jewish prophecy see Josephus, *Wars*, VI.5.3; for others who regard blessing and curse as a formal element of early Christian prophecy, see Heinrich Kraft, 'Die altkirchliche Prophetie und die Entstehung des Montanismus', *TZ* 11 (1955), 255; Siegfried Schulz, *Q: Die Spruchquelle der Evangelisten* (Zürich: Theologischer Verlag, 1972), pp. 61–2; Grundmann, *Lukas*, p. 141; Dibelius, *Fresh Approach*, pp. 32–3.

11 CHRISTIAN PROPHECY IN Q

1 See Schulz, *Spruchquelle, passim*, esp. pp. 47–53. For reviews of Schulz's book that challenge his partition theory see: Richard Edwards, *JBL* 94 (December 1975), 609–12; Ulrich Luz, 'Die wiederentdeckte Logienquelle', *EvTh* 33 (1973), 527–33; Paul Hoffmann, *BZ* 19 (1975), 104–15.

2 Cf. Georg Strecker, 'Die Makarismen der Bergpredigt', *NTS* 17 (April 1971), 255–75; Eduard Schweizer, 'Formgeschichtliches zu den seligpreisungen Jesu', *NTS* 19 (January 1973), 121–6; Robert A. Guelich, 'The Matthean Beatitudes: "Entrance Requirements" or Eschatological Blessings', *JBL* 95 (September 1976), 415–34.

3 E.g. by Käsemann, *New Testament Questions*, p. 100; Schulz, *Spruchquelle*, pp. 61, 82–4.

4 In addition to the scholars in note 2 above, cf. Schulz, *Spruchquelle*, p. 455, and the literature he gives. T. W. Manson, H. D. A. Major and C. J. Wright, *The Mission and Message of Jesus* (New York: Dutton, 1938), p. 341.

5 Beardsley, *Literary Criticism*, p. 37.

6 Davies, *Sermon on the Mount*, pp. 366–86.

7 Beardsley, *Literary Criticism*, p. 37.

8 Cf. Steck, *Das gewaltsame Geschick*, pp. 25–6; Schulz, *Spruchquelle*, p. 454; Manson, *Mission and Message*, p. 341; *contra* Adolf Harnack, *The Sayings of Jesus* (New York: Putnam, 1908), p. 51.

9   Cf. Schulz, *Spruchquelle*, p. 453; Dieter Lührmann, *Die Redaktion der Logienquelle*, WMANT (Neukirchen-Vluyn: Neukirchener Verlag, 1969), p. 55; Hoffmann, *Theologie der Logienquelle*, p. 148; Philipp Vielhauer, 'Gottesreich und Menschensohn in der Verkündigung Jesu', *Festschrift für Günther Dehn*, ed. Wilhelm Schneemelcher (Neukirchen: Neukirchener Verlag, 1957), p. 52; A. J. B. Higgins, *Jesus and the Son of Man* (Philadelphia: Fortress Press, 1964), pp. 119–20; Heinz Tödt, *The Son of Man in the Synoptic Tradition* (Philadelphia: Westminster Press, 1965), p. 255.

10   See Appendix for the connection of 'Son of Man' and Christian prophecy. The somewhat circular argument above, usually explicitly avoided in this study, is here justified because the saying has already been shown to be prophetic on other grounds.

11   Hoffmann, *Theologie der Logienquelle*, pp. 263–88; Schulz, *Spruchquelle*, pp. 404–19.

12   Dibelius, *Tradition to Gospel*, p. 224, Bultmann, *Synoptic Tradition*, pp. 145, 149.

13   Hoffmann, *Theologie der Logienquelle*, p. 238.

14   Jeremias seems to assume too easily that proving that the Twelve were a pre-Easter group proves the historicity of their mission, though his point is well taken that the lack of christology in the mission address argues in favor of the historicity of the event (*New Testament Theology*, pp. 231–40). But Bornkamm's arguments for the pre-Easter historicity of the Twelve and their mission of preaching and healing seem cogent enough (*Jesus of Nazareth*, pp. 144–50).

15   *New Testament Theology*, p. 15.

16   Cf. the frequent use of ἰδού in Revelation; for ἀποστέλλω ὑμᾶς see on Luke 11: 49–51 below, also a prophetic saying.

17   *Contra* O. Böcher, 'Wölfe in Schafspelzen. Zum religionsgeschichtlichen Hintergrund von Matt. 7, 15', *TZ* 24 (1968), 405–26.

18   IQpHab 1.5; 2.2; 8; Cf. Matt. 12: 39, 41–2, 45; 16: 4; 17: 17; 23: 36.

19   Walter Bundy, *Jesus and the First Three Gospels: An Introduction to the Synoptic Tradition* (Cambridge, Mass.: Harvard University Press, 1955), p. 159; Sand, *Das Gesetz*, p. 168; Bultmann, *Synoptic Tradition*, p. 158.

20   Hoffmann, *Theologie der Logienquelle*, pp. 264–7. Note that Q originally included the prohibition of the ῥάβδος, now in Matt. at 10: 10 and Luke at 9: 3.

21   Albert Schweitzer, *The Quest of the Historical Jesus* (London: A. and C. Black, 1910), pp. 330–403.

22   Cf. pp. 209–11 below.

23   Hoffmann, *Theologie der Logienquelle*, p. 268; Käsemann, 'Matthäus' (unpublished lecture series), p. 121.

24   Bundy, *Jesus*, p. 355; Grundmann, *Lukas*, p. 209; Käsemann, 'Matthäus', p. 121; Hoffmann, *Theologie der Logienquelle*, p. 267, argues that 10: 8–9 is from Jesus.

25   Cf. Grundmann, *Lukas*, p. 210.

26   Ernst Haenchen, *Der Weg Jesu: Eine Erklärung des Markus-Evangeliums und der kanonischen Parallelen* (Berlin: Töpelmann, 1966), p. 225.

27   That ἀμήν belonged to the original Q-version is affirmed by Hoffmann,

Theologie der Logienquelle, p. 283, and Alfred Plummer, *The Gospel according to St. Luke*, ICC (Edinburgh: T. and T. Clark, 1922), p. 276, against Schulz, *Spruchquelle*, p. 407.

28   Richard Edwards, *A Theology of Q: Eschatology, Prophecy, and Wisdom* (Philadelphia: Fortress Press, 1976), p. 104, against Schulz, *Spruchquelle*, p. 407.

29   See pp. 159–64 below on Luke 12: 10 par.

30   Käsemann, *New Testament Questions*, p. 100; G. Schille, *Das vorsynoptische Judenchristentum* (Stuttgart: Calwer Verlag, 1970), p. 25; Bundy, *Jesus*, p. 335; Edwards, *Theology of Q*, p. 105.

31   So Schulz, *Spruchquelle*, p. 362, who gives an extensive list of exegetes who regard the saying as secondary, and Haenchen, *Weg Jesu*, p. 226.

32   So Eduard Schweizer, *The Good News according to Matthew* (Atlanta: John Knox Press, 1975), p. 253.

33   Bundy, *Jesus*, p. 336; Haenchen, *Weg Jesu*, p. 226; Bultmann, *Synoptic Tradition*, p. 143; Tödt, *Son of Man*, p. 249.

34   Hoffmann, *Theologie der Logienquelle*, p. 305, and Boring, 'Johannine Portrayal of the Paraclete', pp. 114–17.

35   E.g. Grundmann, *Matthäus*, p. 302; Rengstorf, 'ἀπόστολος', p. 426.

36   I agree here with the analysis of Bundy, *Jesus*, pp. 332–6, and Hoffmann, *Theologie der Logienquelle*, pp. 263–86, except that it includes verses 21–2 as the conclusion of the speech in Q.

37   The comment is from Schulz, *Spruchquelle*, p. 215, who summarizes and documents the more recent study, and cf. Suggs, *Wisdom*, pp. 79–81.

38   The point is elaborated by both Hoffmann, *Theologie der Logienquelle*, pp. 108–9, and Schulz, *Spruchquelle*, p. 215.

39   Hoffmann, *Theologie der Logienquelle*, pp. 111–12, correctly sees this latter point but does not notice that it clashes with his view that the Q-community regards this saying as from the *earthly* Jesus (pp. 293–4). Schulz, *Spruchquelle*, pp. 213, 217, likewise insists that this *Apophthegmatisierung* of the saying is to be attributed to the Q-community, which wanted to represent the *earthly* Jesus as speaking in these words. Hoffmann's conclusions are inconsistent on this point: an inconsistency from which Schulz saves himself only by positing two Q-communities. All the evidence is better accounted for by seeing the Q-community as (unconsciously?) resisting the historicizing tendencies already present in the pre-Q tradition, re-presenting even historicizing-sayings as the word of the exalted Lord.

40   For Matt. 28: 18–20 as Christian prophecy, see below, pp. 204–6.

41   Bultmann, *Synoptic Tradition*, p. 166, and cf. Jeremias, *New Testament Theology*, 1: 59.

42   J. Dupont, *Gnosis: La connaissance religieuse dans les Épitres de Saint Paul* (Louvain: Paris, 1949), pp. 58–62, and Hoffmann, *Theologie der Logienquelle*, pp. 107–8, who gives further bibliography.

43   The wisdom motifs are pointed out by Edwards, *Theology of Q*, p. 107; Lührmann, *Redaktion*, p. 99; Hoffmann, *Theologie der Logienquelle*, pp. 187 *et passim*; Schulz, *Spruchquelle*, pp. 225–8. Suggs, *Wisdom*, is correct that Q did not identify the earthly Jesus with Wisdom, but has failed to observe the wisdom motifs used by the Q-community to interpret the present role of the exalted Jesus.

44 E.g. Hoffmann, *Theologie der Logienquelle*, pp. 113, 130–3; Schulz, *Spruchquelle*, pp. 217–18; W. D. Davies, *Christian Origins and Judaism* (London: Darton, Longman and Todd, 1962), p. 143.

45 It is thus unnecessary to posit a missing antecedent for ταῦτα, which was supposedly to be found in the context of the lost wisdom book from which this *logion* was taken (Bultmann, *Synoptic Tradition*, p. 160).

46 Suggs, *Wisdom*, pp. 81–3, summarizes recent discussion of this point.

47 Manson, *Mission and Message*, p. 371, who refers to C. F. Burney, *The Poetry of our Lord: An Examination of the Formal Elements of Hebrew Poetry in the Discourses of Jesus Christ* (Oxford: Clarendon Press, 1925), pp. 133, 171–2. Cf. Jeremias, *Theology of the New Testament*, 1: 56–9, and Schulz, *Spruchquelle*, p. 220.

48 James Robinson, 'Die Hodajot-Formel in Gebet und Hymnus des Früh-christentums', in *Apophoreta: Festschrift für Ernst Haenchen*, ed. W. Eltester and F. H. Kettler (Berlin: A. Töpelmann, 1964), pp. 221–6.

49 Barrett, *Holy Spirit*, p. 102; Howard Clark Kee, 'Matthew' in *The Inter-preter's One-Volume Commentary*, p. 623; Frank W. Beare, *The Earliest Records of Jesus* (Nashville: Abingdon, 1962), p. 89.

50 Bultmann, *Theology of the New Testament*, 1: 6; *Synoptic Tradition*, p. 126; Hoffmann, *Theologie der Logienquelle*, pp. 38, 210, 299.

51 Edwards, *Theology of Q*, pp. 47–9; Schille, *Das vorsynoptische Juden-christentum*, p. 24; Käsemann, 'Matthäus', p. 155.

52 Edwards' detailed argument regarding the history of this cluster of sayings is most persuasive to me, though he stops short of attributing the oldest elements to Jesus himself (*Sign of Jonah*, pp. 71–87). Cf. also the similar analysis of Paul D. Meyer, 'The Gentile Mission in Q', *JBL* 89 (1970), 405–10.

53 Bultmann, *Theology of the New Testament*, 1: 8; Käsemann, *New Testament Questions*, p. 95; his 'Matthäus', pp. 145–6, assigns these verses specifically to Christian prophets.

54 Meyer, 'Gentile Mission', pp. 407–9; Schulz, *Spruchquelle*, pp. 250–7; Edwards, *Sign of Jonah*, pp. 71–83.

55 See Appendix.

56 So Manson, *Mission and Message*, p. 389. Cf. Bultmann, *Synoptic Tradition*, p. 128, 'In its original form the discourse against the Pharisees ... is to be traced back to Jesus', but he does not attempt to separate out this 'original form'.

57 It has not been clear to all scholars that Q contained precisely seven woes. (E.g. Manson, *Mission and Message*, p. 388, argues for six woes, as in Luke.) But the argument of Schulz, *Spruchquelle*, p. 95, is compelling: 11: 39 was a woe-oracle in Q, because it is such in the Matthean parallel, because νῦν does not occur elsewhere in Q but is found twenty-five times in Acts (= a Lukan favorite term), and because Luke's change from οὐαί to νῦν is readily explainable as his effort to have the speech begin less abruptly at the dinner-party he has constructed as a setting. The careful redaction-critical work of Lührmann also indicates that Q contained seven woes (*Redaktion*, p. 45).

58 Bultmann, *Synoptic Tradition*, pp. 131–2; Schulz, *Spruchquelle*, p. 101.

59 Cf. Rev. 22: 10–11 and the discussion of Luke 12: 10 par. below, pp. 160–3.

60 Schulz, *Spruchquelle*, pp. 336–45; Bultmann, *Synoptic Tradition*, p. 113; Manson, *Mission and Message*, p. 388; Hoffmann, *Theologie der Logien-quelle*, pp. 40, 73, 158; Suggs, *Wisdom*, pp. 14, 16.

61 Steck, *Das gewaltsame Geschick*, p. 30, and Schulz, *Spruchquelle*, p. 336, include the term in their reconstruction of Q; most others do not. Strongly contested by Günther Klein, 'Die Verfolgung des Apostel, Lu. 11, 49', in *Neues Testament und Geschichte*, ed. Heinrich Baltensweiler and Bo Reicke (Tübingen: J. C. B. Mohr, 1972), pp. 113–14.

62 Even Edwards, who attempts to avoid a speculative reconstruction of Q by including only words appearing in both Matthew and Luke, and hence omits ἀμήν from his concordance of Q, still includes '(Truly) I say to you' in his discussion of prophetic formulae in Q in *Theology of Q*, p. 48, albeit with the 'truly' in parentheses.

63 This διὰ τοῦτο corresponds to the לָכֵן that often introduces the oracular conclusion of a series of threats in the Old Testament prophets, including especially a series of woes, as in Is. 5: 24, and is used in the same way in New Testament prophecy (Rev. 12: 12; 18: 8).

64 Bultmann, *Synoptic Tradition*, p. 114; Suggs, *Wisdom*, pp. 16–19.

65 Plummer, *Luke*, p. 313; Lührmann, *Redaktion*, p. 46; Hoffmann, *Theologie der Logienquelle*, p. 164; Steck, *Das gewaltsame Geschick*, p. 47; Schulz, *Spruchquelle*, p. 341.

66 Manson, *Mission and Message*, p. 394; A. R. C. Leaney, *The Gospel according to St. Luke*, HNTC (New York: Harper, 1966²), p. 194.

67 Lührmann, *Redaktion*, p. 46. So also Müller, *Prophetie und Predigt*, p. 177.

68 Suggs, *Wisdom*, p. 19.

69 Felix Christ, *Jesus Sophia: Die Sophia-Christologie bei den Synoptikern*, ATANT (Zurich: Zwingli Verlag, 1970), pp. 130–1.

70 E.g. 11: 42, cf. Ecc. 7: 18. For an elaboration of this point see Hoffmann, *Theologie der Logienquelle*, pp. 98, 162–4, 169–71, 182–3; Schulz, *Spruchquelle*, pp. 101–2, and Hengel, *Judentum und Hellenismus: Studien zu ihrer Begegnung unter Besonderer Berücksichtigung Palästinas bis zur Mitte des 2. Jh.s. v.Chr.*, WUNT (Tübingen: J. C. B. Mohr, 1973), p. 457.

71 See Schulz, *Spruchquelle*, pp. 66–75, 157–61, 247, 442–4, 463.

72 For the whole, cf. Bultmann, *Synoptic Tradition*, p. 145; Beare, 'Mission of the Disciples', p. 13; Gaston, *No Stone on Another*, p. 60. For verses 2–3: Schulz, *Spruchquelle*, p. 463; Käsemann, *New Testament Questions*, p. 99. For verses 4–7: Schulz, *Spruchquelle*, pp. 160–1; Bultmann, *Synoptic Tradition*, p. 119. For verses 8–9: Käsemann, *New Testament Questions*, pp. 77, 99; Philipp Vielhauer, 'Gottesreich und Menschensohn in der Verkündigung Jesu', in *Aufsätze zum Neuen Testament* (Munich: Chr. Kaiser Verlag, 1965), pp. 78f; Norman Perrin, *Rediscovering the Teaching of Jesus* (New York: Harper and Row, 1967), pp. 22f, 185f; Gaston, *No Stone on Another*, p. 404; Theissen, 'Wanderradikalismus', pp. 245ff; Schulz, *Spruchquelle*, p. 69. For 12: 10: Hans Windisch, 'Jesus und der Geist nach synoptischer Überlieferung', in *Studies in Early Christianity*, ed. S. J. Case (New York: Century, 1928), p. 212; Robin Scroggs, 'The Exaltation of the Spirit by Some Early Christians', *JBL* 84 (1965), 364; Ferdinand Hahn, *Titles of Jesus*, p. 324; Schulz, *Spruchquelle*, p. 248; Hoffmann, *Theologie der Logienquelle*, pp. 150–1. For verses 11–12: Schulz, *Spruchquelle*, p. 444.

73 In addition to the reference being discussed, the Holy Spirit is referred to in synoptic sayings of Jesus only in Matt. 12: 28, Mark 13: 11 par. and Luke 11: 13.

74 Perrin, *A Modern Pilgrimage in New Testament Christology* (Philadelphia: Fortress, 1974), p. 44.

75 For a detailed reconstruction of the history of this saying in the tradition, see my article 'The Unforgiveable Sin Logion', from which the following summary is taken.

76 *Ibid.* pp. 274–6.

77 For more details concerning the following, see my article 'How May We Identify Oracles of Christian Prophets in the Synoptic Tradition?', from which the following summary is taken.

78 This point is strengthened by the fact that ἁμάρτημα may be a translation of the Aramaic חוֹב, 'judgment', so that the meaning would be 'liable to the eternal judgment (which is rapidly approaching)'. Cf. Matthew Black, *An Aramaic Approach to the Gospels and Acts* (Oxford: Clarendon Press, 1954²), p. 102, note 2 (= 3rd ed. (1967), p. 140, note 3).

79 Barrett, *Holy Spirit*, pp. 104–6. Cf. also Evald Lövestam, *Spiritus blasphemia: Eine Studie zu Mk. 3: 28* (Lund: Gleerup, 1968), pp. 14, 25–6, 42.

80 Boring, 'Unforgiveable Sin Logion', pp. 265–7.

81 Schulz, *Spruchquelle*, p. 247, supports this view and lists as examples of recent scholars who concur: Bornkamm, Tödt, Hahn, Conzelmann and Hoffmann. In addition, cf. Grundmann, *Lukas*, p. 255, and Perrin, *Pilgrimage*, p. 71.

82 Edwards, *Theology of Q*, p. 122.

83 Cf. Friedrich Büchsel, 'παραδίδωμι', *TDNT*, 2: 169–70.

84 W. G. Kümmel, *Promise and Fulfillment: The Eschatological Message of Jesus*, SBT (London: SCM, 1957), p. 99.

85 W. G. Kümmel, 'Das Verhalten Jesus gegenüber und das Verhalten des Menschensohns, Markus 8: 38 par und Lukas 1: 8 par Matthäus 10: 32f', in *Jesus und der Menschensohn*, ed. Rudolf Pesch and Rudolf Schnackenburg (Freiburg: Herder, 1975), p. 217; Schulz, *Spruchquelle*, p. 70; Tödt, *Son of Man*, p. 55; Martin McNamara, *Targum and Testament: Aramaic Paraphrases of the Hebrew Bible: A Light on the New Testament* (Grand Rapids: Eerdmans, 1972), pp. 94–5.

86 Bultmann, *Synoptic Tradition*, pp. 128, 151; Tödt, *Son of Man*, pp. 42–3, 55–60; Jeremias, *New Testament Theology*, pp. 15, 254, 275f; Perrin, *Rediscovering*, pp. 190–1.

87 Käsemann, *New Testament Questions*, p. 77; Vielhauer, 'Gottesreich und Menschensohn in der Verkündigung Jesu', pp. 55ff; Howard Teeple, 'The Origin of the Son of Man Christology', *JBL* 84 (1965), 213ff; Hans Conzelmann, *An Outline of the Theology of the New Testament* (London: SCM, 1969), p. 136; Lührmann, *Redaktion*, p. 51; Hoffmann, *Theologie der Logienquelle*, pp. 155f; Schulz, *Spruchquelle*, pp. 69f.

88 Käsemann, *New Testament Questions*, p. 77; Grundmann, *Matthäus*, pp. 33f; Vielhauer, 'Jesus und der Menschensohn', p. 104; Lührmann, *Redaktion*, p. 51; Edwards, *Theology of Q*, pp. 40–1, 52; Schulz, *Spruchquelle*, p. 69.

89   Müller, *Prophetie und Predigt*, p. 180.
90   Tödt, *Son of Man*, points out the legal character of the saying (p. 42), its 'quality as a rule' (p. 43), and its 'legally binding manner' (p. 56).
91   *Contra*: Jeremias, 'Die älteste Schicht der Menschensohn-Logien', *ZNW* 58 (1967), 159ff, and his students Carsten Colpe, 'ὁ υἱὸς τοῦ ἀνθρώπου', *TDNT*, 8: 442; Perrin, *Rediscovering*, pp. 190–1. *Pro*: A. J. B. Higgins, '"Menschensohn" oder "ich" in Q: Luke 12: 8–9/Matt. 10: 32–33', in *Jesus und der Menschensohn*, ed. Pesch and Schnackenburg, pp.117–23; Frederick H. Borsch, *The Son of Man in Myth and History* (Philadelphia: Westminster Press, 1967), pp. 5ff, 16f, 27f; Kümmel, 'Verhalten', pp. 219–24.
92   However logically problematic it may appear, *both* sides seem to be right in the debate as to whether the Son of Man will function as judge (Schulz, *Spruchquelle*, pp. 72, 75; Hahn, *Titles of Jesus*, pp. 30–1) or as the guarantor–Paraclete (Tödt, *Son of Man*, p. 46; Grundmann, *Lukas*, p. 254). The Son of Man's roles as judge and Paraclete blend into each other. As in other prophetic thinking, the exalted Jesus is the mediator of God's will to man, which results in his role alternating between that of God himself (the judge) and that of the intermediary. Cf. the way the exalted Christ's roles in representing God to man collapse into each other in the Apocalypse.
93   Schulz, *Spruchquelle*, pp. 463–5.
94   Kümmel, *Promise and Fulfillment*, p. 79, attributes verse 4 to Jesus; Bultmann, *Synoptic Tradition*, p. 119, designates verses 4–5 as one of the 'characteristically prophetic' sayings.
95   Schulz, *Spruchquelle*, p. 157, ascribes τοῖς φίλοις μου to Luke on the basis of his frequent use of the term (fifteen times in Luke, three times in Acts). But only here in the synoptic gospels does Jesus use the word φίλοι of his disciples, the only other instance being found in John 15: 14, where the designation by the risen Lord of those to whom he grants revelations is φίλοι, as is the case with the heavenly Wisdom in Wis. Sol. 7: 27.
96   Lührmann, *Redaktion*, p. 84; cf. Hoffmann, *Theologie der Logienquelle*, p. 5, who considers 22–31 one unit, and 33–4 a closely-related unit.
97   Schulz, *Spruchquelle*, p. 153; cf. pp. 143–5.
98   The only possible exception, Luke 12: 32, is considered by most scholars not to belong to Q (Manson, *Mission and Message*, p. 405, and Lührmann, *Redaktion*, p. 84, are isolated exceptions) and consequently will be discussed with the Lukan materials.
99   E.g. Bultmann, *Synoptic Tradition*, p. 163; Hoffmann, *Theologie der Logienquelle*, pp. 41, 72–3; Käsemann, 'Matthäus', p. 127; Schulz, *Spruchquelle*, p. 260. The apocalyptic interpretation of Mic. 7: 6 was widespread in late Judaism: Enoch 99.5; 100.2; Jub. 23.16, 19; Syr. Bar. 70.6; Sota 9.15; T. b. Sanh. 97a.
100 Schulz, *Spruchquelle*, pp. 298–309.
101 Bultmann, *Synoptic Tradition*, p. 117.
102 Schulz, *Spruchquelle*, p. 311.
103 Cf. Bultmann, *Synoptic Tradition*, p. 117, and Lührmann, *Redaktion*, p. 71, who already finds *Parusieverzögerung* here.
104 Schweizer, 'Observance of the Law', p. 226; Hahn, *Titles of Jesus*, p. 91; Schulz, *Spruchquelle*, p. 425.
105 Cf. Beare, *Earliest Records*, p. 174.

106 So even Bultmann, *Synoptic Tradition*, p. 116; cf. also Lührmann, *Redaktion*, p. 43.

107 Käsemann, *New Testament Questions*, p. 100; Dieter Zeller, 'Das Logion Mt. 8: 11f/Luke 13: 28f und das Motiv der "Völkerwallfahrt" ', *BZ* (new series) 16 (January 1972), 87–91; Schulz, *Spruchquelle*, pp. 327–8.

108 Manson, *Mission and Message*, p. 419; Strack-Billerbeck, *Kommentar, ad loc.*

109 Cf. Bultmann, *Synoptic Tradition*, p. 114, and Suggs' comment, *Wisdom*, p. 71: 'The "how often" has nothing to do with the number of trips made to Jerusalem by the historical Jesus, but with how Wisdom in every generation has appealed to men through her prophets and has not been heeded.' (Against Manson, *Mission and Message*, p. 419.) The saying is regarded as genuine by, e.g., Jeremias, *New Testament Theology*, pp. 151, 177, 284, and Kümmel, *Promise and Fulfillment*, pp. 80–1.

110 Steck, *Das gewaltsame Geschick*, p. 239; Steck gives a thorough argument for rejecting the authenticity of the saying, pp. 53–5. His principal reasons are: (1) ποσάκις ἠθέλησα (verse 34) comprehends a broader scope of time than that of the earthly life of Jesus; (2) verse 35*a* announces the abandonment of Jerusalem by God, but we know nothing of this from the preaching of Jesus; (3) verse 35*b* portrays Jesus as speaking about his own *parousia* in the first person singular, which is incredible in the mouth of the historical Jesus. He elaborates each point.

111 Cf. Christ, *Jesus Sophia*, who lists more than twenty scholars who so argue.

112 Steck, *Das gewaltsame Geschick*, pp. 57–8.

113 A. H. McNeile, *The Gospel according to St. Matthew* (London: Macmillan, 1915), p. 296.

114 ᾿Εν/ἐπὶ ὀνόματι κτλ is used explicitly of Christian prophets in Mark 13: 6 par. and Matt 7: 22 (for the interchangeability of ἐν and ἐπί see Mark 9: 38–9), with which may be compared John 5: 43; 10: 25; 14: 26; Acts 3: 6; 4: 10, 17, 18, 30; 5: 28, 40; I Cor. 1: 10; 5: 4; II Thess. 3: 6.

115 Independently of the argument developed above, Edwards has also applied the phrase to the Q-prophets, *Theology of Q*, pp. 67, 133.

116 In addition to Ps. 118: 26, there may also be a prophetic 'peshering' of Jer. 22: 5.

117 Mark 9: 1 (see p. 186 below); Mark 13: 30 (see pp. 186–95 below); Matt. 10: 23 (see pp. 209–12 below); and for the whole series, see Gaston, *No Stone on Another*, pp. 451–5.

118 Something analogous happened in Christian tradition in relating Jesus to the Holy Spirit.

119 See the discussion of this prophetic form included in the analysis of Matt. 10: 23 below, pp. 209–12. R. G. Hamerton-Kelly, 'Attitudes to the Law in Matthew's Gospel', *Biblical Research* 17 (1972), devotes much attention to the chiastic form and trajectory of this saying.

120 E.g. E. Earle Ellis, *The Gospel of Luke*, NCB (London: Nelson, 1966), p. 211; Bundy, *Jesus*, p. 389; Bultmann, *Synoptic Tradition*, p. 130 ('possible'); Conzelmann, *Theology of St. Luke*, p. 105.

121 So according to many scholars, e.g. Leaney, *Luke*, p. 231; Lührmann, *Redaktion*, p. 72; Grundmann, *Lukas*, p. 342; Schulz, *Spruchquelle*, p. 278; Conzelmann, *Theology of St. Luke*, pp. 153–4, gives reasons.

122 *Mission and Message*, pp. 324, 436.

123 Cf. detailed evidence in Schulz, *Spruchquelle*, p. 280.

124 Schulz, *ibid.* p. 278, regards this as simply copied by Luke from Mark, as
do several other scholars, e.g. Leaney, *Luke*, p. 231; J. M. Creed, *The
Gospel according to St. Luke* (London: Macmillan, 1930), p. 218. It is
supposed to fit a temporal event but not an eschatological one; but Grundmann's discussion, *Lukas*, p. 344, shows how the Q-form fits perfectly the
eschatological expectation of the Son of Man. Thus numerous scholars
affirm that a Q-form of the saying was Luke's *Vorlage* here, e.g. Kümmel,
Promise and Fulfillment, p. 78; G. B. Caird, *The Gospel of St. Luke*, PGC,
(Baltimore: Penguin Books, 1963), p. 198; Manson, *Mission and Message*,
p. 436.

125 Bultmann, *Synoptic Tradition*, p. 117.

126 See Edwards, *Theology of Q*, p. 142, supported by Norman Perrin, *The
New Testament: An Introduction* (New York: Prentice-Hall, 1974), p. 75,
and Schulz, *Spruchquelle*, pp. 280, 285.

127 Streeter, *Four Gospels*, and Manson, *Mission and Message*, p. 508, omit this
passage from their reconstructions of Q. It has recently been included by
Lührmann, *Redaktion*, p. 109; Hoffmann, *Theologie der Logienquelle*,
pp. 5, 42; Schulz, *Spruchquelle*, pp. 330–6; Edwards, *Theology of Q*, pp.
144–5.

128 E.g. by Hasler, *Amen*, p. 41, though the other supposed examples he gives
of Matthew detaching ἀμήν from a Markan saying and applying it to a
Q-saying are not parallel to the phenomenon of this text (Matt. 5: 18/
Mark 13: 30; Matt. 17: 20/Mark 11: 23), and Jacques Dupont, 'Le logion
des douze trônes (Matt. 19: 28/Luc. 22: 28–30)', *Biblica* 45, 3 (1964),
362.

129 Already Dalman, *Words of Jesus*, p. 177, had pointed to the Aramaic of
the Kiddush prayer הַדְתָּא עָלְמָא as practically the equivalent of
παλιγγενεσία, and now IQS 4: 25 is even closer: קֵץ וַעֲשׂוֹת חֲדָשָׁה
עַד ... There is thus no difficulty in seeing the Q-sayings as having had a
phrase that Matthew could have accurately rendered παλιγγενεσία.

130 Bultmann, *Synoptic Tradition*, p. 159; Käsemann, 'Matthäus', p. 235.

131 See Ps. Sol. 17.28, the tenth petition of the Eighteen Benedictions, and
Grundmann, *Matthäus*, p. 435.

132 Dupont, 'Le logion', p. 388. Kümmel, *Promise and Fulfillment*, p. 47, also
argues for the authenticity of the saying.

133 Cf. Dupont, 'Le logion', p. 386, and Gaston, *No Stone on Another*, pp.
406–7.

134 Cf. e.g. Tödt, *Son of Man*, p. 265; Käsemann, *New Testament Questions*,
pp. 119–20; Philipp Vielhauer, 'Propheten, NT', in *RGG³*, 5: 633–4;
Norman Perrin, 'The Son of Man in the Synoptic Tradition', in *Pilgrimage*,
p. 70; Hoffmann, *Theologie der Logienquelle*, pp. 102, 236, 329–33 *et
passim*; Schulz, *Spruchquelle*, pp. 33–4, 57–165 *et passim*; Edwards,
Theology of Q, p. 56. For the opposite point of view see Athanasius Polag,
Die Christologie der Logienquelle, WMANT (Neukirchen-Vluyn: Neukirchener Verlag, 1977), pp. 27–30, 191, who argues that Christian
prophets had little to do with the formation and transmission of Jesus'

words in the Q-community and that prophetically-formed sayings under-
went an *Entprophetisierung* before being accepted into the tradition.

135 Not only the older critics, such as Johannes Weiss, in *Die Schriften des
     neuen Testaments*, vol. 1, 'Die drei älteren Evangelien' (Göttingen:
     Vandenhoeck and Ruprecht, 1917[3]), pp. 58–71, but some recent scholars
     see the purpose of the collection of the Q-materials as primarily to preserve
     the words of the historical Jesus: A. R. C. Leaney, in *Biblical Criticism*,
     vol. 3 of The Pelican Guide to Modern Theology (Baltimore: Penguin
     Books, 1970), p. 265; Boman, *Jesus-Überlieferung*, p. 107.
136 *Contra* James Robinson, 'ΛΟΓΟΙ ΣΟΦΩΝ: On the Gattung of Q', in
     Trajectories through Early Christianity, pp. 71–113.
137 The phrase is from Taylor, *Formation of the Gospel Tradition*, p. 182, but
     the view is not peculiar to him. Cf. the refutation of it by Davies, *Sermon
     on the Mount*, pp. 366–86.
138 Streeter, *Four Gospels*, p. 291.
139 E. G. Selwyn, *The First Epistle of St. Peter* (London: Macmillan, 1952),
     pp. 439–58; cf. Davies, *Sermon on the Mount*, p. 376, and Hoffmann,
     Theologie der Logienquelle, pp. 159ff.
140 Cf. Schulz, *Spruchquelle*, pp. 78–9. The above represents my modification
     of his view.
141 Cf. Stendahl, *School of St. Matthew*, pp. 46, 88ff, 149. Lührmann also
     notices this characteristic style of dealing with Scripture in Q but attributes
     it to the influence of wisdom. As we have seen, wisdom and prophecy are
     not alternatives.
142 This point is elaborated by Hoffmann, *Theology der Logienquelle*, pp. 113,
     130, 132.
143 In agreement with Robinson, 'ΛΟΓΟΙ ΣΟΦΩΝ', pp. 71–113; Helmut
     Koester, in *The Nag Hammadi Library*, ed. James Robinson (New York:
     Harper and Row, 1977), p. 117, and Suggs, *Wisdom*, pp. 6–9.

12 CHRISTIAN PROPHECY IN MARK

 1 See Appendix.
 2 Perrin, 'Mark 14: 62; the End Product of a Christian Pesher Tradition',
    Pilgrimage, pp. 10–22, and John Donahue, *Are You the Christ?*, pp. 199–
    77, argue convincingly that ἐγώ εἰμι was already in the narrative before
    the remainder of Jesus' response was added by Mark on the basis of an
    extensive early Christian exegetical tradition.
 3 See above, pp. 165–7.
 4 See below, pp. 186–95.
 5 See e.g. Bultmann, *Synoptic Tradition*, pp. 14–16; Erich Klostermann, *Das
    Markusevangelium*, HC (Tübingen: J. C. B. Mohr, 1950[4]), p. 22; Vincent
    Taylor, *The Gospel according to St. Mark* (New York: Macmillan, 1955),
    p. 191.
 6 Cf. Bultmann, *Synoptic Tradition*, pp. 11, 61ff.
 7 So, e.g. Ernst Lohmeyer, *Das Evangelium nach Markus*, KEK (Göttingen:
    Vandenhoeck and Ruprecht, 1937[10]), p. 66; A. E. J. Rawlinson, *St. Mark*,
    WC (London: Methuen, 1936[4]), p. 34; C. E. B. Cranfield, *The Gospel
    according to St. Mark*, CGNTC (London: Cambridge University Press,
    1959), p. 118; Taylor, *Mark*, p. 220.

8   Cf. Bultmann, *Synoptic Tradition*, pp. 143–4; Jürgen Roloff, 'Anfänge der
     soteriologischen Deutung des Todes Jesu (Markus 10, 45 und Lukas 22,
     27)', *NTS* 19 (October 1972), 51. For a different understanding of the
     history of the tradition, see Higgins, *Son of Man*, pp. 36–50.

9   Although 'Son of Man' and λύτρον ἀντὶ πολλῶν are properly taken as
     'late' features of the Markan form in contrast to the Lukan form, Higgins,
     Son of Man, p. 38, equally properly points out that the Lukan form has
     adopted later church language in contrast to the Markan form, as is
     apparent in the pairs of antitheses:

Mark	Luke
μέγας – διάκονος	μείξων – νεώτερος
πρῶτος – δοῦλος	ἡγούμενος – διακονῶν

10   Tödt, *Son of Man*, pp. 135–8, 206–11, so argues.
11   Burney, *Poetry of our Lord*, pp. 63–4; Taylor, *Mark*, p. 444.
12   *Synoptic Tradition*, p. 146.
13   Scholars have been perplexed by the relation of this phrase to Is. 53. It 'has
     as its main background elements derived from Isaiah 53. It is not a plain
     and straightforward Greek translation of any single verse' (Higgins, *Son of
     Man*, p. 46). While 'it does not have a background of its own other than
     Isaiah 53, neither can it be said to point unambiguously to that chapter',
     says C. K. Barrett in 'The Background of Mark 10: 45', in *New Testament
     Essays*, ed. A. J. B. Higgins (Manchester University Press, 1959), pp. 7–8.
     Thus while λύτρον κτλ cannot be *directly* related to Is. 53, it must yet be
     understood in some kind of relation to it. This corresponds to the freedom
     exercised in the pneumatic exegesis of the Old Testament among Christian
     prophets.
14   Roloff, 'Anfänge der soteriologischen Deutung', p. 51.
15   See above, pp. 159–64, and my articles 'Oracles of Christian Prophets' and
     'The Unforgiveable Sin Logion'.
16   Bultmann, *Synoptic Tradition*, p. 145.
17   So Taylor, *Mark*, p. 303.
18   So Rudolf Pesch, *Das Markusevangelium*, HTKNT (Freiburg: Herder,
     1976), 1: 326.
19   See above, pp. 141–9, and cf. Käsemann, *New Testament Questions*,
     pp. 94–5, 103.
20   Günther Bornkamm, 'Die Verzögerung der Parusie', in *In Memoriam Ernst
     Lohmeyer*, ed. W. Schmauch (Stuttgart: Evangelisches Verlagswerk, 1951),
     pp. 118–19; Erik Grässer, *Das Problem der Parusieverzögerung* (Berlin:
     Töpelmann, 1960), pp. 128–37; Schulz, *Die Stunde der Botschaft* (Zurich:
     Zwingli Verlag, 1970[2]), pp. 98–9; Müller, *Prophetie und Predigt*, p. 151;
     Norman Perrin, *What is Redaction Criticism?* (Philadelphia: Fortress Press,
     1969), p. 73.
21   Timothy Colani, *Jésus Christ*, pp. 202ff. G. R. Beasley-Murray's
     'magnificently one-sided' *Jesus and the Future: An Examination of the
     Criticism of the Eschatological Discourse, Mark 13, with Special Reference
     to the Little Apocalypse Theory* (London: Macmillan, 1954) traces the
     history of the theory from Colani to the mid-twentieth century.
22   Beasley-Murray is the most ardent advocate of the view that Mark 13 is
     composed essentially of sayings of Jesus, but cf. also J. A. T. Robinson,

Jesus and His Coming (London: SCM, 1957), pp. 118–39. The Markan redactional emphasis is illustrated by Jan Lambrecht, *Die Redaktion der Markus-Apocalypse: Literarische Analyse und Strukturuntersuchung* (Rome: Päpstliches Bibelinstitut, 1967).

23 Rudolf Pesch, *Naherwartung: Tradition und Redaktion in Mk 13*, KBANT (Düsseldorf: Patmos Verlag, 1968).

24 E.g. the predestined wars and tumults that must happen as part of the End Time events (verses 7–8); the dissolution of families (verse 12); the profanation of the temple (verses 14ff); the expected breakdown of biological processes, producing monstrous births (verse 17); and especially the cosmic breakdown of the universe and the coming of the Son of Man (verses 24–7).

25 Cf. Gaston, *No Stone on Another*, pp. 50–1; Grundmann, *Markus*, p. 251; Lohmeyer, *Markus*, p. 267; William L. Lane, *The Gospel according to Mark*, NIC (Grand Rapids, Michigan: Eerdmans, 1974), pp. 444–5.

26 The only comparable speech-complex in the gospel, the 29 verses of ch. 4, contains only one exhortation, the general ὃς ἔχει ὦτα ἀκούειν ἀκουέτω of 4: 9, repeated in slightly different form in 4: 23. This is clearly a traditional saying, found also in Matt. 11: 15; Luke 14: 35, so that we may say that Mark's other large speech-complex contains no Markan exhortations to the reader. There is no added γίνεσθε διὸ ἡ γῆ ἡ καλή after 4: 20, no ἀπὸ δὲ τοῦ κόκκου σινάπεως μάθετε τὴν παραβολήν.

The 154 verses of speech material outside ch. 13 contain altogether only 10 imperatives that could be taken as exhortations to the reader (1: 15; 1: 17; 4: 9; 6: 6–10; 7: 14; 8: 34; 9: 43–4; 11: 22; 12: 17; 12: 38). Of these, 6 are clearly from Mark's tradition, leaving only 1: 15; 7: 14; 8: 34 and 11: 22 that could possibly be Markan exhortations.

The 5 imperatives in 13: 31–7 are also a disproportionately large number for Markan material and so all seem to appear in the redactional verses 33, 35, 37. These may be explained as a Markan development in the same line as the material he is immediately using in verses 5–30. Hartmann, *Prophecy Interpreted*, pp. 174–5, concurs in this latter point.

27 Cf. e.g. Beasley-Murray, *A Commentary on Mark Thirteen* (London: Macmillan, 1957), p. 13 (messianic pretenders); W. Manson, 'The ἐγώ εἰμι of the Messianic Presence in the New Testament', *JTS* 48 (1947), 137–45 (false Christian teachers); Taylor, *Mark*, p. 504 (the returned Jesus himself); Theodore Weeden, *Mark: Traditions in Conflict* (Philadelphia: Fortress, 1971), pp. 70–100 (θεῖοι ἄνδρες).

28 Haenchen, *Der Weg Jesu*, pp. 449–50; Hartmann, *Prophecy Interpreted*, pp. 145ff; Pesch, *Naherwartung*, pp. 212–13, who correctly points out that Hartmann's analysis is limited too much to Daniel.

29 Hartmann, *Prophecy Interpreted*, pp. 145ff, 174.

30 *Ibid.* p. 175.

31 *Ibid.* p. 106–10.

32 See above, pp. 164–5.

33 Lohmeyer, *Markus*, pp. 269–80; Lambrecht, *Redaktion*, pp. 261–97 and Appendix; Pesch, *Naherwartung*, pp. 74–82 and Supplement.

34 Ferdinand Hahn, 'Die Rede von der Parusie des Menschensohnes Markus 13', in Rudolf Pesch and Rudolf Schnackenburg (eds.), *Jesus und der*

Menschensohn, pp. 240–66; Pesch, *Das Markusevangelium*, 2: 226–312, which represents a shift from his earlier view in *Naherwartung*.

35 Beasley-Murray, *Commentary on Mark Thirteen*, p. 64.

36 Norman Perrin's investigation of the vocabulary reveals that of the 165 words in verses 5–27, 35 (21.2%) do not occur elsewhere in Mark, and of these 35, 15 are found in Revelation. See his *The Kingdom of God in the Teaching of Jesus* (London: SCM Press, 1963), pp. 131–2.

37 I would accept in general the thesis of Rudolf Pesch, that an eschatological Christian prophetic document that was having an influential circulation in Mark's church was included by him partly in order to neutralize the false theology and inflammatory effects it was causing in the hands of those Mark considered false prophets. (See Pesch, *Naherwartung*, chs. 5–6). Because of this special circumstance, Mark included an extensive product of Christian prophecy, which he otherwise would not have done. Even so, I consider Pesch's 1968 conclusion, that this was an old, traditional prophetic oracle, dating from the 39–40 Caligula crisis and made *au courant* by the 66–70 crisis, to be more probable than his later view (*Markusevangelium*, vol. 2 (1978) that the oracle was first *promulgated* at that time. Mark himself probably considered it authentic tradition from the pre-Easter Jesus.

38 The figures are based on a comparison of Mark 1: 1 – 16: 8 with Matt. 3: 1 – 28: 10 and Luke 3: 1 – 24: 11, those parts of Matthew and Luke which correspond to Mark 1: 1 – 16: 8. If Matt. 1: 1 – 28: 18 is calculated, Matthew has 51.3% sayings of Jesus. If Luke 1: 1 – 24: 53 is calculated, Luke has 41.7% words of Jesus.

Robert Morgenthaler, *Statistische Synopse* (Zürich: Gotthelf-Verlag, 1971), on the basis of a more strict definition of 'sayings of Jesus' that could have circulated independently, which he calls '*logia*', counts 2206 words in the Markan *logia*, 6462 in the Matthean and 5083 in the Lukan. On this reckoning, Mark's *logia* represent 21.2% of his writing, Matthew's 38% and Luke's 30.5%.

39 That Mark knew Q has been argued e.g. by the early Streeter, 'St. Mark's Knowledge and Use of Q', in *Oxford Studies in the Synoptic Problem*, ed. W. Sanday (Oxford: Clarendon Press, 1911), pp. 165–84; Dibelius, *Tradition to Gospel*, pp. 235ff; F. C. Grant, *The Gospels: Their Origin and Their Growth* (New York: Harper, 1957), p. 45; Lambrecht, *Redaktion*, pp. 256–8. That Mark did not know Q has been argued e.g. by Julius Wellhausen, *Einleitung in die drei ersten Evangelien* (Berlin: Georg Reimer, 1911²), pp. 120, 157, 169; the later Streeter in *Four Gospels*, pp. 186–91; Harnack, *Sayings of Jesus*, p. 226; B. H. Throckmorton, 'Did Mark Know Q?', *JBL* 67 (1948), 319ff; E. Best, 'An Early Sayings Collection', *NovT* 18 (1976), 1–16; Taylor, *Mark*, pp. 87–8.

40 E.g. in Throckmorton, 'Did Mark Know Q?', pp. 319–27; Streeter, *Four Gospels*, pp. 186–91; Taylor, *Mark*, p. 87.

41 Dibelius, *Tradition to Gospel*, p. 260; Bultmann, *Synoptic Tradition*, p. 347.

42 This argument was presented already in H. A. W. Meyer's 1866 *A Critical and Exegetical Handbook to the Gospels of Mark and Luke*, which appeared in English in 1884 (New York: Funk and Wagnalls), p. 4, and has been often repeated.

43   F. C. Burkitt, *The Earliest Sources for the Life of Jesus* (Boston: Houghton
     Mifflin Co., 1910), pp. 50–7; C. F. D. Moule, *The Phenomenon of the
     New Testament*, SBT (London: SCM, 1967), pp. 100–14.

44   Morton Scott Enslin, *Christian Beginnings* (New York: Harper, 1938),
     p. 375.

45   R. H. Lightfoot, *History and Interpretation in the Gospels* (New York:
     Harper, n.d.), pp. 112–13, 124–5.

46   Étienne Trocmé, *The Formation of the Gospel according to Mark*
     (Philadelphia: Westminster, 1975), pp. 38–9, 45, 84–5, 109; Eduard
     Schweizer, 'Mark's Contribution to the Quest of the Historical Jesus', *NTS*
     10 (1963–4), pp. 421–32.

47   Trocmé, *Formation*, p. 109.

48   Schweizer, 'Mark's Contribution', p. 423.

49   E.g. Weeden, *Traditions in Conflict*; Schulz, *Die Stunde der Botschaft*,
     pp. 1–156, esp. pp. 46–78, 114–42; Ulrich Luz, 'Das Geheimnismotiv in
     und die markinische Christologie', *ZNW* 56 (1965), 9–30; Eduard
     Schweizer, *The Good News according to Mark* (Atlanta: John Knox Press,
     1970), pp. 382–3.

50   In 6: 4 Jesus no more names himself a προφήτης than he claims to be a
     ἰατρός in Luke 4: 23. In both cases he is simply using a popular proverb.

51   Burkitt,'St. Mark 8: 32: A Neglected Variant Reading', *JTS* 2 (1900),
     111–13; Lohmeyer, *Markus*, p. 167.

52   *Mark the Evangelist* (Nashville: Abingdon, 1969), pp. 126–38.

53   Friedrich, 'προφήτης', p. 723.

54   *Die Funktion der alttestamentlichen Zitate und Anspielungen im Markus-
     evangelium* (Gerd Mohn: Gütersloher Verlag, 1965), esp. pp. 157ff.

55   E.g. Perrin, *What is Redaction Criticism?*, pp. 42, 73, 77–8; 'Towards an
     Interpretation of the Gospel of Mark', in *Christology and a Modern
     Pilgrimage*, ed. Hans Dieter Betz (Claremont: New Testament Colloquium,
     1971), pp. 21, 33, 36, 59–61; Karl-Georg Reploh, *Markus: Lehrer der
     Gemeinde* (Stuttgart: Verlag Katholisches Bibelwerk, 1969), pp. 24–5;
     Marxsen, *Mark the Evangelist*, pp. 117–50, 166–88 and *Introduction to
     the New Testament* (Philadelphia: Fortress, 1970), p. 141; Leander Keck,
     'Mark 3: 7–12 and Mark's Christology', *JBL* 84 (1965), 358 and 'The
     Introduction to Mark's Gospel', *NTS* 12 (1966), 369; Werner Kelber (with
     reservations), *The Kingdom in Mark* (Philadelphia: Fortress, 1974), pp. 5–
     6, 12, 127–8, 135. This view is opposed by, e.g., Georg Strecker, *Der Weg
     der Gerechtigkeit: Untersuchung zur Theologie des Matthäus*, FRLANT
     (Göttingen: Vandenhoeck and Ruprecht, 1966), pp. 185–6; and Philipp
     Vielhauer, 'Erwägungen zur Christologie des Markusevangeliums', in *Auf-
     sätze zum Neuen Testament*.

56   Pesch, *Naherwartung*, pp. 48–73.

57   Perrin, 'Towards an Interpretation of the Gospel of Mark', pp. 4–5, 31–5.

58   Trocmé, *Formation*, pp. 215–59.

59   Vernon K. Robbins, 'Last Meal: Preparation, Betrayal, and Absence', and
     John Dominic Crossan, 'Empty Tomb and Absent Lord', in *The Passion in
     Mark* (Philadelphia: Fortress Press, 1976), pp. 21–40, 125–52; Neil Q.
     Hamilton, *Jesus for a No-God World* (Philadelphia: Westminster Press,
     1969), pp. 62–3; Weeden, *Traditions in Conflict*, pp. 106–11.

60 'Eγώ εἰμι is used only three times in Mark: 6: 50; 13: 6; 14: 62. It is properly Jesus' word, which he speaks through his true prophets, falsely used by the prophets Mark opposes.

61 Both quotations are from Kelber, *Passion in Mark*, p. 164, *Kingdom in Mark*, p. 5. A Markan dialectic is involved here.

13 CHRISTIAN PROPHECY IN MATTHEW

1 Hubbard, *Matthean Redaction*, pp. 73–99, 127–9.

2 *Ibid.* p. 101. Hubbard cites the works of Bultmann, Brown, Dodd, Delling, Evans, Fuller, Marxsen and Kilpatrick, which support this conclusion. Cf. also Günther Bornkamm, 'The Risen Lord and the Earthly Jesus, Matt. 28: 16–20', in *The Future of our Religious Past*, ed. James Robinson (New York: Harper and Row, 1971), pp. 206–8.

3 Peter Ellis, *Matthew: His Mind and His Message* (Collegeville: Liturgical Press, 1974), p. 24; Xavier Léon-Dufour, *Resurrection and the Message of Easter* (New York: Holt, Rinehart and Winston, 1973), p. 96.

4 Gillespie, 'Prophecy and Tongues', p. 76, correctly regards this as 'a variation of the ἐγώ εἰμι formula'.

5 Cf. Hubbard, *Matthean Redaction*, p. 80; Trilling, *Das wahre Israel: Studien zur Theologie des Matthäus-Evangeliums* (Leipzig: St. Benno, 1959), pp. 6ff; Tödt, *Son of Man*, p. 288.

6 Cf. P. Boyd Mather, 'Christian Prophecy and Matthew 28: 16–20: A Test Exegesis', in *SBL 1977 Seminar Papers* (Missoula: Scholars Press, 1977), pp. 106–7.

7 See Appendix.

8 Cf. John 14: 16, Johnston, *Spirit-Paraclete*, p. 5, and my 'Johannine Portrayal of the Paraclete', p. 119.

9 See above, pp. 36–70, 40–1, 121.

10 Although he presents no evidence, the saying is regarded as prophetic by Beare, 'Sayings of the Risen Jesus', pp. 164–5; Reginald H. Fuller, *The Formation of the Resurrection Narratives* (New York: Macmillan, 1971), p. 90; Dunn, *Jesus and the Spirit*, p. 173; Sand, *Das Gesetz*, p. 168.

11 So, e.g., Suggs, *Wisdom*, pp. 123f; Douglas Hare, *The Theme of Jewish Persecution of Christians in the Gospel according to St. Matthew*, SNTS (Cambridge University Press, 1967), p. 116; Eduard Schweizer, *Matthew*, p. 97; Grundmann, *Matthäus*, p. 134. On the other hand, Strecker, 'Die Makarismen der Bergpredigt', p. 271, argues that Matthew intends only to compare his hearers with the Old Testament prophets, placing their sufferings in a *heilsgeschichtlich* perspective, not to declare that they are also prophets, and Guelich, 'Matthean Beatitudes', p. 433, sees the Matthean form as moving away from prophecy in the direction of wisdom 'entrance requirements'.

12 Cf. above, pp. 171–3, 186, on Mark 9: 1; 13: 30 and Luke 13: 35, and below, pp. 209–12 on Matt. 10: 23.

13 Cf. Grundmann, *Matthäus*, pp. 33–4, 148–50, Käsemann, *New Testament Questions*, p. 78, 'Matthäus', pp. 51–4; Hans-Theo Wrege, *Die Überlieferungsgeschichte der Bergpredigt*, WUNT (Tübingen: J. C. B. Mohr, 1968), p. 41.

14 Käsemann, *New Testament Questions*, pp. 78, 85–6; Grundmann, *Matthäus*, pp. 33–4, 148–50; Schweizer, *Matthew*, p. 105.

15 Käsemann, *New Testament Questions*, p. 99; cf. p. 77; 'Matthäus', p. 82.
16 Cf. Stendahl, *School of St. Matthew*, pp. 88–90.
17 So also Schweizer, 'Observance of the Law', p. 226; Hahn, *Titles of Jesus*, p. 91; Müller, *Prophetie und Predigt*, p. 176. On the other hand, Michael Krämer, 'Hütet euch von den falschen Propheten. Eine überlieferungs-geschichtliche Untersuchung zu Mt. 7, 15–23/Lk. 6, 43–6/Mt. 12, 33–7', *Biblica* 57 (1976), 349–77, considers the sayings Matthean redaction.
18 *Contra* e.g. Ellis, *Matthew*, p. 49; Heinz Schürmann, 'Mt. 10: 5*b*–6 und die Vorgeschichte des synoptischen Aussendungsberichtes', *Traditionsge-schichtliche Untersuchungen zu den synoptischen Evangelien*, KBANT (Düsseldorf: Patmos-Verlag, 1968), p. 138, gives good evidence that the saying is old tradition.
19 Käsemann, *New Testament Questions*, p. 88; Dunn, 'I Sayings', p. 178.
20 Grundmann, *Matthäus*, p. 292, thinks Matthew gets the pericope from Q.
21 See above, pp. 186–95, 206–7, and below, p. 216.
22 Cf. J. Dupont, 'Vous n'aurez pas achevé les villes d'Israel avant que le Fils de l'homme ne vienne', *NovT* 2 (1958), 228–44; W. F. Albright, *Matthew*, AB (New York: Doubleday, 1971), p. 125; Ellis, *Matthew*, p. 51, for these alternative explanations.
23 See Appendix.
24 Colpe, 'ὁ υἱὸς τοῦ ἀνθρώπου', p. 437. Cf. also A. L. Moore, *The Parousia in the New Testament*, NovTSupp (Leiden: Brill, 1966), p. 99; Vincent Taylor, *The Life and Ministry of Jesus* (Nashville: Abingdon, 1955), p. 115.
25 Cf. Lindblom, *Prophecy*, pp. 199–200.
26 Bultmann, *Synoptic Tradition*, p. 145; Cf. Beare, 'Mission of the Disciples', p. 13.
27 Brown, *Gospel According to John*, 2: 570.
28 Beare, *Earliest Records*, p. 89; Dunn, who is quite cautious about such matters, considers this saying one of the 'more plausible' instances of Christian prophecy in the synoptic tradition ('I Sayings', p. 178; cf. his *Jesus and the Spirit*, pp. 26–34).
29 This is one of only three synoptic sayings of Jesus where ἐγώ appears; cf. Stauffer, 'ἐγώ', *TDNT*, 2: 348. For the Scripture citation see Stendahl, *School of St. Matthew*, pp. 141–2.
30 Sand, *Das Gesetz*, p. 168; Cf. Käsemann, *New Testament Questions*, p. 106; Fuller, *Resurrection Narratives*, pp. 141, 166.
31 The analysis of Christoph Kähler, 'Zur Form- und Traditionsgeschichte von Matth. xvi. 17–19', *NTS* 23 (1976), 36–58, fits neatly into this hypothesis.
32 E.g. Bultmann, *Synoptic Tradition*, pp. 141, 258–9; Käsemann, 'Matthäus', p. 217; Heinrich Zimmermann, 'Die innere Struktur der Kirche und das Petrusamt nach Mt 18', *Catholica*, 30 (1976), 168–83.
33 Bultmann, *Synoptic Tradition*, pp. 149, 158; Grundmann, *Matthäus*, p. 420; Sand, *Das Gesetz*, p. 168; Dunn, *Jesus and the Spirit*, p. 173; 'I Sayings', p. 73.
34 So Grundmann, *Matthäus*, p. 429; Schweizer, *Matthew*, p. 383.
35 See above, pp. 94–5 and Michel, *Prophet and Märtyrer*, pp. 65–71.
36 Jack Kingsbury, *Matthew: Structure, Christology, Kingdom* (Philadelphia: Fortress Press, 1975), p. 72.

37   J. Ramsey Michaels, 'Christian Prophecy and Matthew 23: 8–12: A Test
     Exegesis', *SBL 1976 Seminar Papers* (Missoula: Scholars Press, 1976),
     pp. 305–10.
38   Julius Schniewind, *Das Evangelium nach Matthäus*, NTD (Göttingen:
     Vandenhoeck and Ruprecht, 1950⁴), *ad loc*; Käsemann, *New Testament
     Questions*, pp. 98, 276f; Ernst Haenchen, 'Matthäus 23', *ZThK* 48 (1951),
     43–53.
39   For a more detailed treatment, see my 'Christian Prophecy and Matthew
     23: 34–6', pp. 117–26.
40   Cf. Bultmann, *Synoptic Tradition*, p. 122.
41   Cf. Stendahl, *School of St. Matthew*, p. 80; Gaston, *No Stone on Another*,
     p. 60, argues that all of chs. 24–5 was transmitted by Christian prophets.
     I can find only minimal prophetic influence on the tradition between
     Mark/Q and Matthew in this section.
42   *Contra* Strecker, *Weg der Gerechtigkeit*, pp. 45, 87–91, 185–6; cf. Lloyd
     Gaston, 'The Messiah of Israel as Teacher of the Gentiles', *Int* 29 (1975),
     33: 'This attempt to impose a Conzelmannian understanding of Luke onto
     the theology of Matthew cannot be said to have succeeded.' Cf. Kingsbury,
     Matthew, pp. 31–9.
43   Bornkamm, Barth and Held, *Tradition and Interpretation in Matthew*
     (Philadelphia: Westminster, 1963), pp. 41–3. As a correction to this
     perspective, see Jack Kingsbury, 'The Title "Kurios" in Matthew's Gospel',
     JBL 94 (1975), 246–55.
44   This is suggested by Gaston, *No Stone on Another*, pp. 445–6; Grant,
     Gospels, p. 150; Robert Guelich, 'Early Christian Prophecy and the Sayings
     of Jesus in the Sermon on the Mount', (unpublished paper presented to the
     SBL Seminar on Early Christian Prophecy, 29 December 1977).
45   For a more complete discussion, see Kingsbury, *Matthew*, pp. 27–31.
46   Gaston, 'Messiah of Israel', pp. 38–9, seems to suggest that this view,
     appropriate to Mark, is also correct for Matthew.
47   So Marxsen, *Mark the Evangelist*, pp. 123–4, 138–49.

14 CHRISTIAN PROPHECY AND THE GOSPEL OF LUKE

 1   Bultmann, *Synoptic Tradition*, p. 127.
 2   Heinz Schürmann, *Traditionsgeschichtliche Untersuchungen*, p. 213; *Das
     Lukasevangelium*, HTKNT (Freiburg: Herder, 1969), 1: 339–40.
 3   Steck, *Das gewaltsame Geschick*, pp. 21–2, gives good evidence against a
     purely Lukan composition.
 4   Jacques Dupont, *Les Béatitudes* (Paris: Gabalda, 1969/73), 1: 299–342
     decides for Lukan composition with some hesitation; W. J. Harrington,
     The Gospel according to St. Luke (New York: Newman Press, 1967), p.
     109, readily accepts Lukan composition as 'the simplest solution'.
 5   Johannes Weiss, *Jesus' Proclamation of the Kingdom of God* (Philadelphia:
     Fortress Press, 1971), pp. 80–1; Ulrich Müller, 'Vision und Botschaft.
     Erwägungen zur prophetischer Struktur der Verkündigung Jesu', *ZThK* 74
     (1977), 416–48; A. J. B. Higgins, 'Jesus as Prophet', *ET* 57 (1945), 52–3.
 6   *Princ.*, I.5.5; *Orat.*, 26.5; *Contra Cels.*, IV.92.
 7   This point is developed by Bornkamm, 'Risen Lord and Earthly Jesus',
     pp. 213–29.

8 Manson, *Mission and Message*, pp. 405–6, and Lührmann, *Redaktion*, p. 84, include the saying in Q, but the majority, including Harnack, Streeter, Bussmann, Schulz, Edwards and Hoffmann, do not.

9 Jeremias, 'ποίμνη', *TDNT*, 6: 501.

10 Rudolf Pesch, 'Zur Formgeschichte und Exegese von Lk. 12: 32', *Biblica* 41 (1960), 33–8.

11 This last feature was pointed out to me by David Aune in a letter dated 18 January 1979.

12 Luke leaves the ἀμήν, which he usually changes to ἀληθῶς; the Jewish division of the night into three watches is not adjusted to the Roman four.

13 Bultmann, *Synoptic Tradition*, pp. 118, 127; J. C. O'Neill, 'The Six Amen-Sayings in Luke', *JTS* 10 (1959), 1–9.

14 Bundy, *Jesus*, p. 420; Bultmann, *Synoptic Tradition*, pp. 36, 56, 127; Ellis, *Luke*, p. 228 (cautiously, with a saying of the historical Jesus as the core of the prophetic 'peshering').

15 Cf. 1: 21–6; 10: 34–41, which express an understanding of full apostolic witness that excludes Paul, and 13: 24–31, where 'Paul' himself expresses this understanding. Only in 14: 4, 14 does Luke use ἀπόστολος of Paul, but in the usual non-technical sense of 'missionary', (as in John 13: 16; Rom. 16: 17; I Cor. 15: 7; II Cor 8: 23; 11: 5, 13; Gal. 1: 19; Heb. 3: 1; Rev. 2: 2), which in this context also includes Barnabas.

16 Conzelmann, *Theology of St. Luke*, pp. 170–206.

17 Minear, *To Heal and to Reveal*, pp. 102–21, gives a full discussion of this point.

18 Bauer, *Lexicon*, p. 113: 'Ac 1: 1 = simply *what Jesus did*', and so most recent scholars, e.g. Haenchen, *Acts*, p. 137; Barclay M. Newman and Eugene A. Nida, *A Translator's Handbook on the Acts of the Apostles* (London: United Bible Societies, 1972), p. 13; Conzelmann, *Die Apostelgeschichte*, (Tübingen: J. C. B. Mohr, 1963), p. 20. On the other side cf. Minear, *To Heal and to Reveal*, pp. 84, 170 note 5, and I. Howard Marshall, *Luke: Historian and Theologian* (Grand Rapids: Zondervan, 1970), p. 87.

19 Perrin, *Pilgrimage*, p. 59.

15 SUMMARY AND CONCLUSIONS

1 See Appendix.

2 Werner Harenberg, *'Der Spiegel' on the New Testament* (New York: Macmillan, 1970), p. 34.

3 Bultmann, *Form Criticism*, pp. 58–60. Cf. Leander Keck's cautious affirmation of this approach, in *A Future for the Historical Jesus* (Nashville: Abingdon, 1971), which he relates to Schleiermacher and John Knox, and his criticism of the New Hermeneutic's version of this approach, which Keck relates to Wilhelm Hermann's reliance on 'the inner life of Jesus', pp. 162–9.

4 Rudolf Bultmann, 'New Testament and Mythology', in *Kerygma and Myth*, ed. Hans Werner Bartsch (New York: Harper, 1961), pp. 42–4. Cf. also Bultmann's argument that the repeatedly-present, once-for-all Jesus addresses us in the *kerygma*, the preaching of the church, and thus 'there is no faith in Christ without faith in the church as bearer of the kerygma; that is ... faith in the Holy Ghost'. 'The Primitive Christian Kerygma and

the Historical Jesus', in *The Historical Jesus and the Kerygmatic Christ*, ed.
Carl Braaten and Roy Harrisville (Nashville: Abingdon, 1964), p. 41.

5 John Knox, *Criticism and Faith* (London: Hodder and Stoughton, 1953),
pp. 51—2; cf. *The Death of Christ: The Cross in New Testament History
and Faith* (New York: Abingdon, 1958), pp. 43—4; *The Church and the
Reality of Christ* (New York: Harper and Row, 1962), *passim.*

6 Cf. Knox's own discussion of his relation to Bultmann, *Reality of Christ*,
pp. 13—36.

7 E.g. Hans Küng, *On Being a Christian* (Garden City: Doubleday, 1976),
p. 159; Vielhauer, 'Apocalypses', pp. 605—6; Lucien Cerfaux, *Jésus aux
origines de la tradition* (Louvain: Desclée de Brower, 1968), p. 269—71;
John Reumann, *Jesus in the Church's Gospels* (Philadelphia: Fortress,
1968), p. 189; Mitton, *Jesus*, pp. 49—52 (cautiously); F. W. Beare, 'Sayings
of the Risen Jesus in the Synoptic Tradition: An Inquiry into Their Origin
and Significance', in *Christian History and Interpretation: Studies Presented
to John Knox*, ed. W. R. Farmer, C. F. D. Moule and R. R. Niebuhr (Cambridge University Press, 1967), pp. 178—81; Bornkamm, 'Verzögerung der
Parusie', p. 126; *Jesus of Nazareth*, pp. 13—27, 191; Schweizer, *Jesus*, p. 7;
Fuchs, *Zum hermeneutischen Problem*, pp. 302—4; Amos Wilder, *The
Language of the Gospel: Early Christian Rhetoric* (New York: Harper and
Row, 1964), p. 90.

8 See above, pp. 19—21, and Karl Barth, *Church Dogmatics*, 1/1, pp. 235, 320;
Bonhoeffer, *Act and Being*, pp. 142—3; Bultmann, *Glauben und Verstehen*,
3: 30; Xavier Léon-Dufour, *Resurrection*, p. 234.

APPENDIX

1 Besides 'Son of Man', Q contains only 'Son of God' in the temptation story
(in the mouth of the devil!), the absolute use of 'the Son' in Luke 10: 22
par., and the vague 'the one who is to come' in Luke 7: 19 par. Completely
missing are the titles 'Christ', 'Servant', 'Lord', 'Prophet'.

2 Tödt, *Son of Man*, p. 32. No effort will be made to list even the major
contributions to the debate here. Tödt gives a thorough bibliography up to
1964. Post-Tödt research up to 1974 is listed in the bibliography of
Norman Perrin, *Pilgrimage*, pp. 133—41.

3 Norman Perrin, 'The Son of Man in Ancient Judaism and Primitive
Christianity', *Biblical Research* 11 (1966), 17—28, now reprinted in Perrin,
Pilgrimage, pp. 23—40; Ragnar Leivestad, 'Exit the Apocalyptic Son of
Man', *NTS* 18 (April 1972), 243—67. On the other hand, see, e.g., Tödt,
Son of Man, pp. 22—31; Fuller, *Foundations*, pp. 34—43; Carsten Colpe,
'ὁ υἱὸς τοῦ ἀνθρώπου', *TDNT* 8: 420—30 (cautiously).

4 The debate as to the Aramaic usage continues. Bultmann continued to
maintain that בר אנש was a common expression for 'man' or 'I', which
Jesus used of himself but meant nothing extraordinary by it. (So in the
latest of Bultmann's works on the subject available to me, the fourth
edition of *Theologie des Neuen Testaments* (Tübingen: J. C. B. Mohr,
1961), p. 31.) Dalman, *Words of Jesus*, p. 236, had argued that this usage
was rare, being confined to Aramaic translations of *Hebrew*. Borsch, *Son of
Man*, pp. 23—4, contends that the expression was not in use in the vernacu-
lar and so must be considered a title wherever it occurs in the gospels. Geza

Vermes, in Appendix *E* of the third edition of Matthew Black's *Aramaic Approach*, pp. 310ff, on the basis of a re-examination of all the evidence, argues that בר אנש *was* a common periphrasis for man, but only in the first person. Black declared that the evidence presented in this investigation was convincing (p. 328), while Joseph Fitzmyer, 'The Contribution of Qumran Aramaic to the Study of the New Testament', *NTS* 20 (July 1974), 396–7, questions Vermes' results. However this debate among Aramaists may turn out, it is patently clear that in two categories of the synoptic Son-of-Man sayings, the 'coming' and the 'suffering' groups, 'Son of Man' is a title. See the arguments of Tödt, *Son of Man*, pp. 106–40, Bornkamm, *Jesus of Nazareth*, pp. 229–30, and Fuller, *Mission and Achievement*, pp. 98–101. Colpe's mediating view that in three instances Jesus did use בר אנש in a generalizing sense to refer to himself as a man (Mark 2: 10; Matt. 11: 19 par.; 8: 20 par.) is perhaps a possible way of positing a non-titular use of 'Son of Man' in the life of Jesus, but this still would not have been so understood by the Q-community.

5 Käsemann, *New Testament Questions*, pp. 66–137; Hans Conzelmann, 'Present and Future in the Synoptic Tradition', *JThCh* 5 (New York: Harper, 1968), 26–44; Vielhauer, 'Gottesreich und Menschensohn', pp. 51–79, who reasserted his view (after Tödt's challenge) in 'Jesus und der Menschensohn', *ZThK* (new series) 49 (1962), 133–77. For responses to Vielhauer *et al.*, see Jeremias, *New Testament Theology*, 1: 267f; Colpe, 'ὁ υἱὸς τοῦ ἀνθρώπου', p. 438; Hahn, *Titles of Jesus*, pp. 23–34; Fuller, *Foundations*, pp. 119–24; Tödt, *Son of Man*, pp. 329–47; I. Howard Marshall, *The Origins of New Testament Christology* (Downers Grove: Inter-Varsity Press, 1976), pp. 72–3; Wolfhart Pannenberg, *Jesus: God and Man* (London: SCM 1968), pp. 59–60.

6 This categorization is maintained in the present discussion because it has become traditional and is still somewhat useful, but it is obvious that the hypothesis proposed here calls for new categories. The 'present' sayings, for example, would no longer be the 'present' of the pre-Easter Jesus, within the narrative framework of his life, but the 'present' of the Q-community, between Easter and the *parousia*, during which the Son of Man speaks with authority. Hoffmann, *Theologie der Logienquelle*, p. 133, has noted that this early Christian understanding of the Son of Man who sends prophets between Easter and the *parousia* is a radical departure from that of Jewish apocalyptic, in which the Son of Man is thought of as presently doing nothing except waiting in heaven. In Q, there is 'eine *Offenbarungstätigkeit* des Menschensohns in der Gegenwart'.

7 E.g. Ethelbert Stauffer, *Jesus and His Story* (New York: Knopf, 1960), pp. 162ff; Cullmann, *Christology*, pp. 152ff; Borsch, *Son of Man*, pp. 314–60; Marshall, *New Testament Christology*, pp. 76–8.

8 *Contra* esp. Eduard Schweizer, 'The Son of Man', *JBL* 79 (1960), 119–29; 'The Son of Man Again', *NTS* 9 (1962–3), 256–61, who sees only this category of sayings as containing authentic sayings.

9 So Colpe, 'ὁ υἱὸς τοῦ ἀνθρώπου', pp. 431–2.

10 Fuller, *Mission and Achievement*, pp. 103–8.

11 Borsch, *Son of Man*, p. 360.

12 Georg Strecker, 'The Passion and Resurrection Predictions in Mark's

Gospel', *Int* 22 (October 1968), pp. 421–2, and the literature he discusses.
13 In attributing even the sayings that make this distinction to the early
church, thus making the distinction between Jesus and the Son of Man
both *originate* in, and, when it becomes problamatic, *be dissolved* by, the
early church, Vielhauer and those who hold his view labor under an in-
superable difficulty. To the objection that the church would not have
distinguished Jesus and the Son of Man, Vielhauer replies: so long as 'Son
of Man' had an apocalyptic meaning, it could not be applied to an earthly
being. Thus the church had to distinguish between the earthly Jesus and
the Son of Man ('Jesus und der Menschensohn', pp. 143, 170ff). But this
very argument militates against Vielhauer's other key point, that it was
Christian prophets who first spoke Son-of-Man sayings in Jesus' name. The
prophets did not, however, retroject sayings into the *Sitz im Leben Jesu*; it
was not the earthly Jesus to whom they were attributing their sayings. The
Jesus-ego with which they spoke was that of the exalted Lord, not the
earthly Jesus, so they would not have distinguished Jesus from the Son of
Man on the grounds given by Vielhauer. Thus the sayings that distinguish
Jesus and the Son of Man must be either genuine, modeled on genuine
words of Jesus, or secondary but non-prophetic. But if they are non-
prophetic, they must belong to that later stratum of secondary Son-of-Man
sayings that are dependent for their Son-of-Man terminology on the earlier,
prophetic sayings. In Vielhauer's view this cannot be, for he properly
regards these sayings as the oldest precisely because of the distinction they
make between Jesus and the Son of Man. These are then used as the
pattern for the later, secondary Son-of-Man sayings, thereby accounting for
the fact that 'Son of Man' occurs only in the third person in them. Unless
the sayings in which the distinction between Jesus and the Son of Man is
made are prophetic, the whole structure of Vielhauer's reconstruction
collapses – yet they cannot be regarded as prophetic on his grounds. He
sees a flaw in his construction and attempts to mend it, but without
success. Käsemann, Perrin, Conzelmann and Haenchen do not discuss this
problem in their view.
14 Tödt, *Son of Man*, p. 226.
15 Bultmann, *Theology*, 1: 30; Bornkamm, *Jesus of Nazareth*, pp. 226–31;
Tödt, *Son of Man*, pp. 32–112, 224–31, *et passim*; Hahn, *Titles of Jesus*,
pp. 15–42; Higgins, *Son of Man*, p. 193; Fuller, *Foundations*, pp. 34–42,
119–25, 142–51; Günther Haufe, 'Das Menschensohn-Problem in der
gegenwärtigen wissenschaftlichen Diskussion', *EvTh* 26 (1966), 130–41;
Eberhard Jüngel, *Paulus und Jesus: Eine Untersuchung zur Präzisierung der
Frage nach dem Ursprung der Christologie* (Tübingen: J. C. B. Mohr, 1962),
pp. 215–62; John Knox, *The Death of Christ: The Cross in New Testament
History and Faith*.
16 Davies, *Sermon on the Mount*, refers to these elements in Q as 'immediately
post-Easter'; Schulz, *Spruchquelle*, p. 53, attributes a fairly late date to Q
as a whole, and refers to these elements as representing the *'Geburtstunde
des Urchristentums'*; I accept this view of Q and thus agree with Tödt's
argument that Q from its inception was a christological document. There
was never a time when it was concerned only to preserve the teaching of the
historical Jesus as that of a past authority. See Tödt, *Son of Man*, pp. 253–60.

17 Bultmann, *Theology*, 1: 33.

18 Bousset, *Kyrios Christos*, pp. 49–51, argues that it was the disciples' subjective visions that led to the belief that Jesus was alive, but a deductive process, following on this, that led to the equation Jesus = Son of Man. For similar views see Willi Marxsen, *The Beginnings of Christology* (Philadelphia: Fortress Press, 1969), pp. 22–43; Higgins, *Son of Man*, p. 203; Karl Kundsin, 'Primitive Christianity in the Light of Gospel Research', in *Form Criticism*, ed. F. C. Grant (New York: Harper, 1962), p. 97.

19 Pannenberg, *Jesus: God and Man*, p. 68.

20 Cf. Teeple, 'The Origin of the Son of Man Christology', pp. 237–50; Wm. O. Walker Jr, 'The Origin of the Son of Man Concept as Applied to Jesus', *JBL* 91 (1972), 482–90; Perrin, *Pilgrimage*, pp. 5, 10–22, 36, 55–9; Hendrikus Boers, 'Where Christology is Real', *Int* 26 (1972), 300–27; Barnabas Lindars, *New Testament Apologetic* (London: SCM Press, 1961); Tödt, *Son of Man, passim*; Higgins, *Son of Man, passim.*

21 Teeple, 'Origin of the Son of Man Christology', p. 245.

22 This *'formgebend'* character of the earliest sayings is noticed by Viel-hauer, 'Jesus und der Menschensohn', p. 171; Tödt, *Son of Man*, pp. 61, 65; Fuller, *Foundations*, p. 144; Haufe, 'Menschensohn-Problem', p. 140; and Hahn, *Titles of Jesus*, p. 32, but varying conclusions are drawn from it.

23 See note 20 above. Unfortunately, this process of Scripture reinterpretation is usually attributed to the anonymous 'community', without inquiring who within it would claim the authority to give new eschatological interpretations. Tödt, *Son of Man*, p. 223, and Perrin, *Pilgrimage*, p. 34, refer lamely to 'scribes'. But scribes typically work on a tradition once it has *become* tradition. The tradition-creating impulse inherent in the radical re-understanding of the Scriptures in earliest Christianity should be attributed to prophets.

24 Ulrich Wilckens, 'The Tradition-History of the Resurrection of Jesus', in *The Significance of the Message of the Resurrection for Faith in Jesus Christ*, ed. C. F. D. Moule, SBT (London: SCM, 1968), pp. 68–9; Schulz, *Spruchquelle*, p. 73; Hoffmann, *Theologie der Logienquelle*, pp. 140–54; Wellhausen, *Einleitung*, p. 150.

25 See above, pp. 122–4.

26 Gal. 1: 15–16, pp. 30–6, 88–90, above, and cf. Willi Marxsen, *The Resurrection of Jesus of Nazareth* (Philadelphia: Fortress Press, 1970), pp. 98–129, esp. 115; Xavier Léon-Dufour, *Resurrection and the Message of Easter* (New York: Holt, Rinehart and Winston, 1971), pp. 49–51; Küng, *On Being a Christian*, pp. 374–7.

27 Ernst Lohmeyer, *Markus*, p. 192.

28 Tödt points out in this connection that the 'killing' (instead of the specific 'crucifying') of the Son of Man in the passion predictions is a point of contact with the tradition of the murder of the prophets (*Son of Man*, p. 175).

29 Compare 1: 13–15 and 2: 18, and Colpe, 'ὁ υἱὸς τοῦ ἀνθρώπου', p. 464.

30 C. H. Dodd, *The Interpretation of the Fourth Gospel* (London: Cambridge University Press, 1953), pp. 241–50.

31 Cf. Higgins, *Son of Man*, pp. 183ff. The connections between Son of Man and Paraclete (= the function of Christian prophecy, see p. 49

above) pointed out by Bornkamm, 'Der Paraklet im Johannesevangelium', and Martyn, *History and Theology in the Fourth Gospel*, pp. 122–5, 132–4, 135, 140, need to be noted in this connection.

32 Käsemann, 'The Beginnings of Christian Theology', in *New Testament Questions*, pp. 82–107.

33 This is Käsemann's term for *heilsgeschichtlich* eschatology, which he uses because he considers the term 'eschatology' to have been colored by an existentialist interpretation that he rejects.

SELECT BIBLIOGRAPHY

Abrahams, Israel, 'The Cessation of Prophecy', in *Studies in Pharisaism and the Gospels*. New York: Ktav Publishing House, 1967.

Aune, David, 'Christian Prophets and the Sayings of Jesus: An Index to Synoptic Pericopae Ostensibly Influenced by Early Christian Prophets', in *SBL 1975 Seminar Papers*. Missoula: Scholars Press, 1975.

The Cultic Setting of Realized Eschatology, NovTSupp. Leiden: Brill, 1972.

Bacht, H., 'Die prophetische Inspiration in der kirchlichen Reflexion der vormontanistischen Zeit', *Scholastik* 19 (1944), 1–18.

'Wahres und falsches Prophetentum', *Biblica* 32 (1951), 237–62.

Bacon, B. W., *The Gospel of Mark: Its Composition and Date*. New Haven: Yale University Press, 1925.

Barrett, C. K., *The Holy Spirit and the Gospel Tradition*. New York: Macmillan, 1947.

'The Old Testament in the Fourth Gospel', *JTS* 48 (1947), 155–69.

Bauckham, Richard, 'Synoptic Parousia Parables and the Apocalypse', *NTS* 23 (January 1977), 162–76.

Beare, Frank, W., *The Earliest Records of Jesus*. Nashville: Abingdon, 1962.

'The Mission of the Disciples and the Mission Charge: Matthew 10 and Parallels', *JBL* 89 (March 1970), 1–13.

'Sayings of the Risen Jesus in the Synoptic Tradition: An Inquiry into Their Origin and Significance', in *Christian History and Interpretation: Studies Presented to John Knox*, edited by W. R. Farmer, C. F. D. Moule and R. R. Niebuhr. Cambridge University Press, 1967.

Beasley-Murray, G. R., *A Commentary on Mark Thirteen*. London: Macmillan, 1957.

Jesus and the Future: An Examination of the Criticism of the Eschatological Discourse, Mark 13, with Special Reference to the Little Apocalypse Theory. London: Macmillan, 1954.

Benz, Ernst, *Paulus als Visionär*. Wiesbaden: Steiner Verlag, 1952.

Berger, Klaus, *Die Amen-Worte Jesu: Eine Untersuchung zum Problem der Legitimation in apokalyptischer Rede*. Berlin: Walter de Gruyter, 1970.

295

'Zu den sogenannten Sätzen heiligen Rechts', *NTS* 17 (October 1970), 10–40.

Betz, Hans Dieter, ed., *Christology and a Modern Pilgrimage*. Claremont: New Testament Colloquium, 1971.

'Ursprung und Wesen christlichen Glaubens nach der Emmauslegende (Luke 24: 13–32)', *ZThK* 66 (1969), 7–21.

Betz, Otto, *Offenbarung und Schriftforschung in der Qumransekte*, WUNT 6. Tübingen: J. C. B. Mohr, 1960.

Der Paraklet: Fürsprecher im häretischen Spätjudentum, im Johannes-evangelium und in neugefundenen Gnostischen Schriften. AGSU. Leiden: Brill, 1963.

Bieler, Ludwig, ΘΕΙΟΣ ANHP: *Das Bild des 'göttlichen Menschen' in Spätantike und Frühchristentum.* Vienna: Buchhandlung Oskar Höfels, 1935.

Blenkinsopp, Joseph, 'Prophecy and Priesthood in Josephus', *JJS* 25 (Summer 1974), 239–62.

Böcher, O., 'Wölfe in Schafspelzen. Zum religionsgeschichtlichen Hinter-grund von Matt. 7, 15', *TZ* 24 (1968), 405–26.

Boismard, E., 'Jésus, le Prophète par excellence, d'après Jean 10: 24–39', in *Neues Testament und Kirche*, edited by Joachim Gnilka. Herder: Freiburg, 1974.

Boman, Thorleif, *Die Jesus-Überlieferung im Lichte der neueren Volks-kunde.* Göttingen: Vandenhoeck and Ruprecht, 1967.

Boring, M. Eugene, 'The Apocalypse as Christian Prophecy', in *SBL 1974 Seminar Papers*. Missoula: Scholars Press, 1974.

'Christian Prophecy and the Gospel of Mark'. Unpublished Ph.D. disser-tation, Vanderbilt University, 1969.

'Christian Prophecy and Matt. 10: 23', in *SBL 1976 Seminar Papers*. Missoula: Scholars Press, 1976.

'Christian Prophecy and Matt. 23: 34–36: A Test Exegesis', in *SBL 1977 Seminar Papers*. Missoula: Scholars Press, 1977.

'How May We Recognize Oracles of Christian Prophets in the Synoptic Tradition? Mark 3: 28–29 as a Test Case', *JBL* 91 (1972), 501–21.

'The Influence of Christian Prophecy on the Johannine Portrayal of the Paraclete and Jesus', *NTS* 25 (1978), 113–23.

'The Paucity of Sayings in Mark: A Hypothesis', in *SBL 1977 Seminar Papers*. Missoula: Scholars Press, 1977.

'The Unforgiveable Sin Logion Mark 3: 28–29/Matt. 12: 31–32/Luke 12: 10: Formal Analysis and History of the Tradition', *NovT* 17 (1976), 258–79.

'What Are We Looking For? Toward a Definition of the Term "Christian Prophet" ', *SBL 1973 Seminar Papers*. Missoula: Scholars Press, 1973.

Bornkamm, Günther, *Jesus of Nazareth*. New York: Harper and Row, 1960.

'Die Komposition der apokalyptischen Visionen in der Offenbarung Johannes', in *Studien zu Antike und Urchristentum*, edited by E. Wolf. Munich: Chr. Kaiser Verlag, 1959.

'Der Paraklet im Johannesevangelium', in *Neutestamentliche Studien für Rudolf Bultmann zu seinem 70. Geburtstag am 20. August 1954*, edited by W. Eltester. Berlin: Töpelmann, 1957.

'The Risen Lord and the Earthly Jesus, Matt. 28: 16–20', in *The Future of Our Religious Past*, edited by James M. Robinson. New York: Harper and Row, 1971.

'Die Verzögerung der Parusie', in *In Memoriam Ernst Lohmeyer*, edited by W. Schmauch. Stuttgart: Evangelisches Verlagswerk, 1951.

Bornkamm, Günther, Barth, Gerhard, and Held, Hans Joachim, *Tradition and Interpretation in Matthew*. Philadelphia: Westminster, 1963.

Bousset, Wilhelm, *Die Offenbarung Johannes*, KEK. Göttingen: Vandenhoeck and Ruprecht, 1906[2].

Die Religion des Judentums im späthellenistischen Zeitalter, HzNT. Tübingen: J. C. B. Mohr, 1966.

Brockhaus, Ulrich, *Charisma und Amt: Die paulinische Charismalehre auf dem Hintergrund der frühchristlichen Gemeindefunktionen*. Wuppertal: Brockhaus, 1972.

Brosch, Joseph, *Charismen und Ämter in der Urkirche*. Bonn: Peter Hanstein Verlag, 1951.

Brown, Raymond, 'The Paraclete in the Fourth Gospel', *NTS* 13 (1967), 113–32.

Buber, Martin, *The Prophetic Faith*. New York: Macmillan, 1949.

Bultmann, Rudolf, *The Gospel of John: A Commentary*. Philadelphia: Westminster, 1971.

The History of the Synoptic Tradition. New York: Harper and Row, 1963.

Jesus and the Word. New York: Scribners, 1934.

Theology of the New Testament, 2 vols. New York: Scribners, 1951–5.

Bultmann, Rudolf and Kundsin, Karl, *Form Criticism: Two Essays on New Testament Research*. Chicago: Willet, Clark and Co., 1934.

Bundy, Walter, *Jesus and the First Three Gospels: An Introduction to the Synoptic Tradition*. Cambridge, Mass.: Harvard University Press, 1955.

Burney, C. F., *The Poetry of our Lord: An Examination of the Formal Elements of Hebrew Poetry in the Discourses of Jesus Christ*. Oxford: The Clarendon Press, 1925.

Burrows, Millar, 'Prophecy and the Prophets at Qumran', in *Israel's Prophetic Heritage*, edited by B. W. Anderson and Walter Harrelson. New York: Harper and Row, 1962.

Caird, G. B., *A Commentary on the Revelation of St. John the Divine*. New York: Harper and Row, 1966.

Campenhausen, Hans Freiherr von, *Ecclesiastical Authority and Spiritual Power in the Church of the First Three Centuries*. London: Adam and Charles Black, 1969.

'Tradition und Geist im Urchristentum', *Studium Generale* 4 (June 1951), 351–7.

Charles, R. H., *A Critical and Exegetical Commentary on the Revelation of St. John*, 2 vols., ICC. New York: Scribners, 1920.

Christ, Felix, *Jesus Sophia: Die Sophia-Christologie bei den Synoptikern*, ATANT. Zürich: Zwingli Verlag, 1970.

Colani, Timothy, *Jésus Christ et les croyances messianiques de son temps*. Strasbourg: Treuttel and Wurtz, 1864².

Colpe, Carsten, 'Der Spruch von der Lästerung des Geistes', in *Der Ruf Jesu und die Antwort der Gemeinde*, edited by Eduard Lohse. Göttingen: Vandenhoeck and Ruprecht, 1970.

'ὁ υἱὸς τοῦ ἀνθρώπου', *TDNT*, 8: 400–77.

Conzelmann, Hans, *Die Apostelgeschichte*, HzNT. Tübingen: J. C. B. Mohr, 1963.

First Corinthians: A Commentary on the First Epistle to the Corinthians, Hermeneia. Philadelphia: Fortress Press, 1975.

An Outline of the Theology of the New Testament. London: SCM Press, 1969.

'Present and Future in the Synoptic Tradition', *JThCh* 5 (1968), 26–45.

The Theology of St. Luke. New York: Harper and Row, 1960.

Cothonet, É., 'Les prophètes chrétiens dans l'Évangile selon saint Matthieu', in *L'Évangile selon Matthieu: Rédaction et théologie*, edited by M. Didier. Duculot: Gembloux, 1972.

'Prophétisme dans le Nouveau Testament', *DBS* 8. Paris: Ceffonds, 1972.

'Prophétisme et ministère d'après le Nouveau Testament', *Maison-Dieu* 107 (1971), 29–50.

Crone, Theodore, 'Early Christian Prophecy: A Study of Its Origin and Function'. Unpublished dissertation, Tübingen University, 1972.

Cullmann, Oscar, *Early Christian Worship*, SBT. London: SCM Press, 1953.

' "Kyrios" as Designation for the Oral Tradition concerning Jesus', *Scottish Journal of Theology* 3 (1950), 180–97.

'The Tradition', in *The Early Church*, ed. A. J. B. Higgins. London: SCM Press, 1956.

Daniel, Constantine, ' "Faux Prophètes": surnom des Esséniens dans le Sermon sur la Montagne', *Revue de Qumran* 7 (1969), 45–79.

Dautzenberg, Gerhard, *Urchristliche Prophetie: Ihre Erforschung, ihre Voraussetzungen im Judentum und ihre Struktur im ersten Korintherbrief*, BWANT. Stuttgart: Kohlhammer, 1975.

'Zum religionsgeschichtlichen Hintergrund der διάκρισις πνευμάτων (I Kor. 12, 10)', *BZ* (new series) 15 (1971), 93–104.

Delling, Gerhard, 'Geprägte Jesus-Tradition im Urchristentum', *Communio Viatorum* 4 (1961), 59–71.

Worship in the New Testament. London: Darton, Longman and Todd, 1962.

'Zum gottesdienstlichen Stil der Johannes Apokalypse', *NovT* 3 (1959), 107—37.

Dibelius, Martin, *Botschaft und Geschichte: Gesammelte Aufsätze von Martin Dibelius,* vol. 1: 'Zur Evangelienforschung'. Tübingen: J.C.B. Mohr, 1953.

Die Formgeschichte des Evangeliums, 3rd edition with a supplement by Gerhard Iber. Tübingen: J. C. B. Mohr, 1959.

A Fresh Approach to the New Testament and Early Christian Literature. New York: Scribners, 1956.

From Tradition to Gospel. New York: Scribners, 1935.

Dodd, C. H., *According to the Scriptures: The Sub-structure of New Testament Theology.* New York: Scribners, 1953.

'Jesus as Teacher and Prophet', in *Mysterium Christi,* edited by G. K. A. Bell and Adolf Deissmann. New York: Longmans, Green and Co., 1930.

Dungan, David, *The Sayings of Jesus in the Churches of Paul.* Philadelphia: Fortress, 1971.

Dunn, James D. G., *Jesus and the Spirit.* Philadelphia: Westminster Press, 1975.

'Prophetic "I"-Sayings and the Jesus Tradition: The Importance of Testing Prophetic Utterances Within Early Christianity', *NTS* 24 (January 1978), 175—98.

Dupont, Jacques, 'Le logion des douze trônes (Matt. 19: 28/Luc. 22: 28—30)', *Biblica* 45, 3 (1964), 355—92.

Les Béatitudes, 2 vols. Paris: Gabalda, 1969—73.

Easton, B. S., *The Gospel before the Gospels.* New York: Scribners, 1928.

Edwards, Richard, 'Christian Prophecy and the Q Tradition', in *SBL 1976 Seminar Papers.* Missoula: Scholars Press, 1976.

A Theology of Q: Eschatology, Prophecy, and Wisdom. Philadelphia: Fortress Press, 1976.

Ellis, E. Earle, 'Luke 11: 49—51: An Oracle of a Christian Prophet?', *Expository Times* 74 (1963), 157—8.

Paul's Use of the Old Testament. Grand Rapids: Eerdmans, 1957.

'The Role of the Christian Prophet in Acts', in *Apostolic History and the Gospel: Biblical and Historical Essays Presented to F. F. Bruce on His Sixtieth Birthday,* edited by Ward Gasque and Ralph P. Martin. Grand Rapids: Eerdmans, 1970.

Fascher, Erich, ΠΡΟΘΗΤΗΣ: *Eine sprach- und religionsgeschichtliche Untersuchung.* Giessen: Alfred Töpelmann, 1927.

Fiorenza, Elizabeth Schüssler, 'The Quest for the Johannine School: The Apocalypse and the Fourth Gospel', *NTS* 23 (1977), 402—27.

Foerster, Werner, 'Der Heilige Geist im Spätjudentum', *NTS* 8 (1961), 117—34.

Fohrer, Georg, *Die symbolische Handlungen der Propheten.* Zürich: Zwingli Verlag, 1953.

Ford, J. Massyngberd, 'A Note on Proto-Montanism in the Pastorals', *NTS* 17 (April 1971), 388—46.

Revelation, AB. New York: Doubleday, 1975.

Freedman, David N., 'History and Eschatology: The Nature of Biblical Religion and Prophetic Faith', *Int* 14 (1960), 143–54.

'Pottery, Poetry, and Prophecy: An Essay on Biblical Poetry', *JBL* 96 (March 1977), 5–26.

Friedrich, Gerhard, 'προφήτης', *TDNT* 6.

Fuchs, Ernst, *Gesammelte Aufsätze*, vol. 1: *Zum hermeneutischen Problem in der Theologie: Die existentiale Interpretation*. Tübingen: J. C. B. Mohr, 1965[2].

Studies of the Historical Jesus, SBT. London: SCM Press, 1964.

Fuller, R. H., *The Mission and Achievement of Jesus*, SBT. London: SCM Press, 1954.

Funk, Robert, *Language, Hermeneutic, and Word of God*. New York: Harper and Row, 1966.

Gager, John, *Kingdom and Community: The Social World of Early Christianity*. Englewood Cliffs: Prentice-Hall, 1975.

Gaston, Lloyd, *No Stone on Another: Studies in the Significance of the Fall of Jerusalem in the Synoptic Gospels*, NovTSupp. Leiden: E. J. Brill, 1970.

Gerhardsson, Birger, 'Die Boten Gottes und die Apostel Christi', *Svensk Exegetisk Arsbok* 27 (1962), 110–21.

Memory and Manuscript: Oral Tradition and Written Transmission in Rabbinic Judaism and Early Christianity. Uppsala: Almquist and Wiksells, 1961.

Tradition and Transmission in Early Christianity. Lund: Gleerup, 1964.

Giblet, J., 'Prophétisme et attente d'un Messie prophète dans l'ancien Judaïsme', in *L'Attente du Messie*, edited by L. Cerfaux. Paris: Desclée de Brouwer, 1954.

Gillespie, Thomas W., 'A Pattern of Prophetic Speech in I Corinthians', *JBL* 97 (March 1978), 74–95.

'Prophecy and Tongues: The Concept of Christian Prophecy in the Pauline Theology'. Unpublished Ph.D. dissertation, Claremont Graduate School, 1971.

Gils, F., *Jésus prophète d'après les évangiles synoptiques*. Louvain: Publications Universitaires, 1957.

Grant, F. C., 'The Authenticity of Jesus' Sayings', in *Neutestamentliche Studien für Rudolf Bultmann zu seinem 70. Geburtstag*, edited by Walther Eltester. Berlin: Töpelmann, 1957.

Greeven, Heinrich, 'Propheten, Lehrer, Vorsteher bei Paulus', *ZNW* 44 (1952), 1–29.

Grundmann, Walter, *Das Evangelium nach Lukas*, THNT. Berlin: Evangelische Verlagsanstalt, 1971.

Das Evangelium nach Markus, THNT. Berlin: Evangelische Verlagsanstalt, 1965.

Das Evangelium nach Matthäus, THNT. Berlin: Evangelische Verlagsanstalt, 1972[3].

Guelich, Robert A., 'The Matthean Beatitudes: "Entrance-Requirements" or Eschatological Blessings', *JBL* 95 (September 1976), 415−34.

Gunkel, Hermann, *Die Wirkungen des heiligen Geistes: Nach der populären Anschauung der apostolischen Zeit und nach der Lehre des Apostels Paulus.* Göttingen: Vandenhoeck and Ruprecht, 1888.

Guy, H. A., *New Testament Prophecy: Its Origin and Significance.* London: Epworth Press, 1947.

Haenchen, Ernst, *The Acts of the Apostles.* Philadelphia: Westminster Press, 1971.

Der Weg Jesu: Eine Erklärung des Markus-Evangeliums und der kanonischen Parallelen. Berlin: Töpelmann, 1966.

'Matthäus 23', *ZThK* 48 (1951), 38−63.

Hahn, Ferdinand, *The Titles of Jesus in Christology.* London: SCM Press, 1969.

'Die Rede von der Parusie des Menschensohnes Markus 13', in *Jesus und der Menschensohn*, edited by Rudolf Pesch and Rudolf Schnackenburg. Freiburg: Herder, 1975.

'Die Sendschreiben der Johannesapokalypse: Ein Beitrag zur Bestimmung prophetischer Redeformen', in *Tradition und Glaube: Das frühe Christentum in seiner Umwelt: Festgabe für Karl Georg Kuhn zum 65. Geburtstag*, edited by Gert Jeremias, Heinz-Wolfgang Kuhn and Hartmann Stegemann. Göttingen: Vandenhoeck and Ruprecht, 1971.

Mission in the New Testament, SBT. London: SCM Press, 1965.

Hare, Douglas R. A., *The Theme of Jewish Persecution of Christians in the Gospel according to St. Matthew*, SNTS. Cambridge University Press, 1967.

Harnack, Adolf, *The Constitution and Law of the Church in the First Two Centuries.* New York: Putnam, 1910.

The Mission and Expansion of Christianity in the First Three Centuries. New York: Putnam, 1904.

The Sayings of Jesus. New York: Putnam, 1908.

Hartmann, Lars, *Prophecy Interpreted.* Lund: Gleerup, 1966.

Hasler, Victor, *Amen. Redaktionsgeschichtliche Untersuchung zur Einführungsformel der Herrenworte 'Wahrlich ich sage euch'.* Zürich: Gotthelf-Verlag, 1969.

Hawthorne, Gerald F., 'Christian Prophecy and the Sayings of Jesus: Evidence of and Criteria for', *SBL 1975 Seminar Papers*. Missoula: Scholars Press, 1975.

Hengel, Martin, *Judaism and Hellenism: Studies in their Encounter in Palestine during the Early Hellenistic Period.* London: SCM Press, 1974.

Nachfolge und Charisma: Eine exegetisch-religionsgeschichtliche Studie zu Matt. 8: 21f und Jesus Ruf in die Nachfolge. Berlin: Töpelmann, 1968.

Henneken, Bartholomäus, *Verkündigung und Prophetie im 1. Thessalonicherbrief*, SBS. Stuttgart: Verlag Katholisches Bibelwerk, 1969.

Higgins, A. J. B., *Jesus and the Son of Man*. Philadelphia: Fortress Press, 1964.

'Jesus as Prophet', *ET* 57 (1945).

' "Menschensohn" oder "ich" in Q: Luke 12: 8–9/Matt. 10: 32–33', in *Jesus und der Menschensohn*, edited by Rudolf Pesch and Rudolf Schnackenburg. Freiburg: Herder, 1975.

Hill, David, 'Δίκαιοι as a Quasi-Technical Term', *NTS* 11 (1965), 296–302.

'Prophecy and Prophets in the Revelation of St. John', *NTS* 18 (1972), 401–18.

'On the Evidence for the Creative Role of Christian Prophets', *NTS* 20 (1974), 262–74.

Hoffmann, Paul, *Studien zur Theologie der Logienquelle*. Münster: Verlag Aschendorff, 1972.

Hubbard, Benjamin J., *The Matthean Redaction of a Primitive Apostolic Commissioning: An Exegesis of Matt. 28: 16–20*, SBLDS. Missoula: Scholars Press, 1974.

Jeremias, Gert, *Der Lehrer der Gerechtigkeit*, SUNT. Göttingen: Vandenhoeck and Ruprecht, 1963.

Jeremias, Joachim, *New Testament Theology*, vol. 1: 'The Proclamation of Jesus'. New York: Scribners, 1971.

'Zum nicht-responsorischen Amen', *ZNW* 64 (1973), 122–3.

Johnston, George, *The Spirit-Paraclete in the Fourth Gospel*, SNTS. Cambridge: Cambridge University Press, 1970.

Käsemann, Ernst, *Essays on New Testament Themes*. London: SCM Press, 1960.

'Geist und Geistesgaben im Neuen Testament', *RGG*³. Tübingen: J. C. B. Mohr, 1958.

New Testament Questions of Today. London: SCM Press, 1969.

Perspectives on Paul. Philadelphia: Fortress Press, 1971.

The Testament of Jesus. London: SCM Press, 1968.

'Der Urchristliche Enthusiasmus', Seminarprotokol des Neutestamentlichen Seminar im Wintersemester 1964–65, Tübingen.

Keck, Leander, 'The Introduction to Mark's Gospel', *NTS* 12 (1966), 352–70.

'Mark 3: 7–12 and Mark's Christology', *JBL* 84 (1965), 341–58.

Kelber, Werner, *The Passion in Mark*. Philadelphia: Fortress Press, 1976.

Klein, Günther, 'Die Verfolgung des Apostel, Lu. 11, 49', in *Neues Testament und Geschichte*, edited by Heinrich Baltensweiler and Bo Reicke. Tübingen: J. C. B. Mohr, 1972.

Knox, John, *The Church and the Reality of Christ*. New York: Harper and Row, 1962.

Criticism and Faith. London: Hodder and Stoughton, 1953.

Kraeling, C. H., *John the Baptist*. New York: Scribners, 1951.

Kraft, Heinrich, 'Die altkirchliche Prophetie und die Entstehung des Montanismus', *TZ* 11 (1955), 249–71.

Die Offenbarung des Johannes, HzNT. Tübingen: J. C. B. Mohr, 1974.
'Zur Offenbarung des Johannes', *TR* 38 (1973), 81–98.

Kragerud, Alv., *Der Lieblingsjünger im Johannesevangelium: Ein exegetischer Versuch*. Oslo: Osloer Universitätsverlag, 1959.

Krämer, Michael, 'Hütet euch von den falschen Propheten. Eine überlieferungsgeschichtliche Untersuchung zu Mt. 7, 15–23/Lk. 6, 43–46/Matt. 12, 33–37', *Biblica* 57 (1976), 349–77.

Kretschmar, G. 'Ein Beitrag zur Frage nach dem Ursprung frühchristlicher Askese', *ZThK* 61 (1964), 27–67.

Kümmel, W. G., *Promise and Fulfillment: The Eschatological Message of Jesus*, SBT. London: SCM Press, 1957.

Kundsin, Karl, 'Zur Diskussion über die Ego-eimi-Sprüche des Johannesevangeliums', in *Charisteria Iohanni Kopp: Octogenario Oblata*, edited by J. Aunver and A. Vööbus. Holmiae, 1954.

Lambrecht, Jan, *Die Redaktion der Markus-Apocalypse: Literarische Analyse und Strukturuntersuchung*. Rome: Päpstliches Bibelinstitut, 1967.

Lanckowski, G., 'Propheten', in *Lexikon für Theologie und Kirche*, edited by Joseph Höfer and Karl Rahner, 14 vols. Freiburg: Herder, 1963.

Leisegang, Hans, *Der Heilige Geist: Das Wesen und Werden der mystisch-intuitiven Erkenntnis in der Philosophie und Religion der Griechen*, vol. 1: 'Die vorchristlichen Anschauungen und Lehren vom πνεῦμα und der mystisch-intuitiven Erkenntnis'. Leipzig: Verlag B. G. Teubner, 1919.

Pneuma Hagion: Der Ursprung des Geistsbegriffs der synoptischen Evangelien aus der griechischen Mystik. Leipzig: J. C. Hinrichs'sche Buchhandlung, 1922.

Leivestad, R., 'Das Dogma von der Prophetenlosen Zeit', *NTS* 19 (April 1973), 288–99.

Leroy, Herbert, *Rätsel und Missverständnis: Ein Beitrag zur Formgeschichte des Johannesevangeliums*, BBB. Bonn: Peter Hanstein Verlag, 1968.

Lindars, Barnabas, *New Testament Apologetic*. London: SCM Press, 1961.

Lindblom, Johannes, *Gesichte und Offenbarungen: Vorstellungen von göttlichen Weisungen und übernatürlichen Erscheinungen im ältesten Christentum*. Lund: Gleerup, 1968.

Prophecy in Ancient Israel. Philadelphia: Fortress Press, 1962.

Loisy, Alfred, *The Birth of the Christian Religion*. London: George Allen and Unwin, 1948.

Les Évangiles Synoptiques, 2 vols. Paris: Ceffonds, 1907.

The Origins of the New Testament. New York: Macmillan, 1950.

Lührmann, Dieter, *Die Redaktion der Logienquelle*. WMANT. Neukirchen-Vluyn: Neukirchener Verlag, 1969.

Manson, T. W., 'The Sayings of Jesus', in Manson, Major and Wright, *The Mission and Message of Jesus*. New York: Dutton, 1938.

Manson, W., 'The ἐγώ εἰμι of the Messianic Presence in the New Testament', *JTS* 48 (1947), 137−45.

Marxsen, Willi, *The Beginnings of Christology: A Study in Its Problems.* Philadelphia: Fortress Press, 1969.

   Mark the Evangelist. Nashville: Abingdon, 1969.

Mather, P. Boyd, 'Christian Prophecy and Matthew 28: 16−20: A Test Exegesis', in *SBL 1977 Seminar Papers.* Missoula: Scholars Press, 1977.

Meyer, Paul D., 'The Gentile Mission in Q', *JBL* 89 (1970), 405−17.

Meyers, Jacob M. and Freed, Edwin D., 'Is Paul Also Among the Prophets?', *Int* 20 (1966), 40−53.

Michaels, J. Ramsey, 'Christian Prophecy and Matthew 23: 8−12: A Test Exegesis', *SBL 1976 Seminar Papers.* Missoula: Scholars Press, 1976.

   'The Johannine Words of Jesus and Christian Prophecy', in *SBL 1975 Seminar Papers.* Missoula: Scholars Press, 1975.

Michel, Otto, *Prophet und Märtyrer.* Gütersloh: Verlag Bertelsmann, 1932.

   'Spätjüdisches Prophetentum', *Neutestamentliche Studien für Rudolf Bultmann zu seinem siebzigsten Geburtstag am 20. August 1954*, edited by Walther Eltester. Berlin: Alfred Töpelmann, 1954.

Minear, Paul, 'False Prophecy and Hypocrisy in the Gospel of Matthew', in *Neues Testament und Kirche*, edited by Joachim Gnilka. Freiburg: Herder, 1974.

   I Saw a New Earth. Washington: Corpus Books, 1968.

   To Heal and To Reveal: The Prophetic Vocation according to Luke. New York: Seabury Press, 1976.

Miranda, J. P., *Der Vater, der mich gesandt hat.* Bern: Lang, 1972.

Moore, George F., *Judaism in the First Centuries of the Christian Era*, 3 vols. Cambridge, Mass.: Harvard University Press, 1927−30.

Mowinckel, Sigmund, *Prophecy and Tradition: The Prophetic Books in the Light of the Study of the Growth and History of the Tradition.* Oslo: I Kommisjon Hos Jacob Dybwad, 1946.

Müller, Ulrich, 'Die Parakletenvorstellung im Johannesevangelium', *ZThK* 71 (March 1974), 31−78.

   Prophetie und Predigt im Neuen Testament: Formgeschichtliche Untersuchungen zur urchristlichen Prophetie. Gütersloh: Gütersloher Verlagshaus Mohn, 1975.

Mussner, Franz, 'Die joh. Parakletsprüche und die apostolische Tradition', *BZ* 5 (1961), 56−70.

Neugebauer, F., 'Geistsprüche und Jesuslogien', *ZNW* 53 (1962), 218−28.

Panagopoulos, John, ed., *Prophetic Vocation in the New Testament and Today*, NovTSupp. Leiden: Brill, 1977.

Patsch, H., 'Die Prophetie des Agabus', *TZ* 28 (1972), 228−32.

Perrin, Norman, *A Modern Pilgrimage in New Testament Christology.* Philadelphia: Fortress Press, 1974.

   Rediscovering the Teaching of Jesus. New York: Harper and Row, 1967.

What is Redaction Criticism? Philadelphia: Fortress Press, 1969.

Pesch, Rudolf, *Das Markusevangelium*, HTKNT, 2 vols. Freiburg: Herder, 1976−7.

Naherwartung: Tradition und Redaktion in Mk 13, KBANT. Düsseldorf: Patmos Verlag, 1968.

Rad, Gerhard von, *Old Testament Theology*, 2 vols. New York: Harper and Row, 1962−5.

Reiling, J., *Hermas and Christian Prophecy: A Study of the Eleventh Mandate*, NovTSupp. Leiden: E. J. Brill, 1973.

Reitzenstein, Richard, *Die hellenistischen Mysterienreligionen: Nach ihren Grundgedanken und Wirkungen*. Leipzig: B. G. Teubner, 1927[3].

'Paulus als Pneumatiker', in *Das Paulusbild in der neueren Deutschen Forschung*, edited by K. H. Rengstorf. Darmstadt: Wissenschaftliche Buchgesellschaft, 1969.

Robinson, James, 'Die Hodajot-Formel in Gebet und Hymnus des Früh-christentums', in *Apophoreta: Festschrift für Ernst Haenchen*, edited by Walther Eltester and F. H. Kettler. Berlin: A. Töpelmann, 1964.

Robinson, James, and Koester, Helmut, *Trajectories Through Early Christianity*. Philadelphia: Fortress Press, 1971.

Roetzel, Calvin, 'The Judgment Form in Paul's Letters', *JBL* 88 (1969), 305−12.

Rousseau, François, *L'Apocalypse et le milieu prophétique du Nouveau Testament: Structure et préhistoire du texte*. Paris: Tournai, 1971.

Russell, D. S., *The Method and Message of Jewish Apocalyptic*. Philadelphia: Westminster Press, 1964.

Sand, Alexander, *Das Gesetz und die Propheten: Untersuchungen zur Theologie des Evangeliums nach Matthäus*. BU. Regensburg: Verlag Friedrich Pustet, 1974.

'Propheten, Weise, und Schriftkundige in der Gemeinde des Matthäus-evangeliums', in *Kirche im Werden: Studien zum Thema Amt und Gemeinde im Neuen Testament*, edited by Josef Hainz. Munich: Verlag Ferdinand Schöningh, 1976.

Sandmel, Samuel, *The Genius of Paul*. New York: Schocken Books, 1970.

Sasse, Herman, 'Der Paraklet im Johannesevangelium', *ZNW* 24 (1925), 260−77.

Satake, Akira, *Die Gemeindeordnung in der Johannesapokalypse*, WMANT. Neukirchen-Vluyn: Neukirchener Verlag, 1966.

Schelke, Karl Herman, 'Jesus: Lehrer und Prophet', in *Orientierung an Jesus*, edited by Paul Hoffmann, Norbert Brox, Wilhelm Pesche. Freiburg: Herder, 1973.

Schmeichel, Waldemar, 'Christian Prophecy in Lukan Thought: Luke 4: 16−30 as a Point of Departure', *SBL 1976 Seminar Papers*. Missoula: Scholars Press, 1976.

Schmidt, Joseph, 'Propheten. (b.) P. im NT', *Lexikon für Theologie und Kirche*, 10 vols. Freiburg: Herder, 1957−65.

Schmithals, Walter, *The Office of Apostle in the Early Church.* Nashville: Abingdon, 1969.

Schnider, Franz, *Jesus der Prophet.* Göttingen: Vandenhoeck and Ruprecht, 1973.

Schniewind, Julius, *Das Evangelium nach Markus: Mit einer Einleitung zum Gesamtwerk, die Entstehung und der Wortlaut des neuen Testaments* (by Hermann Strathmann). NTD. Göttingen: Vandenhoeck and Ruprecht, 1960[9].

'Zur Synoptiker-Exegese', *TR* (new series) 2 (1930), 129–86.

Schoeps, H. J., *Aus frühchristlicher Zeit: Religionsgeschichtliche Untersuchungen.* Tübingen: J. C. B. Mohr, 1950.

Schulz, Siegfried, *Q: Die Spruchquelle der Evangelisten.* Zürich: Theologischer Verlag, 1972.

Die Stunde der Botschaft. Zürich: Zwingli Verlag, 1970[2].

Schürmann, Heinz, *Traditionsgeschichtliche Untersuchungen zu den Synoptischen Evangelien*, KBANT. Düsseldorf: Patmos-Verlag, 1968.

Ursprung und Gestalt: Erörterungen und Besinnungen zum Neuen Testament. Düsseldorf: Patmos-Verlag, 1970.

Schweizer, Eduard, ΕΓΩ ΕΙΜΙ: *Die religionsgeschichtliche Herkunft und theologische Bedeutung der johanneischen Bildreden, zugleich ein Beitrag zur Quellenfrage des vierten Evangeliums.* Göttingen: Vandenhoeck and Ruprecht, 1939.

'Formgeschichtliches zu den Seligpreisungen Jesu', *NTS* 19 (January 1973), 121–6.

The Good News according to Matthew. Atlanta: John Knox Press, 1975.

The Good News according to Mark. Atlanta: John Knox Press, 1970.

Jesus. Richmond: John Knox Press, 1971.

'Mark's Contribution to the Quest of the Historical Jesus', *NTS* 10 (1963–4), 421–32.

Matthäus und seine Gemeinde, SBS. Stuttgart: KBW Verlag, 1974.

'Observance of the Law and Charismatic Activity in Matthew', *NTS* 16 (April 1970), 213–30.

'πνεῦμα', *TDNT*, 6: 332–451.

Scobie, Charles H. H., *John the Baptist.* London: SCM Press, 1964.

Scott, Ernest F., *The Validity of the Gospel Record.* London: Nicholson and Watson, 1938.

Scroggs, Robin, 'The Exaltation of the Spirit by Some Early Christians', *JBL* 84 (1965), 359–73.

Seitz, O. J. F., 'The Commission of Prophets and "Apostles", a Re-Examination of Matt. 23: 34 with Luke 11: 49', in *Studia Evangelica 4*, edited by F. L. Cross. Berlin: Akademie Verlag, 1968.

Selwyn, E. C., *The Christian Prophets and the Prophetic Apocalypse.* London: Macmillan, 1900.

The Oracles in the New Testament. New York: Hodder and Stoughton, 1911.

St. Luke the Prophet. London: Macmillan, 1901.

Smith, D. Moody, 'Johannine Christianity: Some Reflections on its Character and Delineation', *NTS* 21 (1975), 222–48.

Stählin, Gustav, 'τό πνεῦμα Ἰησοῦ (Apostelgeschichte 16: 7)', in *Christ and Spirit in the New Testament*, edited by Barnabas Lindars and Stephen Smalley. Cambridge University Press, 1973.

Steck, O. H., *Israel und das gewaltsame Geschick der Propheten*, WMANT. Neukirchen-Vluyn: Neukirchener Verlag, 1967.

Stendahl, Krister, 'The Gospel of Matthew', in *Peake's Commentary on the Bible*, rev. ed., edited by Matthew Black and H. H. Rowley. London: Nelson, 1962.

The School of St. Matthew and Its Use of the Old Testament. Uppsala: Gleerup, 1954.

Strecker, Georg, *Der Weg der Gerechtigkeit: Untersuchung zur Theologie des Matthäus*, FRLANT. Göttingen: Vandenhoeck and Ruprecht, 1966.

'Die Makarismen der Bergpredigt', *NTS* 17 (April 1971), 255–75.

Stroker, William Dettwiller, 'The Formation of Secondary Sayings of Jesus'. Unpublished dissertation, Yale University, 1970.

Strugnell, John, ' "Amen I Say Unto You" in the Sayings of Jesus and in Early Christian Literature', *HTR* 67 (1974), 177–90.

Suggs, M. Jack, *Wisdom, Christology and Law in Matthew's Gospel.* Cambridge, Mass.: Harvard University Press, 1970.

Swete, H. B., *The Holy Spirit in the New Testament: A Study of Primitive Christian Teaching.* London: Macmillan, 1910.

Taylor, Vincent, *The Formation of the Gospel Tradition.* London: Macmillan, 1933.

Teeple, Howard M., 'The Oral Tradition that Never Existed', *JBL* 89 (1970), 56–68.

'The Origin of the Son of Man Christology', *JBL* 84 (1965), 213–50.

Theissen, Gerd, *Sociology of Early Palestinian Christianity.* Philadelphia: Fortress Press, 1978.

'Wanderradikalismus. Literatursoziologische Aspekte der Überlieferung von Worten Jesu im Urchristentum', *ZThK* 70 (1973), 245–71.

Tiede, David, *The Charismatic Figure as Miracle Worker*, SBLDS 1. Missoula: Scholars Press, 1972.

Tödt, Heinz E., *The Son of Man in the Synoptic Tradition.* Philadelphia: Westminster Press, 1965.

Torrey, Charles C., *The Lives of the Prophets: Greek Text and Translation.* Philadelphia: Society of Biblical Literature, 1946.

Trocmé, Étienne, *The Formation of the Gospel according to Mark.* Philadelphia: Westminster, 1975.

Unnik, W. C. van, 'A Formula Describing Prophecy', *NTS* 9 (1963), 86–94.

Vielhauer, Philipp, 'Apocalypses and Related Subjects: Introduction', in *New Testament Apocrypha*, edited by Edgar Hennecke and Wilhelm Schneemelcher. Philadelphia: Westminster, 1964.

Aufsätze zum Neuen Testament. Munich: Chr. Kaiser Verlag, 1965.
'Propheten, NT'. *RGG*³, 5: 633–4.

Weber, Max, *The Sociology of Religion.* Boston: Beacon Press, 1963.

Weeden, Theodore, *Mark: Traditions in Conflict.* Philadelphia: Fortress, 1971.

Weinel, Heinrich, *Die Wirkungen des Geistes und der Geister im nach-apostolischen Zeitalter bis auf Irenäus.* Freiburg: J. C. B. Mohr, 1899.

Weiss, Johannes, *Das älteste Evangelium: Ein Beitrag zum Verständnis des Markus-Evangeliums und der ältesten evangelischen Überlieferung.* Göttingen: Vandenhoeck and Ruprecht, 1903.

Wellhausen, Julius, *Einleitung in die drei ersten Evangelien.* Berlin: Georg Reimer, 1911².

Westermann, Claus, *Basic Forms of Prophetic Speech.* Philadelphia: Westminster Press, 1967.

Wilder, Amos, *The Language of the Gospel: Early Christian Rhetoric.* New York: Harper and Row, 1964.

Windisch, Hans, 'Jesus und der Geist nach synoptischer Überlieferung', in *Studies in Early Christianity*, edited by S. J. Case. New York: Century, 1928.

Paulus und Christus: Ein Biblisch-religionsgeschichtlicher Vergleich, UNT. Leipzig: J. C. Hinrichs'sche Buchhandlung, 1934.

The Spirit-Paraclete in the Fourth Gospel, edited by John Reumann. Philadelphia: Fortress Press, 1968.

Wink, Walter, *John the Baptist in the Gospel Tradition*, SNTS 7. Cambridge: Cambridge University Press, 1968.

Wrege, Hans-Theo, *Die Überlieferungsgeschichte der Bergpredigt*, WUNT. Tübingen: J. C. B. Mohr, 1968.

Zimmermann, Heinrich, 'Das absolute Ἐγώ εἰμι als die neutestamentliche Offenbarungsformel', *BZ* (new series) 4 (1960), 54–69, 266–76.

INDEX OF REFERENCES

Apocrypha

New Testament

Qumran

Other Sources

A. Jewish

INDEX OF AUTHORS